THE PERFORMANCE
OF HEALING

THE PERFORMANCE
OF HEALING

Edited by
Carol Laderman & Marina Roseman

ROUTLEDGE

New York ◆ London

Published in 1996 by

Routledge
29 West 35th Street
New York, NY 10001

Published in Great Britain in 1996 by

Routledge
11 New Fetter Lane
London EC4P 4EE

Library of Congress Cataloging-in-Publication Data available

CONTENTS

INTRODUCTION

Carol Laderman and Marina Roseman

Twenty or so years ago, when we were undergraduates, medical anthropology existed as a small and often narrow enterprise. Reflecting the split in American society between "hard science" and "humanism," and the greater respect accorded "hard science," many medical anthropologists adopted medical models even as others resisted compromising their anthropological vision. In fact, editors of mainstream anthropology journals, with the notable exception of *Ethnology*, often rejected articles on medical subjects, advising their authors to publish their work in specialized medical journals. Over the course of the last two decades, however, medical anthropology has resoundingly joined the anthropological mainstream. Medical anthropologists are increasingly rejecting the role of being an adjunct to the healing arts in favor of using questions of health, illness, and treatment as points of entry into the understanding of human thought and behavior.

All medical encounters, no matter how mundane, are dramatic episodes. The protagonists, often without conscious thought, play out their respective roles of patient and healer according to their society's expectations. In some cultures, the dramatic aspect of healing is overt. Performers' costumes can add to the specialness of a healing encounter, ranging from obviously theatrical dress to a medical white coat, or a stethoscope around the healer's neck. Foods may be forbidden or necessary; odors of perfumes and flowers or the medicinal fumes of herbs or antiseptics may be used; sounds may be hushed, seductive, triumphant, mechanical. The treatment of the patient may be judged as a scientific procedure, appropriate or lacking, or as an art form whose elements are all working toward a specific end.

1

In this book we discuss the music, movement, players, audience, props, plots, comedy, poetry and dialogue that constitute the performance of healing. We speak about views of the self and its components, the use of healing sounds, and the messages, both spoken and silent, conveyed in these performances. The approaches to the performance of healing represented in this volume emerge from the convergence of several theoretical orientations which have reinvigorated research in medical anthropology. These include performance and practice, experience and embodiment. Each of the articles traces a slightly different theoretical lineage, but all share a concern for the notion of healing as performance: as purposive, contextually-situated interaction; as multimedia communication and metacommunicative or "framed" enactment; as historically contingent evocation fusing past traditions and memories with present circumstances and problems; as emotionally, sensuously and imaginatively engaging; as reflective and transformative.

The essays which make up this book are generally concerned with rituals and other performative genres of locally recognized significance that Singer collectively termed "cultural performances" (1955, 1968), while focusing in particular on those which concern culturally-constructed expressions of illness and health (Kleinman 1980; Good 1977). Our authors partake of what Schieffelin (this volume) characterizes as a theoretical "shift from viewing such enactments primarily in terms of structures of representation to seeing them also as processes of practice and performance."

Victor Turner and other symbolic and interpretive anthropologists writing in the 1960s sensitized the field of anthropology to the representative power of key symbols in ceremonies. Indeed, Turner's recognition of properties such as the multivocality and polyvalence of symbols prompted such later developments as the re-evaluation of aspects of ambiguity in the imagery of healing performances (Turner 1967; Laderman 1987, this volume; Desjarlais, this volume). The attention of symbolic anthropologists to the meanings of symbols in context, and their analyses of the social repositioning enabled by the ceremonial enactment of symbols, set the stage for what Csordas (this volume) identifies as one of the four streams of research which have converged "to define the contours of the theory of performance adequate to the questions raised by healing." This first stream, the "cultural-performance approach of interpretive anthropology," formulates performance as an active event, rather than merely an arena for reflective representation. The other three are the performance-centered approach from sociolinguistics, the performance-utterance approach which spans the first two, and the rhetorical-persuasive approach developed in the study of therapeutic processes. The first formulates performance as event, the second as genre, the third as act, and the fourth as rhetoric. The power of the performance is a heightened intensity of communication, an enhancement of experience.

The performance-centered approach in sociolinguistics, anthropological linguistics, and folklore drew attention from text to context, from language as a cognitive system to language use in social interaction, from author to speech community. The insights of Jakobson (1960, 1968) into the multimedia nature of communication and the multifunctionality of signs encouraged a new theoretical orientation toward the subtle interrelationships between aesthetic form, function, meaning, and context. A sign might figure in several communicative functions, keeping a channel open while clarifying comprehension. Jakobson's analyses of the foregrounding of form inspired attention to the manipulation of formal or stylistic patterns in verbal arts (Bauman 1984 [1977]; Tedlock 1972, 1983). Bateson (1936, 1972 [1955]) and Goffman (1974) also contributed to the awareness of the metacommunicative acts whereby performance in ritual and everyday life is "framed" or "keyed."

These developments converged in the "ethnography of communication." Recognizing that communicative competence assumes different forms in different settings, the concept of "genre" was invoked to comprehend relations between formal features, thematic domains, and potential social usages in the analysis of situated events (Hymes 1981 [1975]; Ben-Amos 1976 [1969]; Briggs 1988). This perspective problematized the relationship between text and context: texts were not merely inserted into (or easily extractable from) contexts; rather text and context were mutually constitutive of the domain of performance defined as a communicative mode (Bauman 1984 [1977]; Bauman and Briggs 1990). These insights were variably applied, refined, and reconstituted in the discourse-centered approach to language and culture (Sherzer 1983; Urban 1991), ethnopoetics (Tedlock 1983), studies of narrative structure and experience (R. Rosaldo 1980), explorations of the politics of language use (Brenneis and Myers 1984; Duranti 1994), and by others in ways too numerous to mention here.

That text and context are mutually constitutive in performance highlights the active, emergent quality of these events. Indeed, the performative aspect of performance, the extent to which it does not merely refer to or talk about but *does something* in the world, is fundamental to our comprehension of transformative movements from illness to health, from initiate to ritual practitioners, from past to present. Malinowski's investigation into the magical power of words (1965), Austin's examination of the illocutionary or performative aspects of language use (1962), theater studies of the construction of "reality" from "illusion" (Schechner 1985), and Tambiah's exploration of the performative and transformative power of verbal and non-performative effectiveness (1970, 1985 [1977]) were all central to the absorption of the trope of "performance" into medical anthropology. It is in this context that the essays in this volume were brought together.

Reading through these essays, we cannot escape the idea that if healing is to be effective or successful, the senses must be engaged. Think of the belief, common to many mystical philosophies, that the way to the soul is through the senses. Is the way to health also through the senses? Are people simultaneously moved artistically, psychologically and physiologically? Are there specific connections between particular kinds of aesthetic activity in the shaman's performance and the patient's experience of it? Are practitioners who are themselves strongly moved by music, singing, dancing, and language better able to perform as healers? If a patient is unmoved, will the illness be more difficult to treat? Are successful healers psychologically different from other people within their culture? Is what was known in Western culture (before widespread antibiotic therapy) as "the bedside manner" a comment on the satisfactory performance of a healer, whose style of interaction with a patient was understood as contributing to a cure?

As they address these questions, the essays in this volume contribute to, and benefit from, a growing engagement in the field of anthropology with issues of embodiment, experience, sensation, and imagination. Victor Turner's investigation of what he called the condensation of the "ideological" and the "physiological" poles to symbols could be seen as an early formulation of the concern for embodiment (1968). It was here, in the ability of the symbol to bring lofty ideological concepts into resonance with bodily or "gut" processes, that Turner located the transformative power of symbols. By arguing that "techniques of the body" are cultural categories literally taken on or embodied in social interaction, Mauss's concept of the habitus, as adopted by Bourdieu in his theory of practice, undermines both the primordial nature of Turner's "sensory" pole, and the clearcut distinction between the sensory and the ideological (Bourdieu 1977, 1990; Mauss 1979; Kratz 1994).

Medical anthropology itself, in concert with psychological anthropology, has been instrumental in furthering the paradigm of embodiment. Investigations into the cultural construction of illness and health necessitated a re-examination of theoretical constructs distinguishing mind, body, and spirit; person, self, and society; cognition and emotion (Scheper-Hughes and Lock 1987; Csordas 1990; M. Rosaldo 1980; Lutz 1988). Feminist theory, becoming successively bolder in its investigatory categories, also prompted a progression in focus from "kinship" to "gender" to "the body." Reminding us that the *political* is bodily inscribed and experienced in the *personal*, feminist theory legitimated the turn from disembodied, decontextualized words ("phallologocentric") to embodied utterances and gestures of emotion as they accomplish social jockeying. Butler's concept of "gender performativity" (1993) brings performance and feminist theory together, as she examines the constitution of the gendered subject through performative acts embedded in chains of social and historical conventions.

Aesthetic anthropology, through its focus on music, dance, fragrance, and shape, recognizes the symbolic importance of sensuous forms like sounds, movement, odor, and color in performativity. Ethnomusicologists and dance ethnologists were forced to improvise theoretical and methodological approaches to these dimensions of expression and experience, given the relative lack of attention paid to them by mainstream anthropologists. Paying particular attention to nonverbal aspects of cultural action, musical and dance ethnographies have tilted cultural studies in interesting directions and helped refocus the anthropological antennae on the body, sentiment and sensation (Feld 1990 [1982]; Roseman 1991; Ness 1992; Qureshi 1986; Spencer 1985; Royce 1977). These researchers, along with their cohorts in the "anthropology of the senses" (Howes 1992; Stoller 1989), have contributed theoretical and methodological sophistication to the study of healing performances (McAllester 1954; Bahr and Haefer 1978; Roseman 1990; Laderman 1991; Robertson i. p.) Investigating avenues such as how the concept of "performative" shifts when refracted through non-verbal forms, anthropologists of the arts and the senses have generated new insights into the transformative powers of dramatic pacing, fusions and interactions, the poetics of form, and the forging of meaning (Feld and Fox 1994; Kratz 1994).

These issues and orientations percolate through the chapters in this volume; the authors simultaneously push on the performance frame and the boundaries of medical anthropology as they investigate particular healing performances. Questions of efficacy are resituated in relation to issues of embodiment, sensation, imagination, and experience.

Laurel Kendall, in her poignant essay, "Initiating Performance: The Story of Chini, A Korean Shaman," traces the attempts of a young Korean woman to become a shaman. Kendall warns that a simplistic application of performance theory would only "lead us to an appreciation of how drum beats, costumes, dance, and the recognizable theatrical business of particular spirits—the fan over Princess Hogu's face, the pouring of wine for a drunkard father—are implicated in the construction of a successful *kut*, a *kut* that becomes compelling for its universe of participants." The initiatory spirit seance or *kut* during which Chini's "gates of speech" momentarily opened was effective not merely by virtue of manipulation of these multiple media, but through the action of these forms as dramatic resources linking her with her family and ancestral past. Chini's pain and affliction are understood and resolved by engaging family history.

Most of the essays in this volume take for granted that the healer has achieved proficiency in performance of the art, and do not discuss how healers are initiated or how they must behave in order to keep their patients and reputations. Kendall, however, helps us begin to understand the challenge of shamanistic initiation and the reasons why many of those who would like to attain this role will instead continue their lives in poverty and misery.

Korean shamans are usually women who have had signs that the spirits are calling them to the profession, such as sickness, bad luck, poverty, bad marriages, men harming and neglecting them. But learning to be a shaman is very difficult. Chini does not succeed because she fails to act like a shaman: she cannot clear her mind and open herself to feelings, losing herself in performance. For Chini to be successful, her words must go beyond the formulaic. She fails because she is self-conscious and inhibited: She lacks the ability to perform.

What kinds of skills are necessary for a performer-healer to command in order to be accepted in that role? Kendall's story of the failed Korean student shows us how demanding the shaman's role can be, while Edward Schieffelin's account of two competing Kaluli healers, "On Failure and Performance," reminds us that the "bedside manner" must forever be renewed if a healer is to keep his clientele. Schieffelin, like Kendall, uses the conceit of a failed performance to highlight, through its imperfections, how the event "works." Schieffelin asks: "What is involved in the performative creation of presence, verisimilitude, and social effectiveness—and how is this involved in the social construction of reality?" He approaches his answer through the analysis of an ethnographic example, asking specifically: "How is spirit presence created and convincingly sustained and how are curative or predictive powers effected?"

Aiba and Walia, the two Kaluli shamans in the Southern Highlands of Papua New Guinea who appear in Schieffelin's essay, are both accepted healers, but the respect they are accorded by patients and audience depends strongly upon the evaluation of their current performances. Aiba's audience suspected him of "performing" (or pretending), when he should have been opening a path for true spirit voices to sing. His repeated attempts to regain credibility were more and more firmly rebuffed by his audience, who encouraged Walia to take on the evening's major shamanistic role and essentially excluded Aiba from the seance.

The loosely structured and dialogic Kaluli spirit seance directs our attention to "strategic and interactional aspects of performativity," sometimes overshadowed when ceremonial enactments are determined by (or analytic precedence is given to) their form. Aiba failed to successfully employ Kaluli dramatic conventions that might have created mutual participation and group synchrony; in his insensitivity to the rhythms of the other participants, he failed to establish the audience engagement that would lend *him* credibility and the *performance* reality. Although he is accused of being a performer, his audience is really accusing him of being a bad performer, an inexpert showman who mimics the spirits' voices and doesn't really attain a state of trance. Calling a seance a "performance," meaning pretense, judges the reality of ritual situations. Is the spirit the performer, or is the shaman?

A favorite question often asked of medical anthropologists is "How effective are these treatments?" The question of medical efficacy is more complex than it may seem, since beyond any discussion of pharmacology or the placebo effect, further questions must be asked, such as "Who are the recipients of the treatment?" This may seem like a peculiar inquiry to Americans who find an instant connection between the patient and the treatment, but becomes a perfectly reasonable question to an anthropologist attempting to understand why some seemingly minor problems demand a ritual performance while others do not.

It is problematic to insist that our own categories and standards constitute an unquestioned universal given. Even so, it has become increasingly evident that some healing rituals whose aims are improvement in the health or happiness of particular patients can be judged by standards of Western psychotherapies as producing significant observable results. These rituals do more than merely label sicknesses, manipulate these labels, and apply new labels such as "cured" or "well" to the patient's condition. Hypotheses regarding the mechanisms responsible for results of ritual curing have clustered around two levels of human functioning: the psychological and the neurobiological.

Although scientific studies of medical treatments cannot be accepted as valid unless they demonstrate greater efficacy than that achieved by placebos, the placebo effect, which can trigger the body's ability to heal itself, is nevertheless one of the most powerful tools in any healer's armamentarium. Placebos are used by contemporary Western physicians for such purposes as controlling postoperative pain, relieving anxiety, curing warts and ameliorating peptic ulcers (and, we must not forget, placebos may also cause unexpected and negative reactions). The placebo effect is not necessarily limited to the administration of substances, but may also include words and actions, such as occur in a shamanistic seance or a Western physician's diagnosis. The healer, in engaging the mind and affecting the emotions of his patient, might also initiate physiological repair.

For healing to take place in this manner, aesthetic distance must be achieved—the balance point must be established between feeling painful emotions that have been repressed in the past and reliving these feelings from a point of safety in the present. The healing effects of performance are, on one level, caused by the catharsis that can occur when a patient's unresolved emotional distress is reawakened and confronted in a dramatic context. Techniques of aesthetic distancing often rely upon a willing suspension of disbelief, and combine experiences of pleasure and pain, as evidenced by the interweaving of awesome scenes with comic episodes that not only relieve tension but also provide critical comments about status, class, religion, politics, and relations between the sexes.

A growing number of scientists—from biochemists and pharmacologists to psychiatrists and anthropologists—have speculated that another key to the healer's success may be found in the biochemistry of endorphins, endogenous morphine-like substances that act on the nervous system and are generated in the human brain in response to pain, stress, or certain kinds of peak experience. Given the proper cues, the brain may also generate other endogenous chemicals, as effective as Librium or Valium in their tranquillizing effects. Interestingly, it is usually the patients (and the shaman) who attain trance, while the audience, hearing the same music and chanting, and feeling the vibrations of the shaman's hands beating on the floor where they are also seated, enjoy the experience in full command of their conscious minds, not subject to the biochemical changes taking place in the principal actors.

Thomas Csordas tackles the issue of how healing performances work by conducting an in-depth examination of patients' engagement with the Catholic Charismatic healing process. He situates the approach taken in his article, "Imaginal Performance and Memory in Ritual Healing," within a review of prior variants of performance theory, outlining both their contributions and shortcomings. Csordas demonstrates how performance-oriented approaches can be enriched by theories of experience and embodiment, imagination and memory, self and other. Using a combination of ethnographic techniques, including patients' introspective reports, Csordas investigates how participants in religious healing become existentially engaged in the healing process. Grasping the "experiential specificity of participants," he argues, subverts the researcher's need to leap from action to interpretation. Rather, "performance thus invites us—though we do not yet always accept the invitation—to go beyond the sequence of action and the organization of text to the phenomenology of healing and being healed."

Csordas locates performative transformation in "imaginal performance"; sequences of imagery are not merely elements in a healing performance, but performances in their own right. They do not represent phenomena, they *are* phenomena. Working with a charismatic healer, a patient uses her imagination to place people who have hurt her in the past into a Eucharistic cup, then offers them to the deity. The desired effect is "growing up" and "coming to know who I am in Christ," enacted in the merging of adult and childhood selves in the divine embrace. The result is not just a metaphor but a feeling, as in the case of a patient who commented, "I felt their heart in mine."

Bringing personal experience into relation with symbolism, and memories of past traumas into the imaginal experience of divine embrace effects autobiographical transformations. These contingent and emergent aspects of imaginal performance—like the cries of the Songhay violin fusing past and present, an archetypal personality animating a patient in a Malay spirit seance, or a Kaluli spirit singing through a medium—are grounded in embodiment. "For

Charismatics, efficacious healing is predicated not only on a cultural legitimacy that says healing is possible, but on an existential immediacy that constitutes healing as real."

Grounding images in the body enacts a geography of healing. Metaphor ceases to be merely a referential trope, but becomes performative in the sense of motion suggested by Fernandez (1986). The polysemous overlay of terrestrial and body parts in Malay seances, the images of places uttered by Yolmo shamans, the places mentioned in Kaluli songs and those of a group discussed below, the Temiar, recalling relations between people and remembered occurrences, create a participatory poetics engaging bodies and selves, capable of effecting therapeutic transformation.

Carol Laderman elaborates on the performative dimensions that constitute healing as *real* in her essay "The Poetics of Healing in Malay Shamanistic Performances." She traces the links between Malay theories of illness etiology and treatment, and indigenous concepts of self and personality. She demonstrates how Malay spirit seances evoke these understandings of person and personality as dramatic resources in performance. Most illness is believed by Malays to be caused by humoral imbalance and cured by dietary changes, medicines, massages, and the body's own strength and curative powers. Occasionally, however, the human body becomes imbalanced due to an increase of heat and air brought by spirit attacks, through the loss of *semangat* (universal spirit), or because of the build-up of unexpressed *angin* (Inner Winds which all people carry from birth and which, much like the archetypes discussed by Jung, are responsible for talents and personalities). Some of these problems may be treated by prayers or spells, others may demand a seance. These seances, where through words and rhythms the ritual healer aids the patient in achieving a trance, provide an arena within which the patient can express, through dramatic enactments of archetypal personalities, sentiments and dispositions that are at other times inappropriate. In spirit seances, Malays can periodically heal the need to be "other" than their daily selves.

In his essay "Presence," on the elaborate healing rites of the Yolmo Sherpa, a Tibetan Buddhist people, Robert Desjarlais argues that shamans change the way a body feels by altering *what* it feels, activating the patient's senses, altering his sensory grounds, and waking him up. To the Yolmo Buddhists, presence equals health. If the spirit leaves its body, the body feels heavy, the person has bad dreams, suffers from insomnia, and withdraws from social relationships. The patient needs to be reengaged in life, and his shaman must engage in a struggle with malevolent forces. The shaman's body shakes as he hooks a spirit that appears on the surface of his drum. He drops a "flower" into food that the patient eats and is healed.

Yolmo criteria of efficacy do not rest upon a shaman's statement that life and health have returned, but upon the presence of visceral evidence within the patient that his body *feels* better. Healing takes place not merely within some cognitive domain but also within the reaches of the body. When the spirit returns it feels like a jolt of electricity in the body. The patient's senses and imagination have been activated and his body is rejuvenated.

Desjarlais' sensory interpretation of the effect of the shaman's words or "wild images" in the patient's body adds new dimensions to linguistic meaning. The sensory impact of dramatic media, and their activation in relation to indigenous concepts regarding the constitution of the self, are recurring themes in these essays.

In "Sounds and Things: Pulsations of Power in Songhay," Paul Stoller tunes into the sensuousness of sound, and its power to bring the culturally configured past into a performatively reconfigured present. He reminds us that in Western cultures sound has been spatialized into writing, a visually-based textual analysis which can remove us from the sensory world of taste, smell, hearing, and touch. If such textual analyses are left to stand alone for the event, they limit our understanding of cultural sentiment. Stoller's essay thus enters into debates on textual form, content, and meaning that permeate this volume.

Many Songhay villages have possession troupes, loosely organized groups of men and women headed by a possession priest who produces ceremonies like an impresario of a theatrical company. Most healing in possession ceremonies is social healing, featuring offerings to the spirits for a good rainy season or harvest, but some infirmities, such as infertility and paralysis, must be treated by spirits. Stoller's analysis of Songhay incantations focuses upon the sound of words and instruments: the cries of music are the voices of ancestors filled with power of the past. The sounds of violins, drums, and praise-names are not directly implicated in healing acts, but by activating the ancestral past within the present, they effect the fusing of the worlds necessary for a Songhay medium to speak the words of spirits to the human community.

These sounds, acoustically shaped and weighted with cultural significance, bring collective memories into confluence with present circumstances. They point us toward a strategic aspect of performativity that each of the essays in this volume explores: the contingency or historicity of performance. Contingency is one of eight determinative issues in performance theory that Schieffelin (this volume) delineates: performance is of the moment, articulating cultural symbols and ritual genres at that particular time and submitting them to particular circumstances. Performance "works" when it encompasses the particular occasion.

Can features of healing ceremonies that lack semantic content afford insight into ritual processes? Charles Briggs in "The Meaning of Nonsense, the Poetics of Embodiment, and the Production of Power in Warao Healing" considers both meaningful and "non-sense" elements, movement and touch, vital in effecting a cure. Shamanistic discourse provides an auditory tracking of the production, embodiment, and externalization of complex forms of subjectivity by shamans. The rattles used by the Warao shaman contribute to the ceremony through their variations in tempo and loudness, relationship to singing, and distance from patient's body. Rattles also embody the shaman's dual existence in earth and in the spirit world. Quartz crystals within the rattles ignite tiny wood shavings, providing visual evidence that spirit power is being unleashed.

Warao conceive of illness in pneumatic terms, as pathogenic odor, wind, or air, with physical as well as intangible, invisible attributes. The dominant model for healing is displacement of fetid odorous air by healthy sweet air. The shaman can discern the size and hardness of spirits and feel the movement and heat of a spirit's breath. Vocables uttered by the shaman "provide a running indicator of the complex interaction of spiritual entities" taking place in his body. Sounds, not meaningful as human words, are meaningful as signs of what is occurring in the rite, providing ways of understanding overlapping subjectivities and interpenetrating selves, as helping spirits and illness agents move through the shaman. Briggs' close examination of the details of a Warao healing performance, rather than obscuring its purpose, demonstrates how power and agency, social leveling and social differentiation are accomplished. Through his analysis, Briggs shows us the true sense of "nonsense."

Brigg's ethnographic example reminds us that "curing is not just 'about' making people well—it also forms a crucial means of (re)producing relations of power." Marina Roseman's article, "'Pure Products Go Crazy': Rainforest Healing in a Nation-state," investigates relations of power between Temiar "forest people" and "out-foresters" as they are mediated in healing ceremonies. Temiars employ healing ceremonies, traditionally a site for situating themselves in relation to the forest and to one another, to situate themselves as members of the now independent Malaysian nation. Roseman demonstrates how a healing performance directed toward a particular infant also enacts preventive and therapeutic social healing for a social group traumatized by their encounters with deforestation, Islamic religious evangelism, and the transformation of their economy from generalized reciprocity to mercantile and capitalist systems of exchange. Increasingly disempowered by loss of land and resources, Temiars appropriate the power of foreign peoples and commodities for their own purposes in spirit ceremonies.

In the culturally demarcated zone of the healing performance, a Temiar medium embodies the emergent concept of the "State of Kelantan," combining sounds, shapes, and performance formats traditionally employed by these people of the forest with those associated with the culturally diverse populations of

Kelantan, including Chinese Buddhists, Malay Muslims, and Tamil Hindus. Competing social voices are ceremonially interwoven in a multiplicity of sensory modalities. The Temiar medium draws upon the multidimensional "Spirit of the State of Kelantan" to counteract the effects of living in a multicultural world in which "pure products have gone crazy."

What are the goals of the healer's performance? We have seen that the primary goal is not always the cure of a patient. Can a treatment be considered successful if the patient nevertheless dies? Janet Hoskins, in her essay "From Diagnosis to Performance: Medical Practice and the Politics of Exchange in Kodi, West Sumba," deals with these questions through her study of diagnostic decisions that lead toward or away from performance and the moral consequences of these decisions.

The seriousness of illness or injury, judged in Western biomedical terms, is not as important to Sumbanese people as is its location of occurrence and cause. Hoskins analyzes three cases: the first, gonorrhea in a young man, was considered the result of pollution whose treatment did not require a public ritual; the second, a young woman's fall, resulting in a very minor injury which, however, was interpreted as a sign of social troubles below the surface, caused by an angry ancestral spirit; and the third, a ritual healing ceremony for an old man with a terminal case of mouth cancer. His rite was not held to release him from his coming death; rather, it released his children from their otherwise inevitable early deaths and repaired relations between in-laws. Kodi healing performances may "heal the group" at the expense of the individual; they force us to expand the definition of "cure" from its narrower sense of restoring a victim to health, to the larger goal of repairing social relations.

Like Kendall, Hoskins warns against an analysis of performance that might examine dramatic details but miss the overall purpose of the event. The trappings of elaborate performance, she cautions, may confuse certain issues of substance. "Singers, dancers, and orators are summoned to repeat and reiterate points in a complicated visual and auditory experience intended to dissolve difference into consensus. Moral unity becomes the unity of audience, the shared sensory stimulus, and the evocative dramatic presentation. It is through this aesthetic impact of performance that the group is recreated and reconstituted, often over the body of the patient and without much hope of alleviating his suffering."

Hoskins shows us that for Sumbanese, a treatment that ends with a patient's death may still be thought of as successful and satisfying. Would this judgment seem truly bizarre to contemporary Americans, or are there circumstances under which the performance of healing in America becomes a necessary performance of death?

How do Americans (specifically Texans) judge doctors who, by assisting patients in the performance of death, take the role of Charon, ferryman of the ancient Greek dead? In Megan Biesele's and Robbie Davis-Floyd's essay, "Dying as Medical Performance: The Oncologist as Charon," they discuss how an oncologist's words, dramatically ritualizing and repeating pronouncements of his patient's terminal status, convince the patient that death is imminent, and encourage her to prepare herself rather than attempt healing.

The oncologist termed the task of announcing terminal status a central responsibility—to help the patient to a "good death." He needed to help the patient prepare spiritually and make the best use of her remaining time. Yet simultaneously he was reinforcing the claim of the medical establishment to ritual and symbolic hegemony over the bodily processes of life and death. The patient wavered between embracing either a technocratic model of understanding the body, involving medical control over nature, or a more holistically oriented understanding of the interconnectedness between mind and body. Ultimately, she died at home, cared for by her family. Her doctor's medication, provided to hasten death, remained unused. If death is "the final stage of growth," as prescribed by the holistic model of health, there may be some reason for not hurrying the process. "A good death" was reached through the family's participation in an egalitarian conversational context.

This death in Texas is compared to rituals in Africa among the !Kung (Bushmen). For the !Kung, healing and religion are inextricably linked in altered-state performance. Life and death are in hands of God. Healers are not paid or set above others; healing energy only multiplies by being shared. Healers do not announce terminality; they always affirm life and hope. American doctors have a harder task than !Kung healers; they incur personal responsibility as part of their healing mission. Their attitudes toward dying are embedded within Cartesian rationalism and a belief in human potential to control nature and fate. Of course, both !Kung and American beliefs are cultural constructs. Dying is a cultural performance.

Medical systems need to be understood from within, as experienced by healers, patients, and others whose minds and hearts have both become involved in this important human undertaking. We live in a world increasingly aware of the need to address differences theoretically and in applied dimensions such as health-care governance and service. This volume, addressed to members of the medical, psychiatric, and psychological professions, as well as the anthropological and performance-oriented, joins other essays and voices in a call to understanding concepts and textures embodied in different ways of healing. We hope that these articles on the performance of healing in societies ranging from rainforest horticulturalists to dwellers in the American megalopolis will touch our readers' senses as well as their intellects.

REFERENCES

Austin, J. L. 1962. *How to do things with words.* Cambridge, Mass: Harvard University Press.

Bahr, D.M., and J.R. Haefer. 1978. Song in Piman Curing. *Ethnomusicology* 22(1):89–122.

Bateson, Gregory. 1936. *Naven.* Cambridge: Cambridge University Press.

———. 1972/1955. A theory of play and fantasy. Reprinted in *Steps to an ecology of mind,* 177–93. New York: Ballantine Books.

Bauman, Richard. 1984/1977. *Verbal art as performance.* Prospect Heights, Ill.: Waveland Press.

Bauman, Richard and Charles L. Briggs. 1990. Poetics and performance as critical perspectives on language and social life. *Annual Review of Anthropology* 19:59–88.

Ben-Amos, Dan. 1976/1969. Analytical categories and ethnic genres. In *Folklore genres,* ed. Dan Ben-Amos, 215–42. Austin: University of Texas Press.

Bourdieu, Pierre. 1977. *Outline of a theory of practice.* Cambridge: Cambridge University Press.

———. 1990. *The logic of practice.* Stanford: Stanford University Press.

Brenneis, Don and Fred Myers. 1984. *Dangerous words: language and politics in the Pacific.* New York: New York University Press.

Briggs, Charles L. *Competence in performance: the creativity of tradition in Mexicano verbal art.* Philadelphia: University of Pennsylvania Press.

Butler, Judith. *Bodies that matter: on the discursive limits of "sex."* New York: Routledge.

Csordas, Thomas J. 1990. Embodiment as a paradigm for anthropology. *Ethos* 1(18):5–47.

Duranti, Alessandro. *From grammar to politics: linguistic anthropology in a Western Samoan village.* Berkeley, Los Angeles: University of California Press.

Feld, Steven. 1990/1982. *Sound and Sentiment,* 2nd ed. Philadelphia: University of Pennsylvania Press.

Feld, Steven and Aaron A. Fox. 1994. Music and language. *Annual review of Anthropology* 23:25–53.

Fernandez, James. 1986. *Persuasions and performances: the play of tropes in culture.* Bloomington: Indiana University Press.

Goffman, Erving. 1974. *Frame analysis.* New York: Harper and Row.

Good, Byron. 1977. The heart of what's the matter: the semantics of illness in Iran. *Culture, Medicine, and Psychiatry* 1:25–58.

Howes, David, ed. 1992. *The varieties of sensory experience.* Toronto: University of Toronto Press.

Hymes, Dell. 1981/1975. Breakthrough into performance. Reprinted in Dell Hymes, *"In vain I tried to tell you"*: essays in Native American ethnopoetics, 79–141. Philadelphia: University of Pennsylvania Press.

Jakobson, Roman. 1960. Closing statement: Linguistics and poetics. In *Style in language,* ed. Thomas A. Sebeok, 350–77. Cambridge, Mass.: M.I.T. Press.

———. 1968. Poetry of Grammar and Grammar of Poetry. *Lingua* 21: 597–609.

Kleinman, Arthur. 1980. *Patients and Healers in the Context of Culture: An Exploration of the Borderland between Anthropology, Medicine, and Psychiatry.* Berkeley: University of California Press.

Kratz, Corinne A. 1994. *Affecting performance: meaning, movement, and experience in Okiek women's initiation.* Washington: Smithsonian Institution Press.

Laderman, Carol. 1987. The Ambiguity of Symbols in the Structure of Healing. *Social Science and Medicine* 24:293–301.

———. 1991. *Taming the Wind of Desire: Psychology, Medicine and Aesthetics in Malay Shamanistic Performance.* Berkeley, Los Angeles: University of California Press.

Lutz, Catharine. 1988. *Unnatural emotions.* Chicago: University of Chicago Press.

Malinowski, Bronislaw. 1965. *Coral Gardens and their Magic.* 2 vols. Bloomington: Indiana University Press.

Mauss, Marcel. 1979. Body techniques. In *Sociology and Psychology: essays by Marcel Mauss,* trans. Ben Brewster. London: Routledge and Kegan Paul.

McAllester, David P. 1954. *Enemy Way Music.* Papers of the Peabody Museum of American Archaeology and Ethnology, vol. 41, no. 3. Cambridge, Mass.: Harvard University.

Moerman, Daniel E. 1983. Physiology and Symbols: The Anthropological Implications of the Placebo Effect. In Romanucci-Ross, Lola et al. *The Anthropology of Medicine.* New York: Praeger Publishers.

Ness, Sally Ann. 1992. *Body, Movement, and Culture.* Philadelphia: University of Pennsylvania Press.

Rosaldo, Michelle Z. 1980. *Knowledge and passion: Ilongot notions of self and social life.* Cambridge: Cambridge University Press.

Rosaldo, Renato. *Ilongot Headhunting,* 1883–1974. Stanford: Stanford University Press.

Roseman, Marina. 1991. *Healing Sounds from the Malaysian Rainforest: Temiar Music and Medicine.* University of California Press.

Royce, Anya. 1977. *Anthropology of Dance.* Bloomington: Indiana University Press.

Schechner, Richard. 1985. *Between theater and anthropology.* Philadelphia: University of Pennsylvania Press.

Scheper-Hughes, Nancy, and Margaret M. Lock. 1987. The mindful body: a prolegomenon to future work in medical anthropology. *Medical anthropology quarterly* 1 n.s.(1):6–41.

Sherzer, Joel. 1983. *Kuna ways of speaking: an ethnographic perspective.* Austin: University of Texas Press.

Singer, Milton. 1955. The Cultural Pattern of Indian Civilization. *Far Eastern Quarterly* 15:23–36.

———. 1968. *Krishna: Myths, Rites and Attitudes.* Chicago: University of Chicago Press.

Stoller, Paul. 1989. *The Taste of Ethnographic Things.* Philadelphia: University of Pennsylvania.

Spencer, Paul, ed. 1985. *Society and the Dance.* Cambridge: Cambridge University Press.

Tambiah, Stanley. 1970. *Buddhism and the spirit cults in North-East Thailand.* Cambridge: Cambridge University Press.

———. 1985/1977. The Cosmological and Performative Significance of a Thai Cult of Healing through Meditation. Reprinted in *Culture, Thought, and social action: an anthropological perspective.* Cambridge: Harvard University Press.

Tedlock, Dennis. 1972. On the translation of style in oral narrative. In *Toward new perspectives in folklore,* ed. Americo Paredes and Richard Bauman, 114–33. Austin: University of Texas Press.

———. 1983. *The spoken word and the work of interpretation.* Philadelphia: University of Pennsylvania.

Turner, Victor. 1967. *The Forest of Symbols: aspects of Ndembu ritual.* Ithaca, N.Y.: Cornell University Press.

Urban, Greg. *A discourse-centered approach to culture: Native South American myths and rituals.* Austin: University of Texas Press.

1

INITIATING PERFORMANCE

The Story of Chini,
a Korean Shaman

Laurel Kendall

Kendall: They say a shaman's initiation is the most difficult ritual of all.
Young Shaman: It's hard on the disciple and hard on the teacher. The spirits keep coming in and going out again, and hiding themselves, and then restless ancestors come in and interfere with things.
Experienced Shaman: If it goes well, the initiate speaks the true words of the spirits. A lot of customers come and they all receive remarkable divinations, that sort of thing, proof that the initiate has really become a shaman. If she fails, then no one takes her seriously.

PROLOGUE

The three shamans meet again in Chini's dank little rented room on the day before her *kut,* filling their student's cramped quarters with drums and cymbals, cheap vinyl suitcases bulging with the gods' costumes, and the flurry of their preparations. Chini's pitiful accommodations, like her emaciated figure, attest to the hardship of one who is destined to serve the spirits. The three shamans claim to know this well; the tribulations of the calling are their common history. Still, one must stretch the imagination to find in these robust and forthright matrons any trace of a woman like Chini, thin and timid, pale at the prospect of performing a *kut* to claim the gods' authority as her own.

They had taken Chini, in the late spring, to the public shrine on K'amak Mountain for her initiation ritual (*naerim kut*)[1] but the initiate was reticent and the gods stubborn. The shamans, as they told me months later, hit the drum throughout the night while the initiate stood mute. They hit the drum until four o'clock in the morning before Chini began to shout out the names of her gods, the eleven gods whose painted images she has since installed in a narrow shrine against the far wall of her tiny room.[2] That she had even managed this much was the final proof: the gods have chosen Chini. They had caused her the past ten years of bitter suffering, and now offered resolution in her initiation as a shaman. But Chini's words on the mountain had not been enough. Her "gates of speech" (*malmun*) had not opened to pour out inspired oracles (*kongsu*). She lacked suffi-cient inspiration to prognosticate for her clients over a divination tray[3] or while performing at a *kut*. The gods had not yet empowered her to earn her living as a shaman. The first *kut* cleansed Chini of unclean ghosts and ominous forces. Now in the fall, this second *kut* would call in the gods and urge them to make Chini into a successful shaman.[4] To become a shaman, she must find it in herself to perform as one.

INTRODUCTION

In the 1960s and 1970s, avant-garde theater attempted to reenchant perfor-mance by dipping into ethnography. The actor's experience was described as analogous to possession rituals and shamanistic journeys which evoke imagined truths in the experienced immediacy of performance, thereby making them "real." Actors were encouraged to see themselves as shamans (Cole 1975; Kirby 1983 [1975]). Ironically, performance is precisely what Chini, a destined shaman by the classic standards of her own society, found to be so difficult. An initiation *kut*, like all other *kut*, is a healing ritual aimed at securing auspicious consequences—health, prosperity, harmony—by winning the favor of the gods and assuaging the grief and longing of the dead. These aspirations are given tan-gible form when a shaman, in appropriate costume, invokes the spirits in their proper sequence and manifests them through song, dance, mime, comic banter, and oracles. For an initiation *kut* to be judged successful, the initiate must also be able to do this, and at her first *kut*, Chini had failed miserably.

This is the story of Chini's second initiation *kut*, held in the fall of 1989 to open her gates of speech in the presence of three members of her family, an anthropologist (myself), and an ethnographic filmmaker (Diana Lee) with crew

(Kim Asch). Through Chini's story, it is also an exploration of the delicate balance between theatricality and inspiration as shamans work with the initiate and her family to construct compelling idioms of past misfortune and future power, and to perform them into being. Finally because Chini's second initiation was again judged insufficient, her story confounds the ethnographic near-certainty of formulaic passage rites, the near-inevitability of ritual processes which by their own internal dynamic transform mere mortals into shamans and healers.

There is irony in Western theater's having sought its reflection in ethnography before anthropology was prepared to confront the subjects of its own musings in theater. The recognition that ritual is essentially performance is not new to anthropology. Waldemar Bogoras's turn-of-the-century account of a Chukchi shaman's seance, a masterpiece of ethnographic description, is attuned to the beats of the drum, to how the shaman modifies his voice as he chants, to the spectators' shouts and then the cries and whispers of the spirits as they enter the room (Bogoras 1907). Eliade's (1970) opus is riddled with dramatic portrayals of shamanic soul quests and netherwordly journeys. Michel Leiris described the "theatrical" possession rituals of the Ethiopians of Gondar ([1958] cited in Cole 1975), and Raymond Firth (1967) the "dramatic elements" in performances by Malay spirit mediums. The Human Relations Area Files offer numerous descriptions of shaman rituals replete with such "theatrical" business as impersonation, pantomime, dialogue, sound effects, costumes, and lighting (Charles 1953). My point is not that the dramatic element of shaman rituals went unrecorded, but that it was so seldom pursued. Little more than a decade ago, John Beattie (1977) could claim that ethnographers had generally neglected the learned and performed quality of spirit possession.

The shaman as actor has been an uncomfortable notion for a relativistic social science. Our students inevitably ask us if we "believe" in the powers of the shamans we have studied, or if the spirits were "really" there. The question discomfits insofar as it implies, on the one hand, that the ethnographer follows Castaneda's (1968) leap beyond the pale of professional credulity, or on the other, that acknowledgements of simulation make charlatans of one's informants. We bear the burden of Euro-American conventions in which, as Richard Schechner reminds us, "'acting' means make-believe, illusion, lying. . . . In America we say someone is 'only acting' when we detect the seams between the performance and the nonacting surround" (Schechner 1982:63). Bogoras knew that many Chuckchi recognized the ventriloquistic feats and sleights-of-hand that enhanced a shaman's performance, but he attributed this knowledge to a skepticism born of acculturation. He did not ponder how Chuckchi cognizance of, in his words, "deceit," "liars," and "fraud" might yet be reconciled to his informants' perception of the performances as "wonderful" (Bogoras 1907:429).

Lévi-Strauss (1963) gave us the parable of Quesalid, the Kwakiutl shaman who was not so much a great shaman because he was able to cure, as he was able to cure because he was a great shaman, a fine performer. The story highlights our (and initially Quesalid's) equation of theatricality with falsehood, and then subverts it. Quesalid, the cynic who apprenticed himself as a shaman to expose the tricks of the trade, discovers that his sleight-of-hand cures more effectively than the tricks of a rival shaman. In that realization, conveyed from the Kwakiutl shaman to the discipline of anthropology, lies the knowledge of the power of performance, but the parable of Quesalid still separates artful illusion from the truth claims of the ritual text.

It remained for avant-garde theater to insist that elemental drama was something more than the imitation of a reality that existed elsewhere (Brecht 1964 [1957]; Brook 1968; Cole 1975), and to seek in ritual and in ritual dramas a revitalized knowledge of compelling performance (Artaud 1958; Kirby 1983 [1975]; Schechner 1982, 1985; Schechner and Schuman 1977). It remained for anthropology, infected in at least one instance by association with the avant-garde, to blur the distinction between theatrical artifice and ritual process (Turner 1982)[5] and to view ritual as more than the sum of its structure and symbols, as an enacted realization of personal and collective knowledge (Atkinson 1989; Crapanzano 1977; Schieffelin 1985; Tambiah 1977, 1979, and for Korea, Choi 1989; Kendall 1985:Ch. 1; Kim 1989). Enactment implies a broad range of knowledge and skill. Following the influential work of Bruce Kapferer (1983), a number of studies, including several in this volume, trace the realization of efficacious enactments through the complex and varied media of performance (Boddy 1989; Kapferer 1983; Laderman 1988, 1991; Roseman 1988, 1990, 1991). But if music, song, dance, drama, and mime are inextricable from the texts of ritual, it follows that the skilled performances of shamans, mediums, and accompanying musicians are also intrinsic to the efficacy of the event, however "efficacy" might be emically rendered (Atkinson 1989:93, 218; Briggs this volume; Boddy 1989:134; Golomb 1985:81; Laderman this volume; Lambek 1988). We begin to find, here and there, accounts of those who are poor performers and consequently failed shamans (Choi 1987:164; Laderman 1988: 299, n.d.; Shieffelin n. d.; Obeyesekere 1977:289). The road leads circuitously back to Quesalid and his Chuckchi cousins, to an acceptance of artistry as an attribute of healing power, and on to Korea, to Chini, feeling neither skilled nor yet sufficiently empowered. Her three shaman teachers would struggle to construct for her a world in which the promise and burden of her calling might at last be made manifest.

It would be tempting to call Chini's story a "case study," but this scientifically respectable trope obscures the project at hand. A case study would necessarily focus on Chini as "patient," "victim," or "afflicted" and cast the authorial voice as analyst, recounting her "problem" and its resolution. As a narrative strategy, the case study reduces and simplifies the complex interactions of several family members, shamans, gods, and ancestors brought into play by a ritual as rich and complex as a Korean *kut*. Moreover, the "case" implies closure, however ambiguous, while the shaman's initiation represents only an early chapter in the longer story of a shaman career. Chini's story, and its realization in the performance of her *kut*, comes to us linked with other stories; stories from her family who see Chini's calling as tied to their own troubled history, and from the shamans who find resonances with their own experience. In the text that follows, as in the ethnographic film that Diana Lee and I produced, these several voices—of Chini, the members of her family, the three shamans, the anthropologist, and the spirits—speak in, through, and about the performance of Chini's initiation *kut*, sometimes assessing the action in a monologue, sometimes creating it in the heteroglossia of an unfolding performance (Lee and Kendall 1991).

KOREAN SHAMANS

In Korea, shamans (*mudang, mansin*) are both born and made: fated from birth to suffer until they acknowledge and accept their destiny, initiated, and then trained by a senior shaman to perform *kut*, less elaborate rituals, and divinations. Korean shamans draw legitimacy from personal histories of affliction, constructed as evidence of a calling (Kendall 1988), but they become great shamans through their command of ritual knowledge and performance skills acquired during an onerous apprenticeship (Choi 1987). As elsewhere in the ethnographic world,[6] considerable attention has been devoted to the psychodynamics of possession in Korea as recounted in personal histories that culminate in a shaman's initiation (Harvey 1979, 1981; Kendall 1988; K. Kim 1972; T. Kim 1970, 1972, 1981). I have suggested that Korean shamans are themselves willing participants in the construction of this record. A fortuitous convergence of interest links practitioners of the case-history method—adapted from clinical practice into psychological and medical anthropology—and shamans who create legitimizing autobiographical texts, tales of profound suffering, portentous dreams, and visions, all of which bespeak an inevitable calling (Kendall 1988:16, 63–64). Broad ethnographic treatments of Korean shamans' practices, including my own ethnography, give bare passing mention to the initiated shaman's subsequent apprenticeship under the tutelage of her "spirit mother" (*sin ŏmŏni*) (Ch'oe 1981:81, 129; Harvey 1979:126–127; Hwang 1988:21–24; Kendall 1985:65–69; Kim 1981:451–452). The outstanding exception to this lacuna is Chungmoo Choi's (1987, 1989) study of the shaman's competence in performance, a rigorous portrayal of the multifaceted skills of the successful shaman and their realization as both art and power in emotionally compelling performances.[7]

The two motifs, calling and training, intersect during a shaman's initiation when the initiate must perform like a shaman with appropriate chants, dancing, and above all, divine oracles to conjure and convey the inspiration sent by the gods. When her ability to do this is proven, she may begin to receive clients for divinations, build a following, and earn an income as a shaman. At her initiation *kut,* the would-be shaman is the most active agent in her own transformation. By her own performance, she wills the spirits' presence; if she lacks confidence and rudimentary ritual knowledge, if she falters, then she will fail. Not only is she humiliated, she is also burdened with the necessity of sponsoring yet another expensive initiation ritual before she can even begin to earn her living as a shaman. In the words of Chini's spirit mother, the formidable shaman Kim Pongsun, "If the initiation ritual fails, then the initiate has no professional standing as a shaman, she can't divine for clients. No food, no money, an empty belly, illness, she has to go through all that again."[8]

Chini was in precarious circumstances as she faced her second *kut,* since she had already fallen into debt to finance the two rituals. Kim Pongsun explained, with great compassion, "Chini's all alone in the world. She has a parent and an older sister, but there really isn't anyone who can help her make her way. So we'll make a great shaman out of her . . . this time we'll do another *kut* and she'll have more self-confidence, she'll balance on the knife blades, perform like a shaman. Anyone whom the spirits desire is bound to have hardships. When Chini had her *kut* in the spring, her elder sister gave her the money, and of course she paid for this one, too. But after this, Chini will be a great shaman, then she can make money and pay back her debt."

CHINI'S STORY

The stakes, for Chini's success at her second *kut,* are best understood in her own words, a tale that reveals how she, and those around her, came to construct her story as that of a destined shaman, a tale she willing told on camera. I had dreaded the task of interviewing her for the film. In my earlier attempts to solicit Chini's story, always in the company of her spirit mother, Chini's quiet voice was inevitably overtaken by that of the seasoned shaman and veteran informant who poured out her own recounting of Chini's tribulations. We arranged to interview Chini on the eve of her *kut,* choosing a quiet moment when the senior shamans were gone on an errand. Initially, Chini was uncomfortable with the idea, insisting that she "really didn't know anything," displaying an apprentice's insecurity over her partial knowledge of the tradition, compounded in this instance by the senior shamans' teasing insistence that the anthropologist bested Chini's knowledge of the rituals. She nearly giggled with relief at the patent obviousness of my first question, "What are you going to do tomorrow?"

> Tomorrow, of course, that's my initiation *kut*. That's when you receive the spirits and after that you become a shaman. Ever since I was twenty-three years old, for the last ten years, everything has gone wrong. I've been ill and my family too, nothing's worked out for them. If it were just for my sake, then I wouldn't go through with it, but my whole family is affected. I have an aunt and a cousin who got to be the way I am now, and when they didn't accept the spirits and become shamans they lost their minds, they went crazy. Because two people refused the spirits, and because I've been struggling with this for so long, one *kut* wouldn't do it for me. . . . If I'd accepted the spirits when they first claimed me, then everything would have burst out of me and I would have danced like crazy, but now that it's gone on for so long . . .

Chini's own story, like the stories of many other shamans, begins with a portentous dream:

> I dreamed I was with three friends by a mountain stream. There was a big round rock with a great cavity in the base. . . . I went to see what was hidden there, and when I drew it out it seemed to be some sort of clothing, I didn't know what kind, a bright, dazzling garment. I put it on, and then right before my eyes, I saw a building that looked like a temple. It was a shaman's shrine, and that's how I interpret it now, and the clothing was what the shamans wear. Back then, I had no idea what it was or what sort of clothes those were but just as soon as I put on that splendid garment, I saw the old tile-roofed house. There aren't many of them left now, are there? It was the sort of house they used to build in Korea during the Chosŏn Dynasty. The dream was so clear and vivid. I haven't forgotten it, even after all the things that have happened to me since then.
>
> When my teachers, the great shamans, asked me about my most vivid dream . . . [t]hat's when I realized what it meant. . . . Even after so much time has passed, I remembered everything just as soon as someone asked me, 'What have you dreamed?' The clothes . . . that I put on, the old house, I can still picture them although most of my dreams just fade away. When I was twenty-three years old and had that dream, that's when I should have received the spirits and become a shaman. Instead, a matchmaker came by and I was married. My married life was nothing but quarrels and suffering. I couldn't bear it. I had to leave.

The story of her married life was already well-known to Kim Pongsun, her spirit mother, who elaborated on another occasion:

> She was matchmade and married off, but that man did nothing but drink, he did absolutely nothing to provide for his family, just drank. As if that weren't enough, he got himself another woman and fooled around. . . . So she ran away . . . she gave up her children, a boy and a girl, a three-year-old and a six-year-old. She left all that behind.

In Chini's own words:

> I made my own way and earned some money, but I'd loan it to someone who'd make off with it, or I'd have to go to the hospital, or to a psychiatric hospital. Even though I had several examinations, they never could find anything wrong with me. Medically speaking, there wasn't anything wrong. But as far as I was concerned, I was always in pain. In the four years since I left married life, what little money I earned was wasted on bad loans and my medical expenses. . . . That's how it is; I haven't the least bit of money to show for all that time and all those hardships. Why, I even tried peddling. There isn't anything I haven't tried to sell—scrub brushes, rice cake, water—I tried them all, but I couldn't make any money at it . . . and my body is as it is. I used to weigh more than 110 pounds, I've lost twenty-two pounds. I used to have a nice full figure [*she gestures the shape of a plump, shapely body and chuckles*].
>
> I was sitting in a tearoom with some friends when a shaman happened by, come from an exorcism or something. As soon as she saw me she said, 'The spirits want to make an apprentice of someone; aren't you the one? If you don't apprentice yourself, you'll have a hard time surmounting your troubles.'[9] And with that she left. After this, I had a lot of different jobs, but never anything that suited me. I had jobs that didn't pay very well and sometimes they even withheld my pay. When I had work, I would sense that someone outside was calling me, I'd feel an urge to rush outside. But of course there wouldn't be anyone there. It was the spirits who were shaking me up. I didn't realize what was happening.
>
> I'd be out looking for work, roaming around and I'd see a shaman's house; you know, they have a flag. Every now and then I'd go in. They'd tell me, [*she gives a portentous ring to her voice*] 'You must receive the spirits before the next year is out. You must. If you refuse, your health will deteriorate even more and you will have even worse luck. You must accept them.'
>
> I went from job to job until I finally got discouraged and went to my sister's house. Just joking, I said, 'It looks like I have no recourse but to become a shaman.' My sister yelled at me, called me a 'crazy woman' [*laughs*] because I, her own little sister, had said such a thing. In Korea, If you become one, it's still considered really base. She hated the idea. 'Crazy

woman, with all your gadding about, must you go that far to make a living?' Since it couldn't be helped, I went out again and forced myself to find work, but they cheated me out of my pay. . . . I went back to my sister's house. My sister said, 'Mother and I talked it over. If the spirits have gotten such a hold on you, then you have to accept them. Could we hold that against you?'

Chini's story follows upon numerous other shaman autobiographies as a tale of inexplicable illness, marital turmoil, and financial reverses, interlaced with a portentous dream and oracles (Ch'oe 1981; Harvey 1979; Kendall 1988; Kim 1981:196–228). The discovery of shamanistic goods hidden away in the mountains (Choi 1987:114, 121–126), the mysterious compulsion to rush out of the workplace (Kim 1981:202), and even the image of the tile-roofed shrine appear in other stories (Ch'oe 1981:66). Like other shamans in other tales, Chini presents herself as dodging and denying the bald evidence of her destiny through years of pain (Harvey 1979; Kendall 1988). Her tale builds to a relentless sense of inevitability when Chini and her family finally acquiesce to the will of the spirits.

But while Chini presents herself as avoiding the obvious, her actions, even as she describes them, suggest her nagging preoccupation with the intimations of a calling. She visits diviners and their response becomes predictable: "You must serve the spirits." "Just joking," she broaches the idea to her sister. The construction of Chini's tale is a collective enterprise with a long gestation, begun in the divination sessions when she tells her story to a shaman and is in turn told its meaning.[10] By the time of her *kut*, Chini's story has also become a part of her spirit mother's repertoire, a story the older shaman tells about Chini as confirmation of the necessity of initiating her, and as one more example of the kind of person who is a destined shaman. While the oral performance of Chini's story— Chini to a shaman, Chini to our camera, Kim Pongsun to her clients, to the anthropologist, and back again to Chini—is an event peripheral to the performance of Chini's initiation *kut,* by its message and its place among a universe of such tales, it is intrinsic to the ritual's realization (Bauman and Briggs 1990).

FINDING A TEACHER

Between Chini's acceptance of her calling and her first initiation lay a crucial task: finding a shaman who would perform the initiation ritual and train her as a "spirit daughter." "You have to find a good shaman to do the initiation," the old shaman An Hosun insists. "If you meet up with a bad woman—and there certainly are a lot of bad women—if they don't do it right, then the initiate might even lose the force of her inspiration (*myŏnggi*).

Chini explains how her sister took her to Kwan Myŏngnyŏ, a young shaman with whom she was acquainted, but Kwan Myŏngnyŏ was unwilling to preside at Chini's initiation *kut*.

> Kwan Myŏngnyŏ said, 'As soon as you walked in, the General (Changgun) and the Child Gods (Tongja) came right on in after you. Whether I do a divination or not, that's the way it is (the spirits are with you.)' Then she divined and told me that I absolutely had to receive the spirits in the next year. There it was! She said exactly the same thing as the others. Kwan Myŏngnyŏ said, 'I'm just a beginner. I'm going to introduce you to a good, experienced teacher. I'll take you to meet her right now.' And that's how I came to meet my spirit mother Kim Pongsun.

Kwan Myŏngnyŏ is still considered an apprentice "little shaman" (*chagŭn mudang*) or "disciple" (*cheja*) studying with her "teachers" (*sŏnsaeng*), Kim Pongsun and An Hosun. An avaricious but still inexperienced shaman might have claimed Chini as her own client and officiated at her initiation, but Kwan Myŏngnyŏ considered this immoral:

> Would I go and ruin someone else's life for a few pennies? The truth is, it's pitiful enough when someone is forced to become a shaman. When someone gets in that situation, the only right and proper thing to do is see that they get a good teacher . . . I had so many difficulties starting out, the last thing I wanted was for her to go through what I'd endured.

Kwan Myŏngnyŏ had sponsored four *kut* before she was able to burst out with inspired speech and deliver oracles from the spirits. But without further training she was unable to mount *kut* for her own clients. She explained:

> I had a lot of customers for divinations, a steady stream of work, but I couldn't perform *kut*. Even though I had many opportunities for work where I could jump and call up the spirits, I gave it all away to other shamans. Kim Pongsun is the only one [who helped me]. Because I met her, things are working out for me now.
> [*The old shaman, An Hosun, assumes a didactic tone.*] That's right. There are rules and procedures (*pŏpto*). Now you're learning them one by one, huh? You'll get to know them all by and by because you met the right teacher. You know which spirit this is and which spirit that is, rules and procedures. When you perform it properly, then aren't you a shaman who serves the spirits? You've got to know it all, for all twelve segments of a *kut* the way it's been handed down from the old people, sequence by sequence. You have to learn it all to be a shaman, and it's very difficult to learn.

[*Kwan Myŏngnyŏ turns to the anthropologist for sympathy.*] It's really hard. You learn all that and there are still so many different sorts of things to learn, a lot of different spirits, a lot of rules and procedures . . . They say that if you don't concentrate just so, then it goes right past you. . . . since I met Kim Pongsun, I always write everything down. Me too [like the anthropologist], when I go home at night, I write down everything I've learned during the day and fix it in my mind. But of course, the language of the spirits and the way we humans talk isn't the same thing, is it?

Kwan Myŏngnyŏ and Chini were both initiated at a moment when women were embracing the shaman's profession in unprecedented numbers as a consequence of the loosening of government "anti-superstition" policies in the late 1980s, the rising popular interest in officially designated "National Treasure Shamans" whose rituals are often televised, and an intellectual movement that embraces shamans as the wellspring of the Korean spirit (Choi 1987:Ch. 2; Kim n. d.). When I asked Kwan Myŏngnyŏ about the frequency of initiations, she attributed their popularity to "*massŭ kom*," to mass communications. Hwang Rusi (Lucy Hwang) quotes a shaman who joked that one out of every two *kut* is an initiation (Hwang 1988:19), and religious studies scholar Sun Soon-Hwa cites a popular observation that "in poor districts like Kuro-dong if a woman shivers after urinating, she is initiated" (Sun n. d.:34). Hwang sees in this enthusiasm a dilution of the tradition and faults the numerous recent initiates for performing as they please without having subjected themselves to years of rigorous training at the feet of a spirit mother who has genuine knowledge of the tradition (Hwang 1988:19–21). These complaints are echoed by some of Sun's shaman informants (Sun n. d.:35). Some would-be shamans seem even to practice without the benefit of an initiation *kut,* particularly where their attractiveness or performance skills prompt seasoned shamans to include them in their *kut* (Choi 1987:132; Harvey 1979:191–195).[11] An Hosun's remarks and Kwan Myŏngnyŏ's experience suggest, on the other hand, the vulnerability of the neophyte when a less than maternal "spirit mother" regards her initiation as little more than a passing business transaction (see also Choi 1987:179).

An Hosun and Kwan Myŏngnyŏ, from their different perspectives, affirm that even with a proper teacher the training is grueling. Other apprentices complain that the senior shamans exploit them (Kendall 1985:59, 69–70). Kwan Myŏngnyŏ describes how, once she'd "bounced my way through a *kut,* the senior shamans would take all of the money for themselves." Jealousy among junior shamans, or the ambitions of established shamans who would snatch a promising apprentice, can also fracture the relationship between a spirit mother and spirit daughter (Kendall 1985:71, 1988:116–117; Sun n. d.:67). Some women given up in despair at the harshness of their training (Choi 1987: 130). This was An

Hosun's experience, which she juxtaposes to the gentler circumstances of contemporary training:

> When the spirits first came to me, I thought I would go out of my mind. . . .
> Why was I fated to have this happen to me? I was miserable, desolate, I
> would just sob and sob. It was all because I was just a little slip of an
> apprentice. In the old days, the shamans were very strict. When I was an
> apprentice, if you made a mistake over a single word, they'd give you a
> scolding right there and then, no matter who was there to hear it. You had
> to be careful about so many things. If you made a mistake, well, then
> they'd beat you, slap-bang, with the drumstick or the laundry paddle. . . .
> When you're a new shaman what do you know? You don't know the
> sequences, you don't know the rules and procedures. All you've got going
> for you is inspiration.
>
> Of course nowadays . . . they love and protect apprentices. They
> instruct them when no one is around, tell them 'You should do this like
> so.' In the past the old ladies would scold you. I was so miserable, and on
> top of everything else, I had to put up with this. I would go off by myself
> and cry my heart out. When they scolded me, I'd go hide and sob away.
> Sometimes I'd go to the outhouse or I'd go behind the house where I
> could cry by myself. I'd come back and pretend that I hadn't been crying,
> and if I did well after that, then everything would be fine. Nowadays they
> say, 'Well done, well done,' even when the apprentice doesn't know what
> she's doing, isn't that so? It wasn't like that in the past. . . . I wanted to
> escape the beatings. I decided not to go through with it.[12]

An Hosun fled her spirit mother's house and, although she was called upon to
assist at other shamans' *kut,* she was not reconciled to her calling until she was
forty-eight years old. She thinks of the years between her initiation at age thirty-
six and her final acceptance of the spirits twelve years later as empty time,
marked by illness, mental instability, and financial failure. Her remarks betray a
profound ambivalence toward the demands of her tradition. She insists that only
a thorough knowledge of the rules and procedures makes a real shaman (*sinŭi
kija*) and has contempt for the praise now lavished on incompetent apprentices.
Yet she evokes the bitterness of her own experience, picturing herself struggling
through snow drifts on her way to a *kut.*

> Those were the most miserable times. You'd sink into it up to your knees
> and your feet would freeze. . . . You had to walk. No matter if it were 10
> *li,* 15 *li,* 20 *li,*[13] you had to do your work that day. . . . It was a little bit
> better when it rained, but when it snowed, when you were pelted with
> snow, well even slogging through knee-high drifts was all right, but when
> you sank in up to your waist, that was really miserable, yep. You had to

carry everything on your head, even the drum and all the spirits' paraphernalia. No one wanted to go, all the carriers would refuse. Who wanted to wade through the high snow drifts? You had to slog through with everything on your own head. That was when I was the most miserable of all. Would other people have given up a son and given up a husband? All they had to do was keep house and things worked out for them. Why did I have to endure this? At those times I cried a lot. [*She chuckles.*] Isn't what I'm telling you sad and pathetic?

Toward Chini, the teacher's sternness comes mingled with the concern of a fictive "maternal aunt" (*imo*)[14] who enjoins Chini to take her training seriously and be spared wasting her own prime years. On the morning of the *kut* she delivers a sharp lecture to the apprentice, becoming more impassioned as she speaks:

If I had just met you for the first time, then I wouldn't be saying this. I'd think that these are the troubles of someone else's child; it's sad but it doesn't concern me. But now I'm telling you, like your own mother. I'm old, I've had a lot of experience. . . . If you don't go through with it, then in the end you'll be beaten down. That's what happened to me. I refused . . . said I wouldn't follow a shaman's path and left, said I wouldn't make my living this way, but in the end this is what I became. Even if it's the death of you, you have to heed your spirit mother's words and give a good answer. Truly, those who make it through find their minds at ease, they're not longer burdened with sorrow. I've spoken in a fit of passion. Hereafter, just be responsive. If there's something you need to know, don't hide it. Ask, 'Which spirit is this?' 'Mother, how should I do this?' Only if you make a point of asking such things will you ever become a great shaman. If you're stubborn and just do as you please, it won't happen . . . you have to be diligent. Did you hear me? Answer me, 'Yes, right'; that's how you should make a good response.

Even greater than An Hosun's concern is that of Chini's spirit mother, Kim Pongsun, for this is the first spirit daughter whom she has initiated. As Kwan Myŏngnyŏ told me, "We call the shaman who presides at the initiation 'spirit mother' because her responsibilities are as weighty as those of any parent raising a child." Or as Kim Pongsun, the spirit mother, put it, confessing her anxiety over Chini's impending *kut*:

When someone sets out to become a shaman, they agonize over whether they'll make it or not, and now that's my worry too. It would be different if Chini hadn't come to my house, but when you are like parent and child, then you agonize over them. It's that way with Americans, too, isn't it?

Chini had spent the summer in Kim Pongsun's house, following the custom of apprentice shamans who spend a period of training in residence with the spirit mother after their first initiation *kut* (Choi 1981:81, 129; Choi 1987:131–132; Hwang 1988:23). This period was particularly long and intense, perhaps because Chini was bereft of both economic and social capital, and because she had emerged from her first *kut* still unqualified to begin her own practice as a diviner. Chini ran errands and helped in the kitchen while she shared the good food and comfortable accommodations of a prosperous shaman's household. She gained back some of her weight and seemed less high-strung and tense.[15]

In the months between her first and second initiation *kut*, Chini was expected to develop both her practical knowledge of ritual performance and her store of spiritual inspiration. She would learn the former through Kim Pongsun's instruction and by observing Kim Pongsun's work, a process the shaman "Yongsu's Mother" once likened to my own fieldwork (Kendall 1985:67–68). When I visited Kim Pongsun's shrine to discuss our plans for the film, I found Chini perched in a posture of intense concentration while Kim Pongsun performed an exorcism in her shrine.

Chini also made pilgrimages to four sacred mountains seeking the spiritual force or energy that would sharpen her visions and give her the power to convey oracles from the spirits. On the eve of her second *kut*, Chini spoke with some confidence about the powers she had acquired through these efforts:

> When the spirits appear, when they're really touching you, it's like your film rolling on, image by image, the vision comes up and then it disappears [*she said this while facing Diana's camera*]. . . . Each time I went to the mountain, the spirits would come out and play for a while. You see, at first [at my first *kut*] inspired speech didn't burst out of me, but then each time I went to the mountain the spirits gave me a little more power and inspiration. This time I've got to go through with it. They'll give me the power of inspired speech. This time their oracles will pour out.

Chini describes herself as a passive receptor of the spirits' power. Her shaman teachers, on the other hand, will insist that Chini must take the initiative, perform like a shaman to claim the spirits' power as her own. This tension of perceptions will be evident throughout Chini's *kut*. As she helps Chini into her costume on the first morning of the *kut*, Kwan Myŏngnyŏ recalls her own series of failed initiations and tells her, "You have to call the spirits or the spirits won't come, and they won't give you the power of inspired speech. Do you want to spend the rest of your life doing *kut* after *kut*?

SUMMONING THE BUDDHIST SAGE

On the first morning of the *kut* the experienced shamans perform the preliminaries, purifying the ritual space and inviting the spirits into Chini's rented room. After this, as in other initiation *kut,* Chini is dressed, in sequence, in costumes for the spirits of each segment of the *kut.* The costumes that the shamans wear are more than theatrical artifice; they are vehicles for the spirits' presence. Each robe has been dedicated to a particular spirit, either a member of the shaman's own pantheon or a particularly potent spirit of a client household. In particularly dramatic manifestations, spirits with unusually pressing business may appear out of turn when a shaman reaches spontaneously for their costume, clothes herself, and then gives them voice. During her *kut,* the shamans will urge Chini to follow her impulses and select from a random array of costumes; the garment she chooses will reveal the claims of a particularly potent spirit.

Once dressed, she dances to ready herself for the descent of the spirits, encouraged by the three shamans who beat the drum, gong, and cymbals. Then, charged with divine inspiration, she must proclaim the long lists of spirits associated with each segment of the *kut* as the visions appear before her eyes, and transmit the spirits' oracles. Her performance implies a spontaneous flow of visions, but in fact the lists of spirits are learned and difficult to master. Kwan Myŏngnyŏ still receives occasional coaching before she performs, and Oggyŏng's Mother, three years a *mansin* when I began my first fieldwork in 1977, was often criticized for the mistakes she made (Kendall 1985:67).

The first segment of the *kut* honors the Buddhist Sage (Pulsa) and the Seven Stars (Ch'ilsŏng), and Chesŏk (associated with birth and fertility)—pure high spirits honored on the mountains. To receive these spirits, Chini must balance on the rim of an earthen jar filled with water and call them to this pure high place. Dressed in the white robes and peaked cowl of Buddhist liturgical dances she faces the three shamans who pound the drum, cymbals, and gong. The drum provides the essential rhythm of a *kut,* the sounds that rouse the spirits at the start of a ritual and pick up pace when the dancer seems ready to assume the series of jumps, on the balls of her feet, that signify inspiration. The presence of a strong drummer is essential to coax a timid initiate like Chini to contact with the spirits. Only Kim Pongsun and An Hosun, the two experienced shamans, will wield the drumstick during Chini's *kut.* The cymbals and gong seem to have been borrowed from Buddhist practice and are used to punctuate the arrival of spirits or the high drama of an exorcism.

Chini, dancing with timid steps, moves her lips, attempting to follow the shamans' chant of invocation. She begins to jump, encouraged by the drum beats. She hesitates, wide-eyed and uncertain. In the distance, her mother and sister kneel on the floor beside the earthen water jar, hugging it steady in tense anticipation of Chini's ascent.

"Now look here," yells Kim Pongsun, the spirit mother, "it takes concentration to do it. Set your mind on it. You've got to get up on that jar."

Kwan Myŏngnyŏ shouts encouragement. "The spirits are coming! When you're jumping, when you feel an urge to grab a spirit's costume, then grab it and jump like crazy." The power comes through the costume. "Today all you have to do is dance with the costume, go up on the jar, and give it a try. This behavior is really too much, stupid." She says this last with a touch of affection, as to a recalcitrant child.

Kim Pongsun vents her frustration. "I'm losing my patience. What's there to deliberate? Do you think that the spirits will show up if you just stand there waiting for them?" The drum pounds its *tonk, tonk, tonk, ta kung* rhythm, the pace accelerates as Chini approaches the jar, still dancing, still hesitating.

> **An Hosun:** Go on, go on, get up, go right on up. The spirits will only give you the force of their inspiration when you get up on the jar. The Buddhist Sage is giving you inspiration! Go on up! That's right!
>
> **Kwan Myŏngnyŏ:** The spirits are coming through! Go up, the spirits are pushing you up! Bow, bow, bow, bow! [*Chini stands on the rim of the jar and bows to the four directions, but still she does not speak. The shamans address not Chini now, but the spirits.*]
>
> **An Hosun:** Are you here? Who are you? Who are you?
>
> **Kwan Myŏngnyŏ:** Please open the great front gate for the apprentice of the Yi family.
>
> **Chini as the Buddhist Sage:** [*in a voice that is breathy and uncertain*] The Buddhist Sage of the Sun and Moon, the Buddhist Sage of the Heavenly Palace, just so, the Buddhist Sage of the village shrine, just so, pray to the Buddhist Sage, the Buddhist Sage, the Buddhist Sage, [*she falters, shakes her head in frustration, recovers*] the Buddhist Sage of the village shrine, [*she draws a deep breath as if fighting panic*] the Buddhist Sage from the village shrine in our ancestral home. For years we have intended to help our apprentice, just so, but our apprentice does not accept us.
>
> **Kwan Myŏngnyŏ:** Because she doesn't know any better. [*This is a common rejoinder in* kut, *intended to mollify the spirits.*]
>
> **Chini as the Buddhist Sage:** All this year she must bow in the shrine, yes, and honor the spirits, offer many more prayers, and then next year we'll give her the power of inspired speech. [*The shamans are livid.*]
>
> **Kwan Myŏngnyŏ:** *Aigo!* You'll put it off to next year? We've done all this so that you'll give her the power of inspired speech now. Why should we wait until next year? You keep coming through with visions, keep right on transmitting the words of the spirits.

Kim Pongsun: Give us the true words of the spirits, an inspired divination!
Chini as the Buddhist Sage: This year the spirits will just come and
go . . . the apprentice will not gain the power of inspired speech.
Something is blocking her.
Kwan Myŏngnyŏ: Go on! Haven't we given you everything you asked for
to make you unblock her gates of inspired speech?
Kim Pongsun: It's no good. We gave you everything you wanted. What's
this about next year, next year? In the meantime, your apprentice will
have starved to death!

Chini descends from the jar. Her foot slips on the paper covering over the
mouth and splashes into the water. Her sodden stocking is removed. She returns
to the shrine, her face red with silent weeping. Back in the shrine, she sways on
her feet to the slowed pace of the drum beats, like the ticks of a lethargic
metronome. Chini speaks no more. The old shaman An Hosun urges her, once
again, to give vent to the spontaneous impulses that will unleash the spirits: "If
you want to insult someone, insult them; if you want to cry, then cry your fill; do
whatever you feel like, this is the spirits' day." Kwan Myŏngnyŏ, aware of Chini's
peril, tries again to coax her into positive action: "If all you're going to do is
stand there praying for something to happen, then the spirits will just keep on
going their merry way without doing anything for you. . . . All you have to do is
say, 'I'm the Seven Stars' and give an oracle. Come on, whether the spirits have
made you into a shaman or not." An Hosun suggests a stiff beating, such as she
once endured.

The shamans begin to consider Chini's/the Buddhist Sage's assertion that
something, some spirit out of sequence, is blocking her. Noting Chini's timid
prances, Kim Pongsun, the spirit mother, offers the wry comment that Chini has
been possessed by the ghost of a dead deer. As Chini continues to sway in silence,
Kim Pongsun scolds her in mounting desperation.

> What are you up to? Come on, you've got to talk, why can't you give us
> an oracle from the spirits. Isn't this what you asked for? We decided to
> do this because you thought that you could bring it off. [*And still Chini
> hesitates.*] You've already given us one oracle, now shouldn't you give us
> the true words of the Seven Stars? You can't? What are you thinking of?
> You've let yourself get distracted, filled your mind with other things,
> otherwise you'd feel the spirits from the top of your head to the tips of
> your toes. Come on, say, 'It's the Seven Stars! Here's how it is with
> Chini.' [*She draws out her words for emphasis in the manner of spirits pro-
> claiming their presence through the shaman during* kut]. Tell us she's
> frustrated; tell us she's pitiful. Hey, do you think some spirit would go so

far as to move your tongue for you? [*And as a muttered aside*] I'm struck
dumb by her stupidity.

Kim Pongun's scolding betrays the paradox of agency and performance that
marks Chini's struggle. Chini has failed to "feel the spirits," but she has also
failed to *act* inspired, to convey the presence of the spirits through her own
words and actions. For her part, Chini is unable to act inspired because she does
not feel the presence of the spirits. Chini gives up and bows her head for a scowl-
ing Kim Pongsun to remove her white cowl. Chini giggles with embarrassment,
perhaps heightened by the realization that she is in full view of Diana's camera.
This earns the wrath of Kim Pongsun: "Laughing? Don't you have any pride?
How dare you laugh after that?" Kwan Myŏngnyŏ gives Chini a gentle repri-
mand, telling her to listen attentively to her spirit mother's words. "Listen to
what?" snaps Kim Pongsun. "If you tell her something, it just goes in one ear and
out the other. Today, I don't have a single shred of patience left. Just wait and
see what I've got in store for you." In the corner of the room, the old shaman, An
Hosun, wipes away a tear.

Chini's sister embraces her and comforts her. Later she will tell the shamans,
"This child never cries and that's a worry. She holds it in." Chini admitted this
herself when I asked her how she felt on the eve of her *kut*, "Other people might
get depressed and cry about it but I'm the sort of person who doesn't shed tears;
I'm always happy." Her inability to give vent to emotion is, in this context, a
liability. Her sister calls it "a worry," believing that pain held too long inside fes-
ters into pathology; she may even be thinking of Chini's past treatment for
mental illness.[16] For the shamans, Chini's emotional resistance prevents her from
clearing her mind and opening herself to the spirits' inspiration. She does not
heed the impulse to draw down a particular spirit's costume and take it to herself as a vehicle of that spirit's presence and power. She neither weeps nor shouts
insults, thus resisting the very acts of emotional release and surrender that would
bring on the force of the spirits.[17] Above all, she has failed to act like a shaman.
The shamans tell her that the spirits will not move her tongue for her, that performing inspired speech "whether or not the spirits have made you into a
shaman" is more constructive than succumbing to stage fright in stony silence.
Their metaphor, that Chini's gates of inspired speech are "blocked" (*makhida*),
works on two nearly indistinguishable levels: she is blocked because an
obstreperous spirit stand in her path, and she is blocked because she cannot
clear her mind and open herself to feelings, impulses, and spirits by losing herself in performance.

Because Chini is unable to continue, Kwan Myŏngnyŏ performs in her place,
manifesting the Seven Stars and the Birth Grandmother (Chesŏk)[18] who must

also appear in this segment of the *kut.* These spirits, like the shamans, scold Chini for her lack of resolve, then threaten to leave her:

> **Chini:** How can you leave me? Please give me the power of inspired speech.
> **Kwan Myŏngnyŏ as the Seven Stars:** Didn't you close your lips when we were going to give you speech? . . . Quick, quick, unless you set your mind to it, you won't be able to receive it. This time, try for it with all your heart and soul.

PRINCESS HOGU

Kim Pongsun, the spirit mother, performs next, seeking the identity of the spirits that are blocking Chini. As the Mountain god who presides over the dead in their hillside graves, she senses the presence of two restless souls (*malmyŏng*) who died young.[19] She orders that two sets of spirit clothes be purchased to appease the restless shades of Chini's father, a heavy drinker and poor provider who died away from home while in his prime, and a pock-marked sister who committed suicide at age nineteen. But when Kim Pongsun, now in the costume of the Special Messenger (Pyŏlsang), offers meat to the spirits, balancing the offering on her trident,[20] she sees a vision of Chini's dead sister in a more formidable guise, not merely as the ghost of a maiden suicide but as a destined shaman who, through the force of her calling, asserts herself as a guardian spirit (*taesin*) who assists the shaman in her practice. She appears in the guise of Princess Hogu, the smallpox maiden in the shaman's pantheon. Kim Pongsun's chant alternates the observing voice of the shaman with the voice of the spirit.

> It's Chini's sister who has come here as Princess Hogu, blocking Chini's path. It's clear, she's come here wearing a crown and a court robe, she's come as Princess Hogu to be Chini's guardian spirit.
> I'm full of resentment, full of regret. Chini, you're not as bright as your sister. I'm so very bright, and filled with jealousy, but you, for some reason, you're cowardly, you don't take initiative, you're always anxious and troubled. If you honor me as your guardian spirit, Princess Hogu, if you give me a robe and a crown, then all will be well. The calamities will cease. . . .
> I see the child, flickering before my eyes. What's to be done? It's clear, she's Princess Hogu. Had she lived, Chini's sister was fated to become a shaman, to be renowned far and wide. She died without fulfilling her destiny so now its come to you, but however you look at it, Chini, you can't measure up to your dead sister.

Figure 1. A Korean shaman places thousand-wŏn bills on the meat offering. She will balance this pig's head to determine if the spirits accept the *kut*. Photograph by Homer Williams.

Figure 2. Princess Hogu in an antique painting from a shaman's shrine.
Photograph by Homer Williams.

The shamans immediately seized upon the logic of this apparition, identified with pock-marked maidens and dead shamans. With the women of Chini's family, they reconstruct a story about the dead girl who is now a potent spirit.

> **Kwan Myŏngnyŏ:** They say she was pock-marked, Chini's dead sister.
>
> **Kim Pongsun:** And she was bright, really bright.
>
> **Chini's mother:** She'd say 'What's the point of living?' We couldn't give her plastic surgery. She'd get upset when she went out in public. She thought that everyone was staring at her. And then she'd say that she was going to kill herself. I'd say, 'What's this talk of dying? You'll find a nice husband and things will work out.' That's what I told her. [*She speaks with great speed and heat, reliving the force of her old argument against the fact of her daughter's death.*]
>
> **Kwan Myŏngnyŏ:** [*breaking in on Chini's mother*] She took poison? When she was still a maiden? Well then of course she would come back as Princess Hogu; she died a maiden.
>
> **Kim Pongsun:** [*authoritatively*] Of course, if she died as a maiden she would be Princess Hogu.
>
> **Chini's mother:** She was nineteen years old.
>
> **Shamans:** There, you see!
>
> **Kwan Myŏngnyŏ:** Chini, your sister's come to guide you, to be your guardian spirit and make you into a successful shaman.

And now Chini claims that she sensed her dead sister's presence when she was unable to perform: "It was so strange. She said that she had come to me because I'm so pathetic. No one else in the family has suffered the way I have." The words Chini attributes to her dead sister could as easily be her own or an echo of the old shaman An Hosun's "Why did I have to endure this?"—the common question of a shaman's life.

The sister is to become a permanent symbol of Chini's destiny, indeed a partner in it. The spirit mother orders that a crown and robe be purchased to honor the dead girl as Princess Hogu, Chini's guardian god (Hogu Taesin). Chini's elder sister goes back to the shaman supply shop. But Princess Hogu is, and is more than, Chini's personal idiom (Boddy 1989:136, 166; Crapanzano 1977; Obeyesekere 1970, 1977, 1981). The shamans construct the logic of her story from a common history of family suffering even as family history is implicated in Chini's crisis, and family fortune hangs upon Chini's cure. By Kim Pongsun's logic, the spirits were determined to make a shaman of someone in the family, but the family consistently misread the signs. An aunt and a cousin were judged to be "crazy" and did ultimately lose their minds. The pock-marked sister committed suicide. Chini endured ten years of suffering and a bad marriage because her portentous dream was ignored. Chini's story also "belongs" to her mother and sister, and they tell it in order to make sense of their common history, to cast Chini's destiny as one manifestation of a common fate. More of their story will be enacted, and interacted, when the family's ancestors appear later in the *kut*.

To Western ears, the spirit mother's words sound callous: "Chini, your sister was bright as a button. She was the one who was destined to become a shaman, but the family didn't realize what was going on." Yet here her blunt comparison—"You can't measure up to your dead sister"—expresses compassion, not cruelty. Chini should have been spared this ordeal and the necessity of embracing a profession for which, it is now obvious, she is temperamentally ill-suited. Her sister would have made the better shaman, but when she died, the spirits turned to Chini.

Because Chini herself ignored the spirits, she cannot now easily claim their power. As she acknowledged on the eve of her second *kut*, "If I'd accepted the spirits when they first claimed me, then everything would have burst out of me and I would have danced like crazy, but now it's gone on for too long. . . . I won't be cured just like that." Kim Pongsun affirms this during a break in the *kut:*

> There is a difference between someone who's been sitting quietly and then bursts out with it like a sudden peal of thunder, and someone who has been stuck with a stubborn spirit through a long, hard, and bitter experience. From what I've seen and those I've helped along at the other initiation *kut,* she's been too hasty (in holding this second *kut*). . . . It isn't a matter of foresight, it's just how things have turned out . . . If I take her on, then she's got to become a shaman. We can't give up, even if we don't succeed this time. Not a single one of her siblings is doing well, right? If they don't have anything, then they can't help her out; it can't be helped. But even if they can't support her, they should find it in their hearts not to slander her. When she hears that, how can she muster the strength to go on? If they help her, as loving brothers and sisters, then in a year or two, by the time Chini is thirty-three, thirty-four, thirty-five, she will be a success.

She addresses Chini's mother, and through Chini's mother, Chini herself, evoking the bond of suffering that she and Chini share:

> The first time I talked to you, Auntie, didn't I tell you that I also had difficulties starting out? But now I have a house, I'm comfortable, and everyone comes to me for handouts. . . . Look, Chini has a bad fate and I have a bad fate. There's nothing we can do about it. Didn't she come to my house and didn't I meet her and that's how it happened [that she became my apprentice]? Have I ever denied her food to eat or clothes to wear? . . . I'm quick-tempered. I scold with my lips but inside, my heart aches for her, all alone in the world. I've been through it all myself.

ANCESTRAL AFFIRMATIONS

When the old shaman An Hosun performs the ancestors' sequence of the *kut*, the dead sister appears twice, first as the Great Spirit Princess Hogu (Hogu Taesin), filling the role of a dead shaman who leads the souls of the family dead to the *kut*. This appearance further validates the dead sister's thwarted destiny as a shaman and her claim to the status of a guardian spirit. She asks, "How is my little sister going to fill my big shoes with her tiny feet?" She reappears later in the persona of a family ghost, trailing after the family ancestors, as must the unquiet soul of one who died unmarried and without issue, a maiden lachrymosely complaining of her unmarried state.

When Chini's dead father appears, he affirms his role in the family's misery, first by neglect, then by dying and abandoning Chini's mother to fend for herself and her children.

> **An Hosun as Chini's father:** You think I died away from home because I was too fond of friends, food, and spending money? You think that's why I died, don't you?
> **Mother:** Yes.
> **An Hosun as Chini's father:** And because I died, look at how much pain you've suffered. All because I died, you've had reason to cry [*sobs*]. . . . When I was alive I thought of my own pleasure, I didn't provide for my family at home. I used what was in my pockets to entertain my friends.

The ancestor shares a cup of wine with his long-suffering wife: "I haven't seen you, dear, for such a long time." The shamans titter at An Hosun's repeated requests, in character, for yet another cup of wine.

As in any *kut*, the appearance of the ancestors gives voice to a larger family story of pain, recrimination, and reconciliation. In the guise of restless ancestors, An Hosun gives back as drama what has already been told as story, inviting Chini's family to confront visions of their common past. Everyone present, including Diana Lee and myself, knew the basic structure of their story before the *kut* began."[21] Other bits and pieces are revealed and elaborated from the sidelines of the *kut* in dialogic interpretations of the unfolding action—*"She took poison? When she was still a maiden?"*—a process that will climax in Chini's possession by her own dead sister. Ancestral appearances, ancestors turned into gods, and stories told about the dead affirm that bonds of kinship and history are implicated in Chini's plight, and that mother, sister, and sister-in-law thus act with appropriate complicity in Chini's initiation.

CHINI TRIES AGAIN

The shamans dress Chini in Princess Hogu's robes. She stands tense with antici-pation, then rushes to the street and scatters coarse grain to drive off malevolent forces. She leaps while the drum throbs, but when she stops, she is still unable to speak. In near desperation, the shamans clothe Chini in the gold satin robe of the Heavenly King (Ch'ŏnha Taewang), a high spirit in her pantheon whose presence she proclaimed on the mountain. This spirit came to her from her mother's lineage, a consort line in dynastic times.[22] The spirit mother would explain later that no intrusive spirit could block the high King.

No longer jumping, Chini sways on her feet to the slowed pace of the drum, eyes vacant, a smile on her lips.

> **Kim Pongsun:** Has the Heavenly King arrived?
> **Chini:** Just so, the Heavenly King.
> **Kim Pongsun:** [*to the spirits*] Now that you've descended into the appren-tice, please speak. Such a dignified spirit as yourself should instruct her so that her every phrase is eloquent and each word fragrant. Give us the true words of the spirits.
> **Kwan Myŏngnyŏ:** Chini's spirit mother has gone to so much trouble. Give the spirit mother your words of knowledge and then divine for all the other shamans here too.

Chini has lapsed back into silence, swaying on her feet and tugging at her ear as if struggling to hear a faint or distant voice. Kim Pongsun the spirit mother kneels in front of Chini's altar and rubs her hands in supplication, petitioning the spirits:

> If you've really descended into the apprentice, give her inspiration, give us the true words of the spirits. . . . What does the apprentice know? She's like a child, a three-year-old baby. . . . You're such a renowned spirit, please let her have her wish. Ah, we human beings don't know anything. Please give her the power to see and express the spirits' knowledge. She's been clumsy and stupid. Now your shaman is going to have sore legs from kneeling here for so long honoring you this way.

She asks Chini, "Don't you have the least little vision? Who is that standing beside you, huh? Who's the one at your side? No response. Chini continues to sway. The spirit mother directs her frustration to the painted images of the spir-its above Chini's altar, telling them that in all of her seventeen years as a shaman, she has never picked a fight with the spirits, not even once, but now she is reaching her limit. Chini's sister-in-law catches my eye, stifling a giggle at Kim Pongsun's performance.

> I'm going to tear you off the wall and burn you up! [*Kim Pongsun controls herself and gives slow emphasis to her next statement*] I mean it, if I get any angrier . . . because you've been tormenting the apprentice to death. I said that we should do the initiation next spring but because you harassed her so much, we're doing it now, quick as a flash. Why can't you speak? [*sarcastically*] All you nobles, you're really something. You're heartless as an empty can. That's the truth. If I get any angrier I'll cast you all out, I will. [*She says this last with great heat.*]

The shamans continue to coax Chini, reminding her of the effort that they have all undertaken on her behalf, telling her to let it all burst out of her, asking her for "just one little word." Kim Pongsun, with reckless humor, asks, "Shall I chant you some sutra?" Still kneeling, she taps lightly on her gong in imitation of a monk beating a wooden clapper and intones the Ch'ŏnsu Kyŏng, the sutra she plays on tape at home when she has a headache or feels depressed. "You like that?" she asks with a coy roll of her eyes. "Well then, talk."

And at last, Chini speaks:

> **Chini as the Heavenly King:** From now on, the great Heavenly King will help the apprentice Yi become a successful shaman. The apprentice must make many offerings in her shrine and then bit by bit we will help her gain recognition. Princess Hogu has become a pupil of the Heavenly King.
> **Kwan Myŏngnyŏ:** That's the way!
> **Chini:** I am Princess Hogu. I have not harmed my family. I have received the teaching of the Heavenly King.

The shamans tell her to deliver an oracle to her sister-in-law, who has provided the divination tray Chini will use in her practice when, aided by her guardian spirit, she divines for clients. The tray was dedicated with a wish for Chini's brother's success. The sister-in-law is called into the room and ordered to "Kowtow! Kowtow! Kowtow!", which she does with great dispatch. Chini, as Princess Hogu, reassures her that "bit by bit, things will improve," that she will help her family from now on. She tells her mother "If you honor me, then your children will be free from misfortune and strife," and again promises good fortune and the spirit's protection to her elder sister.

Kim Pongsun complains that this was not an impressive oracle, that what she said was not enough (and indeed it was formulaic and predictable). Kwan Myŏngnyŏ defends Chini: "It's her nature." "Her nature is her nature, but the spirits come on with a bang," Kim Pongsun reminds her. She continues to urge

Chini on, using a now familiar formula: "If there's a costume the spirit wants to wear, then put it on! Jump and keep shouting out the spirits' commands. That's what we mean by the true words of the spirits, shout out what the spirits have to tell us. That's what it's all about." The shamans pound cymbals, drum, and gong with great enthusiasm, the boom, boom, boom of percussion reverberating against the *tonk, tonk, tonk, ta kung* rhythm of the drum, as Chini reaches again for Princess Hogu's robe.

> **Spirit mother:** Cry your heart out. Then everything will burst out.
> **Chini:** [*racked with sobs as she buries her tear streaked face in her open fan*[23]] Mother! Mother! Mother!
> **Kim Pongsun:** You see, she's letting it all come out.
> **Kwan Myŏngnyŏ:** Chini's mother, come up here, come up here.
> **Chini:** [*She gasps out her words between sobs while her mother rubs her hands in supplication, her eyes brimming over with tears.*] Mother! Mother! I wanted so much to be beautiful. Mother. . . . I'll help my little sister as a shaman, Mother. I want your blessing, but you don't respond. Mother, how many times I've called you! . . . When my mother raised me she wasn't able to give us decent food. I'm full of pity for Chini. How can it be helped, Mother? . . . That's why I've come.

Weeks later, Kim Pongsun would comment on the pathos of this encounter:

> She was telling her mother what she couldn't say when she was alive. She had to die to do it. 'Mother, did you give me good food to eat? Did you ever buy me a persimmon? Did you ever make me pretty clothes?' . . . By possessing her younger sister, she attacks her mother. The mother was heartsick when she heard that. . . . She never realized how her daughter felt. Even in death, her daughter feels such resentment that she possessed her sister and said these things. . . . It was a pathetic death, age nineteen, that should be such a lovely age, but she wasn't able to eat good food, wasn't able to wear nice clothes, wasn't able to feel her mother's love. Now she possesses her younger sister and says, 'I was tormented to death so you had better take care of me.' That's what she meant. Chini's sister cried, her mother cried, even I cried; we all cried.

There is a subtle distinction between Chini's portrayal and Kim Pongsun's recollection of a resentful, spiteful child, as dead children are commonly portrayed in *kut*. In fact, Chini portrayed the dead girl in a more benevolent guise consistent with her acceptance of the spirit as a divine alter ego.[24] Just as Chini has claimed that Princess Hogu received the elevated instruction of the Heavenly King and has not harmed her family, here the dead sister/Princess Hogu seeks her mother's blessing and acceptance (as does Chini). Again, the dead girl's pain merges with

Chini's story and with the painful history of her family. After this confrontation the mother recounts the story of the dead girl's suicide by poison on a lonely hillside. Kwan Myŏngnyŏ remarks that she heard the dead girl mention white trousers when Chini spoke, and taps a well of remorse in Chini's elder sister:

> White trousers, she said she wanted to wear white trousers. It wasn't easy for me then either. I wasn't more than twenty-two or twenty-three years old. I said, 'Crazy woman, what's so important about white trousers?' I was hateful. It was her nature not to be bothered by little things. When she came to my house, she didn't just sit and visit. She'd wash the diapers for me, help me out however she could, fix the food, even boil up the stew. My younger siblings, when they come round, *ahyu!* They won't so much as lift a dish rag, except for Chini, of course.

While still possessed by her dead sister/Princess Hogu, Chini is led to the divination tray in the expectation that she will cast rice on the lacquered surface and from its configurations, offer oracles in the manner of a shaman giving divinations. Chini collapses on the floor in a bow of supplication at Kim Pongsun's feet. "Teacher, help me!" she sobs. Between them, they spread and count rice grains as Chini, still shielding her tear-streaked face in Princess Hogu's fan, produces simple divinations for her mother, elder sister, and Kwan Myŏngnyŏ, confirmed as Kim Pongsun flicks the rice grains with her own fingertips.

Chini stands while the shamans give her the rhythm for the spirit's praise song (*t'aryŏng*), a chance for the singer to proclaim triumphantly, "There is no guardian spirit so wonderful as my guardian spirit, so wonderful I just can't say." Half-dancing, half-staggering, Chini flails her arms and sobs her way through a few bars of the usually lively song. Encouraged by the drum rhythm, she jumps to the point of exhaustion and collapses in a bow on the floor in front of the altar to receive the shaman's praise.

> **An Hosun:** You did well.
> **Kim Pongsun:** That was A-1! Cry your heart out, let go of all your resentment. Cry your heart out and next time don't cry. Just give a terrific performance.[25]
> **Kwan Myŏngnyŏ:** Today is a day for crying, a day to let all your feelings out.

The story of a successful ritual process might have ended here. Chini's triumphant unblocking came after the appropriate personal and familial symbols, drawn from a larger cultural lexicon, had been identified and set at play (cf. Kessler 1977; Obeyesekere 1977; Turner, 1967, 1981 [1968]). The transformative power of spiritual manifestations in this and other *kut* thickens a common family history of pain, casts individual affliction amid a web of family experience, and offers a promise of common resolution for both the afflicted initiate and the members of her family, living and dead. Performance theory would lead us to an appreciation of how drum beats, costumes, dance, and the recognizable theatrical business of particular spirits—the fan over Princess Hogu's pock-marked face, the pouring of wine for a drunkard father, the sobbing cry of "Mother!"—are implicated in the construction of a successful *kut*, a *kut* that becomes compelling for its universe of participants (cf. Kapferer 1983). Chini's *kut* has "worked" in the sense that ordinary *kut* work, as a collective mustering of family, gods, and ancestors, conjoined in the performance of their story (Kendall 1977, 1985:Ch. 1).

If we were to interpret Chini's initiation as fundamentally a healing ritual, we would find reassurance in Chini's seeming catharsis through the persona of her dead sister (Scheff 1979), and the remainder of her *kut* would be but denouement. But the stakes are different in an initiation *kut* and a moment of catharsis is insufficient to the expectations of a fully realized shaman. Chini has made progress. An Hosun and Kwan Myŏngnyŏ confirm this later that night at Kwan Myŏngnyŏ's home, when Kim Pongsun has stayed behind to instruct Chini on the next day's performance. "After all, she did manage to give us some words from the spirits," says An Hosun, contrasting Chini's performance today with her recalcitrance on the mountain last spring. Yet in their guarded comments, the shamans recognize that Chini is not yet empowered to pour out compelling oracles on command and minister to clients. Except for the brief encounter with her dead sister, come back as Princess Hogu, her words have been formulaic and limited. She is not yet a shaman; the successful outcome of her *kut* remains uncertain.

THE KNIFE-RIDING GENERAL

The next day, Chini faces a final ordeal. She must summon the fearless Knife-Riding General (Chaktu Changgun) and through the force of his power, balance on blades used to chop fodder. The blades are set high atop the earthen water jar. From that perch, Chini must again try to deliver the true words of the spirits. An Hosun, the old shaman, helps her to dress. As she fastens the ribbon of a blue court robe, worn under the Knife-Riding General's red brocade, she tells Chini, "Wear this and think of Auntie," loaning Chini the added power of one of her own spirits along with her robe. Chini is optimistic: "I feel it today; . . . the Heavenly King and the jade Immortal [his consort] are taking me away. It's good; your star pupil is going to be fine."

Chini starts to dance, then stops, reaches for the Heavenly King's robe, and puts it on, doing spontaneously what yesterday had to be urged upon her. She dances, announces the presence of the Heavenly King, and then the Generals. She declares that she is going to ride the blades. The shamans again urge her to deliver the true words of the spirits, but Chini just continues to dance. Again, they urge her to follow her impulses and grab another costume, or to pick up the blades and dance with them. When this fails, they clothe her in Princess Hogu's robe. When this fails, they dress her in the robe for Kim Pongsun's own Knife-Riding Guardian God (Chaktu Taesin). Kim Pongsun scolds her for staring up at the images on the altar while she dances, rather than casting her eyes to the ground, clearing her mind, and allowing the spirits to descend. She bumps and waddles in a comic imitation of Chini's dancing style. Chini struggles to keep dancing, then gives up and mops her brow.

> **Kim Pongsun:** She's dumbfounded, panic-stricken. How can she go through with it? . . .
> **An Hosun:** [*to Chini in a gentle, instructive tone*] You have to have faith in the spirits for it to work. . . .
> **Kwan Myŏngnyŏ:** You even said, 'Now I'm going to ride the knife blades.' Did the very thought of it make you freeze in your tracks? . . . She's made herself too nervous. She might get up there and hurt herself.
> **Chini:** That's not it; I'm not nervous about the blades.
> **Kim Pongsun:** What do you mean?
> **Kwan Myŏngnyŏ:** Then what's this all about?
> **Chini:** I just can't.
> **Kwan Myŏngnyŏ:** She says she doesn't know. That's her answer. She says she doesn't know.
> **Kim Pongsun:** Bitch! Is that all you have to say for yourself?
> **An Hosun:** Like they used to say in the old days, beat her with the drumstick.
> [*But now Kim Pongsun suggests another spirit-engendered cause for Chini's difficulty.*]
> **Kim Pongsun:** You were so stupid you must have concrete for brains. When the Heavenly King kept coming up in your visions, maybe you didn't know enough to say, 'I'm the Heavenly King, I need a crown,' but couldn't you at least have made the right gestures for a crown? Couldn't you have done that much with the King coming up in your visions like that? . . .
> **Kwan Myŏngnyŏ:** When you see the vision you should say, 'You're insolent. Why didn't you give me a hat?'
> **Chini:** How would I know?
> **Kim Pongsun:** He was telling you, in the vision.
> **Kwan Myŏngnyŏ:** You can't ignore that when you're divining. Speak up about each and every vision. . . . [*to Kim Pongsun*] What does it mean? Is it because we didn't buy the King a hat?

Kim Pongsun: He's telling us, 'Buy one.' That's what it means.

Kwan Myŏngnyŏ: Of course. She should buy one and then he will bring boundless good fortune.

Chini's sister: [*to Chini in anger and frustration*] If you knew it, you should have spoken up. If you have a vision of a hat, or the knife blades, then you should come out with it. Then your teachers will understand. Even if it's painful to say it, what's the point of speaking up when it's all over and done? . . .

Kwan Myŏngnyŏ: You get the vision and then you speak. Understand? How can we understand the words of the spirits?

Kim Pongsun: [*to Chini*] If the spirits come up right before your eyes and you don't announce them, then what's the point?

Chini: Uhm, this time, the Heavenly King appeared; I saw him. I thought it was him; I thought I saw the Heavenly King.

Kim Pongsun: *Ahyu!* If he appeared, then why didn't you gesture with your hands, 'I need a crown like such and such?' [*She demonstrates the appropriate gesture.*] You've got to come out with it.

Chini: [*surprisingly feisty*] The vision was really clear. The Heavenly King appeared. I thought it was the Heavenly King, but how could I know what to do?

Kwan Myŏngnyŏ: You say, 'I've arrived.' You say, 'I've come down from heaven wearing my hat.' Couldn't you even say that? [*She gives Chini a playful punch.*]

Kim Pongsun: When the Heavenly King dances, you show his hat like so. [*She mimes the appropriate posture and gesture for the Heavenly King, thrusting her hands up into the air to indicate his crown.*] When you've gotten the message, when you see what he wants, you say, 'I'm the Heavenly King; why haven't you done this for me?' You've got to have confidence; you're the one who says it. [The spirits don't say it for you.] It's what you see, a vision. And when you're doing *kut,* the General or the Special Messenger comes up, like so. [*For each of these spirits, she strikes the pose she would take when performing them in* kut.] Or someone with pock marks takes shape in your eye, a woman, that's Princess Hogu, isn't it? . . . And again, when it's the Warrior Spirits, don't you recognize the Warrior Spirits? And all the Generals from long ago look like so. [*She places her hands on her hips and thrusts her chest forward, imperiously, her characteristic pose when manifesting a divine General during* kut.] When you see those gentlemen, say, 'I'm this General, I'm that general.'

Then right when you take up the blades—didn't I teach you that this morning?—take the blades in hand like this and test them like this [*she pantomimes striking her cheek*], and here too [*she strikes her forearms*], and then when you've done that, and you're ready to go up, wash your feet and climb on up, that's how it's done.

Now Kim Pongsun herself takes on the costume and invokes the Knife-Riding General. Wearing the imperious scowl of a disgruntled spirit, she performs the gestures that she has just demonstrated to Chini, pressing the blades against her cheeks and forearms with zealous shouts and rapid dancing. She removes her costume and Chini tries again, dressed in Kim Pongsun's costume, holding the blades with tense concentration during the invocation, while Kim Pongsun, at her side, rubs her hands in supplication. This time, Chini dances with the blades and tests them against her arm as Kim Pongsun has shown her. She pumps her arms in a frenzied dance as the drum throbs. The blades are placed over the water jar in anticipation now of Chini's ascent. Kim Pongsun burns thin white paper over them as an act of purification. The women wash Chini's feet. She approaches the jar, climbs up, and gingerly rests her feet on the blades, turning and bowing to the four directions. She pivots toward the wall and steadies herself against it, sobbing.

> An Hosun: Yes? Yes?
> Chini: [*gasping out her words between sobs*] It's the Knife-Riding General!
> Shamans: Yes!
> An Hosun: Help her succeed! . . .
> Chini as the Knife-Riding General: [*with great emotion, weeping*] Just so, from now on, we'll keep her busy with work and help her to succeed as a shaman. We will give her boundless good fortune.
> Kim Pongsun: Yes, that's right.
> Kwan Myŏngnyŏ: You say her gates of speech are open?
> Chini: [*still racked with emotion*] They're all coming. All the spirits all here.
> Kim Pongsun: [*almost chuckling*] Well of course they're all here now. If you had gone all the way up there and they hadn't come, then that really would have been a disaster.

AFTERMATH

When Chini stood upon the blades, we thought that we had just filmed our happy ending: that Chini, coached by her spirit mother, encouraged by her sister shamans, and supported by the women of her family, had finally called in the spirits. The results were, alas, more ambiguous. Even after standing on the knives Chini did not deliver oracles. When she descended from the jar, she did not speak again, and the senior shamans finished the *kut*. While the shamans praised Chini for ascending the blades, a feat Kwan Myŏngnyŏ had not managed after several *kut*, they were disappointed. The initial oracle, and Kim Pongsun's assessment during the *kut*, still held: Chini had been too hasty. She was still not prepared to perform as a shaman; her "gates of speech" were not yet fully open. She must spend the next year cultivating the source of her inspiration through devotions to the spirits and prayers on sacred mountains as the Buddhist Sages required.

Immediately after the *kut,* Chini seemed relieved. Her step was lighter and she smiled. We saw her at a *kut* hitting the cymbals and gong, a simple task allotted to apprentice shamans (and occasionally to visiting anthropologists). Often corrected for rhythm and style, she watched the *kut* intently and moved her lips to follow the invocations. Then, for a while, she disappeared. The shamans would offer little more than "Chini's off praying on some mountain." A month after her *kut,* on the eve of my departure from Korea, we saw her again, assisting at a *kut* at her spirit mother's shrine. The small store of confidence that she had mustered for her own *kut* seemed to have withered. When she hit the gong or the cymbals, she was immediately corrected and sometimes summarily relieved of this charge by a more experienced shaman. Like an overly disciplined piano student, her mistakes increased. When I dressed to dance *mugam,* the interval at a *kut* when clients dance in shaman's costumes,[26] I noticed Chini watching me intently. I recalled her having told me that shamans chided her with unfavorable comparisons between her dancing and my dancing. "Damn," I thought as the drumming started, "She's taking their teasing seriously." So it seemed. Chini was clothed to dance *mugam,* but after a few desultory jumps, she gave it up and retreated to a distant part of the house.

Kim Pongsun described Chini's demoralized state of mind and her own disappointment. Chini had gone to pray on a sacred mountain after her *kut,* but this time she had not been granted a single vision. "Chini was impulsive when she said she wanted to have a *kut.*" She was not ready. "She wasn't able to deliver the true words of the spirits, was she?" She gave no memorable oracles. "Of course I'm heartsick too. It isn't as though she had the money to do this. She borrowed the money for her *kut,* so she has to start earning to pay off the debt. But she doesn't have the power of inspired speech. She isn't ready to earn money as a shaman. She got discouraged. She tried to [give it all up and] go find work in Seoul. But when the spirits want her for a shaman, do you think they're going to let her find another job? Now she's really upset and her eyes are bothering her." (At this moment, Chini entered the room.) "Isn't that right? You've started wearing glasses?"

"I think the kitchen smoke got in my eyes."

That is, for now, my final image of Chini, retreating from the camera, smiling faintly and shaking her head as Kim Pongsun urges her, "Fix your hair and take your glasses off; you want to look pretty for the video." Two years later, I learned that like many discouraged apprentices, she had broken with her spirit mother and was working with another shaman. She had also remarried, this time to the son of another shaman.

CONCLUSION: WILL CHINI EVER BECOME A SHAMAN?

Kim Pongsun attributed Chini's difficulties to temperament:

> If the spirits are strong, if the initiate is strong then the spirits come on strong, but if the initiate is a weakling, a spirit wanders in, you sit around for a while waiting, and then another spirit wanders in. It's frustrating. If someone is going to become a shaman, then they should just burst out with it while they're sitting or sleeping, suddenly shouting, 'I'm this spirit, I'm that spirit, I'm the Heavenly King.' But with someone like Chini who just sits there waiting, things drag on. That's so frustrating! [*She chuckles at the memory.*]

Even as she states that there are "people like Chini" to whom the spirits come slowly, Kim Pongsun affirms a cultural ideal wherein destined shamans burst forth with spontaneous oracles from the spirits. "The visions take shape in their eye, and then even without their realizing it, they're shouting out 'I'm so-and-so, I'm such-and-such,' even though they have no idea who the Spirit Warrior is, or the Generals, or Princess Hogu, or the Special Messenger. You take an ordinary housewife who knows nothing about the shaman profession. Would she know anything about the Special Messenger?"

The Korean shaman world's own myths fit tidily with a scholarly tradition that celebrates shamanistic initiation as an experience of profound psychological and spiritual transformation (Eliade 1970:Ch. 2; Lewis 1971:188–190; Peters 1982; and for Korea, Hwang:31, 41–49; Kim 1981:245, 417). But if the spontaneous metamorphosis of a haunted young woman into an inspired shaman is the cultural ideal, ethnographic accounts of the Korean shaman's practice contain a tacit acknowledgement that becoming a shaman is a slow and by no means certain process. Pyong-yang Mansin, Youngsook Kim Harvey's informant, claimed that a spirit mother would be lucky if three out of ten spirit daughters she initiated became successful shamans (Harvey 1979: 126–127). An Hosun's story, and other women's accounts recorded by Ch'oe (1981:66–67), Choi (1987:117, 129–130), and Harvey (1979:37–83), tell of disjunctive careers. And while ethnographic overviews of Korean shaman practice do contain firsthand descriptions of initiation rituals which match classic expectations (Kim 1981:357–372; Kim and Ch'oe 1983; Hwang 1988:Ch. 1; Guillemoz 1988–1989),[27] more discursive accounts by Chung-moo Choi (1987:136), Soon-hwa Sun (n. d.:14–29) and myself (Kendall 1985:65–66) describe initiations that were far less compelling than even Chini's *kut*. Diana Lee (personal communications) observed two such *kut* in the summer before we filmed Chini's initiation and felt, on at least one occasion, that she had a better idea, from her background reading, of what was supposed to happen than did the initiate. Even a renowned Seoul shaman has been heard to admit that she barely managed to utter a few words at her initiation (Chung-moo Choi, personal communication). Kwan Myŏngnyŏ's unabashed admission of previous failure suggests that the necessity of holding more than one initiation *kut* is by no means uncommon (see also Choi 1987:179).

Chini's experience, and the expectations and instructions the shamans placed upon her, allow us to bridge our own dichotomization of "true inspiration" and "pure performance." Throughout her *kut* the shamans chided Chini for naively assuming that the spirits would move her tongue for her. She was repeatedly prompted in performative business that would transform the passive stuff of visions, inference, and intuition into an active spiritual presence: "Say, 'I'm the Seven Stars! Here's how it is with Chini.' Tell us she's pitiful, tell us she's sad." "When you see the vision [of the Heavenly King] you should say, 'You're insolent. Why didn't you give me a hat?'" "And all the generals from long ago look like so. When you see those gentlemen, say, 'I'm this General, I'm that General.'" It was the ability to perform that Chini lacked. She failed, the shamans acknowledged because she was too self-conscious and inhibited. By their logic, she was unable to perform because she could not give herself over to the flow of inspiration conjured by drum beats, dancing, costumes, and by their own suggestive comments—"The spirits are coming!" "Who is that standing beside you?" To feel the spirits and transmit their will and power to others, she must be willing to perform for the spirits, to simulate the spirits. From Chini's perspective, the spirits had not matched her expectations; but for the encounter with her dead sister, she could not feel their presence, and lacking inspiration, she could not perform. Throughout her *kut*, Chini seldom transcended her mundane identity as a timid young woman with a diminished store of self esteem. In the discouraged apprentice, we find the mirror image of the successful avant-garde actor who becomes "like a shaman," inspired to inhabit an alien presence.

If frustrated by Chini's performance and her subsequent loss of nerve, Kim Pongsun was also sympathetic, noting in a private moment that novice shamans were often embarrassed and inhibited. "Even you, mother?" her bemused daughter-in-law asked, and the now-formidable shaman admitted that this had been the case. I have seen, first hand, the growth to shaman stature of "Oggyŏng's Mother," the soft-voiced, bumbling apprentice of my first fieldwork, who "forgets to pick up a fan, misses whole portions of an invocation, or uses incomprehensible words from the dialect of her native Kyŏngsang Province"

(Kendall 1965:67). Today, Oggyŏng's Mother is a plump and commanding presence, belting out chants with a great baritone voice, a younger shaman in deferential tow. Recalling the teasing she endured long ago, she tells me, "They used to say that even you danced better than I did, but which of us is the better dancer now?" So it may be with Chini. For now, Kim Pongsun, the spirit mother, has the last word:

> Look at it this way. It isn't as if anyone could become a successful shaman right when they got the calling. They must make a great effort and change completely. If it happened automatically, then wouldn't everyone be making their living as a shaman? Everyone has their moment and all things happen in their season. If this time the spirits vacillated, then by and by the time can come when they make her into a successful shaman.

ACKNOWLEDGMENTS

The ritual described in this paper was observed and recorded during the filming, in September 1989, of an ethnographic video produced by Diana Lee and Laurel Kendall (Kendall and Lee 1991). My own notes have been supplemented by fifteen hours of tape filmed by Diana Lee with sound work by Kim Asch. Kim Sŏngja, Pak Hyŏnsuk, and Yi Sujong provided written transcripts in Korean script. Dr. Chungmoo Choi saved me from many embarrassing errors of translation and generously shared her insights during my work with this material. Tom Miller offered helpful suggestions during his careful editing of this manuscript. Alexandre Guillemoz and the editors of this volume also offered helpful suggestions. The project was supported by the Department of Anthropology, American Museum of Natural History Belo-Tanenbaum Fund; The Center for Visual Anthropology, University of Southern California; and the Committee on Korean Studies of the Northeast Asia Area Council, Association for Asian Studies.

NOTES

1. Because the process of a *naerim kut* does not require a period of isolation and secrecy, Alexandre Guillemoz suggests that it be called a "passage rite" rather than an "initiation" (Guillemoz 1987–1988). Hwang Rui-si (1988:41–49) also characterizes this ritual as a "passage rite" (*t'onggwa cheŭi*) to underscore the total transformation of the shaman's identity and world view. Because notions of isolation and secrecy are not implicit in the English term "initiation," and because the term is usually associated with admission to more exclusive statuses or associations than those implied by "passage rites," I have retained this usage here.

2. These were the Five Direction Generals (Obang Sinjang), The Heavenly Guardian God (Ch'ŏnha Taesin), the Knife-riding Guardian God (Chaktu Taesin), Hogu Special Messenger (Hogo Pyŏlsang), the Heavenly King (Ch'ŏnha Taewang), the Mountain God (San Sinryŏng), the Healing Sage (Yaksa Tosa), the Seven Stars (Ch'ilsŏngnim), Sambul Chesŏk (birth and fertility—the "Birth Grandmother" in my gloss), and the Buddhist Sage (Pulsanim).

3. Shamans divine (*mugori*) through the visions and sensations that come to them as they cast rice and coins on the slick surface of a varnished tray. Such a divination may provide the diagnosis that leads a client to sponsor a *kut* or less elaborate ritual. Some women routinely seek out a shaman and acquire a divination before the first full moon of the new year; others come at a time of crisis, and still others come to satisfy their curiosity in an idle moment (Kendall 1985:71–79).

4. The shaman An Hosun distinguished between a *hŏt'ŭn* (or *hŏch'in*) *kut,* to drive out malevolent forces so that the purified initiate can receive her spirits, and a *sosŭl kut* to call in the spirits. She thus presented Chini's second *kut* as a logical stage in the process of becoming a shaman. Hwang Russi (1988) glosses *hŏt'ŭn kut* and *sosŭl kut* as variant names for a *naerimkut,* the blanket term for an initiation *kut.* As we shall also see, there is a cultural expectation that an initiate gain the power of inspired speech during one successful initiation *kut.* As in Chini's case, some initiates sponsor severak *kut* before being recognized, by human and spirit, as proper shamans.

5. The convergence of anthropologist Victor Turner's and avant-garde director Richard Schechner's interests is reflected in the near-parallel titles of their *From Ritual to Theater* (Turner 1982) and *Between Theater and Anthropology* (Schechner 1985).

6. Ethnographies that emphasize shamanistic training and technique are typically conducted by researchers who assume the apprentice role themselves (Castaneda 1968, Peters 1981, Sharon 1978).

7. Choi also portrays an ethnographic moment when renowned shamans have come to captivate middle-class audiences who value the "art" of their performances but who give little credence to its efficacy as healing ritual.

8. To keep consistency with the ethnographic video of Chini's *kut,* I have violated my usual practices, both of using pseudonyms, and of replicating the sorts of tecnonymous names (eg. "Yongsu's Mother") that Korean women would use in direct address or common reference. The three shamans decided, in consultation with me, that their work should be acknowledged under their names of record. For clarity, I have consistently used the names "An Hosun," "Kwan Myŏngnyŏ," and "Kim Pongsun" when the shamans refer to each other in direct quotations although the usage is, to my ears and theirs, artificial.

9. Shamans often claim that they discern a potential initiate by the presence of a powerful guardian god hovering around them.

10. Choi (1987:131) suggests that in bringing such apprehension to a divination session, women "self-select" to enter the shaman profession. This is likely, as in Chini's story, but not inevitable; on one occasion, I heard a shaman laugh away a client's fears of being a destined shaman. On another occasion this same shaman

described another client as destined, but that woman was not initiated, at least not at that time and with that shaman.

11. Assuming the shaman role without the benefit of a spirit mother's training was not unknown in the past. The venerable shaman Cho Yŏng-ja does not claim a spirit mother (Ch'oe 1981:66–67, and my own interview in 1977). According to seasoned ethnographer Ch'oe Kil-sŏng (1981:81), shamans will commonly deny that they "learned" to perform *kut* from other shamans.

12. See Sun (n. d.:53–54) for more tales of rigorous training in the bad old days.

13. There are approximately two-and-a-half li (or ri) to an English mile.

14. Consistent with the use of fictive kinship in shaman circles, An Hosun refers to herself as Chini's "maternal aunt" (*imo*) because she is the sworn sister of Chini's spirit mother, Kim Pongsun. Similarly, Kwan Myŏngnyŏ, as the "disciple" (*cheja*) of Kim Pongsun, is Chini's "sister" (*ŏnni*) and "senior classman" (*sŏnbae*).

15. This was Diana Lee's observation when I arrived in Korea in the early fall. She had first met Chini in the early summer.

16. At risk of mapping western psychological constructs onto Korean perceptions, I make an association, from other field experience, with a certain "Mrs. Kim" who, after years of hardship and grief, suddenly lost her wits. When shamans were summoned to perform a healing *kut,* neighbors explained that Mrs. Kim held things inside, that she never vented her frustration, a diagnosis echoed when the gods and ancestors appeared and spoke through the shamans (Kendall 1977). Being vexed (*soksang hada*) is the emotion commonly attributed to wrathful, potentially dangerous gods and ancestors who have been denied for too long the dancing, feasting, and tears of a *kut*. The ethnomedical construct of "fire sickness" (*kwabyŏng*) affirms that suppressed rage and frustration rise from the belly in a choking and potentially fatal heat (Kendall 1991–1992).

17. Dancing itself carries the potential of release and abandon; as such it is a vehicle both of possession and the expression of strong emotions. Thus dancing is both an instrument of therapy and a potentially dangerous, slightly disreputable activity (Kendall 1983, 1991–1992).

18. I use this gloss for consistency. My informants equate Samsin Halmŏni, the birth spirit of household worship, with Chesŏk who appears in *kut* and is associated with the fertility of wombs and land.

19. A good death is peaceful and occurs at home, in the bosom of one's family, at a ripe old age, with no pressing concerns or grievances. Anything less than this may yield restless souls who cling to the living, ancestors who are cited in a shaman's vision as the source of current trouble.

20. The speed with which the shaman balances the top-heavy trident indicates the willingness of the spirits to accept the offering of a *kut*. The base of the trident rests on a flat surface strewn with salt, both a purifying agent and a means of traction.

21. We have seen how Chini carried her history from divination sessions to divination sessions until she reached Kwan Myŏngnyŏ, then Kim Pongsun, who now speaks on Chini's life with a biographer's authority. Kwan Myŏngnyŏ would probably also

have heard from her own client, Chini's elder sister, of childhood poverty and hardship, of a drunken, spendthrift father who died young, and a widowed mother who worked herself to the bone.

22. The Heavenly King sometimes appears in the pantheons of illustrious lineages (Kendall 1985:133–134).

23. When shamans manifest her in *kut,* Hogu commonly hides her face, either under a red skirt or behind her fan, to conceal her pock marks and to express maidenly modesty. She asks for money for cosmetics to cover her scars so that she might find a husband.

24. I am grateful to Chungmoo Choi for this insight.

25. The verb *nolda* subsumes notions of "play," "amusement," and "performance." Shamans commonly describe the action of spirits at a *kut* as *nolda,* as in "The supernatural Official plays well with me."

26. For descriptions of *mugam,* see Kendall 1983, 1985:10–12, 16–17.

27. Note that two of these sources (Hwang 1988, Kim and Ch'oe 1983) describe what was undoubtedly the most remarked upon and best-documented initiation *kut* of the 1980's. The initiate was a graduate student in dance ethnography at U.C.L.A. and, in contrast to Chini, already a skilled performer. Because this initiate evolved her own eclectic practice in the United States and does not receive clients in the manner of a Korean shaman, some would argue that she is not a *mansin* in the classic sense.

REFERENCES

Artaud, Antonin. 1958. *The Theater and its Double.* Translated by Mary Caroline Richards. New York: Grove Press, Inc.

Atkinson, Jane Monig. 1989. *The Art and Politics of Wana Shamanship.* Berkeley: University of California Press.

Bauman, Richard and Charles L. Briggs. 1990. Poetics and Performance as Critical Perspectives on Language and Social Life. *Annual Review of Anthropology* 19:59–88.

Beattie, John. Spirit Mediumship as Theatre. *Royal Anthropological Institute News* 20:1–6.

Boddy, Janice. 1989. *Wombs and Alien Spirits: Women, Men, and the Zār Cult in Northern Sudan.* Madison: The University of Wisconsin Press.

Bogoras, Waldemar. 1907. *The Chukchee.* The Jesup North Pacific Expedition, editor Franz Boas. Memoir of the American Museum of Natural History VII. Leiden: E. J. Brill.

Brecht, Bertolt. 1964. *The Development of an Aesthetic.* Edited and translated by John Willett. New York: Hill and Wang.

Briggs, Charles. The Effectiveness of Dialogue. Paper presented at the annual meeting of the American Anthropological Association, New Orleans, La., November–December 1990.

Brook, Peter. 1969. *The Empty Space.* New York: Avon Books.

Castaneda, Carlos. 1968. *The Teachings of Don Juan: A Yaqui Way of Knowledge.* Berkeley: University of California Press.

Charles, Lucille Haerr. 1953. Drama in Shaman Exorcism. *Journal of American Folklore* 66:95–122.

Ch'oe, Kil-sŏng. 1981. *Han'gugŭi Mudang* (Shamans of Korea). Seoul: Sŏlhwa Tang.

Choi, Chungmoo. 1987. The Competence of Korean Shamans as performers of Folklore. Ph. D. diss. University of Indiana.

————. 1990. The Artistry and Ritual Aesthetics of Urban Korean Shamans. *Journal of Ritual Studies* 3 (2):235–250.

Cole, David. 1975. *The Theatrical Event: A Mythos, A Vocabulary, A Perspective.* Middletown, Connecticut: Wesleyan University Press.

Crapanzo, Vincent. 1977. Introduction to *Case Studies of Spirit Possession,* ed. V. Crapanzano and V. Garrison, 1–39. New York: John Wiley.

Eliade, Mircea. 1970 [1951]. *Shamanism: Archaic Techniques of Ecstacy.* Translated by W. Trask. New York: Pantheon.

Firth, Raymond. 1967. Ritual and Drama in Malay Spirit Mediumship. *Comparative Studies in Society and History* 9:190–203.

Golomb, Louis. 1985. *An Anthropology of Curing in Multiethnic Thailand.* Illinois Studies in Anthropology 15. Urbana: University of Illinois Press.

Guillemoz, Alexandre. 1988. Récits autobiographiques d'une chamane coréenne. *Résumés des Conférences et Travaux,* Ecole Pratique des Hautes Etudes, Section des sciences religieuses, Tome XCVI:90–92.

————. 1989. La descente d'un chaman coréen. *Résumés des Conférences et Travaux,* Ecole Pratique des Hautes Etudes, Section des sciences religieuses, Tome XCVII: 103–107.

Harvey, Youngsook Kim. 1979. *Six Korean Women: The Socialization of Shamans.* St. Paul: West Publishing Co.

————. 1980. Possession Sickness and Women Shamans in Korea. In *Unspoken Worlds: Women's Religious Lives in Non-Western Cultures,* ed. N. Falk and R. Gross, 41–52. New York: Harper and Row.

Hwang, Ru-si. 1988. *Han'gukinŭi kutkwa mudang* (Koreans' shamans and shaman rituals). Seoul: Munhwasa.

Kapferer, Bruce. 1983. *A Celebration of Demons: Exorcism and the Aesthetics of Healing in Sri Lanka.* Bloomington: Indiana University Press.

Kendall, Laurel. 1977. Caught Between Ancestors and Spirits: Field Report of a Korean Mansin's Healing Kut. *Korea Journal* (August):8–23.

————. 1983. Giving Rise to Dancing Spirits: Mugam in Korean Shaman Ritual. In *Dance as Cultural Heritage, Volume One (Dance Research Annual XIV),* Editor Betty True Jones, 224–232. New York: CORD.

————. 1985a. *Shamans, Housewives, and Other Restless Spirits: Women in Korean Ritual Life.* Honolulu: University of Hawaii Press.

————. 1985b. Ritual Silks and Kowtow Money: The Bridge as Daughter-in-law in Korean Wedding Ritual. *Ethnology* 24 (4):253–267.

————. 1988. *The Life and Hard Times of a Korean Shaman: of Tales and the Telling of Tales*. Honolulu: University of Hawaii Press.

————. 1991–1992. Of Gods and Men: Performance, Possession, and Flirtation in Korean Shaman Ritual. *Cahiers d'Extrême-Asie*.

Kendall, Laurel, and Diana Lee. 1991. An Initiation *Kut* for a Korean Shaman. Honolulu: University of Hawaii Press Videotape.

Kessler, Clive S. 1977. Conflict and Sovereignty in Kelantanese Malay Spirit Seances. In *Case Studies in Spirit Possession,* Edited by V. Crapanzo and V. Garrison, 295–332. New York: Wiley Interscience.

Kim, Seong Nae. 1989. The Chronicle of Violence, a Ritual of Mourning: Ceju Shamanism in Korea. Ph. D. diss., University of Michigan.

Kim, In Hoe and Ch'oe Cong Min. 1983. *Hwanghaedo Naerim Kut* (Initiation Kut of Hwanghae Province). Seoul: Yŏlwa Tang.

Kim, Kwang-iel [Kim Kwang-il]. 1972. Sin-byŏng: A Culture-Bound Depersonalization Syndrome in Korea. *Neuropsychiatry* (Seoul) 11:223–234.

Kim Kwang-Ok. 1994. Rituals of Resistance: The Manipulation of Shamanism in Contemporary Korea. In *Asian Visions of Authority*. Eds. Charles E. Keyes, Laurel Kendall, and Helen Hardacre. 195–219. Honolulu: University of Hawaii.

Kim, T'ae-gon. 1966. *Hwangch'on muga yon'gu* (A study of shaman songs of the Yellow Springs). Seoul: Institute for the Study of Indigenous Religion.

————. 1970. A Study of Shaman's Mystic Illness During Initiation Process in Korea. *Journal of Asian Women* (Seoul) 9:91–132.

————. 1972. Etude du processus initiatique des chamans coréens. *Revue de Corée* 4 (2):53–57.

————. 1981. *Han'guk musok yŏn'gu* [A study on Korean Shamanism]. Seoul: Chimmundang.

Kirby, Ernest Theodore. 1983. Shamanistic Theater: In *Symposium of the Whole: A Range of Discourse Toward an Ethnopoetics,* ed. J. Rothenberg and D. Rothenberg. 257–273. Berkeley and Los Angeles: University of California Press.

Laderman, Carol. 1988. Wayward Winds: Malay Archetypes and Theory of Personality in a Context of Shamanism. *Social Science and Medicine.* 27 (8):799–810.

————. The Performance of Healing: Medicine and Aesthetics in Malay Shamanism. Paper presented at the annual meeting of the American Anthropological Association, New Orleans, November–December 1990.

————. 1991. *Taming the Wind of Desire: Psychology, Medicine and Aesthetics in Malay Shamanistic Performance*. Berkeley: University of California Press.

————. n.d. The Limits of Magic. Unpublished ms.

Lambek, Michael. 1988a. Graceful Exits: Spirit Possession as Personal Performance in Mayotte. *Culture* VIII (1): 59–69.

———. 1988b. Spirit possession/spirit succession: aspects of social continuity among Malagasy speakers in Mayotte. *American Ethnologist* 15/4: 710–731.

Lévi-Strauss, Claude. 1967 [1963]. *Structural Anthropology.* Garden City, New York: Anchor Books.

Lewis, I. M. 1966. Spirit Possession and Deprivation Cults. *Man,* n.s. 1 (3):307–329.

Obeyesekere, Gannath. 1970. The Idiom of Possession. *Social Science and Medicine* 4:97–111.

———. 1977. Psychocultural Exegesis of a Case of Spirit Possession in Sri Lanka. In *Case Studies in Spirit Possession,* ed. V. Crapanzano and V. Garrison, 235–294. New York: John Wiley.

———. 1981. *Medusa's Hair: An Essay on Personal Symbols and Religious Experience.* Chicago: University of Chicago Press.

Peters, Larry G. 1982. Trance, Initiation, and Psychotherapy in Tamang Shamanism. *American Ethnologist* 9 (1):21–46.

Peters Larry and D. Price-Williams. 1980. Towards and Experiential Analysis of Shamanism. *American Ethnologist* 9 (1):21–46.

Roseman, Marina. 1988. The Pragmatics of Aesthetics: The Performance of Healing among Senoi Temiar. *Social Science and Medicine* 27/8: 811–818.

———. 1990. Head, Heart, Odor, and Shadow: The Structure of the Self, the Emotional World, and Ritual Performance Among Senoi Temiar. *Ethos* 18 (3):227–250.

———. 1991. *Healing Sounds from the Malaysian Rainforest: Temiar Music and Medicine.* Berkeley: University of California Press.

Schechner, Richard. 1982. Collective Reflexivity: Restoration of Behavior. In *Crack in the Mirror: Reflexive Perspectives in Anthropology,* ed., J. Ruby. 39–81. Philadelphia: University of Pennsylvania Press.

———. 1985. *Between Theater & Anthropology.* Philadelphia: University of Pennsylvania Press.

Schechner, Richard R. and Mary Schuman, eds. 1977. *Ritual, Play and Performance.* New York: Seabury Press.

Scheff, T. J. 1979. *Catharsis in Healing, Ritual, and Drama.* Berkeley: University of California Press.

Schieffelin, Edward L. 1976. *The Sorrow of the Lonely and the Burning of the Dancers.* New York: St. Martin's Press.

———. 1985. Performance and the Cultural Construction of Reality. *American Ethnologist* 12 (4):707–724.

———. On Failed Performance: Throwing the Medium Out of the Seance. Paper presented at the annual meeting of the American Anthropological Association, New Orleans, November–December 1990.

Sharon, Douglas. 1978. *Wizard of the Four Winds: A Shaman's Story.* London: The Free Press.

Sorensen, Clark W. 1988. The Myth of Princess Pari and the Self-Image of Korean Women. *Anthropos* 83:403–419.

Sun, Soon-Hwa. 1991. Women, Religion, and Power: A Comparative Study of Korean Shamans and Women Ministers. Ph. D. diss., Drew University.

Thambiah, S. J. 1977. The Cosmological and Performative Significance of a Thai Cult of Healing through Meditation. *Culture, Medicine and Psychiatry* 1:97–132.

———. 1979. A Performative Approach to Ritual: Radcliffe-Brown Lecture in Social Anthropology. *Proceedings of the British Academy* 65:113–169.

Turner, Victor. 1967. *The Forest of Symbols: Aspects of Ndembu Ritual.* Ithaca, New York: Cornell University Press.

———. 1968 [1981]. *The Drums of Affliction: A Study of Religious Processes among the Ndembu of Zambia.* Ithaca, New York: Cornell University Press.

———. 1974. *Dramas, Fields, and Metaphors: Symbolic Action in Human Society.* Ithaca, New York: Cornell University Press.

———. 1982. *From Ritual to Theatre: The Human Seriousness of Play.* New York: Performing Arts Journal of Publications.

2

ON FAILURE
AND PERFORMANCE

*Throwing the Medium
Out of the Seance*

Edward Schieffelin

INTRODUCTION

Over the past few years, the anthropological study of ritual[1] has moved from seeing these kinds of enactments largely in terms of structures of representation to seeing them as processes of practice and performance.[2] The focus on performance has appeal for those interested in the nature and power of ritual experience because it is concerned with the experience-near aspects of social phenomena: with actions more than with text, with illocutionary rather than with propositional force—with the social construction, rather than just representation, of reality. The performative perspective is also fundamentally concerned with something anthropologists have always found elusive and hard to deal with: the creation of presence. Performances—whether ritual or dramatic—create and make present realities vivid enough to beguile, amuse or terrify. They alter moods, attitudes, social states and states of mind. Unlike texts, however, they are ephemeral; they create their effects and then are gone, leaving their reverberations (fresh insights, reconstituted selves, new statuses, altered realities) behind them. It is the process of "performatively creating reality" found in many events of interest to anthropologists, that has become increasingly a focus of attention.

This paper, which represents work in progress, contributes to the further development of performative approaches amenable to elucidation of ethnographic materials. It has as its focus the question: "What is involved in the performative creation of presence, verisimilitude, and social effectiveness, and how is this involved in the social construction of reality?" In keeping with the idea that performance is in essence a concrete phenomenon, centrally located in enactment, and fleeting, I think it most useful to pursue the discussion through the elucidation of a particular example drawn from an ethnographic setting.[3] I take as my exemplar a spirit seance I observed in 1976 among the Kaluli people of Papua New Guinea.[4] The question can be raised, however: in what sense is a spirit seance a "performance"? So before proceeding, it is well to consider the way the notion of performance has been used in social science and some of the problems it entails.

There seem to be two principal modes of usage for the term "performance" in the social sciences. The most familiar refers to the domain of particular "symbolic" or "aesthetic" modes of action.[5] In the field of anthropology, this designates ritual—theatrical or folk artistic activities which are enacted as *intentional expressive productions in an established local genre.*

Bauman, in one well-known formulation (1986), defines performance as a display of expressive competence by one or more performers addressed to an audience. Beyond aesthetic virtuosity, however, such enactments fundamentally aim to create or evoke an imaginative reality, a sense of presence, among the participants, in which their awareness becomes (for a time) situated away from the activities of everyday life. Participants undergo a heightening and intensification of experience, an altered awareness of their situation (even if only a new appreciation for the genre), and often a sense of emotional release. In true "ritual" events, not only the participants' attitudes but also their social statuses and relationships to one another (or to the wider cosmos) may be altered. All this depends, of course, on whether the enactment is "properly done," whether it "works." This is the responsibility of the central performer(s), and thus their acts of expression are always open to evaluation by the other participants for the way they are brought off (quite apart from their referential or symbolic value). This points to a performative issue that will be central to our discussion: genres of performance are, for those who participate in them, both fundamentally *interactive* and inherently *risky.* There is always something aesthetically and/or practically at stake in them, and something can always go wrong.

The second usage of "performance," represented especially in the work of Goffman and the symbolic interactionists (and to some degree Pierre Bourdieu) refers to the fundamental practices and performativity of everyday life. The focus here is not on a type of event, but rather on the expressive processes of impression management, strategic maneuver and regulated improvisation through which human beings ongoingly articulate their purposes and relationships in normal social existence. From this point of view, the larger structural and institutional aspects of society provide the context in which people operate, the stakes for which they play, the roles and statuses through which they are positioned, and the dispositions which shape their practices. At the same time these institutions have no reality except insofar as they are reproduced through these practices and activities. Here performativity converges with implications of theories of practice. Social practices, emerging in what Bourdieu has called "regulated improvisations" arising from the socially structured dispositions of ordinary persons (the *habitus*), assert their own forms of intelligibility and organization in human activity.[6] One effect of this is that social and symbolic meanings become altered by the manner in which they are expressed from their significance viewed simply as texts. That is, symbols derive their categorical and transformative powers not only from the cognitive or textual structures of which they are a part, but also from the practices and contingencies involved in how they are put across. Strategic and rhetorical intentions, arrangement of social space, pace and intensity of interaction, and the position and disposition of the other participants all affect the meaning with which they eventually emerge. In this way, every implementation of symbols in the world submits them to the determinations of the manner in which they are presented and the contingencies of the local social-historical situation. The structure of an enactment is inherently subject to the contingencies of the enactment itself.[7]

The continuities between the notion of "performance" as embodied in the performativity of everyday life, and "performance" in the "theatrical" or "ritual" sense can be found in two ways. First, at the level of experience in everyday life, it is possible to move from one mode to the other. This is accomplished through a shift of expressive orientation called by Hymes the "breakthrough into performance" (Hymes 1973). In "breaking through" one moves from the expressiveness of everyday interactional performativity to an expressiveness that calls attention to itself as a genre or an object of appreciation. The shifts in behavioral and linguistic features (or "cues") that bring this about convey the meta-message "I am performing". (See also Bateson 1955, 1956).

Secondly, though aesthetic and symbolic performances may set themselves apart in this way, they rely upon expressive conventions, principles and abilities derived from (or analogous to) those of everyday life. To take an example that will be important for our discussion, a performer's responsibility to make the performance work depends on his or her establishment of interactional credibility with the audience. That is, both performers and audience must establish a basis of trust that the others will sustain the definition of the situation and their identities within it. If the performers are too incompetent, or the audience too uninterested or disruptive, the performance cannot proceed.

Such interactional credibility is, however, also a general requirement for normal sociality. For an interaction to proceed, each participant must create a credible social identity and maintain the definition of the situation sufficient to allow the others to manage their behavior in relation to him/her (Goffman 1967). Interactive credibility is fundamental to aesthetic and symbolic performance because it ratifies the bond between performer and the other participants which is crucial if the performance is to be brought off. Understanding how such credibility is created and maintained is fundamental to understanding how the performance itself works and can have its effect.

Having said this, it is clear that performativity in this sense overflows those genres (ritual or otherwise) that we might normally classify as "performances". We are left in an awkward position: either we call any extended interaction sequence a "performance" when it is subjected to a performative analysis, or we restrict the term "performance" to specific genres of ethnographic events that resemble what we call "performances" (artistic, liturgical, whatever) in the West.[8] For now I propose to grasp both these alternatives and return to the problem later in the paper.

TOWARDS THE PERFORMATIVE ANALYSIS OF A SPIRIT SEANCE

We now return to the main business of this essay, which is to develop and explore a mode of performative analysis through elucidation of a particular ethnographic example. Most of the best studies of rituals and theater-like events in anthropology that take a performative perspective approach them in the full flower of their success (Turner 1969, Kapferer 1991, Drewel 1992). I propose to go the opposite route and analyze an event that was in part a performative failure: In the seance I take as my ethnographic example the principal medium was forced to leave the ritual due to mediocre performance. Moreover, his contribution to the proceedings was disregarded by a hostile audience and overridden by the superior performance of a rival medium. Studying such a performative failure is interesting, since it stands to reveal (through the imperfections that bring them down) the inner construction of the particular "ritual" or "theatrical" experience involved, and thus, on a broader level, to provide insight into the particular ways (at least performatively) a people constructs its own particular social reality.

The Kaluli people, among whom I observed the events in this account, live in twenty longhouse communities in the tropical forest just north of Mt. Bosavi on the island of New Guinea. Traditionally (prior to Christian evangelization), Kaluli believed the forest around them was coincident with an invisible world of spirits. These spirits manifested themselves in everyday life in the voices of the birds in the canopy. However, human beings could communicate with them directly through mediums. A medium was a man who had married a spirit woman in a dream or unusual hallucinatory experience. After having a spirit child by her the medium was able to go out of his body into the spirit world known as ɛs tih'nan (literally, 'going down to the spirits'). Spirits could then enter his body and speak to the community gathered around it at the seance. Spirit seances were sometimes called for no other purpose than pure entertainment—so that people could sing and joke with the spirits. But usually they were called for more serious purposes: to cure the sick, to investigate witchcraft, to uncover the cause of a death, or to locate lost pigs. Kaluli believe illness to be caused when the (invisible) spirit-counterpart of a person's body is dismembered by a witch or injured by other circumstances in the spirit world. The person can be treated by asking the spirits (through a medium) to locate the patient's body-counterpart in the spirit world and repair the damage.

Seances are held at night in the longhouse, and a good one may last until dawn. Typically, the seance begins when the fires are banked to place the area in darkness, and the medium lies down on one of the men's sleeping platforms. In a short while, one hears a long hissing drawn-out breath indicating the arrival of the first spirit. The spirit makes itself known by starting to sing a Gisalo song.[9] Between songs the spirits talk with audience members and are requested to go off on errands, usually of healing. When audience attention wanders, it can be brought back to focus through the singing of another song. This alternation of Gisalo songs and conversation goes on with spirit after spirit late into the night until the work of healing or whatever else the spirits have been requested to do has been completed and the medium returns to his body.

The question with which we are concerned here is how this sort of event is made to work. In concrete terms: how is spirit presence created and convincingly sustained, and how are curative or predictive powers effected? It is usual in anthropological investigations of rituals to focus emphasis on the form or, if you will, overall narrative ordering of the performance—the succession of its phases, the sequencing of its symbolic enactments—as crucial to the understanding of its significance and effectiveness. The logic of symbolic meaning and the transformations of the participants are seen largely in relation to this structure of phases.

A Kaluli seance is a much more loosely structured, dialogic and improvisatory kind of event than rituals are usually characterized as being in anthropological literature (cf. Bloch 1974, Rappaport 1979, Tambiah 1980 etc.).[10] Moreover, the overall structure of the seance does not play as obvious a guiding role as it does in more formal rites. For our purposes, this has the advantage of directing our attention to other, more strategic and interactional aspects of performativity which tend to be overshadowed when ceremonial enactments are largely determined by (or analytic precedence is given to) their form.

The matter, however, is complex. It seemed to me in examining my tapes and transcripts that understanding what is involved in the performative articulation of this seance reality might best be approached in terms of a series of determinative issues—each of which would provide a basis for a set of questions. These issues are *form, agenda, means, authority, strategy, historicity, embodiment,* and *emergence.* Though undoubtedly not exhaustive, or even fully independent of each other, they seem sufficient, for the present, to outline the domain of the problematic that a performative analysis needs to encompass. Moreover, because these are issues rather than terms of analysis, they are open for ethnographic exploration themselves, and hence allow for corrective critique: For instance, we can ask: What do Kaluli people think about a seance participant's "agenda" (i.e., intentions)? Does this enter into their understanding of what happens in a seance? If not, to what degree does our interest in agenda distort our understanding of their experience? And so on.

Though space forbids my tracking all of these issues in detail, we may characterize them and place them roughly in relationship to one another (and to our seance example) as follows:

The effectiveness of a ritual or a theatrical performance revolves around the issue of *emergence.* Emergence is a complex matter, but as a first approximation, we might say emergence is what happens *by virtue of* performance. It refers to an irreducible change in quality of experience or situation of the participants that comes about when the performance "works". It is that aspect of a socially produced reality, which cannot be reduced to any of its means (text, structure, or symbolic manipulation) by themselves. If a performance attempts to evoke or create for the participants some state of affairs, then the emergent appears if that state of affairs does become evoked. A group of novices stripped of all items of social identity may appear to be reduced to a common symbolic and existential state. But the experience of *communitas* (Turner 1969) (rather than, say, individualized terror and embarrassment) is emergent in the situation only if it happens. It may happen, but it also may not. It is part of the work of rituals and performances to bring about such realities and presences. In the case of Kaluli spirit seances, the minimum required emergent would seem to be the convincing presence of spirits. All conversation with the spirits, engrossment with them, anxiety and thrill over the information they impart, indeed the whole forward motion of the performance builds upon the successful creation of the reality of spirit presence. As we shall see, however, all that "emerges" in a performance is not necessarily predictable—or even desired. It might be more accurate to say that a performance is considered "successful" when what emerges from it fulfills the main agenda(s) of its participants.

The *agenda* of the performance refers to its intentionality: what the people who observe or participate in a performance expect to accomplish through it. What a particular performance is about in both its text and all its subtexts depends on the agendas of performers and audience. Thus, in the most conventional sense, the agenda of a Kaluli spirit seance is to cure an illness or locate a lost pig—or for some participants, simply to provide entertainment. There is not necessarily one agenda to a performance; indeed all performances probably have multiple agendas, some overlapping, some conflicting even for each participant in it. We will return to this point later.

Form in performance has been used to refer to a bewildering number of conventions in the arts. Here I intend it to refer to any domain of consistency of performance that has a convention that guides the expectations of performers and audience, and constrains the ways in which the performance may brought off. Form may appear at any level of performance, from the overall genre down to narrative program of events—the arrangement of bodies in space, or a particular performer's style. It may be heavily prescriptive (as in Catholic liturgy) or it may be improvisational (as in Kaluli seances), but it provides, as it were, the orderly set of expectations that enables the participants to think they know where they are going. This does not mean that conventions may not be stretched, bent, or broken for strategic effects. Indeed this is one way that performers stretch the envelope of genre. Yet unless some level of consistency is retained, the performance itself is likely to disintegrate or become unintelligible. Thus Kaluli seances, as a genre, are improvisatory in form, with various norms which guide proper behavior for the attending participants. There are various mini-climaxes or periods of increased intensity in the process, but no overall structure or predetermined trajectory to the event.

The *means* of performance refers to any conventional and/or aesthetic device which may be strategically used to produce particular effects. In Kaluli seances, this may be no more than the startling series of bird calls that above-average mediums use in the darkness to announce the arrival of spirits. But perhaps the most important performative means in Kaluli seances are the *Gisalo* songs. These songs form a genre which calls for chorusing by echo-overlap participation (*dulugu ganalan*). The audience/participants repeat each textual/melodic line by overlapping the spirit's voice a split-second behind the start of his original enunciation (Feld 1990). This requires considerable concentration and the other seance participants are drawn into and involved with the performance as they sing. Beyond this, *Gisalo* songs also often carry important information from the spirits, hidden in veiled poetic form. Listeners attend them closely not only to be able to chorus them properly, but also to figure out what their underlying message is. It is of the nature of spirit seances that the information made available is often elusive and ambiguous. Listeners have to work hard to get the meaning clear. In the process the performance becomes increasingly engrossing, and the audience increasingly committed to it.

Performance *strategy* refers to the way in which means are used within a performance to accomplish performance intentions. Performative strategies may be to some degree programmed into the "script" or "scenario" of a performance. This phenomenon has been analysed by many symbolic anthropologists who sought to explain the transformative power of rituals mainly by following the strategic transformations outlined in their symbolic structures, scripts or texts (see, e.g., Gell 1975, Bloch 1992, Munn 1986, Battaglia 1990). But the most subtle performative strategies lie outside the script, in the activity of the participants, for it is through *their activity* in successfully *embodying* the script (if there is one) that the performance is kept intact and moving forward. From moment to moment the performer must strategically modulate the quality of interaction with the audience/participants to accomplish this. In Kaluli seances, when *Gisalo* songs are sung, when there are periods of silence, when certain spirits come up, or when they leave can all be interpreted as strategic matters in the carrying forward of various seance and performative agendas.

Historicity or *contingency* is usually the most neglected aspect of performance, yet it is one of the most essential. Ritual performances are never timeless. They are ephemeral—they only happen once. While the form of a performance may recapitulate the forms of performances in the past and presage those of the future, the performance itself is of the particular moment, articulating cultural symbols and ritual genre at that particular time and submitting them to particular circumstances. It is only if the performance succeeds in encompassing this particular occasion that the ritual actually "works". Every occasion is different, in its social circumstances, the issues at stake, and the agendas of the persons present. All these must be encompassed in the ritual event. A great deal of the burden of responsibility therefore falls on the shoulders of the *performer.*

All the contingencies and constraints of agenda, form, and historicity converge on the performer(s) since it is through his or their creative embodiment that the ritual is articulated and realized in social life. For all of this, the performer is responsible to the audience and is deeply involved in risk. The risk at the bottom line is that the performance will "fail". At its simplest level, this is a matter of basic performance competence: the ability to create and maintain a credible persona and activity and carry it off acceptably within the limits of the genre. Beyond this, the more talented or experienced performers create the more effectively engrossing and compelling imaginative realities and more deeply affect the audience/participants. Some can embody their activity to the point where the performance seems more real than everyday life.

From a Kaluli perspective, it is actually the spirits who are the performers in seance. But they are made present through the mediums. This leads to a complex ambiguity for Kaluli audiences no less than for western analysts. For Kaluli, the contrast between a good and bad seance is that between the actual presence of the spirits vs. the presence of a "performer" who is consciously trying to deceive them, or in other words, between authentic mediumship (*kobale tih'nan*) and false pretenses (*madali tih'nan*)—or worse, "trickery" (*dikidan*). Kaluli are experienced and critical seance-goers, and are well aware that seances can be simulated. The authenticity of a medium could be judged on several points. Important in the long run was a reputation for successful cures. But in the immediate event it was a medium's quality in seance that was scrutinized. As a basic minimum, the songs had to be well composed, poetically well constructed (with proper framing of place-names within a range of poetic devices) (Schieffelin 1976, Feld 1990), well sung, and capable of occasionally moving audience members to tears. Further, the voices of the various spirits had to be recognizably different from the medium's natural voice and from each other. Various vocal pyrotechnics, such as bird calls (representing spirits who arrived in the form of birds) and other kinds of vocalizations thought to be only producible by spirits, lent further verisimilitude to a seance. Finally if the spirits spoke about matters that the audience believed the medium couldn't possibly know, this was a very strong indication of seance authenticity.

Kaluli were usually very annoyed if they suspected a medium was attempting to deceive them with a false seance. But they would rarely interrupt the performance or confront the medium if they suspected such a thing. This was partly because not everyone at a particular seance was likely to think it was false. Those who were distressed over sick relatives and had a great need for help might be deeply committed to the authenticity of the proceedings despite what others saw as evidence to the contrary. They would naturally be furious if it were disrupted. Even more important, a medium who was exposed as false during seance would feel publicly humiliated, and he or his relatives might be resentful enough to seek revenge of some kind. To avoid these consequences, audience members who believed a seance was not authentic usually communicated their displeasure through the subtleties of their response to the performance, and attempted to engineer an apparently "natural" ending to it as quickly as possible.

THE PERFORMANCE

Mediumship was a source of a certain amount of prestige and social attention in Bosavi and could bring its practitioner occasional strategic advantages (a young man who became a good medium might be a more attractive marriage prospect to potential in-laws, for example). Mediums sometimes revealed veiled rivalries with one another through disparaging remarks or stories of another's dubious authenticity in ordinary conversation. But amongst themselves they were generally cordial, and those who were friends sometimes held seances together in a mutually supportive way.

The two mediums who formed the *dramatis personae* for the performance I wish to discuss here were a man in his late thirties named Aiba, who had been a medium for many years, and Walia, a younger man who had become a medium much more recently. Aiba was the leading man of his community, which was situated some miles away from the village where the seance was held. He was exceptionally well traveled, with acquaintances and relatives among many of the Kaluli communities. Aiba always liked to know what was going on and had an alert watchful manner and a penetrating gaze which other Kaluli found intrusive and unnerving. He struck me as an extremely manipulative person. Aiba was a long-time medium, but people were not enthusiastic about him as a seance performer. By reputation, it was said that his songs were well-crafted, but that the voices of his spirits were all very similar to each other, and worse yet, uncomfortably similar to Aiba's own natural voice.

Walia, the other medium, was a bit of a social non-entity, peripheral to the community in which he lived, and not widely traveled or well connected. At the time I knew him, he was in the unenviable position of being a lone widower with a small child, living in a community with few relatives to help him. He was a weedy-looking individual, who struck me as being rather feckless and unreliable. His general style and demeanor called to mind the stereotype of a 1950s jazz musician. He was, however, a wonderful medium with a highly praised reputation for leading exciting seances.

Aiba and Walia were to all appearances good friends. Indeed, Walia sometimes treated Aiba as though he were a sort of mentor, and the two of them sometimes held seances together.

The circumstances of the seance we are looking at were as follows: I had traveled with a few villagers from my home community at Bona to visit Walia in his community, at Sibalema, to learn from him about the Kaluli spirit world. I had also brought recording equipment, hoping to catch one or more of his seances. While I was there, Aiba showed up from his own village some distance away. I was not sure for what purpose. He showed considerable interest in what I was doing. At the time it was a matter of positive social remark to be "schooling" the anthropologist, and there was a little money involved. Aiba clearly wanted to get a piece of the action. I myself was irked at Aiba's presence since I found it disruptive to the way I wanted to work. Things were not helped, from my point of view, by Walia's apparent deference to Aiba. He praised Aiba's knowledge of the spirit world and his capacity as a medium, and insisted I work with him some of the time. The two seemed on affable terms.

One evening I played a recording of a seance I had recorded elsewhere. Aiba and Walia, motivated by the idea of being tape-recorded themselves, decided to hold a seance jointly. Aiba took charge of gathering the audience around, arranging the chorus, and giving instructions about how the singing should be managed. Aiba told me that a child was sick with a stomach ailment in a nearby community and that relatives had asked him to go out and take a look at it from the spirit side.

Despite this set-up, however, the seance started off under less than ideal circumstances. In the first place, the audience members had mixed agendas. Visitors who had accompanied me from my home village of Bona were excited about the performance since they had not attended a seance for a long time, let alone one with two mediums. Relatives of the sick boy were anxious to learn if he would be all right. However, many of the young men of the village who would be singing the chorus were tired and wanted to go to sleep rather than stay up half the night singing. They were already a restive audience. Finally, though no one mentioned it, Aiba's reputation as a less than terrific medium may have dampened enthusiasm for the seance. All of this meant that Aiba and Walia were facing something of an uphill fight to gain audience rapport, but none of these difficulties was necessarily insurmountable for a good seance.

As the fires were banked and the seance began, the first spirit came up on Aiba. It sang strongly, quieting the background talk and when it was finished announced its name as Odolaba. Odolaba's voice was a diminutive spirit voice, but still sounded recognizably like Aiba's. The audience seemed somewhat inattentive, though not unreceptive, a fairly common situation at the beginning of a seance. Background conversation revolved around rolling tobacco for sharing smoke—people were settling down.

After a pause Odolaba spoke again, this time in the language of the Komuna people who lived some distance away. This usage by the spirit should have marked Aiba's authenticity as a medium since it was thought that he could not speak Komuna. Moreover, ordinarily a spirit speaking in a foreign language grasps an audience's attention as they try to figure out what is being said. However, the audience at this point had not yet developed sufficient interest in the performance to put much energy into it, and their response over the following six turns of conversation was essentially: "So who understands this?" The conversation drifted off into joking repartee.

Presently, Aiba began another song which he skillfully and assertively increased in volume at a pause in the conversation, compelling the audience to focus on chorusing and bringing the performance back on track. When he had finished, one of the Bona visitors remarked, "What about the other one?" (That is, the second medium, Walia.) Almost immediately there was a long, drawn-out spirit breath from Walia's space in the darkness, followed by a loud and dramatic series of bird calls—his signature entrance to a performance. The audience made startled remarks which were also somewhat off-color and led into further joking. Walia's spirit shortly commenced its song which had a much more commanding presence than Aiba's, singing with a better voice and a more assertive and resonant manner. When it was over, Walia returned to silence. He seemed to be maintaining a low profile in this performance so far.

Aiba's spirit once again began to speak to the audience in the Komuna language—and received the same reception that he had before. The spirit became silent and the sound of a long expelled breath indicated that it had left and another was arriving. Some jokester in the background called out, "Hey, do some bird calls!" and was rebuked by an older man in the audience. Presently, Aiba's new spirit began to sing. When the song ended, but before he had a chance to say very much, Walia's spirit started strongly into song, singing without chorus. During the song, in the background, Aiba addressed the people of the longhouse on a topic that should have been arresting. It concerned the sick child: "I searched out the traps in the spirit world," he said, "but I found nothing, so I came back." The audience seemed puzzled. When Walia's song ended and he had once again lapsed into silence, Aiba's spirit asked if anyone of the community were sick. It turned out that most people didn't know about the sick boy since his family had been living at a garden house some distance away. Aiba's spirit then tried to put the audience on the defensive.

"The person is your housemate and you haven't seen him?"

Audience member: "Well since we didn't know about him being sick . . ."

But it backfired: "Hasn't anyone in the house seen him?" asked Aiba.

"We Kaluli don't see if a sick person is going to die. But you (spirits) know if he will die. Say so and we will listen," responded an audience member.

Aiba's spirit was saved from this confrontational question by Walia's spirit which suddenly burst into song, distracting audience attention. After a pause, however, Aiba's spirit continued talking about the sick child in the background of the Walia's song. He repeated that he had searched for the child's reflection in the spirit world but had not been able to find it. This was an ambiguous message. If the child's reflection was not caught in a trap in the spirit world, this could imply that the child was not very sick and that there was no cause for worry. On the other hand, if the child's reflection was not found because it had already been taken from the trap by spirit people—or Aiba's spirit had simply been unable to locate it—the child might die. No fools, the audience pressed him to explain: Did this mean that the child would be all right? Aiba's spirit, his voice audibly fading, avoided an answer but said: "Ask the medium himself when he returns." Shortly afterwards Walia's Gisalo song ended and Aiba began to sing.

After this point the seance stayed at a plateau of moderate intensity for a while. Aiba's song was followed by two more from Walia. The background conversation remained relatively subdued. It was Aiba's next song that led to the first visible turn in the balance of the performance. Aiba, so far in the seance, had not been very successful at getting focused audience attention. This time he had been singing only a short while when his song came to an abrupt halt—suspended in mid-stanza. It was a dramatic moment and the audience was galvanized: Several of the men quickly assessed the situation: "There must be a witch nearby." Aiba's spirit voice, weakened and sounding as if it came from far away, spoke: "There are 'others' [witches] gathering in the houseyard." This is usually a spine-tingling moment in a seance, when the invisible presence of dangerous evil becomes virtually palpable, and the proceedings become riveting, but at this moment, with a drawn out spirit-arrival breath and a series of bird calls, Walia launched loudly into another song. In the west this would have been seen as a classic upstaging maneuver. The audience was distracted and the intensity of the witch situation dissolved. Aiba tried to keep it up but interest rapidly dissipated. Worse, the fact that Walia was cheerfully singing away when witches were supposed to be close enough to silence Aiba's spirits put both the strength of Aiba's spirits and the reality of the presence of the witches into doubt. It would be difficult to recover from this disaster. Aiba fell silent.

When the song was over, Walia's spirit identified itself as Kidel, an affable character known to be fond of tobacco. He and the audience joked good-naturedly as he tried to bum a smoke. Kidel returned the audience to its former jocular mood and the context of the seance was effectively redefined: any notion of nearby witches was forgotten. Presently Aiba began to sing again, and he and Walia alternated singing for several turns. During this time, despite the distractive joking and bantering by the young men in the background, it became clear that the audience was paying much more careful attention to Walia's spirit's songs than they did to Aiba's—and on two occasions women were moved to tears by their nostalgic beauty.

The second turn in performative balance came shortly afterwards, and Aiba's downhill slide continued. Walia's spirit finished a song and became silent. There was a long pause while people waited for Aiba's spirit to pick up and begin to sing. As the pause lengthened, the young men's remarks took on increasingly sarcastic tonalities:

"What's with this one? Is he still here? Or is he gone for good?"

Two of the visitors tried to pick up the performance by remarks that would return the focus to the sick child: "They say a medium can say if he sees the soul of the dead leave the longhouse," suggested one, "but we're not hearing anything about it." Walia for his part remained silent. Eventually Aiba's spirit spoke up to say once again that he had been unable to find the sick child in the spirit world and suggested that Walia's spirit go and look for himself. At this Walia's spirit spoke up sharply. "Who is that?!" This ordinarily represented an opportunity for some lively spirit repartee, but Aiba, apparently taken aback at the tone, came up with only a limp response which led audience members to joke that he seemed like he was running away.

Aiba then changed conversational direction and began talking once again about the sick child. At the same time he switched to speaking in the Sonia language[11] and so forced the audience, only a few of whom knew the language well, to focus attention on him to try to figure out what he was saying. The audience, however, was losing patience

"I looked around and couldn't see him," Aiba's spirit said.

"But you are supposed to be able to see him!" an audience member retorted. Aiba's spirit fell silent again for a while. The audience then began discussing the case among themselves.

"It was just a stomach ache," one man insisted.

"There is a fatal stomach sickness going around amongst kids," said another. "When a kid like this gets stomach pains you are supposed to take him to the aid post right away".

"They said they were going to take him yesterday, but they didn't."

"The parents are risking going to jail," said another man. "If the child dies without being taken to the aid post, the government officer will arrest them."[12] As these potential implications of the case became apparent, Aiba's spirit spoke up again in what looked to me—as an outsider—to be an oblique attempt to gather more information about the nature and seriousness of the child's illness.

"Does it ever happen that a sick child doesn't eat for a whole week?" he asked.

"It can't last a week," answered an audience member.

"Even an adult wouldn't last five days," said Aiba's spirit. They discussed the possible seriousness of the illness for a while, but no one had any specific information about the child's condition, and the conversation simply created the impression that it might be serious. Aiba's continued use of the Sonia language was beginning to become annoying—particularly as it was not masking any significant or interesting information that was worth the trouble of striving for. The young men were becoming restive:

"This is just gabble-gabble-gabble talk," said one finally. "Gabble, gabble." An older man told him to shut up.

"If he doesn't eat, he won't last five days," Aiba persisted.

"You're the one who is supposed to be able to see if he will live or die," retorted another audience member.

"He'll live—but I searched the spirit-world traps and couldn't find him," said Aiba.

"Because you were afraid to look on the other side more thoroughly!" laughed one of the young men, using a mocking broken imitation of Sonia. Aiba was repeating himself, and audience attention was drifting away. Nevertheless, he persisted:

"Do you understand what I'm saying," he asked. He seemed to be unbelievably insensitive to the context.

"We hear," said one of the senior men. "But if you have something to say, you should say it."

"Do *you* hear *us?*" countered another man. "What is going to happen? Will the child live or die? You tell us!" It seemed to me some people were beginning to suspect that Aiba was attempting to fish for information.

"I didn't see a fallen trap," Aiba persisted.

"If you looked and couldn't see—then forget it!" the man responded.

"Give it up. Sing another Gisalo," suggested a woman.

"Have the other one [i.e., Walia] come up!" suggested someone else, "This one just says the same things over and over." The audience response was rapidly becoming overtly negative.

Aiba softly began to sing another song.

"I'm going to sleep!" announced one of the young men of the audience decisively. Aiba stopped singing. A few moments later, a drawn-out spirit breath followed by loud bird calls announced that Walia was back on the scene.

From this point forward Walia dominated the seance. Seen from an outsider's perspective, as a matter of performance strategy, Walia had gained this position partly through undermining Aiba's credibility at a few critical points, but mainly through simply waiting until Aiba had managed to discredit himself with the audience through his own fumbling performance. Repetition of uninteresting information, bad timing, and a lack of rapport with the audience which was not well disposed towards him anyway were his main faults.

When Aiba's rapport with the audience collapsed, Walia simply moved into the breach. From an outsider's perspective, he also had the advantage of having overheard the audience's interaction with Aiba and thus had a take on its mood. He had also been able to gain an impression of the seriousness of the child's illness unencumbered by having taken a position on it of his own.

At first, however, there was the problem of overcoming a tired and hostile audience. Walia's first spirit song evoked several remarks of praise from the young men of the village until they realized that it was not about the lands they themselves knew and started joking among themselves. The lands Walia sung of, however, belonged to the community of the Bona visitors who had given the most enthusiastic support to the seance performance from the start, even to Aiba, but who had been rather excluded during the more recent phases of Aiba's performance, which had been conducted largely in the Sonia language, which they did not understand. Walia's song, while it did not move anyone to tears, had the effect of acknowledging and reincorporating these dependable supporters into the circle of participation. The Sibalema youths, however, still continued their obstreperous joking in the background.

The focus returned to illness when a woman asked for Tigobiya—one of Walia's more effective healing spirits—to come so she could ask about another person who was sick. Amid shouts of ribald jokes and men declaring they were going to go to sleep, the new spirit came up and started to sing. In a short time, however, the jokers fell silent. It became clear, as people deciphered the song's poetic images of birds, waterfalls and journeying, that it contained a heavy underlying message. Directed at members of the sick child's family, the song suggested that they had recently had a dispute in which one antagonist had come off the loser and had angrily left the community to live for a while in another place. The implication was that the dispute was responsible for the illness because the anger among the antagonists drew witches to the family. Most of the people present knew the incident being referred to.

In effect, this was Walia's version of why the young boy was ill. Its implications (which included witchcraft) differed considerably from those of Aiba's, while at the same time deeply engaging audience attention. In the middle of the song, Aiba's spirit spoke up in surprise and protest: "He's singing as if he's actually seen the soul down there [in the spirit world]." Sensitive to Aiba's annoyance, one man suggested that he sing too, but other audience members objected since they wanted to hear Walia's song clearly.

As Walia's song inexorably continued, Aiba's spirit moved in the background to recover whatever credibility he could. At first he said he might go out and take another look for the child again himself. Then, as Walia's spirit's song continued with more revelations, Aiba lost his cool entirely and declared Walia's Gisalo was "to no purpose" and that people should not listen to it since when he went around in the spirit world he couldn't find anything. Aiba was so miffed he fell out of performance and spoke with his own natural voice, not that of the spirit he was supposed to be impersonating. No obvious notice was taken of this by the audience, however, and, recovering himself, Aiba changed tactics and declared that even with a mild illness a soul might go down to the spirit world. The implication he was pushing seemed to be that the child wasn't really very sick at all. "I'm not going to sing Gisalo," his spirit declared, "so that the boy's family won't think I'm working to no purpose and get angry." To me this sounded rather like sour grapes, but to my informants it suggested Aiba was implying he could see some extremely disturbing events in the spirit world concerning the child that prevented him from singing. However, the fact that he left the implication hanging, without pursuing it, also suggested that Aiba might be bluffing and actually didn't have anything to say at all. One of the senior men at the seance ignored him and turned to me saying, "The child is sick; he's going to die." Overhearing this, Aiba's spirit spoke up again saying "He's not seriously sick; he just looks like he's sick." The audience just let this pass. When Walia's spirit's song was over it was greeted with praise by a few audience members. The spirit Tigobiya was then instructed to go out and look at a sick woman and again at the child.

As he was leaving with the sound of the spirit breath, Aiba's spirit spoke up for the first time since he had lapsed into silence and reiterated: "I looked but I couldn't find him. . . ." Aiba acted as if repeating this fact would somehow discredit Walia despite the dramatically vivid picture of dispute and witchcraft conjured by the latter's song.

"Has he come back again already?" a young man responded sarcastically.

"He's come up but he says he won't sing Gisalo [because something heavy is happening in the spirit world]," replied a senior man near where Aiba was stretched out.

"But that one is singing OK," said a visitor, indicating Walia.

"Then tell him (Aiba) to wake up [since he won't sing]," said a young man, to surrounding noises of approval. Several women immediately pointed out that if Aiba was made to end his part in the seance, Walia was likely to do so also, before they had received an answer from Tigobiya about the sick people. The underlying implication was that if Aiba suffered loss of face by being asked to leave the seance, Walia would have been unwilling to continue lest he show up Aiba too badly. Aiba's spirit was then asked to remain but both his and Walia's spirits remained quiet for a long time, and the audience conversation turned to other things. Eventually two of the senior men returned to the topic of the seance, making laudatory comments, mainly about Walia:

"This one really sings Gisalo well," said one man. "We really enjoyed that last one." This was followed by remarks that wondered aloud at issues they hoped the next Gisalo would clarify.

"What is going to happen?"

"Wai, It looks like the sick child's soul has gone out to the spirit world." (i.e., he's going to die.) Speculation arose as to the reason for Tigobiya's increasingly prolonged silence.

"It looks like he has left."

"He hasn't gone."

"He seems withdrawn . . ."

"He's acting like he's having trouble because of something down there."

"I think he's paying attention to something important down there."

Ironically the audience now accorded to Walia's spirit Tigobiya credibility they had not been willing to grant Aiba's spirit when he had tried to claim it for himself earlier: that the spirit was prevented from singing Gisalo due to momentous events in the spirit world that required his attention. Whether it was the humiliation of this or not I can't say, but shortly afterwards Aiba quit the seance. With much gasping and hacking, his own spirit returned to his body and he sat up.

The audience to which he returned was engaged in a worried discussion of the long delay in hearing from Walia's spirit Tigobiya. Presently, however, a spirit-arrival breath came from Walia's direction, followed by a long low whistle. Aiba, now back in the world, but still trying to regain credibility, switched to the role of seance expert. He informed the others that the whistle meant that Tigobiya was returning in the form of a harpy eagle.

Tigobiya began to sing. The song was sung as though by the sick child to his relatives. It pictured him leaving them but fearful of living in another strange place. At the crossover point of the song, the spirits of two of his brothers (who had died previously) called out for him to come stay with them. All this strongly implied that the child would die. There was almost no background talk as the audience listened with rapt attention. As soon as he had finished singing, the audience members asked how the child was. "His stomach is just mush," answered Tigobiya. These symptoms pointed to a poor prognosis.

"It looks like he won't live," one man concluded.

"No! I didn't say he won't live," said Tigobiya.

"Well, then, is he going to be all right?" pressed another man. Tigobiya avoided answering by turning the question back on the audience:

"Why didn't you bring him down to the aid post?" he asked. Here Walia's spirit used exactly the same tactic—trying to put the audience on the defensive when it asked an awkward question—that had failed Aiba earlier in the seance. But Walia had by now thoroughly established his credibility, and people were engaged enough to help create his context for him. Knowledgeable informants later explained to me that Tigobiya, like everyone else, knew the child was going to die, but didn't want to say so. Rather, they said, he was concerned that the parents should not go to jail.

"Quickly, quickly, quickly, take him to the aid post," said Tigobiya, keeping the initiative. "If he stays in the house—woooo!"

At this point the ambiguities in the situation—Tigobiya's Gisalo indicating death for the child, but Tigobiya avoiding direct answers about it—were sensed by Aiba who spoke up to undermine the performance: "One spirit says the child won't die; the other spirit says he didn't see him—the spirits said different things." Tigobiya immediately moved to interrupt this line of approach by launching into another Gisalo song. But Aiba persisted: ". . . Is that the way you do things around here?"

The audience, however, was unreceptive.

"Yeah, sure . . . ," a senior man responded in a fed-up tone. This cut bordered on the shaming. Aiba remained insensitive to the audience's negative attitude towards him. Unlike Walia, he seemed absorbed in his own agenda and unable to vary his style.

The song Tigobiya sang to interrupt him was short, only about ten lines, but it communicated the implication that the child would die, taken by a witch from its own community.

"Go quickly," the spirit repeated when he had finished. "If the child stays at home . . ."

Seeing another opening to put himself forward, Aiba asked: "When the Aid Post Orderly (APO) sees the sick boy, will he not say something?" He implied that if the APO saw that the dying child had been ill for some time without being brought in, he might prosecute the parents anyway. Aiba hoped to frighten the Sibalema people into taking him seriously again.

But he was out of his league. Tigobiya answered scornfully: "Ha! Of course he'll say something!"

Aiba persisted: "Will he not ask, 'Why did you not bring him in earlier?'"

"He won't beat you," Tigobiya answered, "Go carry him in."

"Yeah, that's right," said another audience member. The finality of his tone indicated that the seance was over.

"Wake the medium," he said to Tigobiya.

"I'm off," responded the spirit.

Shortly afterwards Walia, coughing and gasping, returned to the living and sat up.

FAILED PERFORMANCE

What can we learn from this complicated story? If we look at Aiba's role in it, we see he managed to get himself effectively excluded from serious consideration by the audience before the seance was half over. Yet in a technical sense (the types of moves he made, the performative strategies he followed, etc.), it could be argued that he did everything right. What went wrong?

From the beginning Aiba had difficulty judging the mood and energy of the audience. Consequently his timing was awkward, and he seemed more intent in driving forward with his own agenda than synchronizing audience rapport. This insensitivity to the rhythms of the other participants, together with a mediocre ability to impersonate spirits, and a comparatively narrow range of responses to seance situations were responsible for his losing the interest, sympathy and credibility of his audience early on. He never really achieved the *engagement* of the other participants. The fact that he was playing against a much superior seance performer only made things worse.

Walia clearly had a better sense of performance as interaction than Aiba. His ability to sense and synchronize audience rhythms into a strong rapport, to take their distracting noise or flagging interest and work with it,[13] to produce a wide range of intriguing songs and dramatic moves to attract and hold their interest, enabled him to create and dominate the performative space much more skillfully and less heavy-handedly than Aiba.

Aiba's shortcomings undermined his performance on the larger level, even with things that he could do well. The Gisalo songs sung by the spirits are, as mentioned earlier, the principal means by which mediums/spirits create audience engagement, mutual participation and group synchrony. As participants sing, repeating and overlapping each line of the spirit's song,[14] there emerges a concentration of energy and a mutual musical resonance which draws them together into the space of the spirit. This, in turn, normally contributes to the forward motion of the seance. Although Aiba did not have as good a singing voice as Walia, his songs worked well at drawing the group of audience-participants together while they were being sung. However, Aiba lacked the ability to orchestrate his songs into the larger performative momentum of the seance. Once one of his songs was completed, whatever focus and unity participants had achieved was allowed to dissipate and had to be rallied again. On the one occasion when one of his songs seemed about to lead to further developments (the song interrupted by the presence of witches), the situation that was being created was quickly upstaged and sidetracked by Walia. Walia's songs, on the other hand, often played into the movement of the performance. Any local person familiar with Walia's seances and the Sibalema locality could have guessed from the place names being sung that the spirit who arrived to upstage Aiba's witches was probably the jocular Kidel. Indeed it was Kidel, and though he had no particular agenda beyond bumming a smoke, his appearance and comfortable affability effectively carried the seance direction away from Aiba's evocation of witches. Though Walia's spirits were undoubtedly more familiar to the audience than Aiba's, Aiba seemed to make little attempt (beyond the one song mentioned above) to work his songs into the flow of the larger performance in this way. The result was a kind of on-and-off intensity which gave a sense of leading nowhere.

Aiba came off even worse on another level. Part of the fascination of spirit songs is that the audience knows they often contain important information about seance concerns hidden in ambiguous or elusive poetic language. When people sense such a song is being sung they often stop chorusing and listen attentively to figure out what it is telling them. Walia's songs in the latter part of the seance were of this type, with their implications of dispute and witchcraft. Everyone became caught up in trying to clarify what social conflicts were implicated in the boy's illness and whether he would live or die.[15] The questions and discussion that followed were then answered by further songs, and the audience became deeply engaged. From this point of view, Aiba's songs were not only strikingly uninteresting, but also, one might say, bad practice. It is not that spirit songs must always carry implications that carry forward the larger agendas or momentum of a seance, but Aiba's were singularly deficient in this regard. The fact that he came from another village and might not have the details of local domestic disputes that Walia was privy to should not have been a deterrent for a good medium. If a song is sufficiently cleverly constructed, an attentive audience can usually find a meaning in it.

Once Aiba's credibility was lost, the audience was unwilling to grant him the same suspension of disbelief they granted to Walia. The responsibility for finally excluding him from the seance lay largely in their hands. Their most obvious constraint was the fear that humiliating Aiba too obviously might end the seance before Walia's spirits had completed checking out the sick boy. Aiba had to be seen as cooking his own goose and leaving the seance voluntarily. Audience members therefore never directly confronted him with the question of his authenticity. Rather, his limitations were simply allowed to become more and more obvious, and his repeated attempts to regain credibility more and more firmly rebuffed until he had, in effect, no performative legs left to stand on.

The detailed analysis of the causes of Aiba's failure and Walia's success could be extended, but enough has been said to make the main outlines of its performative dimensions clear. I would like, in the space that remains, to outline some more general implications of this discussion for the broader domain of cultural performance, including ritual, and the ethnographic usefulness of the concept of performance itself.

PERFORMATIVITY AND PERFORMANCE

One important point suggested by this discussion is that the enactment of *all* ceremonial (or theatrical) performances is inherently risky. This is because they are necessarily subject to the variable competencies of the major performers, the competing agendas and ongoing evaluations of all the participants, as well as unforeseen contingency and blind luck. It is likely, however, that the nature of the risks involved for a performer vary according to the cultural genre and situation in which s/he is acting.

Kaluli seances are relatively loosely structured. The element of risk in these types of performances derives from their improvisational and dialogic construction: while they may be centered around the spirit medium, they are by no means entirely under his control. Yet the medium (or spirit) bears most of the responsibility for creating the seance reality and holding it together. The difficulties and pitfalls of creatively organizing this kind of complexity are clear from our example.

If we turn, however, to more formalized rituals, such as those Bloch describes for the Merina (1974), we find that letter-perfect performance of a ritual "script" is highly prescribed.[16] According to Bloch, the agenda of the Merina elders who perform the rite is the reassertion of their own social authority. If the text is performed correctly and intact, the ordinary members of the society are automatically placed in submission to them by virtue of the parts they must play in the rite. The risk then would seem to lie largely in the danger of flubbing the ritual text and destroying its (and the elders' own) dignity and authority. Thus, where the risks lie in a given performative event or genre must be ethnographically determined— but they will be there and contribute to the quality of what happens.

Successful mastery of the risks of performing is a necessary condition for the creation of performative *authority*. As exemplified in the Merina example above, ritual performances are often themselves assertions of social rank or political authority (or the vehicles by which these are asserted). But the assertion of a domain of authority is, in fact, an inherent condition for any performance if it is to work and be at all effective. Within the domain where it commands attention, other activities are compelled to pause. Aiba and Walia created their authority by the brisk entry of their songs, clever repartee, and various upstaging maneuvers (amongst other devices), but their performative authority in the event was also emergent in the beguilement and participation of those in attendance. In this way, performance inherently becomes an assertion of power, and, indeed, is often used for that purpose.[17]

The authority of performance is not necessarily ephemeral. It holds the audience-participants in thrall not only while the performance is going on, but may also be so compelling that it influences them in the ways they engage their lives beyond its boundaries in the everyday world. It is in this way that performances may become politically potent or socially creative.

Performative authority is a fundamental condition of *emergence*. The emergent is what performance as performance brings about in social reality—and thus in historical experience. It is precisely the emergence of realities in performance and their movement into the domain of social historical events which constitutes the movement of ritual or symbolic efficacy into the human world. This is true even when what emerges in a given performance is not necessarily predictable or is even the opposite of the performer's intentions.

The emergence in our Kaluli example of a compelling spirit-reality, of possible causes of illness, and of a discredited medium could be tracked continuously through the seance. Aiba's experience reveals poignantly that emergent features may occur unwanted—as unintended consequences arising within the performance process, far removed from the original agenda.

However, while Aiba's performance was a failure, the seance as a whole was not. It continued on after him. The agenda concerning the sick child was carried forward by Walia's spirits until a prognosis emerged and was convincingly established, a course of action was suggested (going to the aid post), and everyone knew there was really nothing to be done (despite the spirit's protest to the contrary).[18] Even though this wasn't much help to the patient (who died a few days later, as expected) the situation had been clarified and reconstructed for the community. The effect was powerful, even to an outside observer.

The way this seance becomes effective is quite different from the sort of account that, for example, sees symbolic healing as a matter of assimilating a problematic situation (illness) to a ritual form whose inner text or logical structure provides a kind of program for its resolution (cf. Lévi-Strauss 1963, Devereux 1956, Turner 1969: ch. 1). In the seance it seems clear that the effectiveness and reality of what we would call symbolic material (spirit world, witch attack) is to be found in *the manner in which it is articulated* or *comes into being*, in the world—that is, in the process by which whatever structure—textuality, logic—it may have becomes subjected to, and articulated with, (local) historical conditions. Thus, in our example, the emerging message about the child's illness gained force and conviction by virtue of the fact that the seance happened to be conducted by two mediums who developed a rivalrous relationship in the course of the procedings. Instead of undermining the seance, the rivalry, by the way it was managed or played, rendered the emerging impression of the boy's illness more powerful and convincing. At a critical point in the audience's growing displeasure with Aiba and its acceptance or rejection of the dramatic implications of Walia's (Tigobiya's) song about the sick boy amounted to their choosing between Walia or Aiba as an authentic medium. In this context, the audience's annoyance with Aiba by itself confered authority and verisimilitude to Tigobiya's performance—*and thus* to the message he encouraged. This was not a matter of textuality so much as the concatenation of boredom and irritation, the rhythm of medium-audience interaction, and the timing of strategic appearances.

It may be argued that this cannot be true of all ritual performances, at least as they have usually been described in the anthropological literature. That is, it might be argued that performativity is of central importance mainly in highly contingent, dialogic, and improvisational kinds of performance like this one. The rituals most anthropologists write about seem to be more formally structured than the Kaluli seance, and their scripts or structures would seem to have more central importance. Certainly most anthropological analyses of rituals suggest that the structures are fundamental to the ways they accomplish their purposes. Nevertheless, the articulation of ritual structure within social reality, insofar as it is actually *enacted,* is unavoidably a performative process. This is because however fixed the ritual script or structure may be, the participants must still work creatively to articulate these forms to the particular contingencies of the living situation if the rite is to be convincing and effective. It is because texts and genres must be accommodated to historical situations that performances are required—and why they are submitted to some determination by history. Otherwise, rituals could be effectively enacted simply by playing recordings of them on video tape.

Throughout this analysis I have focused on the performative dimensions of this seance, including its failures, in order to explore how performatively created realities socially emerge and have an effect—sometimes contrary to the participants intentions—as a matter of practice as well as of fact. But while I have treated the seance as a kind of performance, it should be clear by now that we have already moved considerably beyond the definition of performance given, for example, by Bauman. It would be well, then, in concluding, to reconsider the way the concept may be useful in anthropology.

From a Western perspective, it seems reasonable to treat a Kaluli spirit seance as a genre of performance because it appears to share a number of definitive features with Western performances, the most important being that there is a central performer who bears a responsibility to an audience to create an imaginative reality. This is not quite the way Kaluli see it, however. To them, it is the spirits, not the medium, who are the performers; or rather they are more like interlocutors. For the Kaluli this interaction is not a theatrically created imaginative reality, but rather a sort of culturally specific type of interview. (Kaluli at various times explained to me that speaking with a spirit in seance was like talking with someone over a wireless set.) For them the major issue was not whether the seance was aesthetically good or bad (though they could also make that judgment), but whether they were really speaking with a spirit or with someone who was trying to "trick" or deceive them. Aiba was excluded from the seance precisely because people suspected he was "performing" in this way. A "performance" in the Western sense was precisely what a seance is not—and can not be.

What then is the status of the notion of performance as it may be applied in anthropological analysis? From what we have just said, it might be argued that the ethnocentric implications of the notion of "performance" overwhelm its value as an analytic category. The Kaluli know the forest to be inhabited by spirits who take the form of birds and speak through mediums. Westerners interpret the spirits as being symbolic elements in Kaluli cosmological belief which are impersonated in seances by skilled performers. The difference in ontological status accorded to the spirits is a mark of cultural incommensurability. But if so, extending the notion of theatrical performance across the cultural divide exacerbates the problem of ethnographic analysis, because it imports a judgment about the reality of Kaluli ritual situations from the beginning.[19] In so doing, it misconceives the phenomenology of that experience for its participants and leads us away from what we are trying to understand. In our Kaluli example we have a dramatic "theatrical" social process, which instead of creating an imaginary reality articulates a real one. Indeed, the question of whether they were faced with real spirit presence or deceptive impersonation was a fundamental issue for the Kaluli themselves—one which they resolved within the performance.

I explore this issue of whether seances—or rituals, in general—can be seen in analogy to theatrical performances because I think it is an intellectual red herring. The issue is not really about whether the ethnocentric implications of the notion of "performance" cloud its usefulness as an analytical genre for understanding a range of cultural enactments (including rituals). We should expect such a genre of anthropological discourse to suffer from the shortcomings of any heuristic device. (See Scott 1992 for a useful critique of the notion of ritual in this regard.) The issue is "What are the performative dimensions of the social construction of reality: how are local enactments articulated in the world." The issue is not fundamentally about representation (though representation is certainly involved): it is about *the relative movement of moral and cosmological relationships, power and experience,* such as took place in the seance. The emphasis is on performative processes, not genres of "performance", and thus may be applied to Kaluli seances (or any enactment) whether the "performer" is considered to be the medium or the spirit. The social improvizations and expressive problems are very much the same. The difference arises in the interpretative agenda. If we take the mediums to be the performers, the issues focus around the rivalry between Walia and Aiba and the means by which the former successfully discredited the latter and got him ousted from the seance. If we take the spirits to be the performers, then the question becomes on what basis the audience decided Aiba was a fraud, and how they managed to maneuver him out of the seance. Either way, Aiba's exposure is an emergent part of the performativity of the seance.

The objection might be raised that the two perspectives yield two different stories. This actually provides a unique advantage to the analysis, since it allows us to track both perspectives at the same time. In fact, that is exactly what I have tried to do in this paper. Or at least I have tried to write in such a way that the reader can shift from one perspective to the other at any point along the way. If, as I believe, ethnographic understanding is more of the nature of annotated translation than sociological reduction, then it is through this kind of tacking or alteration between our perspectives and that of the Other, rather than the reduction of the Other's to ours, that we reach our fullest comprehension of our mutual humanity. Within the limits of the objectives of this paper, however, my point has been to show how a performative analysis can contribute to understanding the emergence of consequential realities in the historical world.

ACKNOWLEDGMENTS

Research for this paper was undertaken through grants from the National Science Foundation, the National Institutes of Mental Health and the National Endowment for the Humanities. I am also indebted to Alida Gersie, Steven Feld, Bruce Kapferer, Charles Briggs, Marina Roseman, Debbra Battaglia, Arthur Kleinman, and Jimmy Weiner for comments and critiques of earlier drafts of this paper which have led to its substantial improvement.

NOTES

1. This statement could be expanded to include "cultural performances" generally. The concept of this anthropological genre was developed by Milton Singer (1955, 1968). It includes ritual and numerous other ceremonial pageant- or theater-like performative genres of locally recognized significance.

2. Several trends in recent years have contributed to this. The first was the growing interest of scholars with backgrounds in folklore and theater studies in the ethnography of the performing arts (Schechner 1985, Schechner and Appel 1990, Kirshenblatt-Gimblett 1990, Drewel 1992). This movement was encouraged and influenced by Victor Turner (1979a–b, 1982, 1985). Converging with this were the developing fields of the ethnography of speaking (Hymes 1973, 1981, Kuipers 1990), sociolinguistics of narrative (Labov 1977), linguistically oriented studies in the verbal arts (Bauman 1984, 1986, Sherzer 1990), and ethnographic studies of music and aesthetic systems (Feld 1988, 1990, Keil 1979, Roseman 1991)—not to

mention studies of anthropological rituals and cultural performances themselves (Keeler, 1987, Kapferer 1991, 1984, 1979a–b, Schieffelin 1985).

3. General inspiration for the discussion that follows is drawn from the phenomeno-logical sociology of Peter Berger and Thomas Luckman (Berger 1967, Berger and Luckman 1971). Detailed analysis of the strategies and politics of the performative draws upon the work of Erving Goffman (1959, 1967) and Pierre Bourdieu (1977, 1990). Conceptualization of the process of encounter between structures of social relationship, cultural symbols, and historical contingency is influenced by the work of Marshall Sahlins (1981, 1985).

4. Detailed ethnographic descriptions of the Kaluli or Bosavi people are given in E. L. Schieffelin 1976, Feld 1990, and B.B. Schieffelin 1991.

5. Associated with the work of such scholars as Victor Turner, Bruce Kapferer, Richard Schechner, Richard Bauman, Joel Sherzer, Charles Briggs, Margaret Drewel, and Steven Feld.

6. Practices may from one perspective be seen as both embodied through, and provid-ing general limits upon, the modes of expression by which they are realized.

7. Tambiah provides an example of this in his description of historical changes in Thai royal ritual (Tambiah 1980). "The question," as Sahlins (1985) has put it, "is how the reproduction of structure can also be its transformation."

8. Of course, ethnographically, it is more convincing if the local people themselves also recognize the "performance" as a special event and set it off from ordinary social life.

9. The genre of songs normally sung at Gisalo ceremonies. (See Schieffelin 1976; Feld 1990.)

10. The poetic structure of the songs is generally quite tightly determined (see Feld 1990), but this does not affect the relatively loose structure of the performance as a whole.

11. Sonia was the language spoken by a language group to the southwest of the Bosavi area. Bosavi communities near the border between them often had marital alliances with Sonia speakers and were generally bilingual. Aiba came from one such com-munity and knew Sonia well. Sibalema, however, was located closer to the center of Bosavi country, and only a few people knew Sonia there.

   Gisalo songs all over Bosavi often made use of Sonia words for aesthetic (or eso-teric) effect, and to make them more difficult and ambiguous for the audience to interpret (Feld 1990). Similarly, the use of Sonia by a spirit in seance conversation increases the interpretive tension and work that audiences have to put in to under-stand what he is saying.

12. From 1965–67, Australian government officers on patrol made a point of strongly encouraging people to take their sick to the mission aid post for treatment. In a couple of cases, parents with very ill children who had failed to do this were arrested for child neglect. These events made a strong impression on the Kaluli, and though very few people were actually affected, it was a issue to consider in discussions of ill-ness for years afterwards.

13. As when he reincorporated the visitors from Bona. See also the discussion of Kidel in the ensuing paragraph.

14. This process of "overlapping call-response" singing is known in Kaluli as *dulugu salan* or "lift-up-over-singing." For a detailed account of the music of Gisalo, and Kaluli music in general, see Feld 1982, 1988. For a discussion of Gisalo in ceremonial setting, see Schieffelin 1976.

15. For a more detailed discussion of this process of interpretive search, see Feld 1982 and Schieffelin 1985.

16. In this famous and much-debated article, Bloch describes Merina ritual as so highly prescribed and redundant that he felt confident in asserting that the ritual was almost exactly predictable in every detail, and consequently carried no information (in the information-theory sense) to its participants. Its effect, he claimed, was purely illocutionary. For critiques of this position see Tambiah 1980, and Irvine 1979. These do not, however, contest the rigidity and predictability of the rite's performance, but rather Bloch's claim that they contain no information.

17. Indeed, social and political authorities in many cultures seek to affirm or extend their power through performance of political or religious rituals and pageants. By the same token, they may perceive other kinds of ceremonial activities as subversive or threatening and move to control them. The result is seen in such things as the political proscription of "dangerous" ritual or theatrical activities, the social marginalization of performers, domestication of performances in "legitimate" theatre, and, of course, various forms of disempowering censorship.

18. Informants explained to me that it was clear from the songs that the child would die, and that the spirit (Tigobiya) knew it, but did not want to say so outright.

19. To make the point more strongly: Performance in the Western theatrical sense strongly implies the production of imaginary, "pretend" situations, not real ones. Moreover, the distinction between what is true or real and what is pretense or imaginary is a consequential moral and metaphysical question in Judeo-Christian tradition (as well as among Kaluli). To cast the seance as a "performance" in this sense subjects it to a denigrating moral judgement in relation to our own doxic traditions.

REFERENCES

Bateson, Gregory. 1955. A Theory of Play and Fantasy. In *Psychiatric Research Report* 2:39–51.

———. 1956. The message "this is play". Paper delivered at the second Conference on Group Processes, Josiah Macy Jr. Fnd., New York.

Bauman, Richard. 1984. *Verbal Art as Performance.* Prospect Heights, Ill.: Waveland Press.

———. 1986. *Story, Performance, and Event.* Cambridge: Cambridge University Press.

Bauman, R. and Sherzer, J. 1989. *Explorations in the Ethnography of Speaking.* 2nd ed. Cambridge: Cambridge University Press.

Berger, Peter. 1967. *The Sacred Canopy.* 1st ed. Garden City, N.Y.: Doubleday.

Berger, P. and Luckman, Thomas. 1971. *The Social Construction of Reality.* London: Allen Lane.

Bloch, Maurice. 1974. Symbols, Song, Dance, and Features of Articulation. *European Journal of Sociology* 15:55–81.

Bourdieu, Pierre. 1977. *Outline of a Theory of Practice.* New York: Cambridge University Press.

————. 1990. *The Logic of Practice.* Stanford: Stanford University Press.

Devereux, Georges. 1956. Normal or Abnormal. Some Uses of Anthropology, Theoretical and Applied. Washington D. C. The Anthropological Society of Washington.

Drewel, Margaret. 1992. *Yoruba Ritual: Performers, Play, Agency.* Bloomington: Indiana University Press.

Duranti, A. 1986. The Audience as Co-author. *Text* 6(3):239–247, The Hague, New York: Mouton.

Feld, Steven. 1990. *Sound and Sentiment: Birds, Weeping, Poetics and Song In Kaluli Expression.* 2nd ed. Philadelphia: University of Pennsylvania Press.

————. 1988. Aesthetics as Iconicity of Style, or "Lift-Up-Over-Sounding": Getting into the Kaluli Groove. In *Yearbook for Traditional Music* V(20):74–113. Pub by the International Council for Traditional Music.

Goffman, Erving. 1959. *The Presentation of Self in Everyday Life.* Garden City, NY: Doubleday Anchor.

————. 1967. *Interaction Ritual.* New York: Doubleday Anchor.

Hymes, Dell. 1973. *Breakthrough Into Performance.* Urbino: Università di Urbino.

————. 1981. *"In Vain I Tried To Tell You."* Philadelphia: University of Pennsylvania Press.

Irvine, Judith. 1979. Formality and Informality in Communication Events. *American Anthropologist* 81:773–790.

Kapferer, B. 1991. *Celebration of Demons.* 2nd ed. Washington/London: Smithsonian Institution Press/Berg.

————. 1984. Ritual Process and the Problem of Reflexivity. In *Rite, Drama, Festival, Spectacle,* ed. John MacAloon. Philadelphia, Pa: The Institute for the Study of Human Issues.

————. 1979. Emotion and Feeling in Sinhalese Healing Rites. *Social Analysis* 1(1):153–176.

————. 1979. Entertaining Demons: Comedy, Interaction and Meaning in a Sinhalese Healing Ritual. Social Analysis 1(1):108–152.

Keeler, Ward. 1987. *Javanese Shadow Plays, Javanese Selves.* Princeton, N.J.: Princeton University Press.

Kuipers, Joel. 1990. *Power in Performance.* Philadelphia: University of Pennsylvania Press.

Keil, C. 1979. *Tiv Song.* Chicago: University of Chicago Press.

Kirshenblatt-Gimblett B. 1990. *Getting Comfortable in New York.* New York: The Jewish Museum.

Labov, William. 1977. *Therapeutic Discourse.* New York: Academic Press.

Lévi-Strauss, C. 1963. The Effectiveness of Symbols. In *Structural Anthropology,* 186–206. New York: Basic Books.

Marcus, George and Fischer, Michael. 1986. *Anthropology as Cultural Critique: An Experimental Moment in the Human Sciences,* Chicago, Ill.: University of Chicago Press.

Ortner, Sherry. 1984. Theory in Anthropology since the Sixties. *Comparative Studies in Society and History* 26:126–166.

———. 1989. *High Religion.* Princeton, N.J.: Princeton University Press.

Rappaport, Roy. 1979. The Obvious Aspects of Ritual. In *Ecology, Meaning and Religion.* Richmond Calif.: North Atlantic Books.

Roseman, Marina. 1991. *Healing Sounds from the Malaysian Rainforest: Temiar Music and Medicine.* Los Angeles, Berkeley, Oxford: University of California Press.

Sahlins, Marshall. 1981. *Historical Metaphors and Mythical Realities.* Ann Arbor: University of Michigan Press.

———. 1985. *Islands of History.* Chicago: University of Chicago Press.

Schechner, R. 1985. *Between Theatre and Anthropology.* Philadelphia: University of Pennsylvania Press.

Schechner R. and Appel, W. 1990. *By Means of Performance.* Cambridge: Cambridge University Press.

Schieffelin, B. B. 1991. *The Give and Take of Everyday Life.* New York: Cambridge University Press.

Schieffelin, E. L. 1976. *The Sorrow of the Lonely and the Burning of the Dancers.* New York: St. Martin's Press.

———. 1977. The Unseen Influence: Tranced Mediums as Historical Innovators. *Journal de la Société des Oceanistes* 33(56–57):169–178.

———. 1985. Performance and the Cultural Construction of Reality. *American Ethnologist* 12(4):707–724.

Scott, David. 1992. Anthropology and Colonial Discourse: Aspects of the Demonological Construction of Sinhala Cultural Practice. *Cultural Anthropology* 7(3).

Sherzer, Joel. 1990. *Verbal Art in San Blas.* Cambridge: Cambridge University Press.

Singer, Milton. 1955. The Cultural Pattern of Indian Civilization. *Far Eastern Quarterly* 15:23–36.

———. 1968. *Krishna: Myths, Rites and Attitudes.* Chicago: University of Chicago Press.

Tambiah, S. J. 1981. A Performative Approach to Ritual. Proceedings of the British Academy, V. 65, 113–169.

Turner, Victor. 1969. *The Ritual Process: Structure and anti-structure.* Harmondsworth: Penguin.

———. 1974. *Dramas, Fields and Metaphors.* Ithaca N.Y.: Cornell University Press.

———. 1979a. The Anthropology of Performance. In *Process, Performance and Pilgrimage.* New Delhi: Concept Publishing Co.

———. 1979b. Dramatic Ritual/Ritual Drama: Performative and Reflexive Anthropology. In *Kenyon Review,* n.s., 1(3):80–93.

———. 1985. *On the Edge of the Bush,* ed. E. Turner. Tucson: University of Arizona Press.

3

IMAGINAL PERFORMANCE
AND MEMORY
IN RITUAL HEALING

Thomas J. Csordas

The notion of performance has become increasingly central to the study of religious healing. In the past decade, at least four streams of research have converged to define the contours of a theory of performance adequate to the questions raised by healing. These are the cultural-performance approach of interpretive anthropology (Singer 1958, 1972; Peacock 1968, Geertz 1973, Grimes 1976, Kapferer 1979a, 1983; Laderman 1990, Schieffelin 1985, Manning 1988, Roseman 1991), the performance-centered approach from soci-olinguistics (Abrahams 1968, 1972; Gossen 1972, Hymes 1975, Bauman 1975, Jansen 1975, Fabian 1974, 1979, Goldstein and Ben-Amos 1975, Kuipers 1990, Samarin 1976), the performative-utterance approach which spans both of the former (Austin 1975 [1962], Searle 1969, 1975, Finnegan 1969, Bloch 1974, 1986; Tambiah 1985, Rappoport 1979, Ray 1973, Gill 1977, Fernandez 1986); and the rhetorical-persuasive approach developed in the study of therapeutic process (Frank 1961, 1973, Frank and Frank 1991, Bourguignon 1976, Scheff 1979, Csordas 1983). All share a hermeneutic sense of the importance of con-text, but complement one another in that the first formulates performance as event, the second as genre, the third as act, and the fourth as rhetoric. I shall briefly elaborate each of these approaches.

In Singer's formulation, cultural performances as events are elements of tradi-tion on the "cultural level of analysis," and ways in which "content is organized and transmitted on specific occasions through specific media" (1958:194). For Singer, performances are "the most concrete observable units" of culture, from which progressive analytic abstraction can lead to the structure of kinds of performances, and thence through examination of linkages among these structures to constructs of cultural structure or value system (1972:64). Not only does cultural performance constitute an open window on culture for the observer, but it also has a creative dimension for participants, as aptly summarized by Geertz:

> [Performance, by] ordering [important themes of social life] into an encompassing structure, presents them in such a way as to throw into relief a particular view of their essential nature. It puts a construction on them, makes them, to those historically positioned to appreciate the construction, meaningful—visible, tangible, graspable—real in an ideational sense. (1973:443–44)

Cultural performance has a power to transform both experience and social relations. Singer recognizes that it is not through evocation of emotion that performance acts, but by creation of a specific mood, the constancy and intensity of which become a religious devotee's primary concern (1972:201). This matches Geertz' general formulation that religion "acts to establish powerful, pervasive, and long-lasting moods and motivations . . ." (1973: 90), where moods are kinds of dispositions "which lend a chronic character to the flow of . . . activity and the quality of . . . experience" (1973:95). Thus, cultural performances are primary arenas not for representation, but for the active constitution of religious forms of life.

In contrast to performances as events, the sociolinguistic approach formulates performance as a specific kind of action carried out within a distinct genre:

> . . . there is *behavior,* as simply anything and everything that happens; there is *conduct,* behavior under the aegis of social norms, cultural rules, shared principles of interpretability; there is *performance,* when one or more persons assumes responsibility for presentation. (Hymes 1975:18)

The concept of genre in this approach is a modification of the concept as used in literary criticism. In particular, Frye (1957:246–48) argues that any analysis of the rhetorical functions of language is contingent on a theory of genres. This approach may be even more essential to the cross-cultural study of oral performance than it is to comparative literature, for whereas literature typically deals with a limited number of more or less well defined genres (epic, drama, lyric, novel), anthropologists have encountered a multiplicity of specialized speech varieties and oral performance forms. Bauman suggests that "performance sets up, or represents, an interpretive frame within which messages being communicated are to be understood, and that this frame contrasts with at least one other frame, the literal" (1975:292). The critical aspect of performance for this argument is its emergent quality that "resides in the interplay between communicative resources, individual competence, and the goals of participants, within the context of particular situations" (Bauman 1975:302; see also Abrahams 1968:148–49). The power of performance is in part "that it offers to the participants a special enhancement of experience, bringing with it a heightened intensity of communicative interaction which binds the audience to the performer in a way that is specific to performance as a mode of communication" (Bauman 1975:305).

The third component of the theory of performance shifts analytic focus from the more general domains of event and genre to the specificity of the performative act. This approach originates with Austin's (1975) and Searle's (1975, 1979) notion of "performative utterance." For Austin, not all utterances are "constative" or descriptive of states of affairs. Some are actually ways of *doing* things, so that in certain cases "saying something is doing something," and there is no simple distinction between spoken word and physical act. Austin also distinguishes the force of an utterance from its meaning. "I will come to the party" has a clear sense and reference, but may have either the force of a promise, or only that of a vague intention. In Austin's formulation, illocutionary force is effected in the act of saying itself, as in "I promise." In contrast, perlocutionary acts "produce certain consequential effects of the feelings, thoughts, or actions of the audience, or of the speaker, or of other persons" (1975:101). For example, saying something can perform the perlocutionary act of "persuading" someone of something, but one cannot say, as with illocutionary acts, "I persuade you that . . .'"

Anthropologists have applied the concept of performative acts cross-culturally to conventional forms of ordinary speech as well as to forms of ritual language, and have reinforced the theory's implicit blurring of the line between word and deed by including non-linguistic ritual acts in their analyses. Tambiah (1979) has proposed for the analysis of ritual language a distinction between the illocutionary frame, roughly that which establishes the force of an utterance, and the predicative frame, or that in which qualities are attributed and transferred among persons and entities. This distinction can serve us as long as we recognize that the illocutionary act bears an aura of predication, and that the performance of metaphors carries illocutionary force. It expands the notion of performative act to explicitly include the performance of metaphor, the power of which to create form and movement in expressive culture has been decisively shown in the work of Fernandez (1986).

The fourth relevant aspect of performance theory comes from a stream of work on therapeutic process in healing itself. This approach originates with Frank's (1961) analysis of the arts of therapeutic persuasion, in which he emphasized the analogy between psychotherapy and religious healing. The locus of persuasive activity was the patient's "assumptive world," in essence all that afflicted persons take for granted about themselves, others, their life circumstances, and their surroundings. Frank regards change in the assumptive world as necessary to alleviate the sense of demoralization experienced alike by patients who seek out conventional psychotherapy and religious healing. Recently, Frank has drawn the parallel between these processes and formal rhetoric (Frank and Frank 1991), but throughout his work the emphasis has been on the transformation of meaning in the therapeutic performance. Subsequent work has modified Frank's emphasis on the face-to-face interpersonal encounter between patient and healer, based on the model of psychotherapy, toward an emphasis on rhetorical processes central to performance. Thus Scheff (1979) has compared healing, ritual, and drama to show how catharsis is achieved by the performative creation of aesthetic distance. My own work has shown how the rhetoric of transformation achieves its therapeutic purpose by creating a disposition to be healed, evoking experience of the sacred, elaborating previously unrecognized alternatives, and actualizing change in incremental steps (Csordas 1983, 1988).[1]

The convergence of these four approaches offers the opportunity for something that has been markedly absent from anthropological accounts of religious healing, namely a way to grasp and formulate the experiential specificity of participants. Many earlier accounts are descriptions of healing rituals—there is attention to what is *done to* participants without much attention to what the event *means for* them. Their lack of experiential specificity has had important consequences for our understanding of therapeutic efficacy. With only a descriptive account to go on, anthropologists typically made an interpretive leap and attributed efficacy to some global, black-box psychic mechanism such as trance, placebo, suggestion, or catharsis. There are two obvious problems with this strategy: the grounds for the interpretive leap are weak, and because they are weak the interpretation remains vague. Yes, there may be a catharsis, but what is being catharted? In contrast, a synthetic approach to performance as sketched out above offers analytic purchase on experiential specificity by allowing us to ask in what manner participants in religious healing become existentially engaged in the healing process. Performance thus invites us—though we do not yet always accept the invitation—to go beyond the sequence of action and the organization of text to the phenomenology of healing and being healed.

In this chapter I want to push the issue of experiential specificity by examining sequences of imagery not as elements in healing performance but as performances in their own right, as a kind of performance within performance that may not even be observable. Here is what I mean: The shaman's formal narration of his journey to the realm of spirits is taken as data by anthropologists, but he is rarely questioned about the qualities of that realm and what it is like to move about in it. The shaman's narrative is treated as an element within the ritual performance—is it not the case, however, that the experience he narrates has the structure of performance in itself, prior to narratization?[2] The patient is even less a presence in the healing ceremony, frequently treated as a mere spectator rather than as someone who is caught up in an experience that may be more or less immediate and vivid, and that he may or may not understand. The patient is often treated as a kind of spectator to ritual performance. Could it not be, however, that the mode in which the patient becomes engaged in therapeutic process is critical to the efficacy of religious healing?

This problem was suggested to me by observing the occurrence of imagery in patients of Navajo medicine men and Catholic Charismatic healers. Among the latter, I retrospectively elicited detailed accounts of imagery sequences that occurred in healing sessions. These sequences in many cases amounted to elaborate "imaginal performances" including the patient, significant others, and deities. Yet the details of these performances were not only externally invisible in the healing sessions, but were not necessarily narrated by the patient to the healer afterward. My goal is to examine the significance of imaginal performance in Charismatic healing, in order better to define the need for a cultural phenomenology of existential engagement in religious healing. Specifically, I want to deal with imagination and memory as closely related self processes in a form of Charismatic healing called the "healing of memories."

Let me first, however, offer a thumbnail ethnographic sketch of the movement known as the Catholic Charismatic Renewal (see also McGuire 1982, Neitz 1987, Csordas 1983, 1987, 1988, 1993). The movement began in 1967 among junior faculty and graduate students at Catholic universities, who in a spirit of enthusiastic communitarianism adopted the principal ritual features of Pentecostalism, including baptism in the Holy Spirit, speaking in tongues, and laying on of hands for ritual healing. The movement quickly expanded beyond the campuses, into Catholic parishes, religious orders, and abroad. In the United States, active membership reached a peak of over 600,000 in 1976, whereupon it declined to just under 200,000 by the end of the 1980s. Participants are organized into parochial prayer groups headed by "pastoral teams" of lay and religious leaders, and highly structured intentional groupings called covenant communities and headed by "coordinators." A substantial degree of uniformity in ideology and ritual practice has been maintained by an extensive literature of books, pamphlets, and audiocassettes, as well as a structure of regional, national, and international "service committees."

The Charismatic system of ritual healing can be summarized with respect to the four components of the synthetic performance theory outlined above:

1) Ritual *events* include large public healing services attended by hundreds of people, weekend healing retreats and "workshops," and private sessions in which a single patient is treated by a healer or team of healers. The personnel in these events include a variety of cultural specialists (Singer 1972) who either exercise some divinely granted "spiritual gift," or perform more mundane ritual functions like those of musician or usher.

2) There are three major *genres* of ritual healing, corresponding to a cultural conception of the person as a tripartite composite of body, mind, and spirit. Physical healing is addressed to medical problems, inner healing or healing of memories to emotional or psychological problems, and deliverance to affliction by evil spirits.

3) Performative *acts* in healing are discrete gestures or verbal formulae construed primarily as acts of empowerment, protection, revelation, and deliverance. Among others, they include the laying on of hands, speaking in tongues, the use of Catholic sacramentals, soaking prayer (intense and lengthy sessions in which a patient is "saturated" with prayer), the calling down of the blood of the Lamb (invocation of the redemptive power of the blood shed by the crucified Christ), word of knowledge (divine revelation), and the binding of spirits (ritual command preventing demonic disruption of the interpersonal milieu).

4) Finally, the *rhetoric* of ritual performance is undergirded by an elaborate terminology that designates ideal forms of interpersonal relation, collective organization, personal qualities, and activities, all in service to the divine plan. On the negative side, a well developed demonology recapitulates in mirror image virtually every positive item in this terminology (Csordas 1983, 1987, 1993).

CHARISMATIC IMAGINAL PERFORMANCE

The following are accounts of imaginal performances that occurred in sessions in which the ritual genre enacted is the "healing of memories." These sessions are private events with one patient and either one or two healers. The patient sits on a chair, and the healer either sits facing him/her or stands alongside, laying on hands. Periods of conversation in which the healer asks questions, gives advice, or counsels the patient alternate with periods of prayer. The three imaginal performances which will be discussed occurred during periods of silent or glossolalic prayer, and thus had to be reconstructed from post-session interviews. Each patient/healer dyad allowed me to be present at and to audiotape-record up to five consecutive sessions. Immediately following each session I used a standardized set of questions to elicit an experiential commentary from the patient. On a separate occasion I conducted a three-part interview with each patient, which included questions about life history, questions on the nature and extent of participation in the Charismatic movement, and two standard instruments used for psychiatric diagnosis in research settings (The Hopkins Symptom Checklist-90, and the Schedule of Affective Disorders and Schizophrenia). I conducted a followup interview to assess changes in each patient's life circumstances and experience of psychological distress at least three months after the last healing session I attended with each of them.[3]

1) The Woman Whose Mother Went to Pieces

The healer in the session was a Catholic woman, aged thirty-nine, whose training includes a master's degree in social work from a psychoanalytic perspective, and a doctorate in theology with a concentration in spirituality. The patient had been involved in Charismatic spirituality for 10 years. She was a middle-class woman, forty years of age, married for twenty years and the mother of four children. Her principal complaint was her lack of a close and emotionally satisfying marital relationship. She had recently become seriously depressed and suicidal, and sought out the healer-therapist. In the course of her sessions she realized that no matter what she did, her husband and children would be critical of her. She expressed the feeling that her pattern of emotional response had originated in her relationship with her mother. She especially recalled that her mother slapped her in the mouth because of her generally assertive behavior, and blamed her for being sexually molested by older boys in the neighborhood. She formulated her current state of mind in imagery that juxtaposed a picture of her son in his "inner freedom to get dirty" with herself as a repressed little girl who was always primly dressed.

In the session, the healer instructed her to feel her pain and, in the realm of imagination, invited her to "cry on someone's shoulder," presumably that of Jesus or the Virgin Mary. Instead of being held herself, the patient finds herself holding her own mother, who she perceives as being on the verge of shattering or disintegrating. This breakthrough image emerges in the symbolic inversion of the mother-daughter role, as the patient nurtures her own mother. Onto this scenario the healer superimposes the Virgin Mary as the shoulder to cry on who will provide the absent maternal intimacy and "take" the pain. In complying with the request to sit on the Virgin's lap the patient still holds her mother. The patient subsequently reported the insight that her mother's emotional fragility may account for her own inability to be intimate.

The reversal of nurturing roles is integrated with and supported by the divine presence. In addition, the complex kinesthetic or positional imagery appears to be a compromise for a patient who self-avowedly nurtures others without herself being nurtured—the one who is holding is also being held. In resolution there is a process of "letting go" as the patient is instructed to relinquish her mother into the hands of Jesus. Her response is a complex experience of tingling, which for Charismatics is typically an indexical sign of divine power, and physical pain in the heart, a kind of metaphoric synesthesia based on the conventional under-standing of the heart as seat of the emotions. As physical and emotional pain are synthesized, the image is presented not in the visual modality, but simultaneous-ly in the proprioceptive and affective modalities.[4] The emphasis on spatial orientation, bodily engagement and disengagement, and the kinesthetic quality in this account, as well as the integral role of pain and its removal, attest to the eidetic, engaged, and multisensorial nature of imaginal performance.

2) The Woman Who Merged with Herself

The healer was a fifty-one-year-old married teacher who had been involved in the Charismatic movement for fifteen years. Unlike the healer in the previous case, she had no professional training as a therapist, and worked strictly within the tra-dition of healing of memories. The patient was a forty-two-year-old married mother of three, a high-school graduate, and had also been active in the Charismatic movement for fifteen years. Some years before she had undergone an episode of what was most likely a psychotic depression, and also reported sev-eral other problems including phobias and problem drinking which she claimed were alleviated by ritual healing. There were no current diagnoses at the time of her participation in the study. Partly through a series of images, such as herself hiding from her father in a closet and seeing her father's face superimposed on that of her husband, she had come to realize that she hated her father. Through this insight she concluded that much of her previous behavior was based on the fact that she "hated men and didn't know it."

The healer began by asking, apparently based on a revelational insight, why the patient was angry with her husband. The patient said that it was because her husband reminded her of her father, and the healer instructed her to forgive her father. The patient then began to cry, and reported an image of herself in bed with her father, for the first time acknowledging that she had been sexually abused by him. After thanking Jesus for this revelation, the healer instructed the patient to summon her imaginal childhood self to her side and to imaginally place her father and others who have hurt her in the liturgical Eucharistic cup and offer them to the deity. The breakthrough image came at the moment when Jesus embraced the two selves, as described by the patient:

[T]he child inside me—just went "w-whom," and I saw that. Then they [Jesus and the Virgin] were behind me, enmeshed in me, and he embraced me, and I saw the Blessed Mother embrace me too. And I felt their heart in mine, and he said that I had the same heart that they did, the same Sacred Heart. And I could see that in vision.

Suddenly Jesus and the two selves merged into one.

The patient described the effect of the experience as having "grown up" and come to "know who I am in Christ." The expectation of "growing up" was phenomenologically enacted in the merging of her adult and childhood selves in the divine embrace. The formulaic Charismatic articulation of personal identity as "knowing who I am in Christ" is concretely experienced as a multiple embodied metaphor that includes merging aspects of the self, embracing and enmeshing with the two divine figures, and sharing hearts with them ("I felt their heart in mine"). In the divine embrace and the sharing of hearts, intimacy and identity are mutually determining psychocultural conditions of the sacred self. Intimacy is possible only with the achievement of an identity "in Christ," and identity is a kind of intimacy with oneself, a reconciliation of what I will refer to below as the fundamental alterity of the self.

3) The Man with the German General Within

The healing team of two was led by a Catholic woman, aged thirty-eight, who worked full time in a Charismatic counseling center. Her training included a master's degree in counseling, two years' apprenticeship in inner-healing prayer, and certification as a Catholic spiritual director. She was assisted in her work by a male healer. The patient was a thirty-seven-year-old married man with three children, a college graduate employed in a managerial position. He had participated for several years in the Charismatic Renewal, where he met his wife. He defined his principal problem as stress derived from a long-standing self-image that demanded high levels of accomplishment. This had created a strain on marital intimacy, and he reported having had problems with overeating and with pre-ulcerative stomach problems. Our diagnostic interview revealed a single episode of alternating mania and depression in college, a simple phobia of heights, and a period of dysthymia and generalized anxiety disorder immediately preceding his recourse to healing.

The imaginal performance was prompted by a memory brought forward by the patient of an incident from his high-school years. His mother had become angry upon discovering that he had arranged an overachieving and "superhuman" academic and athletic schedule. The principal healer instructed him to invoke an image of the internal "person" who had insisted on that superhuman schedule, taking on the person's "posture, breathing style and language."[5] Following some additional discussion, the session turned to prayer, in which an imaginal Jesus is asked to "journey with S to meet this person face to face, to begin to dialogue with that person." In his subsequent report to the healer, the patient identified this person as an internal "controller." The patient said that in the imaginal performance he asked this controller, "Why are you so strong?" The latter responded that

> [He's] just following my orders. [The controller says,] "If he [the patient] wants me to be different he just has to tell me. Show me what you want— how you want to relate . . ." Then we [the controller and the patient] were at a very peaceful spot—a garden with flowers around us. He and I were there together relaxing. He was relaxed saying [he doesn't] mind this. "This is fine, if you want to live this way—no problem." It really wasn't his choice. So I feel the door opened up to dialogue there.

In the post-session commentary that was part of our research protocol, the patient discussed the beginning of reconciliation with this aspect of himself:

> [What the imaginal personality] wanted to express was a very externalized facade of discipline, excellence, accomplishment . . . [the experience] helps me become aware of when that kind of stress is going on and how I can control it . . . it's a better sense of making those choices myself rather than having it be an automatic, habitual kind of response.

The patient comes to realize not only that his need to be in control controls him, but that he is the one who by his own choice set up the controller in the first place. He expresses an understanding of control not only as overachievement, but as the inhibition of spontaneity. In subsequent sessions he identified a childhood longing for freedom in the face of external controls imposed by teachers and his father, and, as a defense against insecurity, the overdevelopment of discipline that was "not external but feels external." He discovered a sense of being existentially "lost" between self-indulgence (overeating) and discipline (overwork), and was instructed by the healer to cultivate freedom through his relation to the deity in that in-between space, the imaginal garden.

IMAGINATION AND MEMORY

Imagination and memory are culturally constituted, efficacious self processes in Catholic Charismatic healing performance. I define self not as a kind of metaphysical entity, but as a repertoire of capacities for orienting in and engaging the world. Self processes, then, are characteristic modes of orientation and engagement (see Csordas 1994:5–15). For Charismatics, imagination is a self process in two senses. First, imagery is cultivated as a mode of engaging the world in a variety of domains. This attention to imagery is perhaps the principal feature that distinguishes the Charismatic sacred self from the self characteristic of the surrounding North American culture. In this sense, imagery can be considered as imaginal self process in that it becomes a *general capacity* for orientation and engagement in the world. Second, in ritual healing, discrete occurrences of imagery are endowed with the valence of performative force, and assume a *specific efficacy* in transforming other dimensions of the self. In terms of our synthetic theory of performance, each image or sequence of images is a performative act that puts into play a particular rhetoric of therapeutic transformation, where what is transformed is the patient's orientation and engagement in the world.

In the various modes of Charismatic ritual healing, imagery may be either revelatory or therapeutic. Revelatory imagery on the part of a healer is typically identified as one of the group of charisms or spiritual gifts such as "word of knowledge" or "discernment of spirits." Therapeutic imagery occurs not to the healer but to the patient and may occur spontaneously or in the form of guided imagery, active imagination, or meditation—similar in form but different in content from techniques used in image-oriented psychotherapies.

Memory is also a culturally elaborated self process for Charismatics. The Charismatic elaboration of memory is based on the more general circumstance in North American ethnopsychology that both repressed and conscious memories are regarded as significant constituents of the "self."[6] I would argue that there are two ways in which this is the case. First of all, memory is a powerful *symbol* of the self. Access to memory is access to a privileged zone of communion with other, past selves in a way that is construed as a sense of continuous identity, and objectified as the unitary self of psychocultural experience. The self's integrity is a prominent cultural value, and the role of memory as guarantor of that integrity is what assures its status as a symbol of the self. This is sometimes culturally elaborated in a highly sentimental way: it is as a symbol of the self that memories become "precious."

Yet if memory is a symbol of the self, the array of specific memories invoked and reinvoked by techniques such as healing of memories constitute a pastiche of the self. The healing process undergone by Charismatics is essentially one of autobiographical review by stage of life, typically including an intrauterine period, infancy, childhood and school years, adulthood, marriage, retirement. Whatever emerges spontaneously during a period is focused on and "prayed into." Within this basic procedure, multiple variations are possible. It is sometimes the case in one-on-one healing over multiple sessions (analogous to weekly psychotherapy) that entire sessions will be devoted to a single life stage, or the healer may go through the entire life in each session. It is also possible to review one's life on numerous occasions in public healing services. A patient may bring a particular memory to ritual healing; a healer may adopt the strategy of praying for "whatever comes up" without focus on a particular life stage or problem, or prayer about a particular problem may through revelation uncover a memory presumed to lie at the biographical "bitter root" of that problem. Finally, the same memory can be gone over on more than one occasion, with incremental actualization of change. The spiritual career of any Charismatic is likely to include many such instances of healing, such that the sacred self can be understood as a pastiche of ritually transformed memories of varying degrees of autobiographical significance.

The relation between imagination and memory is widely known to be a close one. Personal memory of events and episodes is frequently experienced in imaginal form (Brewer 1986, Casey 1987), and it is precisely these kinds of memories with which we are concerned. From the standpoint of cultural phenomenology (Csordas 1990, 1994), imagery is a bodily practice insofar as it engages multiple sensory modalities. In addition, the experience of immediacy and self-presence in imaginal performance are reinforced by the engagement of both patient and healer in a process of autobiographical transformation. Finally, it is relevant that a principal component of imaginal performance is the manipulation of the actors' bodies. Imaginal bodies though they may be, there is an essential kinaesthetic and proprioceptive element in sitting on the lap of the Virgin, holding one's disintegrating mother, merging with one's childhood self, or walking in an imaginal garden.

It will be recalled that the actors in imaginal performances typically include the patient in either a child or adult persona, significant others, most frequent among whom are parents, and the divine figures of Jesus and occasionally the Virgin.[7] The concrete experiential presence of these actors and their concern with developmental themes invites their interpretation as a strikingly literal example of "internal object relations." The school of psychoanalytic thought oriented around this concept emphasizes the development of personality through the internalization of relationships (Greenberg and Mitchell 1983, Hamilton 1989). In this view, the "objects" are people in relationships, and the developmentally earliest objects are the parents. I would suggest that imaginal performance can be understood as a manipulation in fantasy of internal objects in order to resolve developmental stalemates. In other words, internal objects are objectified as the actors in imaginal performance.

From this theoretical perspective, the nature of the stalemates addressed in the cases we have examined can be understood with Melanie Klein's concept of "splitting." This is regarded as a primary developmental and psychological mechanism by which infants attempt to protect the integrity of object relationships "... by projecting their innate destructiveness onto the environment and introjecting its good aspects or, reciprocally, by projecting the good aspects of themselves onto the good object and experiencing themselves removed from discomfort or danger. Thus, they split their self-and-object world into all-good and all-bad camps" (Hamilton 1989:1553). In our first case, the woman whose mother went to pieces, we can see the split between good and bad self in the preliminary contrast between the patient's son who had the freedom to get dirty, and her image of herself as a little girl who was always primly dressed. As is characteristic in North American ethnopsychology, a principal characteristic of the good self is spontaneity, while the bad self is repressed. In the imaginal performance the split between good mother and bad mother is dramatized in the central image of the patient seated on the lap of the Virgin while holding her own disintegrating mother. The complex resolution is not a synthesis of good and bad mothers. It is instead a physical conjunction of the three bodies holding one another, along with the insight that the real mother's badness was in fact a product of vulnerability, and a letting go of the bad mother not in the form of an abandonment but as a relinquishing to the divine figure of Jesus.

In the second case, the woman who merged with herself, a preliminary image of good father and bad father appears in the patient's seeing the face of her father superimposed on that of her husband. She repeatedly acknowledges that her husband is good. His resemblance to her actual father allows him to take on the psychological role of the good father, while at the same time becoming the object of displaced anger for the drunken sexual abuse she suffered as a child. In the imaginal performance there is a dramatic merging of the childhood self and the adult self, described by the patient as a concrete experience of "growing up." Here again is a resolution of splitting between the bad childhood self understood as the promiscuous, manipulative man-hater, and good self understood as the mature Christian woman who "knows who I am in Christ." The bad self is not abandoned, but merged with the good self in the embrace of the divine figure.

While these analyses constitute a start toward understanding imaginal performance in the healing of memories, they do not adequately account for the role of the divine figures. An immediate response from a psychoanalytic perspective might be that they are simply and invariably positive introjects, or internalizations, of the parental objects. However, as anthropologists we must regard this easy solution as too easy. We must instead examine the implications of the view held by participants in the ritual themselves, a view that, in effect, grants the divine figures autonomy as internal objects in their own right. Remaining within the framework of internal-object-relations theory, we might first try out

Winnicott's notion that Jesus is a kind of "transitional" object. For the young child the transitional object, such as a blanket or a teddy bear, is a "developmental way station between hallucinatory omnipotence and the recognition of objective reality" (Greenberg and Mitchell 1983:195). Jesus as an actor in imaginal performance is not an external transitional object like a teddy bear, but literally an internal transitional object that combines in itself all the features of omnipotence as well as those of another person to which one can have a mature relationship.

Let us take yet another step, however, for Jesus is not only a protective presence but an intimate presence in healing. In Charismatic thinking, he is the ideal object or other with which one can have a mature, intimate relationship. Now if the capacity for intimacy can be cultivated through intimacy with a divine figure, that intimacy must be a genuine intimacy and its object must be a culturally real other. Is this the case in Charismatics' relation to Jesus? In one of the few empirical studies on the subject, S. Levine (1991) intriguingly characterizes psychological intimacy as an "elusive state of grace" that requires two people but has the additional benefit of coming to know *oneself* through the relationship. A series of intrapsychic processes identified by Levine stand out as qualifying the divine relationship as intimacy: 1) imagined presence of the other, most prominent for Charismatics in ritual healing, but also possible in everyday prayer; 2) invented conversation with the absent other, a vivid characteristic of Charismatic "prayer life"; 3) anticipation of togetherness with the other, which Charismatics express as a hunger for prayer. Not only are the intrapsychic processes of the relation with Jesus similar to those of interpersonal intimacy, but the relationship comes to hold an enduring, intrinsic value, with the consequences identified by Levine as attachment, concern (expressed as wanting to do the Lord's work), and vision of the other as special.

I would suggest that this experience is neither a surrogate nor a transitional intimacy, but a manifestation of genuine intimacy with a primordial aspect of the self—its *otherness* or *alterity*. This otherness is the possibility of experiencing oneself as other or alien to oneself, but it is also the possibility for recognizing the existence of other people with whom one can have a relationship. The philosopher R. M. Zaner has identified its origins in three features of our bodily existence: the limitations of our physical being that leave us with a sense of inescapable contingency, the autonomic functioning of our bodies that insistently goes on without us but which implicates us in anything that happens to our bodies, and the possibility of seeing ourselves as objects from the perspective of another (1981:48–55). I am arguing that the capacity for intimacy begins with an existential coming to terms with the otherness of the self, and that the personal relation with Jesus is a metaphor for that capacity—Jesus *is* the otherness of the self. This is the Jesus that speaks internally with the "still, small, voice" within, and whose presence is an act of imagination. The patient in our second case experienced not only the merger of her childhood and adult selves, but a merger with the divinity who embraced them both. We can now understand that this imaginal act was a coming to terms not only with the memories of traumatic events, but also with that very alterity which is the body as existential ground of self.[8]

We can finally grasp the performative structure of imaginal performance by joining this analysis of the roles played by the imaginal actors to the analysis of memory formulated in the work of Connerton (1989) and Casey (1987). Central to both their arguments about memory is the commemorative ceremony, whether it be the Jewish Passover, the Catholic Mass, the American Memorial Day observance, or the Tanagran festival of Hermes. Both authors argue that commemoration is a totalizing form of memory that includes components of both bodily action and verbal action. By this action, memory is located in space as well as time, and is situated at the juncture of individual reality and social reality. For both authors, commemoration is not a representation of the past but a re-presentation, a "presentation again" that collapses the distinctions between past and present, space and time. Put more precisely, Connerton shows that in commemoration the form of memory in *practice* is not representation but re-enactment, while Casey makes a parallel point by showing that in commemoration the substance of memory as *experience* is best understood as a kind of mystical "participation" between the essences of the memory and what is commemorated.[9]

From this standpoint, we can understand the Charismatic healing of memories as a particular kind of commemorative ceremony. Casey (1987) distinguishes ceremonial commemoration carried out as a public ritual from intrapsychic commemoration that occurs in the psychoanalytic process of identification, in which one person is memorialized in another's psyche. In the Charismatic healing of memories we find a middle ground between the two forms, where intrapsychic commemoration is carried out in explicitly ritual terms. As is all true commemoration, it is profoundly social. Revelatory images and imaginal performance are the experiential substance of the ritual relationship between healer and patient. Further, within the imaginal performance, the patient engages in intimate interaction with both the perpetrators of trauma and the divine figures.

What is being commemorated in these healing rituals? In the first instance, it is the wounded and suffering self. Here commemorabilia (the symbols used to commemorate) are indistinguishable from commemoranda (that which is commemorated), for the memories that are in question are themselves constituents of the patient's self. Far more than this, however, the ritual is at the same time a commemoration of the healing and protective presence of the divinity *in every moment of the patient's past life.* It thus links the perdurance of the person in autobiographical time with the perdurance of the divine in cosmic time. The patient comes to participate in the cosmic, while the cosmic comes to intimately inhabit the traumatic moments of the patient's autobiography. Again, it is also a commemoration in a genuinely collective sense. Connerton notes that anthropologists who emphasize performance typically show how it makes structure explicit, but are generally unconcerned with the persistence of collective identity over time (1989:103). Here is precisely the significance of the Charismatic precept that everyone is in need of healing. For any time a patient undergoes healing of memories, she implicitly acknowledges this universal need, and in so doing participates in a commemoration of the human condition as defined in the Christian doctrine of Original Sin and the Fall. It is in part by this process, regarded as preparation for full life in a Christian community, that Charismatic collective identity is formed, or more precisely that the sacred self is created as a member of that collectivity defined as the kingdom of God.

EMBODIMENT AND EFFICACY IN PERFORMANCE

In a minimal sense, the imaginal performances described in this chapter can be said to have been efficacious in that they were meaningful and significant to the patients. Based on follow-up interviews conducted at least three months after the end of their participation in the study, the patients appear to have integrated that meaning into their everyday lives (see Csordas 1994). What we perceive, however, is an incremental efficacy, rather than a global remission of a syndrome or disorder. Our ability to detect such incremental change comes from requiring experiential specificity in our description of how the performative structure of event, genre, act, and rhetoric is realized, rather than imputing efficacy to global, non-specific mechanisms like catharsis, suggestion, or placebo effect.

As *event,* we have identified an invisible performance within a performance, in which the participants are imaginal actors, including the patient, his/her significant others, and divine figures. The *genre* enacted is the Charismatic "healing of memories," where the desired transformation of memory is enhanced by the senses of immediacy and intimacy evoked when imagination and memory join forces as self processes. The *act* component of performance has a double aspect, insofar as the imaginative act that brings about the performative scenario is itself an experience of empowerment, within which the imaginal actors also perform discrete acts upon one another. Finally, the *rhetoric* of transformation addresses emotional issues of interpersonal relationship by means of commemoration.

With all the elements of performative structure thus laid out before us, we must not make the mistake of slipping into the easy conclusion that the source of its efficacy is the experience of totality, which we have identified as a feature of commemoration. Granted the experiential salience of such totality to the participants, there is no reason to attribute an efficacy to it that would carry us beyond those global mechanisms with which we have expressed dissatisfaction, such as the placebo effect or the power of suggestion. Instead, we will come closer to our goal of experiential specificity by examining the performative interaction of imagination and memory as self processes.[10]

Imagination, as Casey (1976) has shown, is inherently efficacious in three unique ways: first, we can hardly fail to imagine what we intend to imagine; second, imaginative spontaneity is sudden, effortless, and immediate; and third, the contents of imagination are self-evident, being nothing other than what they appear to be. As it turns out, much to the enhancement of performative force in ritual healing, *these are characteristics we expect of divine action.* Insofar as from the religious standpoint imagination gives access to a spiritual realm, insofar as the features of that realm correspond to what is culturally expected of a spiritual realm, and insofar as the imaginal world is rendered coherent by the presence of Jesus for patients and a source of divine inspiration for healers, the imaginal world operates *empirically* as a convincingly efficacious spiritual world.

Imagination's efficacy to transform orientation and engagement in the world is reinforced by its close association with memory, especially autobiographical memory (Brewer 1986). Casey (1976, 1987) argues that both imagination and memory have a degree of autonomy as mental functions. He characterizes the autonomy of imagination as a "thin" autonomy of pure possibility. The autonomy of memory, however, is a "thick" one in that memory is bound up in its origins and at the same time, since it is active in the present, constantly transforms and undermines the determinacy of the past. Because of this thick engagement in the actuality of experience, there is an inherent difficulty in the "expressive exfoliation" of memory (Casey 1987:279–80). Their complementarity in healing consists in that imagination is "thickened" with existential care, while memory is "thinned" by the relative ease of imagination. The specific efficacy within this complementarity lies in the juxtaposition of the divine world of the purely possible and the struggling human world of traumatic autobiographical memory, and in the experiential superimposition of the divine imagination upon human memory in imaginal performance.

A further element of efficacy originates in the very embodiment of healing imagery, insofar as the body is the existential ground for efficacy in general. This point has been made in several ways by theorists of embodiment, including R. M. Zaner (1981), Mark Johnson (1987), and Edward Casey (1987). Zaner, drawing on the work of Jonas and Straus, argues that every execution of a movement involves feelings of kinaesthetic "flow," which reveal a fundamental if/then pattern of cause and effect (1981:42). Johnson (1987) argues that such primordial experiences of creative efficacy become objectified as concepts of force and causality. Casey argues, following Alfred North Whitehead, that if the primordial experience of causal efficacy "is the privileged point of connection to a settled past, then its own bodily basis, i.e., the concrete feeling of bodily efficacy, will be intrinsic to *any* connection with *any* past" (1987:175).

To extend these arguments, I would claim that these primordial experiences of efficacy are also preserved as a prototype for experiencing the force of divine power. It is thus no accident that the divine embrace is the privileged and recurrent act of transforming traumatic autobiographical memory. Because the embrace is imaginal, it encapsulates the pure possibility of intimacy; because the imagery is embodied, it is convincing because it partakes of the existential ground of all causality, force, and efficacy; and because it is enacted by a divine figure, its meaning and intent are beyond question.

There is yet one more element of efficacy in imaginal performance. The efficacious presence of Jesus does not act on memories from the standpoint of the present, reaching back and transforming them as from a distance, or "inserting" the imaginal deity into the past. The efficacy of the divine presence lies in that, through successive episodes of healing, the patient comes to "realize" that *Jesus was always already there* with her. This fundamental "withness" is incorporated as a disposition of the sacred self. There can be no question at this level—the level of the *habitus*[11]—of whether or not Jesus is successful at transforming a particular memory. Recognizing his presence is the transformation of that memory. This observation carries us a step beyond the celebrated paradox posed by Kleinman and Sung that "to the extent that indigenous practitioners provide culturally legitimated treatment of illness, they *must* heal" (1979:24). For Charismatics, efficacious healing is predicated not only on a cultural legitimacy that says healing is possible, but on an existential immediacy that constitutes healing as real. The immediacy of the imaginal world and of memory, of divine presence and causal efficacy, have their common ground in embodiment. The moods and motivations evoked upon this ground in ritual performance are indeed uniquely realistic.

ACKNOWLEDGMENTS

The research upon which this chapter is based was supported by NIMH grant RO1-MH40473. An earlier version was presented to the 1991 Annual Meeting of the Society for Cultural Anthropology, and much of the present version is a condensation of material presented in more elaborated form in Chapters 6 and 7 of *The Sacred Self: A Cultural Phenomenology of Charismatic Healing* (Csordas

1994). Thanks for comments are due to Marina Roseman, Janis Jenkins, Edward Casey, Paul Connerton, and Elizabeth Behnke.

NOTES

1. For other observations about the occurrence of healing without much input from healers see Prince (1980) and Finkler (1985).

2. Compare Friedrich's (1986:Chapter 5) discussion of the poetic structure of dreams, which appears to transcend other kinds of narrative and linguistic structure.

3. These imaginal performances are drawn from a total of sixty sessions of Charismatic healing of memories performed for eighteen patients in southeast New England during 1987–88. The cases summarized here, and the general arguments about therapeutic process, efficacy, and embodiment, are presented in expanded form in Csordas (1993).

4. Not all images are visual images; in principle, imagery can occur in any sensory modality. In this case, the image takes the dual form of bodily orientation (proprioception) and emotion (affect). For more on multisensory and affective imagery, see Csordas (1993).

5. Unlike the previous two cases, the patient in imaginal performance does not reenact his memory by entering a particular situation, but by entering, as it were, its underlying motivation.

6. Here I use the term "self" in its indigenous, popular North American sense of a bounded entity possessed by an individual, and subject to processes like "growth" or "fragmentation" (Johnson 1985).

7. Charismatic ritual healing is not unique in the use of imaginal actors. Watkins (1986), for example, has developed a form of psychotherapy in which the patient interacts with a variety of "invisible guests" that represent aspects of the patient's self.

8. Insofar as it is not so integrated, this essential otherness is also the condition of possibility for demonic presence—but that is the subject of a separate account.

9. Casey explicitly invokes Levy-Bruhl's concept of mystical participation, in which "things are connected so that what affects one is believed to affect others." For example, people participate in their names so that abuse of the name harms the person, or parents participate in their children so that the parent drinks medicine if the child is ill (Evans-Pritchard 1965:85–6).

10. While memory is commonly recognized as autonomous of other types of mental acts, imagination is frequently seen as subordinate to either perception or memory. Let me simply re-assert here Casey's (1976) conclusion that imagination is autonomous in that it is independent of other mental acts, is inherently indifferent to the projects of the life-world, and is characterized by an inherent freedom of mind.

11. I use the term *habitus* in Bourdieu's (1977) sense of an enduring structure of bodily dispositions (see also Csordas 1990).

REFERENCES

Abrahams, Roger. 1968. Introductory Remarks to a Rhetorical Theory of Folklore. *Journal of American Folklore* 81:143–148.

———. 1972. Folklore and Literature as Performance. *Journal of the Folklore Institute* 8:75–94.

Ahern, Emily. 1979. The Problem of Efficacy: Strong and Weak Illocutionary Acts. *Man* 14:1–17.

Austin, John L. 1975. *How to Do Things With Words.* 2nd ed. Cambridge: Harvard University Press.

Bauman, Richard. 1974. Verbal Art as Performance. *American Anthropologist* 77:290–310.

Bloch, Maurice. 1974. Symbols, Song, Dance, and Features of Articulation: Is Religion an Extreme Form of Traditional Authority? *Archives Européennes de Sociologie* 15 (1):55–84.

———. 1986. *From Blessing to Violence: History and Ideology in the Circumcision Ritual of the Merina of Madagascar.* Cambridge: Cambridge University Press.

Bourdieu, Pierre. 1977. *Outline for a Theory of Practice.* Translated by Richard Nice. Cambridge: Cambridge University Press.

Bourguignon, Erika. 1976. The Effectiveness of Religious Healing Movements. *Transcultural Psychiatric Review* 12:5–21.

Brewer, William F. 1986. What is Autobiographical Memory? In *Autobiographical Memory,* ed. David C. Rubin, 25–49. Cambridge: Cambridge University Press.

Casey, Edward. 1976. *Imagining: A Phenomenological Study.* Bloomington: Indiana University Press.

———. 1987. *Remembering: A Phenomenological Study.* Bloomington: Indiana University Press.

Connerton, Paul. 1989. *How Societies Remember.* Cambridge: Cambridge University Press.

Csordas, Thomas J. 1983. The Rhetoric of Transformation in Ritual Healing. *Culture, Medicine, and Psychiatry* 7:333–375.

———. 1987. Genre, Motive, and Metaphor: Conditions for Creativity in Ritual Language. *Cultural Anthropology* 2:445–69.

———. 1988. Elements of Charismatic Persuasion and Healing. *Medical Anthropology Quarterly* 2:121–42.

———. 1990. Embodiment as a Paradigm for Anthropology. *Ethos* 18:5–47.

———. 1994. *The Sacred Self: A Cultural Phenomenology of Charismatic Healing.* Berkeley: University of California Press.

Evans-Pritchard, E. E. 1965. *Theories of Primitive Religion.* Oxford: Clarendon Press.

Fabian, Johannes. 1974. Genres in an Emerging Tradition: An Anthropological Approach to Religious Communication. In *Changing Perspectives in the Study of Religion,* ed. A. Eister, 249–72. New York: John Wiley and Sons.

———. ed. 1979. Beyond Charisma: Religious Movements as Discourse. Special edition of *Social Research,* volume 46.

Fernandez, James. 1986. *Persuasions and Performances: The Play of Tropes in Culture.* Bloomington: Indiana University Press.

Finkler, Kaja. 1985. *Spiritualist Healers in Mexico: Successes and Failures in Alternative Therapeutics.* South Hadley: Bergin and Garvey.

Finnegan, Ruth. 1969. How to Do Things With Words: Performative Utterances Among the Limba of Sierra Leone. *Man* 4:537–552.

Frank, Jerome. 1961. *Persuasion and Healing.* Baltimore: Johns Hopkins University Press.

———. 1973. *Persuasion and Healing.* Rev. ed. Baltimore: Johns Hopkins University Press.

Frank, Jerome, and Julia Frank. 1991. *Persuasion and Healing.* Third ed. Baltimore: Johns Hopkins University Press.

Friedrich, Paul. 1986. *The Language Parallax.* Austin: University of Texas Press.

Frye, Northrop. 1957. *Anatomy of Criticism: Four Essays.* Princeton: Princeton University Press.

Geertz, Clifford. 1973. *The Interpretation of Cultures.* New York: Basic Books.

Gill, Sam D. 1977. Prayer as Person: The Performative Force in Navaho Prayers Acts. *History of Religions* 17:143–157.

Goldstein, Kenneth, and Dan Ben-Amos, eds. 1975. *Folklore: Communication and Performance.* The Hague: Mouton.

Gossen, Gary. 1972. Chamula Genres of Verbal Behavior. In *Toward New Perspectives in Folklore,* ed. A. Paredes and R. Bauman, 145–67. Austin: University of Texas Press.

Greenberg, J. R., and Stephen A. Mitchell. 1983. *Object Relations in Psychoanalytic Theory.* Cambridge: Harvard University Press.

Grimes, Ronald. 1976. *Symbol and Conquest: Public Ritual and Drama in Santa Fe, New Mexico.* Ithaca: Cornell University Press.

Hamilton, N. Gregory. 1989. A Critical Review of Object-Relations Theory. *American Journal of Psychiatry* 146 (12):1552–60.

Hymes, Dell. 1975. Breakthrough Into Performance. In *Folklore, Communication, and Performance,* ed. Goldstein and Ben-Amos, 11–74. The Hague: Mouton.

Jansen, William Hugh. 1975. The Esoteric-Exoteric Factor in Folklore. In *The Study of Folklore,* ed. A. Dundes, 43–51. Englewood Cliffs: Prentice-Hall.

Johnson, Frank. 1985. The "Western Concept of Self." In *Culture and Self: Asian and Western Perspectives,* ed. Anthony Marsella, George De Vos, and Francis Hsu, 91–138. New York: Tavistock.

Johnson, Mark. 1987. *The Body in the Mind.* Chicago: University of Chicago Press.

Kapferer, Bruce. 1979. Ritual Process and the Transformation of Context. *Social Analysis* 1:3–19.

———. 1983. A *Celebration of Demons: Exorcism and the Aesthetics of Healing in Sri Lanka*. Bloomington: University of Indiana Press.

Kleinman, Arthur and Lilias Sung. 1979. Why do Indigenous Practitioners Successfully Heal? *Social Science and Medicine* 13b:7–26.

Kuipers, Joel C. 1990. *Power in Performance: The Creation of Textual Authority in Weyewa Ritual Speech*. Philadelphia: University of Pennsylvania Press.

Laderman, Carol. 1991. *Taming the Wind of Desire: Psychology, Medicine, and Aesthetics in Malay Shamanistic Performance*. Berkeley: University of California Press.

Levin, David Michael. 1985. *The Body's Recollection of Being: Phenomenological Psychology and the Deconstruction of Nihilism*. London: Routledge and Kegan Paul.

Levine, Stephen B. n.d. Psychological Intimacy. Paper presented at Grand Rounds, Case Western Reserve Medical School Department of Psychiatry, Spring 1991.

Manning, Frank. 1983. *Celebration of Society: Perspective on Contemporary Cultural Performance*. Bowling Green: Bowling Green University Press.

McGuire, Meredith. 1982. *Pentecostal Catholics: Power, Charisma, and Order in a Religious Movement*. Philadelphia: Temple University Press.

Neitz, Mary Jo. 1987. *Charisma and Community: A Study of Religion in American Culture*. New Brunswick: Transaction Publications.

Peacock, James. 1968. *Rites of Modernization*. Chicago: University of Chicago Press.

Prince, Raymond. 1980. Variations in Psychotherapeutic Procedures. In *Handbook of Cross-Cultural Psychology*, vol. 6, ed. H. C. Triandis and J. C. Draguns, 291–349. Boston: Allyn and Bacon.

Rappoport, Roy A. 1979. *Ecology, Meaning, and Religion*. Richmond: North Atlantic Books.

Ray, Benjamin. 1973. Performative Utterances in African Ritual. *History of Religions* 13:16–35.

Roseman, Marina. 1991. *Healing Sounds from the Malaysian Rainforest: Temiar Music and Medicine*. Berkeley: University of California Press.

Samarin, William, ed. 1976. *Language in Religious Practice*. Rowley: Newbury House.

Scheff, Thomas. 1979. *Catharsis in Healing, Ritual, and Drama*. Berkeley: University of California Press.

Schieffelin, Edward, L. 1985. Performance and the Cultural Construction of Reality. *American Ethnologist* 12:707–24.

Searle, John. 1969. *Speech Acts*. Cambridge: Cambridge University Press.

———. 1979. *Expression and Meaning: Studies in the Theory of Speech Acts*. New York: Cambridge University Press.

Singer, Milton. 1958. From the Guest Editor. *Journal of American Folklore* 71:191–204.

———. 1972. *When a Great Tradition Modernizes*. New York: Praeger.

Tambiah, Stanley. 1985. *Culture, Thought, and Social Action: An Anthropological Perspective*. Cambridge: Harvard University Press.

Watkins, Mary. 1986. *Invisible Guests: The Development of Imaginal Dialogues*. Hillsdale, N.J.: Analytic Press.

Zaner, Richard M. 1981. *The Context of Self: A Phenomenological Inquiry Using Medicine as a Clue*. Athens, Ohio: Ohio University Press.

4

THE POETICS OF HEALING
IN MALAY SHAMANISTIC
PERFORMANCES

Carol Laderman

For every ill, Malays say, God has provided a remedy, if only one knew where to look. Medicines can be found in all realms of nature; animal, vegetable, and mineral. Incantations, inherited through the generations or learned from a master, may dispel the noxious influence of spirits on their human victims. But sometimes only the performance of words and music, poetry and drama, comedy and dance can restore health where other forms of treatment have failed.

The Malays believe that most illnesses result from a humoral imbalance, and treat them with herbal remedies, dietary adjustments, thermal treatments, blood letting, and massage. Should ordinary health problems not respond, or an illness appear to be unusual in kind or in course, a suspicion may arise that the sufferer's problems are due, at least in part, to attacks of spirits (*hantu*), either sent by ill-wishers or acting on their own initiative; or to an imbalance of the component parts of the patient's Self (Laderman 1984, 1991).

Normally, adults have little to fear from *hantu*. Healthy people are protected by spiritual gates which surround them and guard them from harm. Malays believe that human beings are composed of more than thinking minds, mortal bodies, and souls that live on in Heaven or Hell. Humans also embody two other components. One, *semangat*, is the universal spirit that dwells in all creation, including rocks, earth, and fire, and when startled may leave its container. The other component is *angin,* the Inner Winds inherited from our parents that govern individual talent and personality. If strong Winds are not expressed in daily life, they accumulate in the body, causing physical and emotional pain. Should an imbalance occur, whether through depletion of *semangat* or accumulation of *angin,* the integrity of the person is breached and the body's "gates" no longer protect the "fortress within," but instead open it to the depredations of spirits. Neither medicines nor changes in diet are sufficient to cure these spirit-involved conditions, problems related to stifled Winds, or *semangat* loss. External spirits must be exorcised, *semangat* must be recalled and strengthened, and the Winds must blow freely in order for the patient to be brought back to harmony and health. If simple spells do not suffice, the treatment of last resort is a shaman's seance, called the *Main Peteri* (Laderman 1988, 1991). It is the oldest kind of medicine, according to Pak Long Awang, a prominent shaman, dating, in fact, from the time of Adam and Eve. Pak Long explained:

> In the time of the Prophet Adam, Eve was sick. Adam looked for medicine; he looked and looked but he couldn't find any. Then he looked for a *bomoh* (Malay healer), and he found one. Then he asked the *bomoh,* "Do you have medicine to treat Eve?" This is what Tok Kumar Hakim (the *bomoh*) said: "I have medicine for everything!" He brought over a *gebana* (hand drum); he had a *rebab* (spike fiddle). Adam asked what those things were. "This is a bowl for medicine," he said, pointing to the *gebana.* "This is a medicinal herb," he said, pointing to the *rebab.* Then he treated his patient—he played. After he played, Eve was cured of her sickness. Its name is even older than that. When God made Adam he was just a lifeless image. God called Gabriel and breathed into his hands. He told Gabriel to fly over to Adam's image and put the breath up his nostrils. Adam sneezed, and the breath traveled all over his body. His body was too weak for the breath, and broke into little pieces. God told Gabriel to weld (*pateri*) it back together, to make it whole. That's why it's called *Main 'teri.* When we do it, we weld people together, we make sick people well.

ARCHETYPES OF PERSONALITY

In the Malay seance, healing messages, verbal and nonverbal, are conveyed by the players to the participants and audience, both spirit and mortal. They reach out to all five senses—smell, sight, touch and taste, but the sense most intensely involved is hearing. The actors in the seance include the shaman (*tok 'teri*), through whose agency the unseen spirits speak and sing; the *minduk,* the shaman's earthbound partner in dialogue and duets; and a small band of instrumentalists. Excerpts from legends and songs associated with their personality's archetypes encourage patients to achieve trance, allowing them to express their Inner Winds. The majority of conditions treated by *Main Peteri* are *sakit berangin* (Wind sickness), and the most prevalent is due to the thwarting of the personality type known as *Angin Dewa Muda* (The Wind of the Young Demigod), a personality whose archetype is the hero of a story from the *Mak Yong*, a type of play with music and dancing, performed by Malays on the east coast. The following is the story of Dewa Muda, as told by Pak Long, which explains the meaning of *Angin Dewa Muda*:

> Little Dewa Muda was the Prince of Java, the son of the King and Queen of Java, or so he believed. One night he dreamed about a beautiful princess who lived in Kayangan [an abode in the sky where supernatural beings live]. He fell madly in love with her and wanted to find her, no matter what the danger, no matter what the cost. He saw an old man in his dream, an old man with three humps on his back, who told him that if he ever wanted to meet the beautiful princess he would have to wake up immediately and go to the forest, to the clearing in the forest where the white sand lay, and there he must hunt the golden barking deer [*kijang mas*]. "If you don't go hunt the golden barking deer," said the old man, "your people will riot, your kingdom will be in ruins, there will be great fires and the country will sink beneath a flood." Dewa Muda quickly awoke and called his trusted servant, Awang. He told Awang to fetch a *bomoh* skilled in divination. The *bomoh* did a divination and told Dewa Muda that he had dreamed a true dream. He said, "You had better go hunt the golden barking deer. If you don't, your kingdom will be torn apart." Up in Kayangan, Princess Ulana Mas had dreamed of Dewa Muda. She said to herself, "I want to go see Dewa Muda, who loves me so much. I'll fly down to earth and find him." So she soared down to earth, and she took the form of a golden barking deer. She ran in front of Dewa Muda. He called to Awang, "Quick, let's go catch that golden barking deer." They went chasing after her, but they got thoroughly lost. Dewa Muda began to cry. "I must go hunt that a golden barking deer," he said. "It isn't an ordinary barking deer, it's really Princess Ulana Mas, the daughter of Saksa Bota [an ogre]." Awang found the way out of the forest, but the golden barking deer had vanished. Dewa Muda said, "The only way I can find Princess Ulana Mas is to fly to Kayangan. I have to borrow my mother's golden kite. We'll hold on to the kite strings and fly up to Kayangan." So they climbed on to the golden kite. As they approached Kayangan, Saksa Bota yelled down to Dewa Muda, "Hey, Dewa Muda, there's no use your coming here. You can never marry Ulana Mas, because you are my child as much as she is. Your mother is the Queen of Java, but I am your

real father." When he heard those words, Dewa Muda became so unhappy that he went crazy. He couldn't sleep, he couldn't eat, he couldn't bathe. He was so sick that the King and Queen of Java called a *tok 'teri,* a *tok minduk* and the players to have a *Main 'teri,* so he could be cured.

Dewa Muda is the archetype of a personality whose needs are the needs and privileges of royalty: fine clothing, delicate food, aromatic perfumes, comfortable living, and the love and respect of kin, friends, and neighbors. Many people have inherited *Angin Dewa Muda* but few can satisfy its demands. Such people need to be pampered and admired, provided with life's luxuries and reassured often of their charm and worth. Malay village society, where neither material goods nor overt expressions of affection and admiration are in plentiful supply, is a difficult setting for the Dewa Muda personality. The expression of strong emotions is not only frowned upon in rural Malaysia; most people deny that they ever have any. Malays rarely cry or complain. Women suffer through difficult and prolonged labors without raising their voices, and mourners at funerals remain dry-eyed. Married couples normally exhibit no signs of either connubial affection or outright aggression in public.

While living in Malaysia I would never have known that my next-door neighbor had been almost strangled to death one night by her mistakenly jealous husband had she not confided to me, as stranger and friend, and shown me his finger marks on her throat. No telltale sound had broken the peace of the night. Her husband was a classic example of *Angin Hala,* the Wind of the Weretiger, which makes its carrier quick to anger and heedless of its consequences. The archetype of this personality comes from a folk legend, the following version of which was told by Tok Daud, Pak Long's *minduk,* as part of his teachings about *angin:*

> Once there was a young virgin named Siti Zarah who plucked some *buah kemunting* [a kind of berry] and ate them. After a while her belly began to get big. She was pregnant and she had no husband. The berries she had eaten had drops of Weretiger's semen on them. She gave birth to a son who she named Abdul Jinah. As the boy grew older, he acted more and more like a tiger. He started to demand raw meat for his dinner, and he couldn't learn Koran as quickly as the other children did. Finally, his Koran teacher became furious at his behavior and picked up a cane. He beat Abdul Jinah hard, marking his body with forty stripes like the fur of a tiger. The teacher chased Abdul Jinah into the jungle, where he turned into a dangerous weretiger.

Angin Hala is difficult to express in socially accepted ways, unless its possessor is a fighter or occupies a social position that allows him to vent aggression without fear of retaliation. Those with tigerish personalities may prove dangerous to others if they express their *angin* (as in ordinary wife-beating or, in extreme cases, running amok), or to themselves if they do not.

Angin Dewa Penchil is the heritage of those who are dissatisfied with their lives and their homes. They wander in foreign parts, and dress and behave in a manner inappropriate to their station in life. Their archetype is embodied in a character in the *Mak Yong,* as told by Mat Daud bin Panjak, another east-coast shaman:

> Once there was a king called Dewa Penchil who liked to dress in rough clothing and go out among the commoners. His behavior angered his wife's mother, who raised an army to chase him out of the country. Before he fled, he tore a piece of *kain cindai* [a royal cloth] in two, gave half to his wife and kept the other half. He fled to another land far from his kingdom, and wandered for a long time, looking like a poor man and losing his *kain cindai* along the way. One day he sat down under a tree and heard the voice of a bird in the branches saying, "Your wife is being forced to marry another man, and your kingdom is in danger. Go back to your kingdom and kill your rival." As Dewa Penchil looked up at the bird, a suit of royal garments fell down, along with the lost *kain cindai* and a magical royal *kris.* He put on the clothes and hurried back to his kingdom, where he showed his wife the *kain cindai* to prove he was really her husband. With the magical *kris* he killed his rival and his traitorous mother-in-law, and ruled his country in strength and in peace.

Health problems associated with *Angin Dewa Penchil* appear to be rare among rural Malays. Perhaps the wandering urges of this personality type are satisfied by the frequency with which Malay men resort to migratory labor to earn a living for their families (a pattern known as *pergi merantau mencari makan,* or traveling in search of a living, traditional to peninsular Malaysia and parts of Borneo; see, e.g., Freeman 1970).

Behavior inappropriate to one's station has been discouraged by Malay law and custom. In the past, it was a punishable offense for commoners to employ royal language when referring to themselves. Aside from legal sanctions against transgressing the prerogatives of royalty, commoners who dared to break the social barrier or disobey royal commands might expect to fall ill with an incurable skin disease (*kedal*), or suffer in other respects from the curse (*ketulahan*) that accompanies the flouting of royal power (Mohd. Taib Osman 1976).

Rank has its privileges, but it also has its obligations. A surprising number of rural Malays, including some of the poorest, claim descent from royalty. They express their nobility only during preparations for the birth of their children. Since yellow is the color reserved for royalty, a yellow cloth must be spread above the head of a woman of royal descent in labor, its four corners attached to the four walls. An open umbrella, the symbol of noble rank, must be placed upon the outstretched cloth. If these measures are not taken, it amounts to a denial of the woman's royal heritage, and may increase the difficulty of her labor and delivery.

To help me understand *Angin Dewa Penchil* as a personality type, Tok Daud, the *minduk,* compared the behavior of Australian hippies in Malaysia to Dewa Penchil's behavior in the beginning of the story. "They have $1,000 in their pockets," he said, "but you'd never know it, the way they dress in rags and try to bum rides."

People may be heir to one or several types of *angin.* The strength of the Inner Winds can range from a mild breeze to gale force. These Winds, freely blowing or sublimated in everyday living in ways that satisfy both possessor and society, keep the individual healthy and enrich his community. A person with *Angin Dew Muda* may try his best to earn the love and admiration he so desperately needs. A man with *Angin Hala* may cover himself with glory on the playing field or battlefield. If ignored or repressed, powerful *angin* will make its effects felt in the mind and the body. The symptoms of *sakit berangin,* the Wind sickness, include backaches, headaches, digestive problems, dizziness, asthma, depression, anxiety, in short, a wide range of psychosomatic and affective disorders. Asthma, in particular, represents a graphic example of repressed *angin*—Wind that is locked within, choking its possessor.

The Inner Winds of a patient who has been diagnosed as suffering from *sakit berangin* must be allowed to express themselves, released from the confines of their corporeal prison, enabling the sufferer's mind and body to return to a healthy balance. In healing ceremonies, the band strikes up appropriate music as the shaman recites and sings excerpts from the story of the *angin*'s archetype. When the correct musical or literary cue is reached, the patient achieves trance, aided, as well, by the percussive sounds of music and the rhythmic beating of the shaman's hands on the floor near the patient's body.

WORDS OF POWER

The *minduk*'s words, as he chants his invocation and sings his songs, are not sacred in the sense of Islamic prayer, but are, nevertheless, believed to carry power, a power that proceeds from his breath, the outward manifestation of his *bomoh*'s Wind, without which no amount of study could prepare him for his profession. He must open the shaman's gates and move his Winds through the quality of the poetic language of his song. The tropes of this song reveal the interconnections between the human microcosm and the universal macrocosm: a hurricane, immune from human control, can cause damage to the world, and similarly, a strong uncontrolled Inner Wind may cause its possessor to harm himself or others.

As the shaman sits before him, reciting protective incantations to strengthen and guard his "gates," the *minduk* sings:

> Ah, I utter the name of God with one Alif.
> Alif stands at the gates of Heaven.
> I spread a welcome at the gates of Earth.
> Ninety holy prayers I recite,
> And then I will open the pent-up Wind.
> Wind as small as a sesame seed,
> Wind as small as a mustard seed,
> Wind called a golden bouquet of flowers,
> Wind called a silver bouquet of flowers,
> When it emerges.
> The Winds emerge from the tip of eternity!
> They descend, through the father, to his posterity,
> Along with the welcome Winds of the mother.
> The Wind is lit with five rays of light,
> It stands and recites six magical words.
> The Wind comes out with seven claps of thunder.
> The Wind comes out of a handful of earth,
> A drop of water, a tongue of flame, a puff of air.
> Earth, let there be no oppression.
> Water, let there be no floods.
> Fire, let there be no scorching.
> Wind, let there be no great sin.
> Each of you, wake up and meet face to face
> Near the seven gates, every one of them vanished.
> The gate to the lane, each gate to the valley,
> The gate of lust, the gate of passion, the gate of desire,
> The gate that shuts off elemental desire,
> The swaying together.
> The gate of law, the gate of faith, the gate of wisdom.
> Open the gate with a key,
> Open the latch of the gate,
> Golden gate, latched from without,
> Locked from within.
> Gate fastened shut with Muhammad's needle.
> Now I open the way for the friendly Winds.
> Winds of the father's line, Winds of the mother's,
> Winds that interpret our very souls.

Figure 1. Pak Long Awang teaches an aspiring student in an
impromptu school for shamans.

The symbolism in this song speaks clearly to its listeners. Alif, the first letter of the Arabic alphabet, stands for Allah; the five rays of light are the five senses; the six magical words are the four cardinal directions plus up and down; the seven claps of thunder are the seven major parts of the human body; earth, air (or wind), fire, and water are the universal elements of all Creation; the swaying together is the human sex act.

Both the shaman's rationality (the gates of law, faith and wisdom) and his emotions (the gates of lust, passion and desire) must be mobilized. Although his senses have been figuratively shut with Muhammad's needle, a metaphor for the teachings of the Koran (and in fact his seance is condemned by Islamic ortho-doxy), they must be awakened to allow him to heal the sick.

After the shaman has achieved trance, the first entity to speak through him is one of the body's guardians, who act as a kind of spiritual immune system. "From the very beginning, before Creation was complete, [he says], I guarded the four outer walls, the caverns, the two bends in the river, the fortress of excre-ment, the gateway to wisdom." In other words, the human body, with its protective gate and its inner hollows, containing both the lowest form of filth and the highest rationality, is being protected by the guardians. When all of these guardians have been awakened, spirits suspected of having afflicted a patient must be brought to the seance by the shaman's own familiar spirits. The *minduk* flatters, coaxes, promises offerings, insults and threatens them in order to restore the patient's normal humoral balance which has been disturbed by the spirits' airy heat. They must remove their unbalancing presence: the *minduk* instructs them to "clear every stifling vapor from the body and soul" of the patient. He exhorts them to return to their origins and restore the balance of the universe. The integrity of both this body and the entire universe is threatened by their encroaching upon humanity.

Complications can arise when the patient's own birth-sibling, the afterbirth which s/he was born with, joins the disembodied *hantu*'s attack. This afterbirth is the mirror image of the *hantu*. Both are siblings of humanity and both are incomplete: *hantu* lack the earthy and watery elements of which the body is made, while the afterbirth never receives the airy and fiery Breath of Life that animates its human sibling upon the child's first breath. The birth-sibling feels the unfairness of its inheritance. Although they "traveled down the same path"—the mother's birth canal—the child received the love and property of the parents, while the birth-sibling got only a coconut-shell coffin and a scrap of winding sheet. The *minduk* explains that it is only semi-human: "Body of a beast with a human face, your father doesn't love you; your mother doesn't cherish you. The sky is your roof; the earth is your pillow."

The patient's suffering is ennobled by the tropes of Malay legend, particularly by the story of Dewa Muda losing his reason through thwarted love. The patient's condition is compared by the shaman during the ceremony to a muti-lated tree: "The Jati Jawa tree has many lovely leaves, one shoot, and two boughs. A branch on the left has been trampled on this side. The branch on the left now is drooping. The shoot has been trampled. I fear that the shoot will be chopped down. My speech is becoming confused, my behavior is going awry." The patient is like a traveler who has lost his way: "I came straight from the cape at the river's mouth; I leaped into my little junk, my golden barge. I sailed for two times seven days and two times seven nights upon that junk until I reached the coarse sands at the harbor's edge. Well, where was that—a place with three islands and a harbor? I disembarked, not knowing to what place I had come. Yes, I stared at the islands but could not see them; I stared at the land but could not see the sands. I was completely confused, I was totally lost."

The *semangat* of a patient suffering from soul loss feels pain at its separation. It sings:

> Oh, father, where has my sister vanished? Where has she disappeared? While you sit, sad and compassionate, the flower with seven petals [the body with its seven parts] is being eaten away. My sister, Princess Flowerbud, has vanished who knows where, stolen out of her cradle and taken away, by whom I don't know. They say she was taken by the one

called Make-the-Baby-Laugh [the afterbirth that plays with its human sibling], that it is certain she was taken away from the top of the main mast [the patient's head] by his forces. Day and night she sits, her face pale, her body close to dying. She's just skin and bones. Strew down bouquets of gold and silver flowers, strew down limes. Guard this living, breathing child; return him to health.

The ritual relies upon a variety of tropes to express the fullness of the seance's meaning. Some are common metaphors of Malay poetry and flowery speech, such as "beetle and flowerbud" for "young man and young woman." Others, like "tear the leaf, break the charcoal" (end a relationship past mending), are everyday expressions. Hearing the *minduk* compare a patient to a trampled tree with drooping branches does not puzzle the Malay audience; nor do comical remarks such as a shamans' complaint that "the rains have not yet come" when he was not offered a drink, and "there's no crust here" because sugar wasn't added to his tea. It amuses the audience when a shaman calls his false teeth scissors that don't cut properly (i.e., don't let him enunciate clearly), and compares his troupe to shadow puppets. Malays enjoy the players' puns: spirits are teased by twisting their names into new forms—*polong* (a type of spirit) becomes *talang* (mackerel) in the *minduk*'s mouth; *serupa* (looks like) becomes *sejubur* (asshole). They roar with laughter when a patient's immodest way of sitting is noted by the shaman as showing "the hole in his window" (implying that his anus was visible). In the seance, emotions out of control are like a "great elephant whose driver is stupid, crazed elephant whose driver's a fool."

The tropes of conception used by the *minduk* are densely packed with meaning—a phrase I translated as "The Winds emerge from the tip of eternity" could also be rendered as "The child's personality is inherited from the father, emerging, with semen, from the end of his penis"; or "The Inner Winds have exited from the beginning of Time and will exist forever more." All of these meanings, suggested by the *minduk,* are equally valid and simultaneously understood. Likewise, the fruit of the father, of which the *minduk* sings, is both his offspring (as the fruit is child to the tree) and his own testicles, the core of his fruitfulness.

The language of the seance makes extensive use of the multivocality that Victor Turner called a "fan" of meanings. Corresponding to their dual functions of restoring harmony to both humans and to the universe, references to body parts also refer to terrestrial features: the mountain top is also the human head, the wide fields the human breast, the ocean at once the South China Sea, the human bloodstream and the stomach, the liquid center of the body.

Within the shamanistic ritual, the unsaid becomes the said, the intangible and inaudible take on form and sound, the chaotic becomes controlled. Spirits "borrow the voice of Adam," they speak and sing, joke and complain, express their wishes and agree to withdraw their harmful influence, all through the medium of the shaman. Normally present but unseen, they show their character through the shaman's movements and his tone of voice as he "carries" them in trance.

Concepts unexpressed in daily life come to the fore in the seance. Many are commonplace truisms that Malays assume are universally known and give insight into their conceptions of gender, such as the father's role in conception. Although I regularly assisted traditional midwives in delivering babies, it was not until I heard the *minduk*'s song that I learned about the father's pregnancy. "For forty days and forty nights the baby rests within its father's womb," sings the *minduk*. "A single drop falls from the father's pen . . . thrust, then, into the mother's womb, enclosed there nine months and ten days." According to the text of the *Main Peteri,* human beings possess an animal nature that makes us kin to the beasts. Yet humans are also unique among God's creations in possessing rationality (*akal*). Rationality is what distinguishes humans, and, in this respect, makes them even closer to God than the angels. Men, however, have a greater amount of rationality than do women, in whom animal nature predominates. In this light it makes sense for a baby to begin life within its father's brain, the paternal womb, where it acquires rationality from a developed source.

Much of the symbolism of the *Main Peteri* centers around the mysteries of birth and sex. The patient's birth-sibling often appears at the seance, complaining of their unequal fate. Having begun in the mother's womb rather than the father's brain, the birth-sibling is not only lacking the air and fire that the baby takes in with its first breath; it also lacks human rationality.

The disembodied spirits are kin to humanity in the same manner as the birth-sibling is kin to the patient. In one origin story, the spirits are said to have arisen from the afterbirths that accompanied the emergence of Adam and Eve. The Yellow Genie and the Black Genie were formed from the debris of human childbirth; specifically the Yellow Genie arose from the blood of parturition (yellow is often symbolic of blood in Malay magic), and the Black Genie arose from the placenta.

Sex and other intimate bodily functions are not always serious matters in the ritual. Its humor tends to be broadly sexual and scatological. The names of many female spirits are graphic and uncomplimentary, unlike the awesome and powerful titles claimed by male spirits. While male spirits have such names as "He Who Chastises as He Passes," and "Mighty Hammer," female spirits are known as "Mother Long-breasts," "Miss Tits," the "Moldy Old Maid," and the "Old Maid Who Can't Control Her Urination." One of Pak Long's spirit familiars (*penggawa*), the Old Toddy Tapper, explains that it's a long time since he had a toddy container—his wife is old now. The Mute Spirit (*Hantu Bisu*) is a favorite with audiences in Merchang. All he wants to do is get laid, and he conveys his message by the universal symbol of a finger moving in and out of the circle made by the joined thumb and forefinger of his other hand.

Shamans themselves are teased about their supposed habit of applying their healing touch to pretty women's bosoms more often than they do to less attractive patients. They appear to take such teasing in good part. Sex, after all, is one of life's great pleasures, and what man would not take advantage of such an opportunity? In fact, shamans believe that human woes can sometimes be caused by unsatisfied sexual cravings, and do their best to allow these feelings to be expressed in an atmosphere that does not threaten their possessor. In his treatment of a young unmarried girl who laughed and cried for no apparent reason, the handsome young shaman urged her to act out her repressed feelings in trance by singing to her, "What's the use of wearing pants? Get up and dance!"

Moments of humor in the seance may be reflections of a spirit's known character. For instance, Wak Long, one of the shaman's spirit familiars and a popular figure in the shadow play, claims to be a rich man. The *minduk* laughs at his claims, saying, "Oh, that's a good one! He even has debts piling up at the store . . . That's the kind of rich man he is." A sea spirit, asked to break off relations with his human associate, says that he will "row off." More often, however, humorous episodes involving the spirits reveal ways in which they are inferior to human beings. The *hantu,* for instance, exemplify bad manners. They are noisy, threatening, greedy; they gobble up their feasts, grab their offerings, and show themselves to be not only lacking in a humoral sense, but also in a cultural sense. They may behave like children, demanding bananas and stuffing the entire fruit into their mouths. Female spirits may act immodestly, like Miss Click-clack (*Mek Kutuk-ketak*), who goes so far as to point out a man in the audience whom she would like to meet.

Many of the jokes that the *minduk* makes at the spirits' expense depend upon the *hantu's* lack of reasoning power. They do not understand the (often not very subtle) insults hurled at them. They are deficient in rationality and lack the knowledge essential to every human Malay. Even the Hantu Raya, the most feared spirit on the east coast, when pretending to be a pious Muslim, cannot recite more than the first line of the daily prayer. His ignorance amuses the audience while revealing his true identity.

The behavior of the *hantu* relegates them to a position outside the norms of polite human society, and the aim of the seance is to see that they return to the place in God's scheme where they belong (see Kapferer 1983:224) for similar material in Sri Lanka). Within their own sphere, the *hantu's* society is organized along much the same lines as human society. They have a hierarchy of rulers, headmen, assistant headmen, armies of soldiers, and servants. Their rulers may make demands on humanity, as well as on their ghostly subjects, similar to those of human rulers. For instance, Hitam Seri Penakluk (the Black Conqueror), who rules the crossroads, "levies taxes and demands tribute."

Although human beings are placed in a relationship of superiority to *hantu,* the supernatural beings that appear during a seance are far from pathetic figures of fun, as are the Sri Lankan demons described by Kapferer. Speaking of the dramatic seance, Kapferer says that the demons' howling and crying contribute to the destruction of any sense of awe which may have surrounded the demonic previously (Kapferer 1983:224). In contrast, the Malay sea spirit who breaks off relations with his human partner, remains a noble and tragic figure as he sings and sobs, "My prince, you have the heart to . . . All his words strike me to the quick. He wants to get rid of me; he wants to get rid of me."

Before either an exorcism or a "moving of the patient's Wind" can take place, the inner forces of the ritual pair, *tok 'teri* and *minduk,* and their patient must be invoked. The Four Sultans, Four Commanders, Four Warriors, who dwell within humans must be awakened to the necessity of guarding their possessors. The body's own healers must be aroused: the *minduk* sings, "Awaken the drummers in the palace of bone, Awaken the fiddlers in the palace of flesh." Royal allusions abound in these seances. The shaman is called *inang,* literally the nurse of a royal child; the *minduk* is named *pengasuh,* the body servant and companion of a prince. Both the site of the seance and the patient's body are called "the palace." The body is the palace of the soul, and its parts are like porches or verandas. The mat upon which the patient sits is called the throne room, and his illness is often compared to a civil war, relating the disharmony of disease in the human body to disharmony in the body politic (see Kessler 1977; Laderman 1981).

The *minduk* expresses the philosophy behind the seance when he ends by singing that "those born to be kings are content when they associate with kings, those born noble when they associate with nobles" and when he exhorts the genies to stay "with genies together in ranks, *mambang* [a type of spirit] with *mambang* together in ranks." Everyone, in other words, must act as befits his or her place in society, and everything must be in its proper place in the universe for harmony to prevail.

THE *MAIN PETERI* AS DRAMATIC FORM

Like a play, the seance is composed of a series of scenes within acts, often divided by intermissions. The first act sets the stage for the rest of the play. The spirits are invited to the seance, the inner forces and spirit familiars are invoked, and the first divination takes place, often followed by an intermission. The second act usually consists of several scenes in which tensions engendered by the visitation of threatening spirits alternate with episodes of comedy and other tension-easing devices. Then the patient is put into trance—a tense and exciting moment. The release that follows his trance prepares us for the final duet of the *minduk* and *tok 'teri*—another easing of the night's dramatic tension: "The waves have been put to rest by the strings of the Winds . . . One and all are at ease, each in his place in the palace."

Those who perform *Main Peteri* are individualists, each with his own history, training, and idiosyncracies. The reasons for holding a seance change from case to case. Certain conventions, however, appear to be basic to the genre, although the content can vary within categories. This minimal form of the *Main Peteri,* used in an emergency seance performed to heal a sick shaman, included the following:

1. An invocation sung by the *minduk* as the prelude to the seance. In his introductory song, the *minduk* sends greetings to the ancestral teachers, healers, and saints, and awakens the healing powers within himself. He invokes the spirits of the place, mentioning their domains: the denizens of the earth, fields, village, orchards, water's edge, ocean, jungle, and heavenly abode (*kayangan*). These are not, by far, all the spirits: there is no list of denizens of the spirit world consistent from *bomoh* to *bomoh.* Each *bomoh* invokes the spirits most familiar to him, and apologizes to those he has inadvertently omitted. In this seance the *minduk* accompanies himself in the three-stringed *rebab,* a spike-fiddle played with a bow. During the *minduk's* invocation, the audience mills about, paying little attention to his song; not because it is unimportant—it is a necessary prelude to the action of the seance—but because it is meant primarily for the ears of the invisible powers the *minduk* invokes, not those of his human audience.

2. At the end of the introductory song, the *tok 'teri,* having changed his clothes, seats himself before the *minduk* listening intently while the *minduk* sings *gerak angin,* the Bestirring Song (literally "to move the Wind") that will assist the shaman in achieving trance. Toward the middle of the Bestirring Song, the shaman recites his incantation, invoking his inner resources and spirit familiars.

3. Having achieved trance, the shaman has a conversation and shares a duet with the *minduk,* in the persona of an internal force (one of the Commanders and Warriors within the human body that act as a kind of spiritual immune system).

4. He is replaced by the persona of an ancient and powerful *bomoh,* who sings a duet with the *minduk* and conducts a divination.

5. Following the divination, the shaman and *minduk* sing a duet about the changing nature of Dea Muda. On the sea he is the Young Captain, on land the Young Prince, in heaven the Young Demigod.

6. The first moment of real tension arrives in the persona of the Assistant Headman of the Earth Spirits.

7. He is followed by another dangerous spirit, Anak Jin Serupa Muka (the Genie With the Look-alike Face). The tension of his presence is somewhat lessened by the insults he receives from the *minduk*, amusing to the audience, incomprehensible to the genie.

8. The third ghostly visitor arrives—in fact, they are three spirit-brothers (although only one speaks through the agency of the shaman). The tension they engender quickly dissipates when they agree to help the patient.

9. After a break for tea, the *Main Peteri* resumes. The *minduk* and the shaman (in his own persona) sing a duet, "Let the Winds blow and open the way for the souls of former kings." All of the world is now at ease, and everything is back in its proper place, as the seance comes to an end.

At each point of transition, and at the close of the seance, the musicians play a "traveling" tune, which becomes faster and louder, stopping suddenly as the shaman changes persona. More elaborate *Main Peteri* are built upon this model, with appropriate changes to suit the circumstances, and variations to suit the training, temperaments and moods of the performers.

In addition to the fact that the majority of performers in the seance are also involved with the shadow play (*wayang kulit*) and/or the Mak Yong dance theater, formal connections between the three genres are also evident. The most important of all *wayang kulit* rituals are those called *berjamu* (feasting), performed for the propitiation of spirits. The basic form of *berjamu* follows that of the *Main Peteri*. Unlike other performances of the shadow play, which employ only the *dalang* (puppet master) and his assistants, the *berjamu* requires as well the presence of a *minduk*, who leads the orchestra and plays the three-stringed *rebab* (otherwise used only in the seance). In the *berjamu*, the *dalang*, after achieving trance, engages in dialogues with the *minduk* in the same manner as the shaman in the seance, and the idiom of their language is often that of the *Main Peteri* (Sweeney 1972:278). Many of the shamans' spirit familiars are characters in the shadow play.

Performances of the *Mak Yong* dance-theater which are enacted for reasons of health include the *semah angin* (offering to the Winds), meant to prepare performers for their graduation and to adjust their humoral well-being thereafter, and *sambaut* (catching) or *memanggil* (calling) *semangat*, performed to strengthen or recall the vital spirit. In addition, the *Mak Yong* can combine with the shaman's seance to produce a special genre known as *Mak Yong-Main Peteri*. A patient diagnosed as suffering from an unrealized identification with a *Mak Yong* character is given the opportunity of performing in this special *Mak Yong* as a means of curing his *sakit berangin* (Ghulam-Sarwar 1976:256). In a typical *Mak Yong-Main Peteri* performance, a patient might assume the role of the hero, Pak Yong, while the *bomoh* takes the role of his clown-assistant, Peran. This genre appears to be the type of performance witnessed by Kessler (1977). He describes the seance of a woman with *Angin Hala* (Wind of the Weretiger) who acted out the part of a warrior with a swaggering walk and a threatening stance. In trance, she fought with the officiating shaman as she would not have dared to do with her neglectful husband, thereby alleviating the feeling of powerlessness she suffered in everyday life.

So strong is the actors' belief in the power of even ordinary performances of *Mak Yong* that enacting certain roles, especially that of Dewa Muda, entails not only dramatic rehearsal but psychological and spiritual preparation as well. In the drama of Dewa Muda, the part of Peran Tua (the old clown—assistant to the prince) is played by a *bomoh,* who recites all the incantations and conducts all necessary rituals. Before the portion of the play in which Dewa Muda and his Peran enter the forest, the *bomoh* must ask the spirits for their protection and offer them a feast. His actions are vital to the safety of the performers: They are not merely play-acting, they *become* the characters. Although the performance of a *Mak Yong* drama may take place on several succeeding nights, the action of any night can never end at a place in which one of the characters is in danger, lest the actor's welfare be put in jeopardy.

This strong identification between the actors and their roles benefits the players while increasing their risks. Actors rarely suffer from *sakit berangin* since their performances allow their Winds to blow, and the appreciation of their audiences flatters the players' Winds and keeps them content (Ghulam-Sarwar 1976).

STAGE AND PROPS

Performance of *Main Peteri* requires the establishment of a space set off from everyday uses. A structure may be built especially for the seance, or the shaman's or patient's home may be transformed by the arrangement of floor mats and the seating of the performers and audience. The props of the seance are often used in other types of ritual, since their symbolic value holds true in other circumstances. For example, the spirit feast offered in the *Main Peteri* contains the same ingredients as the feast offered to jungle spirits to placate them before their land is opened to agriculture. The double-slipknot palm-frond "releasers," used to release victims of spirit attacks from danger, are also used by midwives to release new mothers from the perils of childbirth. Patients are often bathed by the shaman at the close of the seance, to cleanse them of any remaining spiritual pollution. This ritually cleansing bath is also performed by patients themselves at the behest of *bomoh* who have treated them for "unusual" ailments; and midwives bathe new mothers, for similar reasons, at the close of the rituals of childbirth.

Some of the props are multivalent, appearing in cognate forms in other ritual settings. For example, the shaman places a loop of cord atop the offering to his spirit familiars. A similar loop of cord becomes a stand-in for the birth canal as a woman pregnant with her first child passes through it at the finale of the *melenggang perut* (a ritual that takes place during the seventh month of pregnancy). It is also used at the end of the postpartum period, when a new mother and her child pass through the lop in a representation of rebirth into a new status. Another multivalent symbolic object is the *keras,* a dish containing money, raw rice, a coconut, and a loop of cord. The shucked coconut, with its suggestion of a face and hair, is a double of the patient's head in the context of the *Main Peteri.* It becomes a stand-in for the uterus in the *melenggang perut.* Hard and round like a pregnant womb, the coconut contains liquid and solid elements that mimic the fetus and amniotic fluid.

THE MUSIC OF HEALING

Apart from performances and ceremonial occasions, I never heard my Malay neighbors play any musical instrument and rarely hard them whistle or sing. On one memorable day, the voice of a man reached my ears as I walked by the house where he cantillated his prayers, yet in Islam, the melodic recitation of Koran is not considered "music". Although I spent a good deal of time with mothers and their babies, I never heard a lullaby. Music is not part of the school curriculum, but before the day's instruction begins the children sing the National Anthem. None of the children in my son's class appeared to agree on the melody, although they sang together loudly and enthusiastically. We had no idea of the tune its composer had intended until we read it from a book.

But although it is not an everyday occurrence, music is important in the fabric of Malay life. Performances of *wayang kulit* and *dikir barat* (a form of male group singing which takes one of two forms, praises to Allah or profane joking songs) cannot be imagined without music. Music accompanies the stylized movements of *silat,* the Malay martial art. The musical prelude of the Mak Yong not only sets the stage for the performance, it also helps the actors to prepare themselves psychologically before the play begins.

Music, both vocal and instrumental, is also an integral part of the healing seance. As other students of Malayo-Indonesian culture have indicated (see, e.g., Errington 1975; Siegel 1979), the mere sound (*bunyi*) of a beautiful voice is considered to produce an effect upon its listeners. Above all talents and skills, a performer must possess a beautiful voice. Inability to produce a "delicious sound" is fatal to a ritual healer's career.

The importance of the voice as brought home to me forcefully during the course of a *Main Peteri*. Several ritual specialists, including a young novice, took turns putting patients into trance. The novice was signally unsuccessful. Clients explained to me later that there was nothing wrong with what he said, the difficulty lay in his unmelodious voice which jarred the ears and prevented the harmonious state of mind and body that allows one to trance. Although ideally, as Errington remarks, sound, meaning, and effect can be thought of as an inseparable whole (the word *bunyi* encompasses the concepts of sound, melody, meaning, content, and purport), in practical terms, each aspect can be judged and found satisfying or wanting.

The music of the *Main Peteri* conducts the participants into the realm of the sacred. Although the *tok 'teri* seemingly ignores the *minduk*'s introductory song, its sound permeates the air, preparing the ritual partners for their encounters with the supernatural. The *minduk*'s duets with the *tok 'teri*, both in his own persona and in the personae of other beings, are in the form of a dialogue with musical overlaps that attest to the interactive harmony of their partnership. While the vocal music shows the relationship between people (or between people and spirits), the instrumental interludes function as transitions into altered states. They occur as the shaman changes from one persona to the next, when a patient is helped into and out of trance, and at the close of the seance. Often the transition music is "traveling music" (*lagu berjalan,* as it is known in the puppet play), played as participants travel from one level of awareness to another.

Much has been written about the power of music, particularly rhythmic percussive sound, to induce trance (e.g., Needham 1967; Neher 1962; Lex 1979), but it seems clear that, by itself, music cannot alter the consciousness of those who are neither sensitized to it nor expectant of its results (Rouget 1980; Blacking 1985; Roseman 1988). The audience at a seance hears the same sounds as the shaman and his patient, but rarely does anyone go into trance who is not *meant* to do so.

The choice of music used in the seance rests, to a large extent, with individual performers and their troupes. For example, Mat Daud bin Panjak begins the seance with *Lagu Kijang Mas Tuah* (Lucky Golden Barking-Deer Tune). He uses *Lagu Pandan Wangi* (Aromatic Pandanus Tune) to move the shaman's Wind, *Lagu Pak Yong Muda* (the tune of the hero of the *Mak Yong*) to send praises to his Grandsire, and *Lagu Sedayung* (Oar or Boat Pole Tune) to call his familiar spirit. He does the divination to the tune of *Lagu Wak Tanda Raja* (Tune of the Old Man with Tokens of Royalty), and puts his patient into trance with *Lagu Mengambul* (Swinging Back and Forth; Submerging and Emerging Tune). If it is necessary to evoke the Wind of the Weretiger (*Angin Hala*), he plays *Lagu Kecubung* (Datura Tune). The seance ends with *Lagu Mengulit* (Lullaby).

The music of the *Main Peteri* punctuates and reinforces the words and action of the drama, and helps to shape its form by means of its rhythm, tonal range, and pitch center. Songs start with a compressed tonal range, and then widen in range as the section repeats, pressing the limits with stresses, ornamentations, and elaborations much like the process of elaborated repetitions found in the European Baroque musical tradition. During the course of the ceremony, the tendencies found in individual songs are replicated in the overall shape of the seance; as the pitch center rises, the rhythms intensify, and then finally ease down. The rhythm often identifies the genre, such as *Lagu Berjalan* (traveling music), while the melody points to specifics (which character is traveling. The extent to which language is transformed by music constitutes the ritual reframing of reality through sound (Basso 1984; Roseman 1991). Sung music expands the parameters of speech, but the sobbing of an abandoned spirit goes beyond both spoken language and music.

Many of these tunes are also used in the *Mak Yong*, where they perform different but related functions. In the *Main Peteri*, *Lagu Kijang Mas* accompanies travel from everyday life to a sacred space. In the *Mak Yong*, it is traveling music for characters who are going from one location to another. In the seance, *Lagu Pandan Wangi* is used to heighten the emotions of the shaman—to move his wind. In the *Mak Yong*, it is played during scenes of lamentation. *Lagu Pak Yong Muda*, the tune which accompanies the shaman's praises to the Grandsire, an even more powerful being, is the tune that introduces the hero of the *Mak Yong*, a royal personage, full of *sakti* (magical power, like mana). *Lagu Sedayung*, played in the *Mak Yong* during magical situations, is used by the shaman to call his spirit familiars. The *Lagu Mengombul*, which sends a message to the patient's inner core in the *Main Peteri*, enabling him to trance, accompanies the transmission of messages with the *Mak Yong*. And *Lagu Mengulit*, which ends the seance, is played during gentle and delicate moments in the *Mak Yong*.

The instrumental music that accompanies the shaman's trance not only marks a transition to a new persona; it is also a transition from sung speech to the sound of the shaman's inarticulate cries of "Eiii, aiii" as he goes from the solidity of one persona into wordless chaos. Then, the oscillating two-note figure played by the spike fiddle in the lowest part of the ensemble's tonal range accelerates and comes to a crescendo, and the shift to a new persona is complete.

The music of the seance ends in the tonal center of its beginning, relaxing from the emotional and tonal high attainted by a forsaken spirit. It moves from the driving sixteenth-note beat found in the sobbing spirit's song, to stately quarter-note beats accompanying the song of Prince Potent Cure, the personification of shamanistic healing. Each beat in these successive sections has a longer duration than the beats in any of the music that has come before. This music eases the Winds that have blown that night. The seance slows down and spirit and mortal are at ease.

MOVEMENT IN THE *MAIN PETERI*

Even more than music, dance in rural Malaysia is usually the province of professionals and ritual specialists. Although I attended celebrations of all kinds, the only dancing I observed was on public ceremonial occasions, such as the birthday celebration of the Sultan of Trengganu in the state capital.

In the village, I witnessed one performance of *silat,* the Malay martial art that incorporates many dancelike movements, held by the village men as a special treat for me shortly before I left for home. Every year, professional players and dancers were invited to perform at the three-day annual *Main Pantai* (festivities at the seashore). Actresses from the *Mak Yong* troupe took turns performing as *joget* girls, dancing alongside daring young village men. The dancers never touched one another, but the experience of men and women moving their bodies to music, facing each other, was considered terribly exciting and verging on the scandalous (particularly in the case of men who were already married). Actresses in the *Mak Yong* usually dance with slow circling movements, while the male players have more complicated and stylized dances that incorporate steps (*langkah*) and turns (*kirat*) often named after the characters they are meant to portray. Rough or brutal characters move with large, sudden, and violent gestures, while noble characters use smaller and more delicate movements. The hand gestures of the *Mak Yong,* such as the fluttering of held-out fingers, denote nobility of character but do not themselves have specific meanings, with the exception of those done in the section called *Menghadap Rebab* (Salutations to the Spike Fiddle).

The *Menghadap Rebab* is the most elaborate part of the *Mak Yong,* both in its music and its dance. The ritual serves the dual functions of paying respect to the rebab and its attendant spirits, and preparing the actresses spiritually and psychologically for the roles they are about to play. Each arm movement in this section has a meaningful name, such as *tangan sembah guru* (obeisance to the teacher), *tangan susun sirih* (arranging the ingredients of the betel quid), *tangan burung terbang* (flying bird), and *tangan sawah mengorak lingkaran* (rice fields unwinding their curves). The body postures are called *liuk ke kiri, liuk ke kanan* (bend to the left, bend to the right) (Ghulam-Sarwar 1976:131–132).

All three performance genres, *wayang kulit, Mak Yong,* and *Main Peteri,* include many scenes of traveling. The music that accompanies walking movements in the shadow play accounts for fourteen pieces in the musical repertoire (Matusky 1980:181). *Mak Yong* players take mincing, circling steps as they pretend to travel from one location to another. The same movements accompany the shaman's transition to another persona as he rises and dances in trance.

As in the *Mak Yong,* not all of the gestures and movements in the *Main Peteri* have specific symbolic content. Personae can be identified by their movements and postures, as well as by their voices and speech, as the shaman portrays them with dramatic gestures and expressive characterizations. The truth of his interpretation is vital to the success of his treatment: he is not merely an actor who must convince his audience; he is the embodiment of entities who are present and real. Human beings who ordinarily can only feel the effect of invisible spirits upon their bodies, visualize them in the seance through the efforts of the *tok 'teri.* Genies arrive with sudden, violent thrusts and crouch threateningly before the *minduk.* Strong but benevolent characters, such as Hanuman the White Monkey (a spirit familiar), make large, heroic gestures. The gentle spirit, Mek Bunga, announces her arrival by her feminine, flirtatious wiggles, which Pak Daud compares to sifting rice, winnowing it up and down. Offerings, on other occasions merely left in strategic places for the spirits, are actually eaten by them before the onlookers' eyes. A *hantu* childishly stuffs his mouth with bananas; the Yellow Genie who guards a mountain top swoops down on a raw egg and sucks it dry.

The movements made by the shaman as he first goes into trance on any particular night are invariable: He seats himself cross-legged before the *minduk.* Towards the middle of the Bestirring Song, after the shaman has begun his incantation, a tremor starts in one foot, going up through his leg and torso until it reaches his head, which begins to shake and whirl faster and faster until trance is achieved, indicated by the cessation of shaking as the shaman claps his palms together overhead. The *tok 'teri*'s initial head-shaking marks the division between his ordinary actions and the shamanistic behavior that his *minduk* and the audience have now been signaled to expect during the rest of the night's work. Successive trances are faster and less strenuous, often requiring only a few moments of head-shaking for one spirit to exit and another to take its place. The seance ends with a final series of head-whirlings and shakings, marking the transition back to everyday life. When the music has ceased and his head has stopped

Figure 2. A shaman sings his opening song during a seance
performed for an asthmatic puppet master.

Figure 3. The shaman brings his patient out of trance. The patient has sunk
to the floor after performing, while entranced, with his puppets.

its shaking, the *tok 'teri* wipes his face, stretches, and speaks once more in his own voice. The drama has come to an end as decisively as though a curtain had fallen.

Spoken dialogues are always done in a seated position. Duets may be sung either while the ritual pair is seated or while the shaman dances (the *minduk* never leaves his seat). The shaman's dance is slow and stately, with small circling steps in the manner of *Mak Yong* actresses. His dance is characterized by bending to the left, swaying to the right (*liuk ke kiri, longlai ke kanan*), like the dance in *Menghadap Rebab*—a fitting gesture, since the *rebab* is a central instrument in the *Main Peteri* ensemble. His bending, swaying body, like a branch waving in the breeze, attests to the blowing of his Inner Winds, stirred into life by the *minduk*'s song.

The shaman's gestures communicate their meaning to his spirit audience as well as to the mortal onlookers. When he points his hand, palm facing inward, to the sky, it bids the spirits to stay calm. An arm outstretched and bent at the elbow, palm outward and fingers lightly raised, asks for protection and favor from the Original Teacher (*guru asal*). When the dancing shaman closes his fist, with the thumb outside, and brings it up to his mouth, or to his temple, he is recalling his magical knowledge (*ingat ilmu*). He joins the little fingers of both hands and lifts them slowly from chest height to his chin as he mentally recites a spell (*baca ilmu*). Lowering one arm behind him, hand brought back and palm up, the other arm elevated obliquely, palm down, sends a call to his familiar. Extending his arms horizontally, the hand of one arm pointing down and the other up, or raising one hand with the fingers bent, the other hand flat on his knee, announces the approach of a spirit. Raising a hand with the index finger extended and the other fingers folded salutes the spirits and asks them to accept his apology (usually on behalf of a patient).

From time to time, the *tok 'teri* dips his hand into the water to which perfume or sweet-smelling flowers have been added and rubs it on his face and neck to cleanse himself of the spirits' hot vapor. The more powerful spirits manifest themselves in the form of a virulent heat that is particularly oppressive to the shaman's face.

When the *tok 'teri* dances before his patient, in the persona of a spirit who has agreed to be helpful, he often takes hold of the patient's head or shoulders, sometimes violently, pulling the oppressive vapor from the patient's body into his own hands. He then claps them together, forcing the vapor to escape into the air and dissipate.

The patient's trance in the *Main Peteri,* unlike those described by Kapferer (1983) for Sri Lanka and Epton (1966) for whirling dervishes, does not develop out of the dance, but precedes it. His trance neither marks a transformation into a demonic self, as in Sri Lanka, nor does it bring the trancer divine intoxication, as it does for dervishes. The Malay patient's trance transforms him by opening the gates of his inner self. His Winds show their mighty nature in his vigorous head-whirling at the height of trance, and their gentle strength as he dances, bending and swaying to their inner breeze. The patient's dance is usually a *pas de deux* with the *tok 'teri*. Occasionally, an onlooker, having achieved trance, electrifies the audience with her uncontrolled violent movements, or joins the shaman in a sedate dance. On one occasion, the participation of an onlooker made the difference between a partial cure and a successful treatment. The shaman had been trying to get his patient to rise and dance, entranced, for three nights, but she only sat "shivering like a bird in the rain," while her sister (who was not a patient) danced with the shaman. On the third night, an old friend of the family arrived: a famous *Mak Yong* actress who sprang up when she saw the shaman's unsuccessful struggle, and pulled the entranced young girl to her feet. To the tune of *Lagu Mengambul* (the Swaying To and Fro tune that delivers messages to the Self) they danced—the shaman, the actress, the young patient and her older sister—until the patient's Wind was refreshed, in spite of herself, and her cure was complete.

ORAL LITERATURE AND PERFORMANCE ARTS

The language of all three performance genres includes both informal, highly improvised speech and formal, relatively fixed language. In general, most of the informal language occurs in comic scenes and in the dialogue of unrefined characters. Even then, the style takes on formality when the circumstances become more formal, or when the characters break into song (Ghulam-Sarwar 1976:95).

As Sweeney points out, the wisdom of an oral culture "is encapsulated in mnemonic patterns which must constantly be repeated if they are to survive. . . . It is for this reason that the discourse of an oral culture is heavily dependent upon the use of relatively fixed utterances in stylized form. . . . [T]heir use of parallelism, assonance, alliteration, etc. ensures that the form produces its own, often distinctive rhythm." (Sweeney 1987:96). But although the patterns for much of Malay ritual speech are relatively fixed, they are by no means frozen. To heal patients, the shaman works within a poetic tradition comparable to the epics of the ancient Western world in that they speak to us across time and space. Like the European singer of tales studied by Lord (1976), the Malay *minduk* and shaman must develop the capacity to generate expressions on the model of fixed formulae, whose ready-made character makes fluency possible. The elaboration of these formulae, the systematic variation, and the use to which they put redundant and "flowery" speech, allow the ritual pair time to collect their thoughts and avoid any hesitancy that might otherwise occur (Brauman 1984:18; Zurbuchen 1987:152).

CONCLUSION

The *Main Peteri* encompasses the totality of performers, audience, words, music, movement, setting and props. The audience does not merely observe, enjoy, and applaud. Members of the audience have personal and immediate stakes in the proceedings and their outcome. They may help prepare the props, interject comments, or even become spontaneous performers, rising in trance to sing or dance.

The words, although preeminent, are not the sole messengers of meaning. The music underlies and complements the message of the words; the movements speak with a clear voice to the audience, both human and spirit. Each prop carries multiple meanings to those who understand their language. The seance takes place in a ritual space, a delimited area marked off from everyday life, but its meanings are embedded in a view of the universe that embraces all aspects of human existence. The Malay shaman exorcises the demons of disease and opens the floodgates of emotion by allowing the Winds their moments of freedom. His vehicle encodes precepts of clever and proper behavior, and reveals truths about flesh and spirit, temperament and power, illness and health, death and birth.

ACKNOWLEDGMENTS

I would like to acknowledge the financial and moral support of the following institutions: The John Simon Guggenheim Foundation, The Rockefeller Foundation, the National Endowment for the Humanities (Translation Program, and Interpretive Research Program), Fordham University, and the City College of New York. My consultants, Profs. Amin Sweeney and Marina Roseman, were invaluable to my research, generously sharing their expertise and insights into the language, drama, and music of the Malay healing seance.

REFERENCES

Basso, Ellen. 1984. *A Musical View of the Universe: Kalopalo Myth and Ritual Performances*. Philadelphia: University of Pennsylvania Press.

Bauman, Richard. [1977] 1984. *Verbal Art as Performance*. Prospect Heights, Ill.: Waveland Press.

Blacking, J. 1985. The Context of Venda Possession Music: Reflection on the Effectiveness of Symbols. *Yearbook of Traditional Music* 17:64–87.

Epton, Nina. 1966. Sumarah and the Ghostly Sultan. In *Trances,* ed. Stuart Wavell, Audrey Butt, and Nina Epton. London: George Allen & Unwin, Ltd.

Errington, Shelly. 1975. A Study of Genre: Meaning and Form in the Malay Hikayat Hang Tuah. Ph.D. diss., Dept. of Anthropology, Cornell University.

Freeman, Derek. 1970. *Report on the Iban.* New York: Athlone Press.

Ghulam-Sarwar Yousof. 1976. The Kelantan "Mak Yong" Dance Theatre: A Study of Performance Structure. Ph.d. diss., Dept. of Drama and Theatre, University of Hawaii.

Kapferer, Bruce. 1983. *A Celebration of Demons: Exorcism and the Aesthetics of Healing in Sri Lanka.* Bloomington: Indiana University Press.

Kessler, Clive S. 1977. Conflict and Sovereignty in Spirit Seances. In *Case Studies in Spirit Possession,* ed. V. Crapanzano and V. Garrison. New York: John Wiley & Sons.

Laderman, Carol. 1981. Symbolic and Empirical Reality: A New Approach to the Analysis of Food Avoidances. *American Ethnologist* 9 (3):468–493.

———. 1983. *Wives and Midwives: Childbirth and Nutrition in Rural Malaysia.* Berkeley, Los Angeles, London: University of California Press.

———. 1988. Wayward Winds: Malay Shamanism and Theory of Personality. *Social Science & Medicine* 27 (8):799–810.

———. 1991. *Taming the Wind of Desire: Psychology, Medicine, and Aesthetics in Malay Shamanistic Performance.* Berkeley, Los Angeles, London: University of California Press.

Lex, Barbara. 1979. The Neurobiology of Ritual Trance. In *The Spectrum of Ritual: A Biogenetic Structural Analysis,* ed. E. G. d'Aquila, C. D. Laughlin, Jr., and J. McManus. New York: Columbia University Press.

Lord, Albert. [1960] 1976. *The Singer of Tales.* New York: Athenaeum.

Matusky, Patricia Ann. 1988. Music in the Malay Shadow Puppet Theater. Ph.D. diss. Dept. of Music, University of Michigan.

Mohd. Taib Osman. 1976. The Bomoh and the Practice of Malay Medicine. *The South-East Asian Review* 1 (1):16–26.

Needham, Rodney. 1967. Percussion and Transition. *Man* II:606–614.

Neher, A. 1962. A Physiological Explanation of Unusual Behavior in Ceremonies Involving Drums. *Human Biology* 34:151–161.

Roseman, Marina. 1986. Sound in Ceremony: Power and Performance in Temiar Curing Ritual. Ph.D. diss., Dept. of Anthropology, Cornell University.

———. 1988. The Pragmatics of Aesthetics: The Performance of Healing among Senoi Emiar. *Social Science & Medicine* 27 (8):811–818.

Rouget, Gilbert. 1980. *Music and Trance: A Theory of the Relations between Music and Possession.* Chicago: University of Chicago Press.

Siegel, James. 1979. *Shadow and Sound: The Historical Thought of a Sumatran People.* Chicago: University of Chicago Press.

Sweeney, P. L. Amin. 1972. *The Ramayana and the Malay Shadow-Play.* Kuala Lumpur: The National University of Malaysia Press.

———. 1987. *A Full Hearing: Orality and Literacy in the Malay World.* Berkeley, Los Angeles, London: University of California Press.

Zurbuchen, Mary S. 1987. *The Language of Balinese Shadow Theater.* Princeton: Princeton University Press.

5

PRESENCE

Robert R. Desjarlais

"We must go like thieves," Meme Bombo, a Yolmo shaman, said to me one afternoon as we sat by the hearth in his one-room house in the Helambu region of north-central Nepal, "without ghosts, demons, or witches knowing of our presence. Otherwise, they will attack." He was speaking of the magical flight he and other healers undertake to search for and "call back" the lost spirit of a patient.

For over a year in the late 1980s I lived in a village in the southwest of Helambu. Serving as a shamanistic apprentice to Meme Bombo, I participated in some two-dozen healing rites and tried to learn something of this "grandfather shaman's" craft. Since the first nights of the apprenticeship, I have been trying to understand if, how, and to what extent his spirit-calling rites work to rejuvenate a spiritless body. My understanding is that the rites do, at times, have a positive effect, tending to work through indirect, tacit means—the less obvious aspects of ritual[1]—to negate a sensibility bound by loss, fatigue, and listlessness and create a new one of vitality, presence, and attentiveness. Simply put, Meme changes how a body feels by altering what it feels. His cacophony of music, taste, sight, touch, and kinesthesia activates the senses. The activation has the potential to "wake up" a person, alter the sensory grounds of a spiritless body, and so change how a person feels.

This take on Yolmo spirit-callings, in which the sensory dimensions are pivotal, goes against the grain of the dominant anthropological interpretations of ritual healing, which tend to privilege the symbolic, intellectual, and social features of such healings. The distinction is, I think, worth exploring. To better appreciate what Meme's rites can tell us about the performance of healing in

Nepal and elsewhere, we need to understand something of the nature of spirit-lessness among the Yolmo people, how the rites work to recover lost vitality, and how the acts intrinsic to these rites compare to those found in other soul-calling ceremonies in the Himalayas.

SPIRIT LOSS

Yolmo wa, or "the Yolmo people," are a Tibeto-Burman people who migrated in the eighteenth and nineteenth centuries from the Kyirong region of Tibet to the forested foothills of the Helambu valley on the basis of religious land grants received from the Nepalese government (Clarke 1980a, 1980b). They speak a language derived from Tibetan as well as from the national language of Nepal. Commerce, land rentals, pastoral grazing, and the farming of maize, potatoes, and other high-altitude crops provide the main sources of food and income, although recently tourism and "factory" employment in Kathmandu and India have brought additional material wealth. Until 1991, the national *Panchayat* governmental system of Nepal officially set political agendas by regulating district elections, but village politics have often been defined by the local power structures of wealth, status, and kinship (one widely found local preference for kinship status is a combination of patrilineal descent and residence, together with cross-cousin marriage). Though devout practitioners of the Ningmapa, or "Ancient School," of Mahayana Buddhism, Yolmo wa with whom I lived (of the southwestern side of the valley) also turn to local shamans in times of physical and spiritual distress.

Many of the rites performed by Yolmo shamans work to recover life-forces lost by their patrons. Yolmo wa possess several kinds of life-forces, each of which can depart from the body (see Table 1). The *bla* or "spirit" is one such force. The absence of *bla* from the body leads to a dysphoric state that we might call "spirit loss." For Yolmo wa, the *bla* or "spirit" implies the vital essence of a living person, a spiritual force that courses through the entire body and upon which rest other psychological functions (volition, motivation, energy). *Bla* (pronounced "la," with the "b" a silent Tibetan prefix) bestows energy to the body and volition to the *sems* or the heartmind—the locus of personal knowledge, desire, and imagination. It is a spiritual essence that provides the volitional impetus to engage in life—the spirit to get out of bed, eat, and walk up a hill to talk with family. The *bla* typically leaves the body when a person is startled: a sudden fall, birds rustling in a dark forest, or a nervous, solitary walk near a cremation ground can spook the spirit from the body. Once parted from the body, the *bla* can fall into the hands of a ghost or witch (*shi 'dre* or *boksi*), and so be carried into the land of the dead.

Table 1. Yolmo Life-Forces

	rNam Shes (pronounced "namshe")	Bla (pronounced "la")	Tshe	Srog (pronounced "sok")
Force	"Conscious-ness"; "soul"	"Spirit"	"Life"; "life span"	"Life support"; physical foundation
Function	Awareness; consciousness	Vitality; energy; volition	Strength; fortitude	Physical support; strength
If Lost	Death (death causes departure from body)	Spirit loss; loss of vitality and volition	Diminished life span; loss of strength and vigor	Loss of physical strength; bodily decay
Ritual Strategy	Transmigration of the soul through funereal rites	Hooking, summoning the spirit (bla 'gug)	Enhancing the life (tshe grup)	Recovering the life supports (srog dgu·mi)

Since a person might not know for several days that his or her *bla* has been lost, spirit loss can be an insidious process. Within a few days or weeks, a person begins to lose the volition to act. The body feels "heavy," lacks energy or "passion," and the afflicted does not care to eat, talk, work, travel, or socialize; he or she has trouble sleeping, witnesses ominous dreams, and is prone to further illnesses. "When the spirit leaves," one villager told me, "no passion comes (*sems pa ma yong*)." "When the *bla* is lost," another recalled, "a man feels tired, sleepy, lazy. He cannot get up quickly, can eat just a little, and wants only to stay at home." "Dullness" (*tum tum*) wells up in the heartmind, dimming the afflicted's thoughts, memory, and sense of alertness. The pulse slows and becomes irregular "like a watch that is not ticking properly," as one woman put it. The ill person also loses the sense of kinesthetic attentiveness or "presence," as I call it, that characterizes local states of health. In contrast to Balinese, who, according to Gregory Bateson and Margaret Mead (1943:7), regularly drift off into detached moments of "awayness," Yolmo wa, wary of life's vicissitudes, constantly attend to the flux of life around them, chatting with others, smoking cigarettes, shooing fluttery chickens (see Figure 1). Yet when the "spirit" is lost, so is the sense of presence.

Figure 1. "Presence"

Although bouts of spirit loss bear a common sensory range, which in many respects compares to what Westerners call "depression," each incident presents a slightly different form and etiology. A middle-aged woman named Nyima lost her spirit while crossing a stream on her way to participate in a funeral rite; she lost the desire to walk, eat, work, and socialize. Yeshi, a young Yolmo bride, also lost her spirit; she displayed a lethargy of body and spirit, a lack of emotionality, and a general apathy towards her surroundings.

SPIRIT-CALLINGS

Dawa, a priest in his early thirties, also lost his *bla* a few years back. "I was so sick," the lama recounted one afternoon. "My body felt dizzy, heavy, and I kept fainting." Several days after falling ill, Dawa's family summoned a renowned shaman who ritually called Dawa's spirit from the land of the dead. "When the spirit returned to my body," Dawa recalled, "I felt well. I felt happy, comfortable. I felt a bit lighter by the next morning. Slowly, slowly, within ten, fifteen days, I was fine." Dawa's newfound health was further signalled by dreams: after the healing, he dreamed of walking uphill and of seeing a bright, clear light—both signs, for Yolmo wa, of health and prosperity.[2]

Other villagers speak of similar events. In general, if a villager suffers from spirit loss, his or her family will summon a *bombo*. This shaman arrives at the patient's home around sunset to perform an elaborate, all-night healing ceremony in which he divines how the *bla* was lost, searches for the itinerant spirit, and tries to return it to the person's body.

Meme Bombo prepares for a night's work by constructing a sacred altar that serves to both represent and embody the various gods that he calls upon. Once the altar is constructed, Meme begins the ceremony proper by singing of the mythic origins of each ritual item in his altar and equipment. Maintaining a fast-paced drumbeat, he similarly consecrates the lamp and the grains of his altar, as well as his bells, belt, rosaries, and drum, by citing the five directions from which each article comes: east, south, west, north, and the center "above." He then offers "incense" (*gtsang rab,* pronounced "sanrap") to the gods and goddesses of Helambu and neighboring lands, including Tibet and India. The "incense-recitation," in which the healer charts a score of place-names, serves to purify deities and their locales by offering a cleansing incense. Beginning in the *sbas yul* (pronounced "beyul") or "hidden country" of Tibet, Meme tours "with his heartmind" (with his *sems*) the numerous locales and shrines to the east of Helambu as they descend south into the Kathmandu valley and India. He returns upon a westerly route back north to the Himalayas, then locates the sacred geography within Helambu itself, situating the divine within a range of "cliffsides, big rocks, and tall trees," speaking of the telluric haunts of his tutelary spirits. After identifying each set of deities, Meme requests the gods to "purify all that has been affected by pollution" (*pho pai drip ci bsangs*). The journey is lengthy and encompasses over four hundred sacred sites: from north to east, south, west, and north again.

After taking a break, during which time the host family serves food and tea to Meme and the various relatives and neighbors who have come to watch the event, Meme calls several gods to "fall" into his body to "show," through the vehicle of his voice, the cause or causes of the patient's malady. If the malady is the result of a lost *bla,* Meme ritually searches for and attempts to "call" the spirit back into the body of his patient by performing a "spirit-hooking" ceremony (*bla 'gug*) in which he journeys on a magical flight to the land of the dead. He begins by playing his drum while summoning the fierce *khyung,* the eagle-like Garuda deity of Buddhist lore. Once the *khyung* responds to the call, the shaman stops drumming and his heartmind leaves his body with a joyful, ecstatic shout and glides through space, clinging to a bird's chest as it escorts and protects him in search of the lost spirit.[3]

While the shaman's heartmind travels through the air, scavenging "like a hawk," his body remains motionless. Occasionally, the shaman confronts malevolent spirits—"witches", angry deities (*lha*), and shades of persons deprived of proper funerals. In a struggle to escape the clutches of these forces, the shaman's body shakes, causing the bells strapped around his chest to ring out in the otherwise silent room in which the patient's family waits. These events Meme described as follows: "We go like a hawk hunting a chicken, looking far away, then coming to snatch it. Sometimes along the way a tiger comes to 'cover' [attack] us. Sometimes an ox comes to hit; some dogs come to bite. We get startled."

While Meme searches everywhere for the spirit, "in someone's house, in the forest, in the land of the dead, the land of the gods, above, below," the patient sits behind the shaman on a sacred symbol composed of rice kernels, with legs crossed, hands held in prayer, and a white shawl draped over the head and body (see Figure 2).[4] Once Meme "hooks" the spirit, which the *khyung* snaps up in his claws, his heartmind returns to the body and a flurry of ritual activity ensues: the participants of the healing shout out in celebration; two assistants pass a bowl of incense around the patient's body to purify it; and a third man touches the bowl containing the enhanced "life" and other sacred objects to the patient's scalp, shoulders, chest, hands, and feet.

As soon as Meme recovers from the flight, he holds his drum so that the skinned surface lies horizontal and drums fiercely upon the bottom surface while chanting sacred prayers. If the spirit has been hooked successfully, it falls onto the drum surface in the "image" of three white "flowers" the size of specks of dust (which are typically spotted by flashlight-bearing assistants). After each flower appears, Meme lowers the drum—while still drumming—closer to the foods and drops the flower into one of the bowls of food (milk, meat, egg, curd) set upon a tray before the patient. By eating from each of the foods, the patient reincorporates lost vitality.

Finally, Meme touches a magical dagger to the patient's forehead to imbue it with renewed "power," and then, after one more break, he ends the ceremony by chanting a prayer of "departure" (*btang shag,* pronounced "shyasal") that asks the various deities to leave the altar and return to their respective "domains" (*dal*). By this time, the patient is usually asleep in bed.

Figure 2. "Hooking the Spirit"

MAKING SENSE OF HEALING

Not all villagers respond to spirit-calling rites. Often the rites evoke a sense of vitality, but occasionally that feeling does not lead to a full recovery.[5] For those who do feel better either during or after a spirit-calling, however, feelings of newfound health typically assume a common pattern: bodies become "lighter," heartminds become "brighter," and the sense of fatigue and listlessness that troubles a spiritless person is "cut" from the body. "When the spirit returns," Nyima said, "it feels like a jolt of electricity to the body. . . . The body feels good, and we feel good in the heartmind. After it returns, you can sleep well. Sleepiness comes. Afterwards, I don't see the bad dreams of before." "After the spirit returns," Lakpa told me, "we feel like eating again. Energy returns. After two or three days, the body feels light; the heartmind brightens; it becomes clear, lucid. The eyes become brighter."

The core phenomena of Yolmo healings, in which eyes brighten, the body electrifies, and the heartmind renews, leads me to advance a model of Yolmo spirit-callings that contrasts sharply with anthropological accounts that focus on the ideational, rhetorical, or symbolic aspects of ritual healing. My thinking on the subject has evolved out of dissatisfaction with the tenets of such approaches—particularly with "intellectualist" and "symbolist" explanations of the effectiveness of ritual healing—for they seem unable to explain either the ritual techniques or the effectiveness of ritual among Yolmo wa.[6]

The intellectualist position of British social anthropology, developed most recently by John Skorupski (1976), holds that the shaman's and patient's concern for efficacy is an intellectual one. The shaman acts in order to instill faith and belief in the patient's mind that something can be done to ameliorate his malady (see Frank 1974). Such acts work because they have worked in the past and are expected to work in the present. As Bronislaw Malinowski (1948) suggests, ritual acts are geared not to mean something, but to enact something. Through this enactment, people are said to gain faith in the curing process and begin to think differently about their conditions.

In contrast to the intellectualist stance, "symbolist" positions, the products of French structuralist and American semiotic approaches to ritual performance, contend that curing rites work chiefly by provoking transformations either of the worldview held by a person or of the symbolic categories that define the lifeworld of that person.[7] Here, the shaman typically evokes symbols or metaphors that provide a tangible "language" through which patients can express, understand, or transform the personal or interpersonal conflicts underlying their illnesses. These orientations follow the spirit of Lévi-Strauss' classic essay, "The Effectiveness of Symbols" (1950), which argues that a Cuna shaman's articulation of a mythic realm affects transformations in the physiology of his patient.

While both the intellectualist and symbolist positions have helped to explain the structural logic of religious rites throughout the world, I find neither to be particularly useful in explaining how or why Yolmo shamans heal. The intellectualist position, for instance, does not account for why Yolmo healers work to the extent they do to recover a patient's vitality. According to this model, ritual acts simply aim to achieve what they purport to achieve. To instill the personal conviction that something substantial is being done to improve a person's condition, Meme would need only to call a spirit back; he does not need to carry out a vivid and lengthy rite. And yet he does. In an attempt to explain why he does so, I want to suggest that how a Yolmo shaman searches for a spirit is as important as actually finding it.

At the same time, I do not believe that Meme recovers a spirit primarily through the use of metaphors, symbolic transformations, or rhetorical tropes, as recent formulations of "symbolic" healing hold. While these representational models, which have dominated ethnographies of healing since Lévi-Strauss, apparently identify the general structure of ritual healings in many societies, they cannot fully account for a Yolmo calling of spirits. Yolmo healings involve the imagining of a symbolic ascent from weakness to strength, fragmentation to integration, disharmony to harmony, and defilement to purity. The symbolic shift from illness to health here is not the method, but simply the scaffolding, of the rites (in fact, the shift often has more political than curative value). Generally, spirit calling for the Yolmo people is less like a mythic narrative, progressing from one stage to another, than an imagistic poem, evoking an array of tactile images which, through their cumulative effect, evoke a change of sensibility in the bodies of its participants—a change, that is, in the lasting mood or disposition that contribute to the sensory grounds of a person's existence. Seen in this light, it is more the poem's visceral impact than its metaphoric structure that affects change.

The impact ties into the senses. Meme's craft involves a healing of bodies, of sensibilities, of ways of being in the world. His spirit-calling rites might change how participants think of their conditions and they might alter the symbolic categories that define those conditions. But if the rite is to be considered successful, it must change how a person feels. This is because Yolmo criteria of efficacy rest largely on the lack or presence of visceral evidence that a person feels better in the days following a rite. These rather sensorial criteria relate to Yolmo epistemologies of illness and healing. In illness, a villager cannot know the cause or course of her plight until its signifying symptoms (bodily pains, bad dreams) become manifest. Similarly, since the spirit is an intangible force, a villager can only determine its return by interpreting how body and heartmind feel in the hours and days after a rite.

The shamans have their own, more divinatory epistemologies to assess a person's welfare, such as the oracular divination and the presence or absence of the "flowers" that, in appearing on the drum, signify the return of life-forces. But while a person can take a healer's word that the spirit has been recovered, such talk, I was told, is occasionally "like the wind," and villagers sometimes consider a shaman's "rhetoric of transformation" (Csordas 1983) to be merely rhetoric. As Lakpa put it, "Shamans and lamas tell us, 'The life has come back,' but we don't know this; we cannot see this. When we feel better, then we think it has returned."

A person, therefore, cannot be sure that the spirit has returned to the body until the sensibility of spirit loss (heavy body, weak eyes, weary heart) has been "cut" from the body. The visceral sense of renewed health, which usually takes hold in the hours after a rite and must last if the rite is to be considered successful, is the major criteria upon which Yolmo wa judge rites efficacious. In Helambu, a person does not feel better after being cured; she is cured after feeling better. Whereas all rites, by definition, affect symbolic transformations, Yolmo wa do not consider all rites to be efficacious. These facts suggest that if we are to develop a model of Yolmo healings, the model must not simply sketch out possible mechanisms of healing, but also tie into the particular ways that patients know themselves to be healed. Except for a few studies, most research on ritual healing attempts to explain how symbolic forms reconstitute the social or "inner" experience of a patient without demonstrating to any extent whether or not (and how) patients feel better in the aftermath of healings.[8]

In an attempt to develop such an understanding, I want to build on the work of several anthropologists who emphasize the performative and dramaturgical aspects of ritual healings.[9] While this research attributes ritual efficacy to a variety of factors, from acts of catharsis and an increase in self-understanding, to resolutions of social conflicts and the ritual reframing of cultural realities, a constant concern is for the ways dramatic actions and aesthetic performances engage participants and evoke emotional responses. To date, however, this work has focused more on the social and psychological, rather than the sensory, dimensions of such engagement. There is something at work in Yolmo healings for which this literature does not fully account: the presence of the senses in the rites and the extent to which ritual performances change how people feel.[10]

WILD IMAGES

Meme's search for a lost spirit parallels shamanistic itineraries in other Himalayan lands. A Bhuji shaman lies in the burial ground and "calls to the soul as if it were a child, luring it from the clutches of its captor or enticer" (Hitchcock 1976:170). A Gurung shaman ventures on an elaborate search of cosmological domains, first calling out the names of goddesses "of rock, soil, rivers, and trees" to ask if the soul has been hidden in these domains, and later enticing the soul from the land of the dead (Mumford 1989:170–175). Tamang healers journey to divine "hidden" lands to recover lost shadow-souls, and Magars descend into the "underworld" to overtake a soul before it reaches "The Waters of Forgetfulness."[11] These searches resemble similar soul-callings throughout the world, including the ecstatic journeys of Siberian shamans, who typically hunt for stray spirits throughout a countryside and on into the land of the dead.[12]

Of particular interest is the way healers carefully pronounce concrete details of what they see during their flights. A Kham-Magar's chant, for instance, mentions a half-dozen hamlets, two river crossings, a cave dwelling, a monastery, a sacred shrine, and a "place of origin and fertility" (Allen 1974:8). A Tamang shaman calls out places where lost souls can "get stuck":

> In a heaven of the homeless,
> In a heaven of confusion,
> In a heaven of distress,
> In a heaven of rumorous gossip,
> In a heaven of cannibals,
> In a heaven of closed mouths,
> In a heaven of licentious sex[13]

If the healer does not leave his body in an ecstatic search for the patient's spirit, he calls out to the spirit, imploring it to return to the body. Callings occur throughout the world: a Siberian shaman calls back the soul of a sick child "Come back to your country! . . . to the yurt, by the bright fire! . . . Come back to your father . . . to your mother! . . ." (Eliade 1964:217). Often these callings, which have been done in Asia for at least two thousand years (Yu 1981, 1987), take the form of elaborate litanies. The ancient Chinese *Elegies of Ch'u* depict a "summoner's" ornate invocation to the strayed soul of a sick king to leave "the earth's far corners" and return to its "old abode":

> O Soul, go not to the north!
> In the north is the Frozen Mountain,
> and the Torch Dragon, glaring red;
> And the Tai river that cannot be crossed,
> whose depths are unfathomable;
> And the sky is white and glittering,
> and all is congealed with cold.
> O soul, go not to the north!
> There is no bourn there to your journeying . . .[14]

In Tibet, lamaic lurings assume a similar form: an elaborate, imagistic litany portrays a tangible expanse upon which the singer plots the soul's travels. In a lamaic rite to "call the *bla*," the summoner enumerates a divine pantheon in the hopes of recovering the soul.

> . . . Ye, the fire god, rakshasas, the wind gods,
> and the powerful ones in the four intermediate points,
> Ye gods of the earth below,
> All ye gods of the ten points of the universe,
> If ye have snatched [the soul] . . .[15]

The litany climaxes with a bystander shouting at the top of his voice:

> Soul and life of such and such a person,
> of such a family,
> of such and such an age,
> bearing such and such a name,
> whether thou hast come to a royal palace,
> or a mansion of a nobleman,
> or a Buddhist temple,
> or a place of worship . . .[16]

The litany ends with a general summons, the power of which might be best grasped if we mold its conclusion into projective verse.

>   . . . or an island or islet,
>   a rock or a cave, or
>   a thoroughfare, or
>
>
>   a place noisy with human activities, or
>   a place inhabited by malignant spirits or
>   mischievous demons,
>
>   or whether thou art traveling or
>   drifting in the wind or
>   floating on the water, or
>   scattered about,
>   whether thou art snatched away or
>
>
>   carried off,
>
>   I bid thee come back.

In contrast to Charles Olson's "projective verse," however, where "one perception must immediately and directly lead to a further perception,"[17] the lama's chant presents a different logic of perception. There is no staircasing of impressions, no evolution of insights. The chant turns on a point by point appeal to the imagination. Each image, standing alone, acts as a lure. The heartmind leaps from island to islet.

The curative power of the chant, it appears, ties into its style of presentation, and into how people respond to that presentation. On many occasions, Himalayan healers do not say whether or not they have found the souls they are looking for. In my estimation, they do not need to, for, in contrast to the intellectualist position, it is the search, rather than any ostensive result, that is of fundamental importance.

To better appreciate what makes the search itself so effective, it is useful to compare the poetics of Himalayan soul-callings to certain tenets of modern European literary theory. In his paper "The Metaphorical Process as Cognition, Imagination, and Feeling," Paul Ricoeur draws on Marcus Hester's (1967) theory of poetic metaphors. Ricoeur writes:

> Describing the experience of *reading*, [Hester] shows that the kind of images which are interesting for a theory of poetic language are not those that interrupt reading and distort or divert it. These images—these "wild"

images, if I may say so—are properly extrinsic to the fabric of sense. They induce the reader, who has become a dreamer rather than a reader, to indulge himself in the delusive attempt, described by Sartre as fascination, to possess magically the absent thing, body, or person. The kind of images which still belong to the production of sense are rather what Hester calls "bound" images, that is, concrete representations aroused by the verbal element and controlled by it (1979:148; emphasis in original).

Such "bound" images, Ricoeur suggests, cohere with and add to the larger metaphoric structure of a poem and "bring to concrete completion the metaphorical process" (1979:149–150). This process eventually leads to "a model for changing our way of looking at things, of perceiving the world" (1979:150).

Ricoeur's discussion of bound images aptly documents the metaphoric process of Western poetics—a process that recalls the transformations of experience portrayed by symbolist accounts of healing.[18] At the same time, his dismissal of "wild" images, images that do not fit into a larger architecture of meaning and so "distract thought more than they instruct it" (1979:149), reflects the rage for order in much of modernist poetry, criticism, and anthropology. In their influential treatise *Understanding Poetry*, Cleanth Brooks and Robert Penn Warren declare, "Poetic imagery must not be idle and meaningless, dead or inert, or distracting and self-serving, like some foolish ornament that merely calls attention to itself. Every bit of image ought to 'make sense' and to aid the poem in *its* making sense" (1961:272). James Baker (1957) advances a similar view in his assessment of Coleridge's theory of poetry. "Images," he writes, "are not pillars supporting vacancy, but caryatids sustaining weight; they are not empty caskets, but barrels containing meaning" (1957:195–6). Poetic images, in other words, must not be empty, light, distracting, or self-serving, like some foolish waif prancing about in the house of Order.

Although highly structured, rhetorical poetry can be found in the Himalayas—in Helambu, for instance, Yolmo funereal laments and healing chants rely on a careful scaffolding of tropes to alter ways of thinking and feeling (Desjarlais 1992)—it is precisely the type of poetic calling whose images that "divert" and "interrupt" that we encounter time and again and that, I contend, work most to rejuvenate bodies. By "wild," I mean those images that leapfrog into the imagination and so engage the listener not through any threaded storytelling but through a random and roundabout slideshow of perceptions—a rock, a cave, a thoroughfare—that excites the senses and entices the imagination in a particular way.

Which way is this? In my own encounters with soul-calling rites, I find that the images intrinsic to the chants are predominantly unbounded ones; they demand, by their very lightness, an attentive ear. The "Frozen Mountain" to the north, a sky "white and glittering"—the images of the Chinese "elegy" succeed one another without any sense of untying, though there is an element of intrigue. The chants set up a chain of alternatives—"*or* a mansion, *or* a temple, *or* a place of worship"—that opens up a range of possibilities. Indeed, it may be that the more bounded the meaning of the chant, the more weighted the imagery within an expected context, the less chance there is of waking those who hear it. If the fabric of sense was a closely knit one, without a wealth of alternatives, people would be less inclined to anticipate, attend to, or interact anew with their environments. By necessity, the images remain open.

The endings of many chants, in turn, which often close with a final invocation to, or for, the lost soul, remain incomplete and provisional, as if the images throughout do not round off a controlled fabric of sense. Instead, the images seem to invite an inconclusive dialogue, an interaction that consists of an initial summons to be answered by a person, and a fictive sketch to be completed by his or her imagination. The suspense created by the chants is therefore not one that is answered by the litanies themselves (as a Greek tragedy answers its own questions). The suspense can only be answered by way of the audience's own mindful participation in a chant. Through this participation, a chant hooks a soul: it draws a person out of his or her spiritlessness to invoke a sense of presence, volition, and attentiveness.

The unboundedness of the images appears similar to the polysemic "fan" of meanings that Carol Laderman, following Victor Turner (1967), identifies as the curative agent in Malay birth incantations: "Incantations," she finds, "cure by analogy, not through their specificity but by their 'fan' of meanings, their multi-layered nature and the ambiguity of their symbols" (1987:301). For Edward Schieffelin, in turn, the tension and suspense engaged in a Kaluli curing seance leads its participants to face a sense of "inconclusiveness and imbalance" (1985:721). The event forces people to make sense of the performance and so "arrive at a meaningful account of what is happening." In so doing, they "complete the construction of its reality" (1985:721).

Yet while the use of ambiguity to draw people into a performance appears basic to a variety of ritual settings, the nature of the ambiguity, and the reasons for such engagement, can vary. Soul-calling rites are generally clear in their meanings, with distinct images more iconic than symbolic in scope, and do not entail the ambiguity or obscurity of some ritual symbols. Rather, the linguistic form of the chants, with their litanies of "if"s and "or"s, prompt alternatives and potentials. And while the Kaluli engage in performance to "reach fundamental symbolic understandings and arrive at solutions to their problems" (Schieffelin 1985:721), it appears that, in the Himalayas, the engagement itself is curative.

The priestly chants do not necessarily facilitate any social construction of reality, but rather help a person to participate, anew, in the everyday.

The Tibetan litany reported by Lessing (1951) hints at such a strategy. The images of the chant compel an acoustic pointillism; they attend, imagistically rather than narratively, to tangible features of the cultural landscape. Its aesthetic form—imagistic, tactile, precise—prompts attention, awareness, and volition. The heartmind opens up to a world exterior to itself and "noisy with human activities," and the heavy slumber marking spirit loss can be countered.

Since any sustained activity prompted by the chants would be the singular antidote for spiritlessness, it is interesting to note that the chants stake out a world of activity and movement, from images of "traveling," "drifting," and "floating" to the excited search for the soul. Indeed, as soon as a Tibetan bystander addresses the wandering soul from the rooftop, he shouts out the favorite dishes and entertainments of the patient: "Come quick and eat this. Come quick and enjoy that. Come quick and do this." In short, distinct elements of the chant carve out a poetics of movement, activity, and presence: the luring begins with a roll call of the heavens, stakes out a person's identity, and then zeroes in on the spatially and temporally immediate aspects of his or her world; but the phrases are set up in such a way that the expansiveness of the heavens seems to carry over into the world, as if the words used to draw the soul closer to home also worked to expand the possibilities of engagement within that world.

That the rites aim to induce sensory attentiveness is further evinced in more recent chants, some two millennia after the *Elegies of Ch'u,* whereby Tibetan and Mongolian Buddhist priests lure vital souls by detailing what exists "here," in the felt immediacies of a person's world:

> Your parents are HERE.
> Your brothers and sisters are HERE.
> Your friends and neighbors are HERE.
> The three white and three sweet foods are HERE.
> If you would drink tasty beer, it's HERE.
> If you would eat fat meat, it's HERE.
> If you would eat boiled-down [thick] food, it's HERE.
> Plentiful, sweet tasty food is HERE.
> If you would wear good clothes, they're HERE.
> If you would ride a good horse, it's HERE.
> Don't go there, there! Come HERE, HERE!
> Don't follow to the land of the deathlords!
> *A-bo-lo-lo,* come HERE![19]

The summons begins by acknowledging, and potentially engaging, the sick person's family and friends, then sets acts of drinking, eating, and riding in a fan of alternatives ("if . . . if . . . if"). "Don't go there, come here, here!"—the hurried deictics suggest that the healer seeks to recover the patient's lost vitality by pointing to the taste and feel of the present. Fat meat, sweet beer, and a fine horse lie at one's side, close enough to touch. I have indicated the radical need for presence in Yolmo life, and how a sense of "hereness" is lost when the spirit is lacking. Possibly this sensibility is salient in other Tibetan societies also. If so, then a calling of souls works to draw a person into the here and now by selectively attending to the sensory footholds of his or her environment.[20] All told, the rites provoke a stance toward that environment, urge a rush of activities, open up a range of possibilities, and instill a deliberate attentiveness that is absent when the soul is lost.

A HEALING TOUCH

In Himalayan soul-calling rites, the soul returns to the body by attending to what lies outside its usual abode. A similar preoccupation characterizes Yolmo healings. By calling forth a distinct spiritual geography throughout an evening of chants and drumbeats, Meme works to recover lost vitality through a selective attention to detail, a quickening of the senses, an invocation of presence, the engagement of action, and the use of wild images to induce attentiveness. The cure tacitly but directly confronts feelings of spiritlessness, crafting apathy into attentiveness and fatigue into vitality.

Common to the opening chants is a flickery, place-by-place slideshow of perceptions that has the potential to divert, excite, and engage. Although villagers often do not grasp the specifics of the chants, they do appear to sense their underlying poetics. The prayers transform. As Meme mumbles his chant, cleansing Helambu's hills and forests, one catches snippets of meaning. The directional notation is clear: *shar . . . lho . . . nub . . . byang . . . bdus* repeatedly mark the five directions: east, south, west, north, center. A person soon finds herself at the heart of the center, the four corners of the earth encircling her form. The articulation of place-names leads a person to imagine and attend to specific locales—well-known hamlets and hillsides realized through a rapid, freeze-frame singsong.

It may be that the presentation of this terrain, which plays such an important role in how Yolmo pastoralists make their livings, kindles attention and recalls healthy ways of moving the body. The leitmotif—focused, complete, controlled—commands attention. As shamanistic speech orchestrates the five directions, bodies become centered, alert, enraptured. And by focusing on an extant geography, a foothilled expanse lodged in mountain and forest, spatial images draw the heartmind out of the body to move imaginatively through a rocky landscape in which a person has walked, climbed, and bathed. From cliff-sides to sacred springs, Meme brings to life a sacred yet tangible geography that centers around a patient's body and induces that person to attend more sensibly to this geography.[21]

A patient's body is a key player throughout a Yolmo healing, and this physiology takes center stage at the conclusion of the spirit-calling rite. The acoustics of the spirit-calling rite—Meme's "startled," bell-clanging body, the driving drum-beats, shouts from the audience—maintain a high level of intensity throughout. The flicker of candles, the aroma of incense, and the taste of foods adds to the supple fusion of senses. Ritual sentience, by whetting the senses, helps to renew a villager's felt participation in the world.

The healing rites proper rely on sensory stimuli of a similar kind. The Buddhist symbols on which a patron sits "awaken" his or her body—just as the various ritual items, which "touch" a person's head, shoulders, chest, hands, and knees when the spirit returns, work to "empower" the body. I once asked Meme why he needed to touch so many parts of the body during this act. "We need to touch everywhere," he said, "to assure that the spirit returns to the body, and to give power to its different parts." The contact takes several forms: incense encir-cles the body to cleanse it of lingering harm, a magical dagger imbues a patient's forehead with renewed vitality, and the body reincorporates its "spirit" by con-suming it with the most desirable (and protein-rich) of Yolmo foods.

The act of incorporating, brought home by sensate means, recurs, as if the sensory dimensions of the rite worked to bring home its symbolic and ideological ones.[22] The symbol of prosperity supporting the patient's form, the touching of a vase to "all the parts of the body," and the butter affixed to the forehead all touch off an integration of the values invested in these forms: prosperity, long life, and empowerment. Villagers often underscore the movement from exterior to interior in discussing the rites: power, life, and spirit, they stress, "enter inside the body."

The empowering of Yolmo bodies thus involves more than symbolic, rhetori-cal, or ideational maneuvers. Physically, sensorially, a person is purified, protected, and empowered. Healing transformations take place not within some cognitive domain of brain or heartmind, but within the visceral reaches of the eyes, the ears, the skin, and the tongue. Indeed, the *feeling* of rejuvenation (rather than just its idea or symbolic expression) is essential.

"When the spirit returns," Nyima tells us, "it feels like a jolt of electricity in the body." Bodies lighten. Eyes and heartminds brighten. A person wants to eat and walk and sleep again. "Bad" dreams are cut from the body. The potent blend of image and sensation intrinsic to Yolmo spirit-callings, and the effect that this blend typically has on people, suggest that shifts in how a person thinks of his or her condition (the spirit has returned), or in the symbolic identity that defines that condition (renewed health, transformed contexts), can only partly explain how vitality is restored. For healing to be effective, Meme must alter the sensory grounds of a spiritless body. How does he do so? Our findings suggest that a less cerebral model than those noted above can account for Yolmo spirit-callings: Meme tries to change how a person feels by altering the sensory stimuli around that person. His cacophony of music, taste, sight, touch, and wild, tactile images activates the senses and the imagination. This activation can "wake up" a person, prompt new sensibilities, and so reform the cognitive and perceptual faculties that, in large part, make up a person. "If the sick person is asleep," Meme once said, "he won't get better." Since much of the ceremony does not require a sick person's participation, Meme's rule speaks more of a craftsman's know-how than any ritual imperative: one cannot feel fully if asleep, and by adding to what a person tastes, sees, touches, hears, and imagines, a Yolmo healer jumpstarts a physiology.

ACKNOWLEDGMENTS

The present paper, which extends the analysis of an earlier publication (Desjarlais 1992:198–222), is based on fifteen months of ethnographic fieldwork conducted, while I was a Ph.D. candidate at the University of California, Los Angeles, in a village to the southwest of the Helambu region, in 1988 and 1989. Research was funded by the Wenner-Gren Foundation for Anthropological Research; the Program for Psychocultural Studies and Medical Anthropology at the University of California, Los Angeles; the Department of Anthropology, UCLA; and a National Institute of Mental Health research fellowship in the Department of Social Medicine, Harvard Medical School. Earlier versions of the paper benefited from comments by John G. Kennedy, Marina Roseman, Carol Laderman, Arthur Kleinman, and Tracy McGarry. Special thanks to the residents of Helambu, especially Meme Bombo, who kindly taught me something of his craft.

NOTES

1. The focus of these concerns might be compared to Rappaport's 1979 essay on the "obvious" aspects of ritual.

2. In everyday conversations, Yolmo wa tend to divide dreams into three categories: those that are "good" or auspicious (ascending a mountain, sighting a rising sun); those that are "bad" or inauspicious (descending a hill, envisioning a fragmenting moon); and those that do not seem to bear significant import. Villagers like Dawa rely most upon this oneiric code in times of distress, for dreams often presage the course of an illness (see Desjarlais 1991).

3. Dreaming among Yolmo wa derives from the ability of a person's *sems,* centered in the chest, to travel about the countryside (Desjarlais 1991); a similar process is at work in the shaman's magical flight.

4. If the patient is female, a swastika is drawn with rice kernels; if male, the *dorje,* a sacred Buddhist symbol, is composed. These two Buddhist symbols, which stand for health, wealth, and fertility, are said to "awaken" the patient's body.

5. The failure can occur either because other dynamics are involved in the illness which spirit-calling rites cannot ameliorate in themselves, or because other pains continue to linger after the ceremony is performed. A person might therefore report a renewed sense of vitality, but will continue to suffer malaise in other domains of life. Or he or she will feel well in the hours and days after a healing, but since Yolmo spirit-callings address only the symptoms—not the causes—of spirit loss, the afflicted suffers the symptoms anew several days after a rite. Since the cure sometimes does not last, shamans often repeat the same rite on several occasions before a person feels that he or she has fully recovered (see Desjarlais 1992 for a more extensive discussion of why Yolmo healings as a whole succeed or fail).

6. These are by no means the only positions. Csordas and Kleinman (1990) note, for instance, the existence of at least four models of "therapeutic process," which attribute therapeutic efficacy to either "structural," "clinical," "social," or "persuasive" elements. In my estimation, however, the most influential orientations towards ritual healing are the "intellectualist" and "symbolist" positions.

7. See Kapferer (1983), Dow (1986), and Kleinman (1988), for instance. I use the term "symbolist" more broadly than Skorupski (1976) defines the term.

8. See Bourguignon (1976), Kleinman and Song (1979), Kleinman and Gale (1982), Finkler (1983, 1985), and Csordas (1994) for studies on the efficacy of ritual and religious healing.

9. See, for instance, Turner (1967), Schieffelin (1976, 1985); Feld (1982); Kapferer (1983); Laderman (1987, 1991); and Roseman (1991).

10. My attention to the sensory dimensions of ritual healing builds upon recent work devoted to an emergent anthropology of the senses (Jackson 1989, Stoller 1989, Howes 1991), as well as cultural analyses of the body and embodiment (Scheper-Hughes and Lock 1987, Csordas 1990). Earlier research along these lines focused on the ability of ritual stimuli (such as drumming and hallucinogens) to excite sympathetic and parasympathetic nervous systems (Lex 1970, Joralemon 1984).

11. See Peters (1978:72), March (1979:231), and Holmberg (1989:164) on this aspect of Tamang rituals, and Watters (1975) on shamanism among the Magars.

12. See Eliade (1964), Frazer (1935), and Cubbs (1986), for instance.

13. Holmberg 1989:164–165.

14. Hawkes 1959:101–114.

15. Lessing 1951:272.

16. Lessing 1951:253.

17. Olson's (1951) experiment with "projective verse" involved an attempt to project the poet's breath and consciousness on paper by regulating the pace, rhythm, and typography of the written line.

18. See, for instance, Lévi-Strauss (1950), Fernandez (1986).

19. Collected by the Tibetan encyclopedist Kong-sprul from some "exorcists" in late 19th century; as cited in Martin (n.d.). Bawden (1962:102) and Mumford (1989:169) report similar litanies of the "here."

20. The articulation of concrete and sensorial features of a patient's environment appears common to a variety of healing traditions (see Turner 1967; Laderman 1991; Roseman 1991).

21. See Schieffelin (1976), Feld (1982), and Roseman (1991) for discussions of parallel uses of geographical imagery in Kaluli and Temiar curing rites.

22. The graphing of "ideological" principles onto "sensory" qualities is discussed by Victor Turner (1967:28) and elaborated on by Marina Roseman (1991:171).

REFERENCES

Allen, Nicholas. 1974. The Ritual Journey, a Pattern Underlying Certain Nepalese Rituals. In *Contributions to the Anthropology of Nepal,* ed. C. Von Furer-Haimendorf, 6–22. Warminster, England: Aris and Phillips.

Baker, James V. 1957. *The Sacred River: Coleridge's Theory of the Imagination.* New Orleans: Louisiana State University Press.

Bateson, Gregory and Margaret Mead. 1942. *Balinese Character: A Photographic Essay.* Special Publication of the New York Academy of Sciences, Vol. 11. New York: Ballantine Books.

Bawden, C.R. 1962. Calling the Soul: A Mongolian Litany. *Bulletin of the School of Oriental and African Studies.* 25:81–103.

Bourgignon, Erica. 1976. The Effectiveness of Religious Healing Movements: A Review of the Recent Literature. *Transcultural Psychiatric Research Review* 8:5–21.

Brooks, Cleanth and Warren, Robert Penn. 1961. *Understanding Poetry.* 3rd ed. New York: Holt, Rinehart and Winston, Inc.

Clarke, Graham. 1980a. Lama and Tamang in Yolmo. In *Tibetan Studies in Honor of Hugh Richardson,* ed. Michael Aris and Aung San Suu Kyi, 79–86. Warminster, England: Aris and Phillips.

———. 1980b. A Helambu History. *Journal of the Nepal Research Centre* 4:1–38.

Csordas, Thomas. 1983. The Rhetoric of Transformation in Ritual Healing. *Culture, Medicine and Psychiatry* 7:333–376.

———. 1990. Embodiment as a Paradigm for Anthropology. *Ethos* 18:5–47.

———. 1994. *The Sacred Self: A Cultural Phenomenology of Charismatic Healing.* Berkeley: University of California Press.

Csordas, Thomas and Arthur Kleinman. 1990. The Therapeutic Process. In *Medical Anthropology: A Handbook of Theory and Method,* ed. T.M. Johnson and C. Sargent, 11–25. New York: Greenwood Press.

Cubbs, Joanne. 1986. *Hmong Art: Tradition and Change.* Sheboygan, Wisconsin: John Michael Kohler Arts Center.

Desjarlais, Robert. 1991. Dreams, Divination and Yolmo Ways of Knowing. *Dreaming* 1:211–224.

———. 1992. *Body and Emotion: The Aesthetics of Illness and Healing in the Nepal Himalayas.* Philadelphia: University of Pennsylvania Press.

Dow, James. 1986. Universal Aspects of Symbolic Healing: A Theoretical Synthesis. *American Anthropologist* 88:56–69.

Eliade, Mircea. 1964. *Shamanism: Archaic Techniques of Ecstasy.* Princeton: Princeton University Press.

Feld, Steven. 1982. *Sound and Sentiment.* Philadelphia: University of Pennsylvania Press.

Fernandez, James. 1986. *Persuasions and Performances: The Play of Tropes in Culture.* Bloomington: Indiana University Press.

Finkler, Kaya. 1983. *Spiritualist Healers in Mexico.* New York: Praeger.

———. 1985. Symptomatic Differences Between the Sexes in Rural Mexico. *Culture, Medicine and Psychiatry* 9:27–57.

Frank, Jerome. 1974. *Persuasion and Healing: A Comparative Study of Psychotherapy.* New York: Schocken Books.

Frazer, James. 1935. *Taboo and the Perils of the Soul. The Golden Bough.* New York: Macmillan.

Hawkes, David. 1959. *Ch'u Tz'u: The Songs of the South.* Oxford: Clarendon.

Hester, Marcus B. 1967. *The Meaning of Poetic Metaphor.* The Hague: Mouton.

Hitchcock, J.T. 1976. Aspects of Bhujel Shamanism. In *Spirit Possession in the Nepal Himalayas,* ed. J.T. Hitchcock and R.L. Jones, 165–196. Warminster, England: Aris and Phillips.

Holmberg, David. 1989. *Order in Paradox: Myth, Ritual and Exchange among Nepal's Tamang.* Ithaca: Cornell University Press.

Howes, David. 1991. *The Varieties of Sensory Experience.* Toronto: University of Toronto Press.

Jackson, Michael. 1989. *Paths Towards a Clearing.* Bloomington: University of Indiana Press.

Joralemon, Donald. 1984. The Role of Hallucinogenic Drugs and Sensory Stimuli in Peruvian Ritual Healing. *Culture, Medicine and Psychiatry* 8:399–430.

Kapferer, Bruce. 1983. *Celebration of Demons.* Bloomington: University of Indiana Press.

Kleinman, Arthur. 1988. *Rethinking Psychiatry.* New York: Free Press.

Kleinman, Arthur and L.H. Song. 1979. Why do Indigenous Practitioners Successfully Heal: A Follow-up Study of Indigenous Practice in Taiwan. *Social Science and Medicine* 130:7–26.

Kleinman, Arthur and J. Gale. 1982. Patients Treated by Physicians and Folk Healers: A Comparative Outcome Study in Taiwan. *Culture, Medicine and Psychiatry* 6:405–423.

Laderman, Carol. 1987. The Ambiguity of Symbols in the Structure of Healing. *Social Science and Medicine* 24:293–301.

———. 1991. *Taming the Wind of Desire: Psychology, Medicine, and Aesthetics in Malay Shamanistic Performance.* Berkeley: University of California.

Lessing, Ferdinand. 1951. Calling the Soul: A Lamaist Ritual. *Semitic and Oriental Studies* 11:263–284.

Lévi-Strauss, Claude. 1950. The Effectiveness of Symbols. In *Structural Anthropology,* 167–185. New York: Basic Books.

Lex, Barbara. 1979. The Neurobiology of Ritual Trance. In *The Spectrum of Ritual: A Biogenetic Structural Analysis,* ed. Eugene G. D'Aquili, C.D. Laughlin, Jr., and John McManus, 117–151. New York: Columbia University Press.

Malinowski, Bronislaw. [1948] 1965. *Coral Gardens and Their Magic.* Bloomington: Indiana University Press.

March, Kathryn. 1979. *The Intermediacy of Women.* Unpublished PhD. Dissertation. Department of Anthropology. Cornell University.

Martin, Dan. n.d. Calling, Hooking and Ransoming: Popular Tibetan Rituals for Recovering Lost Souls. Manuscript.

Mumford, Stanley. 1989. *Himalayan Dialogue.* Madison: University of Wisconsin Press.

Olson, Charles. 1951. *Human Universe.* New York: Grove Press.

Peters, Larry. 1978. Psychotherapy in Tamang Shamanism. *American Ethnologist* 7:397–418.

Rappaport, Roy. 1979. The Obvious Aspects of Ritual. In *Ecology, Meaning and Religion.* Richmond, Calif.: North Atlantic Books.

Ricoeur, Paul. 1979. The Metaphorical Process as Cognition, Imagination, and Feeling. In *On Metaphor,* ed. Sacks, S., 141–157. Chicago: University of Chicago Press.

Roseman, Marina. 1991. *Healing Sounds from the Malaysian Rainforest.* Berkeley: University of California Press.

Scheper-Hughes, Nancy and Margaret Lock. 1987. The Mindful Body: A Prolegomenon to Future Work in Medical Anthropology. *Medical Anthropology Quarterly* 1:6–41.

Schieffelin, Edward. 1976. *The Sorrow of the Lonely and the Burning of the Dancers.* New York: St. Martin's Press.

———. 1985. Performance and the Cultural Construction of Reality. *American Ethnologist* 12:704–724.

Skorupski, John. 1976. *Symbol and Theory: A Philosophical Study of Theories of Religion in Social Anthropology.* Cambridge: Cambridge University Press.

Stoller, Paul. 1989. *The Taste of Ethnographic Things.* Philadelphia: University of Pennsylvania Press.

Turner, Victor. 1967. *The Forest of Symbols.* Ithaca, N. Y.: Cornell University Press.

Watters, David. 1975. Siberian Shamanistic Traditions among the Kham-Magars of Nepal. *Contributions to Nepalese Studies* 2:123–168.

Yu, Ying-Shin. 1981. New Evidence on the Early Chinese Conception of Afterlife. *Journal of Asian Studies* 41 (1):81–85.

———. 1987. 'O Soul, Come Back!' A Study in the Changing Conceptions of the Soul and Afterlife in Pre-Buddhist China. *Harvard Journal of Asiatic Studies* 47 (2):363–395.

6

SOUNDS AND THINGS

Pulsations of Power in Songhay

Paul Stoller

W hen we read a fine book, most of us say it is brilliant. When we see a particularly moving play, most of us say it was illuminating. When we hear an excellent paper at an academic conference, most of us say that it shed light. At a recent conference which I attended in France, a discussant responded in the following manner to a particularly masterful paper delivered by the philosopher Isabelle Stengers:

"When Isabelle Stengers began to speak, the sky was cloudy, but when she finished the clouds had dispersed and the sun shone brightly." This comment is easy for most of us to understand, for in the West the sun has been thought of as a friend. Most of us long for bright, warm and sunny days. That's what we call good weather. Most of us don't like cloudy, damp and rainy days. That's what we call bad weather. And of course, most of us metaphorically associate the sun and its brightness with excellence. If Stengers' paper prompted the sun to break out of its cloud bank, given the Euro-American system of metaphoric categorization, her contribution must have been extraordinary.

To a Songhay in Tillaberi, Niger, however, the discussant's comment would have been incomprehensible. For most Songhay, the sun is an enemy, not a friend. In the Songhay language, one says:

1. *weyna ga hottu* (The sun burns).
2. *weyna ga ni bongo kar* (The sun will hit your head).
3. *weyna ga ni wi* (The sun will kill you).

In Songhay country, a sandy and arid steppe just south of the Sahara, most people don't seek the blistering sun; they move toward the soothing shade. And so for most Songhay a good communicative act would not bring out the sun; rather, it would bring clouds, rain, or, better yet, a storm.

It has taken me a long time, more than a twenty-year period of fieldwork in the Republic of Niger, to grasp fully how differently people perceive across cultures. In Europe and North America, the sun is a friend that is valued metaphorically; in the Sahel of West Africa, the sun is an enemy that is reviled metaphorically. Perceptual differences, however, are not limited to variations of judgement with the range of the visual. In Songhay, people use the senses of sound and taste—more than sight—to organize sociocultural experience. Yet in the past, more often than not, mainstream anthropologists have translated experiential categorization based on taste, smell, or sound into vision. With the notable exceptions of performance theorists (see Tedlock 1983; Drewal 1992) most ethnographic representations of other peoples are limited, and ethnographers all too often use the eye to see what the tongue has tasted or the ear has heard. The ethnographic challenge that I attempt to take up in this essay is to try to perceive other worlds and other peoples more faithfully—in this case a virtual coming to one's senses.

How and why did I come to my senses? In 1969, I went to Niger for the first time to teach English as a foreign language at the secondary school of Tera. Tera was a hot and dry town. Residents of Tera—myself included—suffered from chronic water shortages. Often there wasn't enough water to bathe; sometimes we had to drive to wells in the bush for cooking and drinking water. My colleagues and I soon learned that beer was a good way to quench one's thirst in dessicated Tera. There was one bar in town, Chez Jacob, named after the proprietor, a Christian Yoruba from Nigeria who stocked his temperamental kerosene refrigerator with one-liter bottles of Kronenbourg beer. Soon my colleagues and I were regulars at Chez Jacob. Everyday, we'd have a noontime drink before lunch and a late afternoon drink before dinner.

Late one afternoon in December of 1969, a crowd formed near Chez Jacob, which was situated in Tera's *zongo* (the neighborhood of foreigners). A violinist played his *godji* which sounded more like a haunting lamentation than a monochord violin. Two drummers struck their gourd drums, creating a profusion of clacks, rolls, and clacks which shattered the hot dry air above Tera. The sounds of the music captured me and lured me to the crowd. Suddenly, a young man, who had been standing next to me, vomited black ink, staining his white shirt. I thought he was about to die. Like other members of the audience, I gave him room to maneuver. He threw himself to the ground. He threw sand all over his body. He shoved sand into his mouth. He stood up and scanned the audience.

He stopped and spit sand in my direction. Fixing his gaze on other people in the audience, he lunged menacingly toward them. Three men restrained him before he could strike the crowd. I moved closer and saw him clearly for the first time. His eyes bulged. A blood vessel in his forehead throbbed. He groaned. Saliva frothed from his mouth. He broke loose from his restrainers and came at me. Shaken, I raced to Chez Jacob.

"Is the man crazy?" I asked in my inchoate Songhay.

"Oh no," responded another spectator. "He is not a man; he is one of the Hauka [a family of Songhay spirits]. You must go up and greet him. He will not harm you."

At first I resisted the man's suggestion, but he insisted. And so I approached this terrifying Hauka. He thrust his open hand toward mine.

"Sha vas?" He asked how I was doing in Pidgin French.

"Fine," I answered, still afraid.

"Your mother has no tits."

This provoked great laughter. "Yes, she does!" I protested.

"Your father has no balls."

This provoked even more laughter from the audience, which was being entertained at my expense. The man who accompanied me suggested that I say goodbye to the Hauka, and so I did, having had my first exposure to possession among the Songhay.

I said goodbye to the Hauka that day, but this event only marked the beginning of my experiential path among the Songhay. In 1970 in Tillaberi, Niger, the haunting cries of the monochord violin and the electric clack-roll-clack of the gourd drum beckoned me once again, this time over a dune to witness my second ceremony of Songhay spirit possession. The possession dance was held in the compound of Adamu Jenitongo, who would later become the master of my apprenticeship in Songhay possession and sorcery. The sounds of these instruments so impressed me that I continued to attend possession ceremonies in 1971.

Upon my return to Niger in 1976, I again listened for the "cries" of the violin and the "clacks" of the gourd drum. In 1977 I began to learn about the sounds of spirit poetry in the village of Mehanna. Two years later, I was invited to join the Tillaberi possession troupe as a "servant to the spirits," with such duties as gathering ritual plants and resins, and costuming male mediums. In 1984, the absence of rain threatened the growing season, and in a two-week period in July I participated in 10 possession ceremonies during which people begged their spirits to bring rain. That year drought ravaged Tillaberi. Many people died. Throughout this myriad of experiences, my teachers continually focused my attention upon the sounds of the Songhay world.

"Listen to the *godji* [monochord violin] and let its cries penetrate you. Then you will know the voice of the spirits," they would tell me. "Feel the sound of the drum and know the power of our past."

And so I listened and I felt the music: I began to hear the sounds of Songhay possession. I learned from Adamu Jenitongo to "feel" the pulsations of the incantations of Songhay magic. My experiences in Songhay showed me the importance of honing in on Songhay frequencies of meaning, many of which rely on non-visual faculties. Over time, my experience in Songhay taught me that I could no longer separate thought from feeling or sensation from action.

VISUALISM AND THE WESTERN GAZE

My auditory experiences in Songhay ran counter to Western philosophical tradition, for the eye and its gaze, to use the apt term of Foucault (1970), has had a lockhold on Western thought (see Howes 1992, 1988; Classen 1990; Jackson 1989; Stoller 1989b; Corbin 1986). And scholars have long been fascinated with the power of words. Wittgenstein's *Philosophical Investigations* (1953), for example, focuses on language games. Austin's *How to Do Things With Words* (1962) introduces the notion of word work, or linguistic pragmatics. Searle's *Speech Acts* (1968) extends Austin's influential analysis. The underlying supposition of these linguistic philosophers is that problems of meaning devolve from the misuse of words. In 1959 Ernest Gellner published *Words and Things,* which was a broadside against the arcane intellectualism of the Oxford linguistic philosophers. Although Gellner's felicitous argument against the Oxford philosophers focused on the logical (textual) fallacies and the acontextuality of linguistic philosophy, he did not tune his mind to the question of the sound of words, let alone the sound of music. With the notable exceptions of Sapir (1949), Jakobson (1960), and Bollinger (1986), most linguists have emprisoned sound in the hermetically sealed vault of referential meaning. There is a need to resituate our visual bias and tune into the dimension of sound in ethnographic work.

Ever since the period of alphabetization, of which Walter Ong (1967) writes so eloquently, sound-in-the-world has been spatialized into insightful writing. As a consequence, the oral-aural world has been relegated to the back benches of philosophical debating chambers. Zuckerkandl (1958) suggests that the majesty of vision in the epistemology of Western thought is part of a long tradition of observation of specific material things within a field of vision. From Aristotle on, most of us have been conditioned to see colored illuminated things, not colors or light. Most of us feel hard or smooth things, not hardness or smoothness. "In seeing, touching, tasting, we reach through the sensation to an object, to a thing. Tone is the only sensation not that of a thing." (*Ibid.*:70) In Western discourse we have tended in our acts of seeing to spatialize the phenomena we observe. Foucault (1975:3) provides a medical example:

> For us the human body defines, by natural right, the space of origin and of the distribution of disease: a space whose lines, volumes, surfaces, and routes are laid down in accordance with a now familiar geometry, by the anatomical atlas. But this order of the solid visible body is only one way—in all neither the first nor the most fundamental—in which one spatializes disease.

Even the analysis of music gets spatialized. Pitches move "up" and "down" (Nattiez 1990; see also Seeger 1987; Roseman 1991).[1]

In short, Western thinkers have usually ignored many of the dimensions of sound. For Zuckerkandl, sound can be organized into melodies, rhythms, meters, and most of all into forces. The meaning of a sound "lies not in what it points to, but in the pointing itself" (1958:68). He considers the sounds of music as dynamic symbols: "We hear forces in them as the believer sees the divine being in the [religious] symbol" (*Ibid.*:69). Zuckerkandl's musical view of the universe presents for us an entry into the world of intangibles: "Because music exists, the tangible and visible cannot be the whole of the given world, something we encounter, something to which we respond" (*Ibid.*:71). With our ears fully tuned to the existential nature of sound, we can better appreciate the intangible and can cross thresholds into the deep recesses of a people's experience. Feld (1990[1982]:3) demonstrates this very point. In his book on Kaluli sound as a cultural system, he shows

> how an analysis of modes and codes of sound communication leads to an understanding of the ethos and quality of life in Kaluli society. By analyzing the form and performance of weeping, poetics, and song in relation to their origin myth and the bird world they metamorphize, Kaluli sound expressions are revealed as embodiments of deeply felt sentiments.

In Songhay possession ceremonies, sound is more than a means to the end of trance (Jackson 1968; Sturtevant 1968); it is a foundation of experience. If one cannot hear, Sorko Djibo Mounmouni, one of my teachers, once suggested to me, one can learn little about the world. A deeper appreciation of sound could force us to overturn our static, spatialized world and compel us to consider the dynamic nature of sound, opening a door to the comprehension of cultural sentiment.

POSSESSION IN SONGHAY[2]

The whine of the violin (*godji*), the syncopated "clack" of the gourd drum (*gasi*), the roar of the deities, and the murmur of the audience have long echoed in the dry air above Songhay villages. The Songhay, who trace their origin to the eighth century, have a long and glorious history, the peak of which was the Songhay Empire of Askia Mohammed Toure (1493–1528). Possession ceremonies, which probably date to Toure's reign, are a major component of Songhay religion (Olivier de Sardan 1982, 1984; Stoller 1989a). They are ceremonies in which visions and sounds are fused to recreate Songhay experience from mythic past to realistic present.

Possession and the Songhay Cosmos

Islam, which first spread to Songhay in the eleventh century, has had a long and powerful presence there. Yet Songhay cosmology blends both Islamic and indigenous concepts. According to Adamu Jenitongo, my principal teacher in Songhay, the Songhay world consists of seven heavens, seven hells, and earth, on which there are four cardinal directions. This seven-heaven concept derives from Islam. Most Songhay divide life on earth into two elementary domains: the world of social life and the spirit world, which Songhay call the world of eternal war. Meanwhile, God lives in the most distant, seventh heaven. Since God is so distant, contact with God comes only through the good offices of Ndebbi, God's messenger, who inhabits the sixth heaven. Priests chant their magical incantations to Ndebbi, who then carries the message to God for a decision. Songhay elders are divided about which members of the spirit family reside in the second through fifth heavens. Some, including Adamu Jenitongo, suggest that these heavens house the ancestors (a Songhay notion); others maintain that they are the abode of angels (an Islamic notion).

The first, most proximate heaven is the domain of the spirits or *holle*, which are divided into the following spirit "families": the *Tooru*, nobles of the spirit world which control such natural forces as the wind, the clouds, fire, lightning and thunder; the *Genji Kwari* (White Spirits) which are the Islamic clerics and the arbitrators of disputes of the social and spirit worlds; the *Genji Bi* (Black Spirits) which control the forces governing soil fertility and pestilence; the *Hargay* (Spirits of the Cold) which govern illnesses, and are associated with the reproductive cycle; the *Hausa Genji* (*Doguwa*) which precipitate madness and various kinds of paralysis; and the *Hauka* which burlesque identities of French colonial society.[3]

The proximity of social and spirit domains parallels resemblances between spirits and human beings. Like human beings, spirits are members of various ethnic groups, marry one another, and have master-slave relationships. Yet unlike human beings, the spirits are invisible and live forever (see Rouch 1989; Stoller 1989b).

The primary juxtaposition of the first heaven with earth brings the social and spirit worlds into spatial proximity. These worlds are conjoined during possession ceremonies when the spirits leave their world—the first heaven—to visit the social world through the taking of a medium's body.

Spirit mediumship results from the temporary displacement of a person's double by the force of a particular spirit. In Songhay, the individual consists of three elements: flesh (*ga*); life force (*hundi*), which resides in the heart; and double (*bia*) the immaterial aspect of the body. One major difference between spirits and human beings is that spirits, which have no flesh or life force, must use the medium's body—her flesh—to materialize. When the force of the spirit enters the medium's body, the medium shakes uncontrollably. When the deity is firmly established in the dancer's body, the shaking becomes less violent. The deity screams and dances. The medium's body has become a deity, and her double has been displaced.[4]

The Possession Troupe

In many Songhay villages there exists a loosely organized group of men and women who constitute the local possession troupe. The troupe gathers periodically to stage possession ceremonies. The head of the Songhay troupe is the *zima* or possession priest. Like the impressario of a theatrical company, the *zima* produces possession ceremonies in Songhay. He or she makes sure that the proper sacrificial animals have been purchased. He hires musicians and praise-singers. He requires the attendance of spirit mediums. But the *zima* is more than a producer. During ceremonies he or she directs the ritual action, orchestrating musical arrangements, overseeing costume changes, and interpreting spirit language. She or he is also responsible for the distribution of money that the troupe collects during a ceremony.

If the *zima* is the head of the Songhay spirit possession troupe, the medium is its heart. Spirits invade the bodies of their mediums to speak to people in Songhay communities. Although the majority of mediums in Songhay are women, a large percentage of them are men. Contrary to much of the literature on possession, Songhay mediums come from all the social strata in the Republic of Niger (Stoller 1989a). Despite these social divergences, Songhay mediums share social and experiential bonds. First, mediumship is passed down through the kindred. If ego's close relative is a spirit medium, he or she is likely to inherit one of that mediums's spirits. Second, spirits mark their mediums by making them sick. Pre-possession maladies are cured through initiation into the troupe. Third, each medium, through his or her initiation, is linked perpetually to the spirit world. No matter what their accomplishments may be in the social world, mediums are obliged to pay lifelong homage to the spirits. They are also required to support, directly or indirectly, the activities of spirit possession troupes.

The cast of the Songhay possession troupe is completed by its *sorko* (praise-singers) and musicians. The *sorko* are descendants of Faran Maka Bote, a legendary Niger River fisherman who, according to myth, staged the first possession ceremony some time in the distant past. Praise-singers recite "old words" to lure spirits to the bodies of their mediums.

There are two kinds of musicians who perform at spirit-possession ceremonies in Songhay: monochord violinists and gourd drummers. Often, the musicians learn their art as apprentices to close relatives: father, father's brothers, mother's brothers. However, sometimes a spirit will "appoint" a musician, who may simply be a member of a possession audience (Stoller 1989a). Musicians may also be spirit mediums, *zimas* and *sorkos*. The most illustrious monochord violinist was Wadi Godji, who died in the 1940s. Besides playing his monochord violin in Simiri, Wadi Godji was also a *sorko* and a *zima* in the local possession troupe (Rouch 1989).

Songhay Possession and Healing

Healing among the Songhay usually takes place in the privacy of the practitioner's dwelling. Here, the healer, who can be either a *sorko* or a *zima,* will attempt to divine the illness and prescribe some sort of therapy. In some cases, healers ask their patient to bring offerings of foods, perfumes or animals, which they will use in healing rites. During these rites, healers recite incantations over the offerings and then minister to the patient. They may sacrifice a chicken, prepare medicinal teas, or have the patient inhale incense.

Although the deities do practice healing during Songhay spirit possession dances, possession ceremonies are minor loci of individual healing. In Songhay, spirit possession ceremonies are more often about social healing—community offerings to ensure a good rainy season or a bountiful harvest. There are some infirmities, however, that must be treated by the spirits during spirit possession ceremonies. These include male and female infertility, conditions treated by the *Hargay* spirits, and partial paralysis, a condition remedied by the *Doguwa* or

Hauka spirits. In some cases, *Doguwa* spirits will identify sick people in a posses-sion audience and "lay their hands" on the site of the illness. In other cases, *Hargay, Doguwa* and *Hauka* deities will take on the role of Songhay healer by diagnosing an illness and prescribing a cure. These activities notwithstanding, most healing activities in Songhay are left to knowledgeable mortals.

SOUND IN SONGHAY POSSESSION

Anthropological writers have long discussed the meaning of words in cultural life. From Malinowski to Tambiah, anthropologists have attempted to explain the magical power of incantations from a variety of perspectives. Rarely, howev-er, have these analysts focused upon the importance of the sound of words. Rarer still are mainstream anthropological analyses of the cultural importance of the sound of musical instruments.[5] In the remainder of this essay, I shall describe both the importance of the sound of musical instruments and the sound of praise-poetry in Songhay possession.

The Sound of the Godji

The sound of the *godji,* or monochord violin used by Songhay musicians during possession ceremonies, corresponds to deep themes in Songhay experience. The resonating cavity of the *godji* consists of one-half of a hard gourd which has been cut along the axis of its grain. The opening of the resonating cavity is parallel to the neck of the violin, and its diameter averages about 29 centimeters (Surugue 1972:29). The gourd of the violin is covered by a lizard skin, *bo* (*Varanus niloti-cus*), which is stretched over the opening of the gourd and fastened to the instrument with either small iron nails or the thorns of the *garbey* tree (*Balinites aegytica*). The neck of the instrument is a simple stick of wood carved from the kubu tree (*Combretum micrantum*); it is generally 75 centimeters in length. The neck is inserted into the resonating cavity about three centimeters below the point where the gourd was cut into two halves. The violin string consists of black hair clipped from a horse's tail; it is tied to the end of the neck and to a piece of wood attached at the far end of the resonating cavity. The musician pulls the string taut as he pushes a small wooden bridge into position. The bow is an arc of wood to which is attached more black hair clipped from a horse's tail.[6]

When the musician plays the *godji* he produces a sound that is quite high in pitch—similar to a high-pitched wail. Indeed, in Songhay one says that the *godji* "cries" (*a ga he*). As Adamu Jenitongo, *zima* of Tillaberi, Niger, told me: "The

Figure 1. Ali Godji of Garie

Godji cries for me; it cries for you; it cries for the people of Tillaberi; it cries for all the Songhay" (Stoller 1984:564).

Because the *godji* "cries" for all the Songhay, it is the most sacred of instruments. It was the prize given to Faran Maka Bote when he vanquished the river genie Zinkibaru to gain control of the Niger River spirits. Considering its mythic history, the *godji* and its sound are said to link Songhay of the past to those of the present. Indeed, the *godji* is so sacred that it never should be played on nonsacred occasions. Generally, it is kept in a cloth sack and is placed in a *zima*'s sacred spirit house, along with the *zima*'s other sacred objects.

The sound of the *godji* directly links the Songhay with their ancestors. As Adamu Jenitongo said:

> The sound of the godji penetrates and makes us feel the presence of the ancestors, the ancients (*don borey*). We hear the sound and know that we are on the path of the ancestors. The sound is irresistible. We cannot be

unaffected by it and neither can the spirits, for when they hear it "cry," it penetrates them. Then they become excited and swoop down to take the body of the medium (Ibid.:564).

This sound is a tangible link between Songhay present and past, for the wailing revivifies deep-seated cultural themes about the nature of life and death, the origin of Songhay, the juxtaposition of the social and spirit worlds. These themes, in turn, reinforce Songhay cultural identity. Although the sound of the *godji* has no direct effect on patients attending or sponsoring a possession ceremony, it facilitates the fusion of the worlds, a space in which spirits sometimes speak to patients about illnesses and treatments.

The Sound of the Gasi

The *gasi,* or gourd drum, is also a Songhay instrument of unquestioned sacredness. Like the *godji,* it is played only during possession ceremonies. Although much larger than the gourd used for the *godji,* the hard gourd used for the *gasi* is also cut into two halves along the axis of its grain. When the musician wishes to play his *gasi,* he digs a hole in the sand at the edge of the possession dance ground. When the gourd is overturned and placed over the hole, the drum's resonating cavity is deepened considerably. The gourd is stabilized over the hole by a notched stick which the musician extends from under the place where he sits to a point beyond the edge of the gourd. He strikes the drum with a set of carved bamboo sticks which resemble the human hand; the various parts of the drumstick are called the "wrist" (where the musician grips the drumstick), the "palm" (where the five pieces of bamboo are tied to the "wrist"), and the "fingers" (which when manipulated can strike the drum singly or all together). If the musician strikes the drum with the "wrist" or the "palm," one hears a solid "clack" which echoes in the air. If the musician rolls his own wrist, the "fingers" of the drumstick hit the drum independently, producing a "roll." In this way, musicians playing the *gasi* produce a highly distinctive "clack" and "roll."[7] The ratio of "clacks" to "rolls" corresponds not only to dance movements but to the spirit in the Songhay pantheon which the *zima* is soliciting.

Like the *godji,* the *gasi* appears in Songhay myth. The drum was played originally by river spirits which danced to its beat. The importance of the drum, be it a *gasi* or a *turu* (a long slit drum used by Songhay possession musicians in the nineteenth century), is that it produces a highly charged sound which, like the *godji,* revivifies the ancestral past. *Zima* Adamu Jenitongo told me that drums were played for the great warriors of Songhay to render them invincible to their enemies. "The sound of the drum explodes from the *gasi* and reminds us of the

Figure 2. Dukio Gasi of Mehanna

ancients and their strength (*Ibid.*:565–66). And so the sound of this special drum—its "clack" and "roll"—intoxicates the dancers as they participate in the possession ceremony, a rite of ancestral origin. The drum sound, like that of the *godji*, also excites the spirits, creating for them a context in sound which they find irresistible. And like the *godji*, the sound of the *gasi* brings on the fusion of the worlds, but has no known association with healing.

The Sound of Praise-Poetry

In the western Sahel of Africa, the social-symbolic importance of praise-poetry— and the people who produce it—is widespread. Bards (*griots*) have played major roles in the histories of the great empires of the western Sudan (Ghana, Mali, Songhay). In the epic poetry of these empires, *griots* appear as spokesmen and advisors to kings, and as preceptors for princes; genealogists for families and clans; composers, singers and musicians who perform for all segments of society (Hale 1990; see also Kati 1913; Niani 1974; Johnson 1986). Bards, in fact, continue to play important roles in the nation-states of the contemporary western Sahel. In the Republic of Niger, for example, the late President Kountche traveled with a number of bards who recited praise-poetry not only about the president's accomplishments, but also about the feats of his ancestors. Why has praise-poetry remained so significant in the western Sahel?

Irvine's study of the rhetoric of praise-naming among the Wolof of Senegal provides a significant hypothesis. Praise-naming, she suggests, has a far-reaching "rhetorical effect." People who are named during a bard's performance "are thought to be morally, socially, and even physically transformed by the words that are said"(1980:6). During a praise-naming ceremony among the Wolof, a stratified caste society, the praise-naming increases the addressee's moral standing, augments his rank in a rank-conscious society, and precipitates some kind of physiological transformation. It is believed that these transformations occur because the praise-naming ceremony arouses emotion in the addressee which, in turn, alters the balance of his bodily fluids. According to Wolof theories, these bodily fluids are the biological determinants of social position. The physiological (magical) transformation in the addressee is also influenced by the physical sounds of words.

> Words do not just have meaning—they are breath and vibrations of air, constituted and shaped by the body and motives of the speaker, physically contacting and influencing the addressee. So informants liken the effect of a griot's praise-song on his addressee to the effect of wind upon fire (both metaphorically and literally, since air and fire are supposed to be basic constituents of the body. (*Ibid.*:7)

Similar ceremonies occur throughout the western Sahel, though the rhetorical effect varies from society to society. In Songhay the bard's (*jesere*) performance enables people of high rank (nobles, or *maigey*) to achieve and maintain high moral, social, and political stature. This stature is achieved and maintained, in part, through the sound of the praise-names in the context of a praise-naming ceremony. It is perhaps because the sounds of the words the bards have mastered carry the power of social, moral and physical (magical) transformation, called *nyama* in the Mande world, that bards in the western Sahel continue to maintain their significant social role.

The significance of praise-naming in Songhay, however, extends beyond the political and social domains of life. Praise-naming has an essential role in Songhay possession ceremonies. The sorko is praise-singer to the 150 spirits of the Songhay pantheon. While the *godji* "cries" and the *gasi* "clacks" and "rolls" during possession ceremonies, the sorko shouts out the names of the spirits, recounting their genealogies and their supernatural exploits. When the *sorko* performs his praise-naming, he approaches a spirit medium who is not yet possessed and shouts spirit names into his or her ear. He may even poke the medium's shoulder with his forefinger. These actions, according to Sorko Djibo Mounmouni of Namarigungu (Niger), ensure that the sounds of the praise-names penetrate the medium's body. The sound of the praise-names helps to bring on a transformation as the spirit, now in a frenzy caused by the sounds of the *godji, gasi,* and praise-names, takes the body of the medium and throws her to the sand. Her body is jolted by the paroxysms that mark the onset of possession. Through the sounds of violins, drums and words, the social and spirit worlds have been fused. Through the medium's body, the spirit is ready to speak to the community.

HEARING THE WORLD

Inspired perhaps by Cezanne's notion (and demonstration) that "nature is on the inside," Victor Zuckerkandl (1958) tells us that music (and sound, more generally), too, is on the inside; it penetrates us, fusing the material and nonmaterial, the tangible and the intangible. Indeed, Zuckerkandl's thesis on the "inner" dimension of sound merely reaffirms what informants have been telling anthropologists since the beginning of ethnographic field study: that sound is a dimension of experience in and of itself. The Tiv of Nigeria covet song as power, energy, the veritable force of life (Keil 1979). The Kalapalo of central Brazil have a similar musical orientation to the world.

> The mingling of sounds in various situations of performed Kalapalo art is therefore a truly ecological representation of the universe. Through sound symbols, ideas about relationships, activities, causalites, processes, goals, consequences, and states of mind are conceived, represented and rendered apparent to the world. It is through sound that cosmic entities are rendered into being and represented by the Kalapalo—not as object types but as beings causing and experiencing action in a veritable musical ecology of spirit. (Basso 1985:311)

For the Songhay the "cries" of the monochord violin and the "clacks" of the gourd drum are the voices of the ancestors, voices filled with the power of the past, powers-in-sound that can bring rain, eradicate pestilence, and prevent epidemics. Sound for the Songhay and for other peoples around the world is believed to have an existence separable from the domains of human, animal and plant life. Sounds carry forces which are not only good to think about, but good to feel.

Moving epistemologically from *Words and Things* (Gellner 1959) to "Sounds and Things" suggests some fundamental changes in future anthropological practices. Propelled by Clifford Geertz's notion of textualism, the primary focus of anthropological evocation and analysis has been visual. In his influential paper on the Balinese cockfight, Geertz transforms his cockfight analysis into a general interpretive approach to cultural analysis. The two key metaphors of this approach are "reading" and "text." Echoing Max Weber and Paul Ricoeur, Geertz (1973: 373) wrote: "The culture of a people is an ensemble of texts, themselves ensembles, which the anthropologist strains to read over the shoulders of those to whom they properly belong." This passage, the hallmark of interpretive-hermeneutic anthropology, reduces anthropological analysis to the "reading" of a variety of events: cockfights, fistfights, raids, thefts, births, death, sacrifices, possession rituals, indeed all of social action transformed conceptually into words arranged in some fashion on a printed page—a text. Such anthropologists, therefore, become deep readers of cultural texts which they then analyze the way a literary critic analyzes a novel, a play, or a poem.

At first glance, the interpretive analysis of cultural texts seems a felicitous research strategy. The people of many of the societies that anthropologists study do produce various sorts of texts. Some of our informants may write novels, plays or poems; others may recite for us epics or proverbs, which, through our transcriptions and translations, become texts. These then can be studied from any number of literary perspectives: new criticism, structuralist criticism, or post-structuralist crticism.

Closer study of the analysis of cultural texts, however, reveals some taken-for-granted limitations. The ritual portrayed in a Chinua Achebe novel, which is now part of a published text, is qualitatively different from the "text" of a similar ritual that the "anthropologist strains to read over the shoulders" of the Igbo of Nigeria. Can we apply the same critical standards to "texts" that are substantially different?

A more serious limitation, however, is that transforming cultural experience into texts limits cultural analysis to the sense of sight. We use our eyes to read texts. We use our eyes to transform rituals, the meanings of which may depend on senses other than sight, into visual texts that we can see, dissect and analyze. But what about the importance of sound in Songhay possession? Can the sound of the monochord violin be reduced to notes on a page? In honing in on sound-in-culture, analysts must make the connection between sound and cultural meaning. For the Songhay the "cries" of the *godji* are the voices of the ancestors,

socially healing voices that create the auditory context needed for spirit possession. For the Kaluli of New Guinea bird songs are considered the voices of the
ancestors (Feld 1982). Among the Temiar of Malaysia bamboo tubes are linked
to heartbeats (Roseman 1991). To be blunt, a visually based textual analysis
removes us from the sensory world of taste, hearing, and touch. People in some
of the societies anthropologists study see the world in primarily visual terms; in
other societies people demonstrate auditory, olfactory, gustatory or tactile pro-
clivities in their perception of the world. What happens to the validity of our
cultural analyses if we use exclusively visual categories to analyze a society like
Songhay, which places a good deal of emphasis on non-visual categorization?
(See Howes 1988, 1991, Classen 1990, 1992; Stoller 1989b.)

During the last decade there has been much debate about the science of
anthropology. Critical anthropologists have cast doubt on Enlightenment-based
claims that culture can be "found" or "discovered" when anthropologists follow
prescribed scientific methods. Critical anthropologists have also questioned the
scientific methods of the discipline, which they say were inspired by Eurocentric
functionalist or structuralist assumptions about the universality of discoverable
"rules." Analysts have recently probed the rhetorical assumptions of classic
anthropological texts, finding that the language of ethnography also tends to be
Eurocentric, which, in turn, questions the anthropologist's ability to *represent* the
other's world, the other's culture. For some scholars, the inability to represent
the increasingly autonomous other suggests the end of anthropology (see
Malcomsen 1990; Clifford 1988; Said 1989; Tyler 1987).

Anthropologists of a "scientific" bent have labeled the critical anthropologists
"science-bashers." In so doing they reaffirm past practices and Enlightenment
Truths. In time the fog of this seemingly interminable meta-ethnographic debate
will lift to reveal what was always already there—the hard life of fieldwork and
the hard work of writing and filming ethnography.

The fog has nevertheless kept many of us from appreciating and learning from
the many fine and sensitive ethnographies published during the past 15 years.
Much of this writing has been attuned to sensorial difference. Ethnomusicologists
have have long tuned into the centrality of sound in the construction of cultural
meaning (see Keil 1979; Chernoff 1979, n.d.; Feld 1990[1982]; Basso 1985;
Coplan 1989; Waterman 1991; and Roseman 1991), This work, which has been
largely imperceptible to mainstream anthropologists, deserves a better hearing.[8]

Where does all of this theoretical ferment lead? For me, the result of this
ongoing intellectual debate is neither the end of anthropology nor the retreat to
tried and true (social) science. For me, the ferment leads us back to ethnographic
practice and representation based upon the following premises: (1) that ethnographers visit repeatedly their field sites over a long period of time; (2) that

ethnographers, following the model of ethnomusicology, tune their senses to non-visual frequencies, especially in societies with non-visual sensory preferences; and (3) that ethnographers reinstate the non-visual senses into their ethnographic representations.

It sometimes takes years of painstaking work in one society to discover simple elementary principles such as the importance of sensory preference. I discovered the central importance of sound in Songhay possession on my fifth trip to Songhay some eight years after I began fieldwork there. This realization prompted me to pay more attention to the tastes, smells, sounds, and textures in the field—tastes, smells, sounds and textures that have given me a deeper understanding of Songhay society and culture and a more faithful representation of Songhay in my published work. Perhaps it is time for more mainstream anthropologists to adjust their perceptual antennae and come to their senses.

ACKNOWLEDGMENTS

The research on which this paper is based was funded through grants from West Chester University, the NATO Postdoctoral Fellowship in Science Program (NSF), the American Philosophical Society, and the Wenner-Gren Foundation for Anthropological Research. I thank these organizations for their generosity. This paper was read at the 1989 Society for Ethnomusicology held in Cambridge, Mass. I thank Marina Roseman for inviting me to participate. I thank Dan Rose and Thomas Hale for their comments on early drafts of this article. The comments of Carol Laderman and Marina Roseman have been thorough, incisive and stimulating. Their highly appreciated suggestions have made this a much better essay.

NOTES

1. I thank Marina Roseman for pointing this out to me.

2. For a sustained analysis of Songhay spirit possession, see my *Fusion of the Worlds: An Ethnography of Possession Among the Songhay of Niger* (1989) and my *Embodying Colonial Memories: Spirit Possession, Power and the Hauka in West Africa* (1995).

3. See Jean Rouch's remarkable film *Les maîtres fous*.

4. Rouch (1989:339) provides a rare description of the sentient embodiment that occurs in Songhay possession.

> Following numerous indirect accounts (it is already indicated that the dancer must not remember the possession) the dancer sees the spirit [eventually the old initiates see it too], penetrate the dance circle and direct itself toward him or her; the spirit holds in its

hands the skin of a freshly slaughtered animal and presents the bloody side of it to the dancer three times:

—the first time, tears flow from the dancer's eyes;

—the second time, mucus flows from the dancer's nose;

—the third time, the dancer cries out.

On its fourth pass, the spirit places the bloody skin over the dancer's head. In this way the spirit captures the medium's double and enters the dancer's body. During possession the dancer's double is protected under the bloody skin. When the spirit leaves the body, it lifts off the bloody animal skin, liberating the dancer's double. The medium opens his or her eyes. Sometimes, mediums are unconscious for several minutes. They always cough as if they had just left an airless vault. (*Ibid.*:340)

5. The work of ethnomusicologists in this domain is, of course, exemplary, but undervalued by mainstream anthropologists. One can only hope that much-appreciated recent ethnographies written by ethnomusicologists will raise their profile in mainstream anthropology. Two cases in point are John Chernoff and Carol Robertson. Chernoff's *African Rhythm and African Sensibility* (1979), which is about the cultural meaning of percussion in Ghana, sets a standard for ethnographic fieldwork and writing. His forthcoming book, *A Drummer's Testament,* is a stunning example of how sound leads the ethnographer not into the heart, but the heartbeat of a culture. Among the Dagbamba, drummers not only produce rhythms that pulse with cultural meaning, but are the guardians of the "old words." They are the historians and ethnographers of Dagbamba. Robertson (1979: 408) for her part is interested in the cognitive ramifications of musical communication. She reports that among the Mapuche of Argentina people use public behaviors as vehicles to transform thought into social action and images into sounds. In both cases the authors are ethnomusicologists. In both cases they confronted issues of reflexivity and sensorial anthropology well before the "experimental moment."

6. The string of the *godji* is plucked from only two of the many kinds of horses found in Songhay. These are the *sobe* and the *guro,* which are distinguished by the colors of their bodies and their feet.

7. As far as I know there are no agreed-upon terms for the gourd drum's "clacks" and "rolls." Two drummers I know refer to "clacks" as *kab-gande* or "palm," and "rolls" as *kab'ize* or "fingers." "Clacks" are played with the drumstick's "palm," "rolls" are played with the drumstick's "fingers."

8. Also largely ignored by mainstream anthropologists are anthropological studies of nutrition, which feature sensitive analyses of taste. See Laderman 1983; Laderman and Van Esterik 1988.

REFERENCES

Austin, J. L. 1962. *How To Do Things With Words.* London: Oxford University Press.

Basso, E. 1985. *A Musical View of the Universe.* Philadelphia: University of Pennsylvania Press.

Bollinger, D. 1985. *Intonation and Its Parts. Melody in Spoken English.* London: Edward Arnold.

Chernoff, J. 1979. *African Rhythm and African Sensibility*. Chicago: University of Chicago Press.

———. n.d. *A Drummer's Testament*. Chicago: University of Chicago Press, forthcoming.

Classen, C. 1990. Sweet Colors, Fragrant Songs: Sensory Models of the Andes and the Amazon. *American Ethnologist* 17(4):722–36.

Clifford, J. 1988. *The Predicament of Culture*. Cambridge, Mass.: Harvard University Press.

Coplan, D. 1989. *In Township Tonight*. London: Longman.

Corbin, Alain. 1986. *The Foul and the Fragrant: Odor and the French Social Imagination*. Cambridge, Mass.: Harvard University Press.

Drewal, M. T. 1992. *Yoruba Ritual: Performers, Play, Agency*. Bloomington: Indiana University Press.

Feld, Steven. 1982/1990. *Sound and Sentiment*. 2nd ed. Philadelphia: University of Pennsylvania Press.

Foucault, M. 1970. *The Order of Things: An Archeaology of the Human Sciences*. New York: Random House.

———. 1975. *The Birth of the Clinic: An Archaeology of Medical Perception*. New York: Pantheon.

Geertz, C. 1973. *The Interpretation of Cultures*. New York: Basic Books.

Gellner, E. [1959] 1968. *Words and Things*. Hammondsworth, England: Penguin.

Hale, T. 1990. *Scribe, Griot and Novelist: Narrative Interpreters of the Songhay Empire*. Gainesville: University of Florida Press.

Howes, D. 1988. On the Odour of the Soul: Spatial Representation and Olfactory Classification in Eastern Indonesia and Western Melanesia. *Bijdragen tot de Tall, Land en Volkenkunde* 144:84–113.

Howes, D., ed. 1992. *The Varieties of Sensory Experience*. Toronto: University of Toronto Press.

Irvine, J. T. n.d. Address as Magic and Rhetoric: Praise-naming in West Africa. A paper presented to the 79th annual meeting of the American Anthropological Association, Washington, D.C.

Jackson, A. 1968. Sound and Ritual. *Man,* n.s. 3:292–300.

Jackson, M. 1989. *Paths Toward a Clearing*. Bloomington, Ind.: Indiana University Press.

Jakobson, R. 1960. Closing Statement: Linguistics and Poetics. In *Style and Language,* ed. T. Sebeok. Cambridge, Mass.: MIT Press.

Johnson, J. W. 1986. *The Epic of Son-jata*. Bloomington, Ind.: Indiana University Press.

Kati, M. 1913. *Tarikh al Fattach*. Paris: Maisonneuve.

Keil, C. 1979. *Tiv Song*. Chicago: University of Chicago Press.

Laderman, C. 1983. *Wives and Midwives: Childbirth and Nutrition in Rural Malaysia*. Berkeley: University of California Press.

Laderman, C. and P. Van Esterik, eds. 1988. Techniques of Healing in Southeast Asia. *Social Science and Medicine,* 27(8):747–878.

Malcomsen, S. 1989. How the West Was Lost: Writing at the End of the World. *Voice Literary Supplement,* April 14, 11–14.

Nattiez, J.-J. 1990 *Music and Discourse: Toward a Semiology of Music.* Translated by Carolyn Abbate. Princeton, N. J.: Princeton University Press.

Niani, D. T. 1965. *Sundiata: An Epic of Old Mali.* London: Longman.

Olivier de Sardan, J.-P. 1982. *Concepts et Conceptions Songhay-Zarma.* Paris: Nubia.

———. 1984. *Sociétés Sonay-Zarma.* Paris: Karthala.

Ong, W. 1967. *The Presence of the Word.* New Haven, Ct.: Yale University Press.

Roseman, M. 1991. *Healing Sounds.* Berkeley and Los Angeles: University of California Press.

Rouch, J. [1960] 1989. *La Religion et la magie Songhay.* Brussels: University of Brussels Press.

Said, E. 1989. Representing the Colonized: Anthropology's Interlocutors. *Critical Inquiry* 15(2):205–225.

Sapir, E. 1949. *Language, Culture and Personality,* ed. D. Mandelbaum. Berkeley: University of California Press.

Searle, J. 1968. *Speech Acts: An Essay in the Philosophy of Language.* London: Cambridge University Press.

Seeger, A. 1987. *Suya Sing: A Musical Anthropology of an Amazonian People.* London: Cambridge University Press.

Stoller, P. 1984 Sound in Songhay Cultural Experience. *American Ethnologist* 11:559–70.

———. 1989a. *Fusion of the Worlds: An Ethnography of Possession Among the Songhay of Niger.* Chicago: University of Chicago Press.

———. 1989b. *The Taste of Ethnographic Things: The Senses in Anthropology.* Philadelphia: University of Pennsylvania Press.

———. 1995. *Embodying Colonial Memories: Spirit Possession, Power and the Hauka of West Africa.* New York: Routledge.

Sturtevant, W. 1968. Categories, Percussion and Physiology. *Man,* n.s. 3:133–34.

Surugue, B. 1972. *Contribution à l'étude de la musique sacrée Zarma-Songhay.* Etudes Nigériennes 330. Niamey: Université de Niamey.

Tedlock, D. 1983 *The Spoken Word and the Work of Interpretation.* Philadelphia: University of Pennsylvania Press.

Tyler, S. 1987. *The Unspeakable.* Madison, Wis.: University of Wisconsin Press.

Waterman, C. 1991. *Juju: The Social History of an African Music.* Chicago: University of Chicago Press.

Wittgenstein, L. 1953. *Philosophical Investigations.* Translated by G. E. M. Anscombe. New York: Macmillan.

Zuckerkandl V. 1958. *Sound and Symbol. Music and the External World.* Princeton, N.J.: Princeton University Press.

7

THE MEANING OF NONSENSE, THE POETICS OF EMBODIMENT, AND THE PRODUCTION OF POWER IN WARAO HEALING

Charles L. Briggs

The month I spent in a small settlement located in a moriche palm grove near the Mariusa River in the Delta Amacuro of Venezuela in June of 1990 was a stimulating and enjoyable time. Food was relatively plentiful, as palm starch, fruit, wood grubs, swamp fish, and other delicacies were fairly easy to obtain. I was living with some of my closest Warao friends. They had completed about ten days prior to my arrival the first half of the elaborate ritual cycle that uses tobacco smoke and palm starch, music and dancing in propitiating dangerous *hebu* spirits. The euphoria generated by the all-night dancing and music-making and visits from kinsmen lingered. And everyone was healthy.

This ambiance soon ended as the six-year-old son of a close friend, Manuel Rivera,[1] developed a high fever and respiratory congestion. He slept poorly that night; since houses lack walls, we all slept poorly. By morning he lay weak and listless, his gaze unfocused. He spent the day in the house of his grandfather, Manuel Torres. I supplied aspirin, but this proved to be small comfort. Mr. Torres is a *hoarotu,* a curer skilled in extracting and inflicting *hoa,* one type of spirit in Warao cosmology. On massaging the child's chest and abdomen, the size and relative hardness of the perceived spiritual pathogens led him to believe that other spirits, *hebu,* were to blame.[2] Everyone became concerned that the child might soon die.

Accordingly, the family summoned José Medina, a *wisidatu* who is a specialist in controlling *hebu* spirits, when he returned from the forest in the late afternoon. I saw Mr. Rivera, the boy's father, returning with a rattle from the elevated structure in which sacred objects are kept. Realizing that Mr. Medina was about to sing for the child, I asked the elderly curer whether he would mind if I recorded. As he graciously agreed, I quickly grabbed my tape recorder and arrived, just as darkness was falling. The boy was placed in a hammock on the eastern edge of his house, and Mr. Medina sat on a stool beside him. Mr. Rivera and I were seated just outside the house. After beginning to shake the rattle rhythmically, Mr. Medina started to sing. Throughout the curing ceremony, the combination of singing and rattling alternated with periods in which the rattle was either unaccompanied by voice or was complemented by a spoken dialogue between Mr. Medina and Mr. Rivera. In these dramatic exchanges, a relative of the patient converses not with the curer alone but with a series of malevolent spirits as well. At times, Mr. Medina moved from a seated position to one in which he crouched or stood on the edge of the patient's hammock and moved his rattle just above the child's body. On three occasions he pressed the rattle firmly against the patient's abdomen; I recall having the impression that he was performing a sort of invisible surgery using a gourd decorated with parrot feathers. The performance was divided into seven songs, corresponding to the seven *hebu* spirits that Mr. Medina removed from the boy.

Once all seven *hebu* had been extracted and sent away, the performance ended and the child went to bed. The fever had broken by morning. The child remained rather weak during the morning, but was up and playing by the afternoon. The child's grandfather, the owner of the sacred rattle, commented that the boy would have been dead by morning if the cure had failed.

My research did not initially focus on such events. Indeed, curing was the last thing I expected to study when I began conducting fieldwork with Warao people in 1986. I was much more interested in women's ritual wailing, political rhetoric, "mythic" narratives, and discourses that link Warao to the nation-state. I felt, in part, that the situated use of these types of discourse were less adequately documented for indigenous South American groups than was curing, particularly for Warao communities; furthermore I had no urge to poke around in areas in which my interest might not be welcome. I soon found, however, that discourse about illness—accounts of who is sick, who was trying to cure these individuals, who is responsible for the illness, why spirits might be 'grabbing' children, and the like—penetrated all other types of discourse. Additionally, Manuel Torres, the boy's grandfather, and his close friend Rafael García decided in 1989 that I should learn the work of the *hoarotu*. Without any warning, Mr. Torres noisily blew a small army of 'helping spirits' into a cigar and told me to smoke it; my training suddenly commenced. Along with another apprentice, I spent much of that summer smoking, practicing songs, learning to interpret my dreams, and becoming familiar with the practices used in transforming words and actions into methods of inflicting and extracting *hoa* spirits.

Clearly, my involvement in this process was shaped not only by the ritual practices I was learning but by the scholarly texts that I have read and the metadiscursive practices (Briggs 1993) that help shape how I perceive such experiences and re-present them to scholarly audiences. Once I began participating in curing rituals, my reflections on these experiences intersected with two problems that emerge from the social scientific literature on such events. The first is related to Victor Turner's (1967) concern with the relationships of "condensation" and "unification," in which dominant ritual symbols stand for "disparate significata." A number of studies by ethnomusicologists and anthropologists have focused on the multiplicity of communicative channels in curing rituals. Rather than simply studying the one facet of such ceremonies that most closely fits their training, a number of practitioners have attempted to grasp the collective role of music, language, movement, gesture, the use of objects, touch, smell, and other modalities.

Once the scope of the analysis is expanded in this fashion, a question arises regarding the relationship between the different media. Claims have long abounded that a particular ritual element is capable of generating some sort of automatic effect on participants; Andrew Neher's (1962) assertion of a causal link between acoustic stimuli and trance states in drumming provides a classic case. John Blacking (1983) and Gilbert Rouget (1977, 1980) have argued, however, that music is only capable of inducing trance when its use is rooted in a belief system that create a predisposition toward trance as well as a performance setting that occasions it. Rather than isolating the effects of individual elements, others have argued that the different media are woven, both formally and functionally, into what Stanley Tambiah (1981:164) terms a "sense of total fused experience." Tambiah suggests that we see a "blurring of boundaries between separate units or modalities through the mixing of modalities." Carol Laderman (1991:305) similarly states that the Malay healing seance is "a dramatic totality, combining performers, audiences, words, music, movement, setting, and props." Marina Roseman (1991) details the way that male mediums and female choruses produce ensembles of text and tune, instrumental accompaniment, and dance in Temiar trancing ceremonies. Some authors argue that such fusion and condensation takes place through the imposition of, in Roman Jakobson's (1960, 1978[1935]) terms, a "dominant" function that reconfigures the role of other components. Donald Bahr and J. Richard Haefer (1978) thus claim that text reshapes music in Pima curing songs, and Laderman (1991:298) suggests that "words are the real midwives of the seance."

Tambiah (1981:164) argues that one of the factors that contributes to the "fused numinous experience" of ritual is an "atrophy of meaning." He suggests that such facets of ritual discourse as the blurring of boundaries between modalities and poetic elaboration through parallelism lessen the importance of denotatively-based meaning, that is, the sort of referential meaning conveyed in dictionary definitions. John McDowell (1983) argues that the formal elaboration of ritual speech increases performative efficacy at the same time that it decreases semantic accessibility, implying that the latter two factors are inversely correlated. Two classic works on ritual take opposite stands with respect to the semantic interpretability of ritual speech. In his study of Trobriand gardening magic, Bronislaw Malinowski points to the importance of semantically "meaningless" and "archaic" words, grammatical abnormalities, and semantic extensions that lend "a very considerable coefficient of weirdness, strangeness and unusualness" to ritual language (1935:II,221–22). He argues that these "nonsense elements" help differentiate ritual from "ordinary conversation" and contribute to its performative efficacy. Claude Lévi-Strauss' (1963[1949]) contrastively argues that a Kuna chant sung to assist in cases of difficult childbirth "provides the woman with a *language,* by means of which unexpressed, and otherwise inexpressible, psychic states can be immediately expressed" (1963[1949]:198; emphasis in original). While Lévi-Strauss suggests that the "symbolic dimension" of the chant effects a cure by reestablishing cognitive coherence for the patient, Macpherson Chapin (1976, 1983) asserts that Lévi-Strauss is off-base in that the chant uses a 'stick-doll language' that is unintelligible to the patient.[3]

A number of positions have been staked out regarding this question. One of the most extreme is advocated by Maurice Bloch (1974), who argues that by invoking the illocutionary power of speech—that is, its status as culturally constituted social action—as a means of achieving coercion, "formalised language" becomes "an inferior form of communication" in which form and content are highly constrained. Bloch sees ritual language as involving no creativity and little relationship to the speaker, who articulates a social status rather than individual identity. In a somewhat contradictory vein, Bloch suggests that the "drifting out of meaning" of ritual words results in greater ambiguity, thus affording such speech enhanced social, emotional, and performative force. In a discussion of Lévi-Strauss' paper on the Kuna birth chant, Laderman (1987) argues that the greater ambiguity of ritual language *enhances* the role of semantic content in curing. Laderman (1987, 1991), Edmund Leach (1976), Tambiah (1970, 1973, 1977, 1981), and others connect the use of multiple channels in ritual with the question of meaning, suggesting that music, movement, ritual objects, and other features facilitate the process of decoding the semantic content of speech. Thomas Buckley (1984), Laderman (1991), Turner (1967) and others point out that ritual specialists are frequently able to interpret esoteric words and phrases that are not accessible to noninitiates.

We are thus left with two empirical problems. First, while most investigators seem to accept the idea that the performance of ritual induces some degree of fusion among signaling modalities and a condensation of their functions, the precise nature of this interweaving process has not been adequately specified. Second, the effect of this fusion on semantic meaning remains controversial. These questions also raise a number of theoretical questions. Can the performativity of ritual language exist independently of its semantic content, as Bloch argues and Tambiah suggests for some cases? Do performativity and semantic meaning stand in an inverse relationship, as McDowell (1983) suggests? These and other writers seem to assert that the power of ritual language to create and sustain social inequality is rooted less in semantic content than in formal patterning and features of the social setting in which it emerges. Several related questions remain greatly in need of clarification: A number of writers seem to hint that semantic content facilitates awareness of what is taking place, while formal patterning provides a mode of aesthetic and kinesthetic participation that is not cognitively accessible. Can features that lack semantic content afford insight into ritual processes? In short, what sorts of gaps—such as between different modalities or contrastive types of signs and functions—are apparent in the processes of fusion and condensation in ritual language? Are these constraints shared by all participants? If not, are differences in reception between specialists and non-specialists qualitative or quantitative?

These questions are relevant to our understanding of Mr. Medina's efforts to cure the young boy. He and other curers deem the use of rattle, melody, text (including both meaningful and "nonsense" elements), movement, and touch to be vital means to effecting a cure. Moreover, his song draws primarily on a curers' lexicon that is not intelligible to noninitiate patients and their relatives. This does not mean that the boy and his father had no idea what was going on; the latter's engagement in a dialogue with the spirit—as it emerged through the larynx of the curer—suggests that Mr. Rivera and his son participated in some fashion throughout.

This paper explores Mr. Medina's use of curing songs. In doing so, I hope to shed additional light on these broader questions. I argue that a fundamental discontinuity characterizes the role of semantically based features of the text as these relate to other dimensions of the performance. These differences emerge when we attempt to grasp the role of both types of elements in the curing process. I suggest that the nature of the intelligibility enjoyed by the curer and by the non-specialist participants is highly contrastive in the case of semantic features and quite similar with respect to nonsemantic elements. Illuminating these similarities and contrasts can yield a number of insights into the production of subjectivity, agency, and power in ritual performance.

THE WISIDATU CURER

A *wisidatu* obtains power over a broad range of ancestral spirits, which are termed *hebu;* except in a very few cases, *wisimo* (the plural of *wisidatu*) are men.[4] In the course of a rigorous initiation, neophyte *wisimo* travel, in their dreams, to one of the principal abodes of the master *hebu* spirits (see Johannes Wilbert 1972). The relationships established during this journey engenders both an obligation to honor these spirits with offerings of moriche palm starch, tobacco, music, and dance as well as a right to negotiate with spirits who express their anger by killing Warao, particularly children. *Wisimo* conduct two basic types of rituals for preventing *hebu*-induced death.

First, the *kanobo* spirits, who are embodied in a rock that is kept in the *kʷaiyanoko,* the 'spirit house,' inform a curer in his dreams that they desire tobacco smoke and palm starch. This revelation inaugurates a palm starch harvest, which generally takes place between March and May. Once the supply is sufficient, the spirits are invoked by the *wisidatu,* the *esemoi* (a single-reed instrument) and rattles are rattles are played, and community members dance all night long, often for nearly a week. A giant basket called a *nahanamu* is constructed from *naha,* the large green stems of moriche palm branches. The ritual cycle is also called *nahanamu.* The basket should be filled to overflowing with palm starch. The *wisimo* then call their respective spirits, inviting them into the *kʷaiyanoko,* feeding them with tobacco smoke, and then 'throwing' them, using the curer's rattle, into the palm starch. After a final afternoon performance of the *nahanamu* dance, the spirits are left in the palm starch until at least the succeeding full moon, at which time the dancing is repeated. On the final night, the *wisimo* call their respective spirits once more. Exhorting the *hebu* to repay the kindness of their hosts by refraining from visiting illness on the community, the spirits are sent home. The ritual cycle ends with the distribution of the palm starch to all participants and a final dance that displays the social hierarchy of the community.

A PERFORMANCE OF *HEBU NISAYAHA* (CURING HEBU SICKNESS)

The *nahanamu* cycle constitutes a collective and prophylactic curing. Another type of ritual is individual and remedial. When an individual becomes ill, family members summon a curer. When curers determine that *hebu* are to blame, the type of curing performance that I described in the opening lines of this paper takes place. I will now examine in detail one of the songs that Mr. Medina, the *wisidatu*, performed during the *hebu nisayaha* (curing *hebu*-sickness) ritual. The following transcription is of the fourth song, one that addresses a spirit named Waba Sinaka Aurohi, 'the *hebu* of the fever that causes strokes.' A sectional schema of the fourth song is presented in Figure 1; a partial musical transcription is provided below in Figure 2.

> José Medina
> Hebu *curing performance for six-year-old-boy* [5]
> *Curer* = José Medina; *father* = Manuel Rivera
> Mariusa, Delta Amacuro, Venezuela
> June 1990

> *Curer (sung)*
> Section 1: 'Starting up the song'
> 1   *Waiya*
> 2   *ho ho ho ho*
> 3   *hoi hoi hoi hi hi*
> 4   *bohotoya, bohotoya botó*
>   You grabbed him, you grabbed him
> 5   *okó boto sinahiayasí*
>   you grabbed him by the head
> 6   *hiwabotuma isiko*
>   with your fevers
> 7   *hiwabotuma isiko*
>   with your fevers
> 8   *himonituma, hiburetuma isiko*
>   with your afflictions, your power for making one crazy
> 9   *kareko aurohi naminatuiné*
>   I myself am the one who knows the fevers of the little rocks
> 10 *hiahokʷanaminatuiné*
>   I myself am the one who knows you
> 11 *hiahokʷaeturatuiné*
>   I myself am the one who softens you

12 *hiahokᵂaehebaratuiné*
   I myself am the one who makes you let go

13 *tatuka abané mamohorabu abané*
   I am immediately grabbing you with my hands

14 *tatuka nakané*
   you are immediately falling into my grasp

15 *mamohorabu aoatuiné*
   I am the one who grabs you with my hands

16 *hiteho aoané, hiehebaraneiné*
   I am grabbing your body, I am making you let go

17 *hiahokᵂaehebarané, ehebarané*
   I am making you let go, I am making [you] let go

18 *hiahokᵂaehebarané, horoya ehebarané*
   I am making you let go, I am making [you] let go all along the skin

19 *horo mutanayá, atoma mutanayá ehebarané*
   between the skin and the flesh, I am making [you] let go all along
   the flesh

Section 2: 'Spanking the *hebu*'

20 *ho ho ho ho*

21 *waiya:*

[*volume of rattle augments and tempo increases to 5 revolutions per
second during 7-sec. pause in singing*]

22 *(hebu) sebuatiné, waba sebuatuiné*
   I myself am the one who takes out *hebu,* I myself am the one who
   takes out *hebu*

23 *waba sebuatiné, ehebaratuiné*
   I myself am the one who takes out *hebu,* I myself am the one who
   makes [you] let go

24 *hiehebarané, hiahokᵂaehebarané*
   I am making you let go, I am making you let go

25 *mahokᵂarima isiko, oborebu aisiko*
   with these helping spirits of which I am the father, with the spirits
   of deceased curers

26 *urusi sanuka sinahiasí*
   [the *hebu*] is lying on the little boy's stomach

27 *himonituma isiko, hiburituma isiko*
   with your power to cause illness, with your power to make one crazy

Section 3: 'The *hebu* reveals its words'

[*rattle returns to lower tempo and volume during a 20-sec. pause in singing*]

28 *ee:aa:*

29 *ee:aa:*

30 *ho ho ho ho ho*

31 *hoi hoi*

32 *ho ho*

33 *iné, iné*
    I myself, I myself

34 *bohoto sanuka siahinaené*
    I myself grabbed his little head

35 *yanomiahainé*
    I myself was watching him

36 *bohoto yanominiahainé*
    I myself was watching his head

37 *tamaha manatoro sanuka, domu hidoiné*
    I myself, with this grandson of mine, with this young child

38 *mehorokoya tuaturuaené*
    I myself wanted to throw him on the ground [i.e., kill him]

39 *maurohituma miaené*
    I myself saw my fevers

40 *mawabototuma miaené*
    I myself saw my fevers

41 *mak*ᵂ*arika tatuka abanaené*
    I myself put myself next to him

42 *manana abanaené*
    I myself put my filth on him

43 *tamahasi ahok*ᵂ*araisainé*
    I myself [grabbed the grandson of] this friend[6]

44 *domukatu hoebo ahok*ᵂ*arima oborebuiné*
    who is a master of 'bird magic', who is a master of *hoa,* who is a
    wisidatu curer, I myself

45 *diaka abané tatuka abaneiné*
    I myself went outside [of the spirit house], and there I put these
    things [on the child]

46 *deri karamunaené, deri karamunaené*
    they played the *esemoi,* they played the *esemoi*

47 *sabainé ewirikataené*
that's how I myself got close to him

48 *maurohituma isikoiné*
I myself with my fevers

49 *mawabototuma isikoiné*
I myself with my fevers

50 *mawabayaroko wabatuma isikoiné*
I myself, the one who loves to kill, with my ways of causing death

51 *Waba Sinaka temonuk^{w}a abaené*
I myself, the Hebu Who Causes Strokes, have similarly struck him

52 *diaka abané tamaha anatoro sanukainé*
I myself went outside [to grab] this little grandson of his

53 *mehorokoya tuaturuaené*
I myself wanted to throw him on the ground

54 *oborebuiné*
I myself am a curer

55 *oborebu mamohorabu oanaené*
I myself, a curer, grabbed [you] with my hands

56 *mamohorabu oanaené*
I myself grabbed [you] with my hands

[Section 4 begins here]

As was the case in all but one of the remaining songs, the third section was followed by a spoken dialogue between the *hebu*, who speaks through the larynx of the curer, and the father. This rich exchange is beyond the scope of this paper, and I analyze it elsewhere (Briggs n.d.). Here I rather focus on the relationship between the curer, the patient, his father, the *hebu*, the 'helping spirits' of the curer, and the spirits embodied in the quartz crystals in his rattle. I analyze in turn the rattle rhythms and the hand and body motions that produce them, the use of vocables or "meaningless" words, the musical structure of the songs, and the poetics of the text.

The curer's rattle and Warao cosmology

Four types of variation are evident in the use of the rattle: tempo, loudness, relationship to the singing, and distance from the patient's body. I have indicated the rattle rhythms in relation to overall song form in Figure 1, and to a selected song section in Figure 2.[7] At the beginning of each song, the rattle is moved slowly and regularly in a circular fashion at the rate of about 1 revolution per second.

Figure 1
Song for curing Waba Sinaka Hebu
(Fourth song in performance for curing *hebu*-sickness)

Section	Lines	Name	Speech/Song	Rattle	Breath	Voices
1	1–20	*dokotebuyaba*, 'starting up the song'	sung	slow	releases helping spirits expresses shaman's 'will' or 'thoughts' 'softens' *hebu* and 'loosens' its grip on child	shaman
2	21–28	*hebu nayaba*, 'spanking the hebu'	sung	rapid	extracts *hebu* from body	shaman
3	29–56	*hebu aribu abyaba* 'the *hebu* reveals its words' [to the shaman]	sung	slow	discerns *hebu*'s 'will' or 'thoughts'	*hebu* shaman
4	57–122	*hebu aobona tana abaya* 'the *hebu* reveals its "will" or "thoughts" [to the father]'	spoken	slow, then rapid	reveals *hebu*'s 'will' or 'thoughts' to father sends *hebu* home	*hebu* father shaman

The rattle is used by itself at the beginning of the performance, but the singing and rattling begin simultaneously in subsequent songs. Lines 20–21 signal a change that is reflected in the use of the rattle; during 7 seconds in which the singing is absent, the tempo increases to 5 revolutions per second and the loudness of the rattling is augmented as well. After line 27, the singing ceases for 20 seconds, the first 10 of which are characterized by the rapid tempo and the last 10 by the slow, one-revolution-per-second tempo. This pace is continued until almost the end of the spoken dialogue (which is not transcribed here), at which point the rapid tempo is resumed.

What is the role of the rattle in the performance, and what is the meaning of this variation? As Johannes Wilbert (1973–4) has argued, the rattle provides an *axis mundi* that connects the earth's surface with the sky vault, providing curers with a means of celestial ascent and access to the points inhabited chiefly by spirits. It embodies the *wisidatu*'s dual existence as a member of the world inhabited by *hebu* and deceased curers as well a member of the human community. Using the rattle enables him to draw out his own spirit powers as well as to gain control over the *hebu* afflicting the patient.

The quartz crystals that lie inside the shell of the calabash gourd are crucial in this regard. Stones of any sort are nearly absent in the lower delta. Bubu Karoní, home of the spirits that are the *hebu*'s leaders, is a stone-capped mountain on the island of Trinidad, a short distance across the Caribbean from the mouth of the Mariusa River. Just as a stone which is carefully guarded in the spirit house (*kʷaiyanoko*) embodies a *kanobo* ancestral spirit, the *kareko* (quartz crystals) in the rattle provide physical manifestations of *hebu* that come from Bubu Karoní or one of the other sacred mountains. These crystals are bodies of particular *hebu* that reside in the rattle, and each stone is named and accorded a kin term (see Basilio Barral 1964:175–7); the *kareko* assist the *wisidatu* in combating invading *hebu*. As Wilbert (1973–4) describes, patients can literally see the heat and light associated with *hebu* inside the rattle. He suggests that the luminescence is produced as the crystals come into contact with the interior surface of the gourd, thus igniting tiny wood shavings; this effect provides concrete evidence that the *kareko*'s power is being unleashed.

In this case, José Medina, the curer, has determined that the illness was caused by *kareko* that lie in Bubu Karoní (to the north) and Bubu Wayaba Karoní (to the southeast). They sent their *aurohi* (fevers) into the boy to express their anger at the community. The *kareko* in the rattle provide the perfect means of establishing contact with these spirits, removing them from the patient, determining the cause of their anger, and sending them home. Nonetheless, the role of the rattle that belongs to Manuel Torres, the boy's grandfather, as a way station for angry *kareko* in search of a victim points to Mr. Torres' complicity in causing the illness. In Section 3, the *hebu* then reveals the manner in which it 'grabbed' the child. Having come from its home on the edge of the Warao universe, it came to rest in the *kareko* inside the rattle. Watching from the *kʷaiyanoko,* the *hebu* saw the child playing on a dance platform that lies between the *kʷaiyanoko* and the village. The *hebu* recounts the emergence of its 'will' (*aobonona*) to attack the child. Lines 41–47 suggest that the *hebu* entered the child when Mr. Torres, who is skilled in three modes of curing (including that of the *wisidatu*), brought the rattle onto the 'dance platform' at the beginning of the *nahanamu* dances. Ironically, it was the very tool that Mr. Torres uses in exercising his power as a *wisidatu* that provided the malevolent *kareko* with an entrée into the community, and it was Mr. Torres himself who brought the now lethal rattle dangerously close enough to his grandson. I turn later to other ways that Mr. Torres's own search for power precipitated the situation.

Returning to the performance, the slow-tempo rattling enables the *kareko* in the rattle to contact the *kareko aurohi* (the fevers of the stones) in the child; this section is referred to as *dokotebuyaha* (starting up the song). The fast tempo rattling that follows is termed *hebu nayaha* (spanking the *hebu*). Here the curer either leans forward or crouches above the patient, placing the rattle directly above his body. With the increase in tempo and the intensity of the movement, the revolutions become more ellipsoidal than circular, with rapid down thrusts constituting the blows to the *hebu*. This 'spanking' loosens the *hebu*'s grip on the child, paving the way for its extraction.

When a *hebu* has lodged itself inside the viscera, the curer places the rattle firmly against patient's abdomen and applies substantial pressure. While the first three 'fevers' were located there, the fourth and subsequent 'fevers' were lodged in the child's head. In this case, the rattle never touches the patient; rather, the *wisidatu* uses his breath to extract the loosened *hebu* (see next section). With a return to the slow tempo in the third section of the song, the voice of the *hebu* emerges from the rattle through the words sung by the curer. The final period of rapid tempo marks the process of sending the *hebu* through the air back to its home. A single rapid thrust in this direction signals the *hebu*'s departure. A few moments of silence generally follow before the next song is 'started up'.

As Anthony Seeger (1987) has noted, rattles only produce sound when the body is moving. Thus, just as the rattle moves in keeping with the motions of the *wisidatu*'s body, his body moves in concert with the sounds created by the quartz crystals in the rattle. While the slow rattling mainly involves the curer's right arm, 'spanking the *hebu*' entails a complete reorientation of the practitioner's body, as does applying the rattle to the abdomen. Just as the linear progression of the song changes the relationship between the rattle and the curer's body, it produces repeated reorientations between the bodies of curer and patient.

Vocables, the curer's breath, and the auditory trail of spirits

Series of untranslated terms recur periodically in the transcript: *waiya, ee:aa:, ho,* and *hoi.* Such semantically vacuous phonological sequences, which appear frequently in Native American song, are generally termed *vocables* (cf. Frisbie 1980; Hinton 1980). A striking linguistic property of vocables is their lack of grammatical productivity—they cannot be inflected for person, number, or tense. Both semantically and grammatically, vocables stick out like a linguistic sore thumb. Vocables are set apart from other verbal elements of *wisidatu* songs musically as well, in that they are clustered together at the beginning of song sections, do not appear in the same musical phrases as other elements, and are rendered in a less "musical" timbre. Quintessential features of the curer's lexicon, vocables signal interactions between curers and spirits, not words addressed to human interlocutors. *Waiya* (or *waiye*) can only be produced by *wisimo* who have acquired the spirit power needed for curing individuals of *hebu,* and its use marks the beginning of a curing session.[8] What is the nature of these sounds and what role do they play in the therapeutic process?

The concept of breath (*hina*) is central in Warao views of disease. Werner Wilbert (1986) suggests that Warao conceive of illness primarily in pneumatic terms. A vehicle of transmission is believed to bring a pathogenic odor into the victim's body; *ahaka,* its 'wind' or 'air,' expands to fill a particular region of the body. Since this 'odor' or 'wind' has physical as well as intangible attributes, a curer can locate illness in a patient by using his hands to discern the size and relative hardness of the spirit, as well as to feel the movement and heat produced by its breath; this technique serves to distinguish *hebu* from *hoa* and *bahana* spirits. *Hebu* have a particularly powerful or large breath (*hinaida*). A common term for *hebu* sickness is *dio,* which refers to the damage it wreaks on the patient's respiration; the child was suffering from respiratory congestion. *Hebu* attack the patient's organs and blood as well as the invisible spiritual entity or "soul" that is associated with that region (see Wilbert 1986:367–68). As Johannes Wilbert (1972, 1987) argues, the curer's breath becomes efficacious in controlling spirits by smoking *wina* cigars. Since the curer cannot (except in his dreams) see *hebu,* his helping spirits, including both those in his chest and in his rattle, are specifically charged with this task. The use of breath in sending his helping spirits into contact with the invading *hebu* provides the curer with a means of making *aobonona* ('his will' or 'his thoughts') known to the hebu and discovering its *aobonona.*

Ho and *hoi* are produced with pharyngeal constriction, and *e:a:* combines this feature with creaky voice. Since this rather raspy voice quality is believed to reflect the difficulty that the spirits encounter in passing through the larynx and pharynx, it indicates a change in the agent who is seen as producing the sound; while the song is initially sung by the curer, it is the helping spirits themselves who produce the vocables. An additional feature, which is termed "voice masking" by Dale Olsen (1973), is the suppression of the singing format that generally lends the singing voice its characteristic timbre. Speech that bears these acoustic characteristics is believed to be intoned by spirits rather than by the curer himself. *Ee:aa:* projects the helping spirits with sufficient force to enable them to drive out the invading *hebu*. The curer's tobacco-enhanced breath renders the *hebu* soft and compliant; 'heavier' than the *hebu*'s fetid air, it expels the *hebu* from the patient's body. The rattle is also used in driving out the *hebu*. This is particularly evident in line 28, where the vocable *ee:aa* along with the rattle is used to expunge the *hebu* from the body, and at the conclusion of the spoken dialogue, where the *hebu* is expelled from the community.

These voice qualities provide acoustic evidence for the status of the sounds as sonic embodiments of the movement of the helping spirits out of the curer's chest, through his mouth, and into the air—and vice versa. *Ho, hoi,* and *ee:aa:* are not invocations of spirits, signs addressed to invisible audiences, but audible traces of the participation of spirits. Since *hebu* are invisible, *ee:aa:, ho,* and *hoi* provide crucial means of charting the curer's success in extracting the *hebu* from the patient and expelling them.

Musical structure

As indicated in Figure 1, each of the songs consists of three parts which are sung, followed by a fourth, spoken section. Section one is termed "starting up the song," while the second is referred to as "spanking the *hebu*." The *hebu* "reveals his words" in the third section, which is followed by a spoken dialogue between the curer and a relative of the patient in which the *hebu* "reveals his will or thoughts."

While the pitches used in Sections 1 and 2 are quite similar, a contrastive pattern emerges in the third. (The opening phrases from Section 1 are transcribed in Figure 2.) Lines in Section 1 begin primarily on two pitches, F and G. Most lines follow a rise-fall melodic contour, retaining the same pitch for most of the line, climbing to the highest pitch, and falling on a glissando to either the lowest pitch of the phrase thus far, or even farther. The rise in pitch ranges between a major second and a minor third. Many lines in Section 2 follow the same pattern,

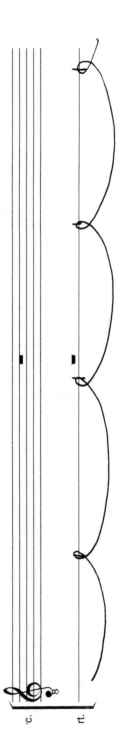

Fig.2. Musical Transcription of Opening Lines from Section 1 of the Fourth Song

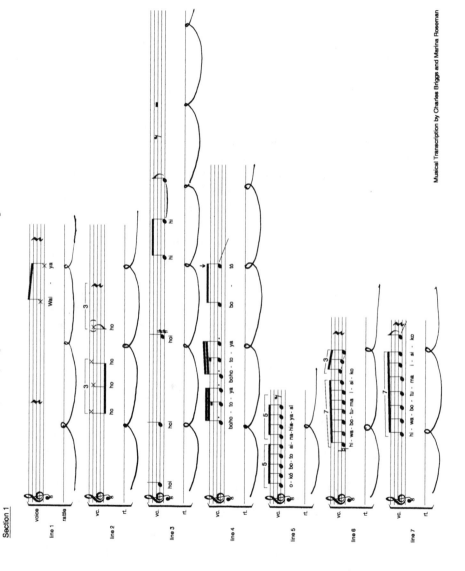

Musical Transcription by Charles Briggs and Marina Roseman

although the glissando is often attenuated in pitch. In both sections, the glissando is usually emphasized rhythmically by its greater duration.

In the majority of the lines in Section 3, on the other hand, the voice does not climb in pitch or trail off into a glissando; it rather ends on an accented note at the same pitch, which is maintained throughout. Given the predominance of the rapid fall in volume and pitch at the end of phrases in the remainder of the song, the pattern evident in Section 3 is musically marked. The initial pitches are generally higher in Section 3, with most lines beginning on B, B-flat, or A. Successive lines generally alternate between initial pitches at an interval of about a half-step.

A recurrent pattern of variation is present in the melodic structure. First, initial pitches of the lines rise in the course of the three sections; while this movement is only slightly noticeable from Section 1 to 2, it is more marked as one comes to Section 3. Suggesting that this "upward drift" signals the curer's entrance into a trance-like state, Olsen (1975) notes that this feature is present in curative performances yet absent in elicited, "studio" recordings. In the case of Mr. Medina's performance, each of the seven songs moved upward in pitch through the three sections, only to drop back to roughly the same pitch at the beginning of each new song. This observation leads me to conclude that the upward drift as a whole conveys involvement in the ritual, while individual rises correlate, at least in this case, with contrastive therapeutic desiderata ("starting up the song", "spanking the *hebu*", and "revealing the words of the *hebu*") and contrastive voices—that of the curer and his helping *hebu* versus that of the invading *hebu*.

The denotative content of the text

With respect to linguistically-coded elements, it does not require a great deal of ethnopoetic sophistication to see that *waiya, ee:aa:, ho,* and *hoi* demarcate sections within each song. These terms, along with the changes in rattling and pitch contour, demarcate the four sections, as shown in Figure 1. In the first section, 'starting up the song', the *wisidatu* addresses the specific *hebu* spirit that he hopes to extract from the child's body through this particular song. After beginning the curative process (line 1) and sending his helping spirits out of his chest (2–3), he refers to the place that this *hebu* has lodged itself in the patient (4–5), the nature of the current symptoms (6–7), and the possible effects of the disease (8).

Starting in line 9, the curer shifts the focus to himself. The line-final, postpositioned *iné* (I myself) is highly marked in an otherwise verb-final language (cf. Andrés Romero-Figueroa 1985). Mr. Medina proclaims his control over *kareko aurohi* (the fevers of the little rocks); note that all seven of the spirits he removed from the boy fall into this class. Mr. Medina asserts his knowledge of the spirits (9–10). Line 8 is crucial in this regard, since it demonstrates his awareness of the identity of the spirit he is attempting to remove, a spirit capable of causing strokes and mental derangement. Beginning in 11–12, Mr. Medina moves to direct manipulation of the *hebu*. These statements are metacommunicative in that they make explicit both the curer's power and the nature of his actions at that moment. In lines 18–19, Mr. Medina reveals the manner in which his helping spirits enable him to view the location of the *hebu* from inside the child's body.

As the first section comes to a close, the *hebu* is no longer wedged deeply into the child's head but is rather close to the surface. He accordingly turns in the second section to rendering the *hebu* weak and compliant by 'spanking' it. He again moves metacommunicatively from a stating his authority over *hebu* in general (22–23) to asserting that he is performing the action (24), making explicit the role of the helping spirits in this process (25). After again showing that he knows the identity of the afflicting spirit (27), Mr. Medina uses his breath (28) to remove it from the patient and place it in his rattle. *Hebu* generally inflict illness in order to express their anger at the entire community. Having been subdued by the *wisidatu*, the *hebu* now speaks to the curer through the medium of the latter's helping spirits and, one might add, the curer's voice. The *hebu*'s statement begins with a series of first-person pronouns (33), strong assertions of its presence and authority, followed by line-final, post-verbal first-person pronouns in each of the succeeding lines. This *hebu* is clearly going to make its voice heard!

As I noted above, the hebu recounts in Section 3 the way it entered the community and made its way into the child's body. After reiterating its malevolent 'will' (48–50), the *hebu* reveals its name—Waba Sinaka, 'the *Hebu* who Causes Strokes', thus confirming Mr. Medina's divination. Mr. Medina's own voice reemerges in the last 3 lines, asserting his status as a *wisidatu* and his success in removing the *hebu*.

The discourse shifts from sung to spoken after the transitional *hoi*'s and *ho*'s of lines 57–60. In 1–60, singing marks the discourse as an exchange between the curer, his helping spirits, and the *hebu*. While both the patient and a relative are present, neither of them is addressed by the song. Warao curers envision such musical discourse as a series of turns in a dialogue in which curer and *hebu* foreground their personal power and the nature of their 'will' or 'thoughts'. With the shift to spoken discourse, first the *hebu* and then the *wisidatu* engage the boy's father in dialogue.

In the spoken section (which is not transcribed), the *hebu* describes the events that induced him to attack the child. The *hebu* again moves the frame of reference to the *nahanamu* ceremony that took place ten days earlier. The *hebu* reports that it became angry because "they were eating the palm starch." As I noted above, sufficient palm starch must be collected in order to fill the *nahanamu* receptacle to overflowing. The two sponsors, the boy's grandfather and another *wisidatu* who heads a settlement 0.4 kilometers away, had collected an adequate supply. The quantity was initially diminished when the father-in-law of the latter curer secreted away about 25 percent of the supply while the two men were upriver. Since they still had just enough palm starch to begin the *nahanamu*, the two curers notified their relatives that the dancing was about to begin. People came in droves from nearby communities. Hungry for palm starch, they insisted that their hosts distribute half of the palm starch for consumption rather than wait for the conclusion of the ritual a month or two later. The guests promised to return and help collect more palm starch, but they failed to do so. As a result, the ritual receptacle was only half full at the time of the ceremony, and the three curers (the two sponsors and Mr. Medina) were unable to call the *kanobo* and other *hebu* spirits to come enjoy the dancing and the palm starch.[9] Hearing the music and seeing the people eat the palm starch that was intended for them, several of these *hebu* attacked the child as a means of expressing their anger.

Toward the end of the spoken dialogue, the curer reasserts his own voice, and the father follows along 'behind' him, in the Warao idiom for this type of dialogue, ordering the *hebu* to leave. Mr. Medina is in full control of the *hebu* at this point, having vanquished it, placed it in the rattle, and provided it with a voice to express its 'will'. He thus minces no words, using bald imperatives in ordering the *hebu* to depart. After telling the boy's father that he has cured the child, Mr. Medina uses his helping spirits in blowing away the *hebu*.

Parallelism and the curers' lexicon

The transcript reveals the importance of parallelism to the text. A host of different types of repetition create classic Jakobsonian (1960) relations of equation and contrast within frames at all levels of the performance. In some cases, the repetition consists of only a single word or grammatical element (as in the use of *boto* in lines 4 and 5). The minimal unit of parallelistic patterning here is the repetition of grammatical constructions, where a series of morphemes are repeated in order from one line to the next, as is apparent in lines 10–12:

		namina- 'know'		
hi- 'you'	*ahokʷa-* (marks for curers' lexicon)	*etura-* 'soften'	*-tu* agentive/singular[10] 'one who'	*-ine* 'I'
		ehebara- 'make let go'		

Here the *wisidatu* places himself in the role of agent and the *hebu* in that of patient (in the grammatical sense of the term); their relationship is established through the curer's actions ("knowing," "softening," "making let go"). The grammatical parallelism is accentuated by the use of the same melodic phrase and placement of stress on the final syllable.[11]

Moving to a more inclusive dimension of the formal organization of the performance, parallelism emerges in the patterning of song sections, the units bounded by two sets of vocables. The *wisidatu* generally moves from asserting his power to performing particular actions (as in 10–12) to stating explicitly that he is doing so (13–19). In the first section, this shift is marked grammatically by a movement from the use of the suffix *-tu* (agentive, 'the one who' performs a particular action) to *-ne* (gerundive, indicating that the action is being performed).

Parallelistic relations between sections of the same song are also crucial. Sections 1 and 2 are grammatically parallel, consisting of assertions by the curer of his power over the *hebu,* followed by declarations that he is exercising that power. Section 3 maintains the line-final first-person pronouns and thus the self-assertions of agency. These lines contrast, however, by virtue of the nearly consistent use of the past non-durative at the beginning of lines—*tuaturuaené* ('wanted to throw him') (38), *miaené* ('saw') (39, 40) *abanaené* ('put') (41), etc. This grammatical form places the *hebu*'s agentive power squarely in the past, having been surrendered earlier in the song. The absence of second person prefixes (*hi-*) in Section 3 similarly suggests that the *hebu* has abandoned its combative and oppositional relationship to the curer. The grammatical parallelism between all three sections draws the *hebu*'s voice into the same discursive arena as the *wisidatu.*

Parallelism is also evident in the repetition of form, content, and function of all seven songs. Tapping the parallelistic power of both equation and contrast, the songs differ fundamentally only in details, but these differences—particularly the name of the *hebu*—are crucial.[12] The movement in each from "starting up the song" to "spanking the *hebu*" to making the *hebu* "reveal its words" provides a reassuring indication that the performance is likely to be successful. Each performance is also related to other performances by the same *wisidatu* through the repetition of essentially the same songs and movements. Like the other types of parallelisms, this broadest level helps provides a strong sense of familiarity for patients and their relatives in the face of an incomprehensible illness. Parallelism occasionally fails due to the curer's inability to identity the *hebu* or to force it to leave the patient's body. Thus, if the *hebu's* voice does not emerge at all, the lack of parallelism signals the failure of the curing performance, and another *wisidatu* will be sought.[13] This equation between multi-layered parallelism and the therapeutic efficacy of curing performances is evident in other types of Warao curing as well (see Briggs 1994).

A crucial feature of the text is that it consists largely of *nobahatu aribu* (the curers' lexicon), which is largely incomprehensible to the patient. The resulting difficulty in interpreting the text is exacerbated by its grammatical complexity. These factors create a profound difference in the experience of the curer and the non-specialist participants. While the referential function of language—the use of semantic content in creating meaning—plays a central role for the *wisidatu* (and, reportedly, for the *hebu*), the boy and his father are excluded from this dimension of the performance.

Why use the curers' lexicon? Practitioners assert that it is the only language that *hebu* understand and thus that will be efficacious in expelling them. Nonetheless, *wisimo* freely admit that *hebu* have no aversion to the use of "everyday" Warao words alongside the curers' lexicon. Some words are indeed based on "everyday" verb and noun stems, although they are grammatically more complex than usual. For example, *himonituma* (your afflictions) (8), *kareko* (quartz crystals) (9), and some whole lines, such as *tatuka abané mamohorabu abané* (I am immediately grabbing you with my hands) (13), are intelligible to both child and father. Clearly, the verb-final *iné,* (I) is unmistakable. The degree to which the semantic content is transparent to noninitiates jumps markedly with the transition from music to speech. While the curers' lexicon is still used (e.g., *yawaramutu yere-banaha,* [because they were eating the palm starch]), more of the dialogue emerges in "everyday" Warao, and some lines are restated in "everyday" Warao.

In other words, just as curers use their specialized lexicon in producing unin-telligibility, they can increase the semantic accessibility of the text to the boy and his father *when they choose to do so.* This should provide a warning against simply accepting eufunctional explanations of the use of curers' lexicon, either of the sort offered by Warao curers or as adopted by many students of curing perfor-mances. The analysis often centers on asking what role each ritual element plays in effecting a cure. Such an approach oversimplifies our understanding of curing performances and naturalizes the techniques that practitioners uses in attempting to establish the authority of their practices. To return to the example of Lévi-

Strauss's (1963[1949]) analysis of the Kuna birth chant, neither Warao nor Kuna curers single-mindedly attempt to render their patients' experience intelligible, but rather they manipulate the borderline between intelligibility and opacity. This facet of curing performances should accordingly sensitize us to the need to examine the way that curing practices produce social power just as they generate spiritual power and curative effects. (More later on this point.)

METAPRAGMATIC DIMENSIONS OF WARAO CURING

I thus turn now to the issues of intelligibility and power. If patients are unable to understand most of what is sung and said, what sort of awareness do they have of what is taking place in the course of the performance? How do such constraints on intelligibility shape their position within the curing process?

This question brings us face to face with issues of discursive reflexivity—the ways that metadiscursive practices use music, gesture, movement, and other signaling modes in shaping the production and reception of discourse. Our understanding of this facet of human conduct has been greatly expanded by Bateson's (1972[1955]) work on metacommunication, Goffman's (1974, 1981) concepts of "framing" and "footing," work by philosophers of language and students of pragmatics on presupposition, entailment, and inference (cf. Grice 1975, 1989; Gumperz 1981; Levinson 1983; Strawson 1952), and Gumperz (1982) on contextualization cues. The emphasis that Jakobson (1957, 1960) and his Russian and Prague School colleagues placed on the multiple functions of signs, the array of socially-defined effects that they achieved through situated use, is also crucial.

For the purposes of this analysis, I would like to draw specifically on a distinction introduced by Silverstein (1976, 1993) that facilitates the recognition of subtle yet important differences in types of reflexivity in discourse. The way language is patterned by the use of signs in context is generally referred to as pragmatics. Studying pragmatics involves expanding notions of language to include indexical as well as symbolic or semantic signs. Indexes are established in particular events of speaking or writing, and they link words or other linguistic forms to elements of the interactional and linguistic context. Interpreting use of the indexes *now* or *here*, for example, involves more than familiarity with semantic definitions, such as one finds in dictionaries; knowing such contextual facts as when and where they were uttered is crucial. Silverstein uses the term metapragmatics to draw our attention to language forms that structure both pragmatics as well as our awareness of pragmatic phenomena. He defines metapragmatic signs in terms of their objects of representation, arguing that they "have pragmatic phenomena—indexical sign phenomena—as their semiotic objects; they thus have an inherently 'framing,' 'regimenting,' or 'stipulative' character with respect to indexical phenomena" (1993:33).

Silverstein's distinction between "degrees and kinds of metapragmatic explicitness," the extent to which the significance of a particular metapragmatic sign is based on the referential function of language, can provide a useful tool for exploring differences between the types of metapragmatic awareness enjoyed by *wisimo* as opposed to patients and their relatives in curing performances. *Denotatively explicit* metapragmatic signs are tied to some discourse element by virtue of their semantic content. *Denotatively implicit* metapragmatic signs, on the other hand, designate some discursive element apart from their semantic content—if they possess semantic content at all. In other words, a denotatively explicit form tells you directly what it is doing; grasping the role of denotatively implicit forms involves picking up on such features as intonation, speech style, poetic patterning, and the like.

To give an example, let us consider two ways of breaking off a relationship. Saying "We're through, you bastard—I never want to see you again!" would constitute a denotatively-explicit approach, while being "cold"—adopting verbal, intonational, proxemic, and gestural features that indicate affective distance—without ever speaking directly about the relationship would form a denotatively-implicit strategy. Friedrich's (1972) well-known analysis of Tolstoy's use of shifts between "formal" and "familiar" second-person pronouns in Russian to indicate changes in affect provides an example of an excruciatingly effective implicit metapragmatic sign.

Bearing this distinction in mind, let us return to Mr. Medina's curing song. The metapragmatic character of the vocables becomes clearer through comparison with what Goffman (1981[1978]) refers to as *response cries*—"exclamatory interjections which are not full-fledged words," such as "Whoops!" or "Ouch!" Goffman argues that the power of such sounds lies in their two-fold nature. As "natural" expressions, that is, as automatic and quasi-involuntary reflections of a presumably ongoing internal state, they enable listeners to monitor what is taking place *inside the speaker*. On the other hand, response cries reflect what Sacks referred to as "recipient design," meaning that the selection of a response cry and how it is uttered are shaped by the identity and state of *the listener*. The use of response cries indexes (that is, designates contextually rather than semantically) parameters of the social situation as a whole. For example, we often avoid using taboo words in response to a sharp pain when in the presence of individuals who would be offended by such speech.

In Native American songs and stories, speakers often use onomatopoeia and other types of sounds in conveying the "natural expressions" of non-human characters. Hymes (1979), Langdon (1978), and others have pointed to the use of particular onomatopoetic sounds and systematic phonological substitutions in quoting animal characters. Basso (1985:67) suggests such forms do not simply reproduce the characters' sounds, but indicates the narrator's knowledge of "some quality of their essence, what they do, or what happens to them when acted upon." Reproducing such characteristic sounds is often seen as demonstrating the ability to control that being. Note that the vocables used by *wisimo* differ in their precise phonological shape and voice timbre, the order in which they are uttered, or the frequency of particular vocables. The individuality of the vocables emitted by a particular *wisidatu* points to the basis of his power in intimate relations with particular spirits rather than simply general knowledge regarding spirits.

As I noted above, vocables are treated distinctly from other parts of the song text. Curers refer to vocables as *koita* (non-speech sounds), a category which also includes animal calls and snores. Their distinctiveness from words (*dibu*) becomes evident when using the standard Warao elicitation device, *Katukane waraya?* (What does it mean?) in attempting to obtain a referential gloss. The response is inevitably *Ekida!* (Nothing!). Warao are clearly aware that such expressions lack denotative content, do not pattern grammatically like other words and morphemes, and are only meaningful when uttered in context—that is, when spirits are entering or exiting the larynx of a *wisidatu*.

Taken together, these points indicate how "meaningless" sounds can be quite meaningful. By indicating the movement of helping spirits through the larynx of the curer, vocables constitute implicit metapragmatic signs that point reflexively to the nature of the complex process that is taking place. They direct attention to the curer's body, metonymically represented by his throat, as a locus of action that is being used simultaneously by a variety of agents. Vocables indicate to the boy and his father that the helping spirits are assisting the *wisidatu* in effecting a cure. Since *hebu* and *kareko* are important elements of Warao conceptions of the universe, the role of vocables as an auditory trail draws attention to the status of the curer's body as a small-scale icon of the spiritual cosmos, as well as of the curing process itself.

Nevertheless, vocables hardly constitute the *only* metapragmatic signs of the progression of the therapeutic process that are intelligible to the patient and his father. The other features that I analyzed above—the rhythmic contours of the rattling, the curer's movements and gestures, musical patterning of the singing, and the poetic patterning of the songs and spoken dialogues—are accessible to lay persons, and these features also function as implicit metapragmatic signs.

Like the curer himself, the rattle is comprised of a number of distinct beings, each having physical and spiritual counterparts. Like the curer's breath and body, the rattle provides a home base for both the *kareko* spirits that ordinarily reside in the rattle and malevolent *hebu* spirits. Just as the use of vocables provide a running gauge of the movement of spirits into and out of the curer's body, the rhythm of the rattle provides a guide to the movements of spirits into, out of, and within the rattle. The rapid beat of the rattle signals an attempt on the part of the curer and his helping spirits to move a *hebu* from one location to another; the vigorous thrusts in a straight line signal its departure. Beyond their specific effects, the rhythmic patterning of the rattling as a whole provides a running monitor of the nature of the curer's actions at each point in time vis-à-vis categories of therapeutic action and song structure ("spanking the *hebu*," "revealing the words of the *hebu*," and so forth).

Use of the rattle is associated not only with the production of sound but with movement of the curer's body and arms. The changing locus of the therapeutic action is signaled by the curer's movement from a seated position away from the patient to a standing or crouching position just above the patient's body. As the child sees and, at times, feels these changes in the position of the curer's body and the rattle vis-à-vis his own body, he gains a stronger sense of the progression of the performance and the extraction of malevolent spirits than would be obtained through details of linguistic and textual patterning alone.

The melodic contours and the alternation between sung and spoken discourse similarly provide indexes of the progression of the ritual. The movement from the rise-glissando pattern to level pitch contours indicates a switch from the control of the *wisidatu*'s larynx by the curer and his helping spirits to its usurpation by the *hebu* spirit. The upward drift in pitch indicates the linear progression of song sections and the growing intensity of the curer's engagement as the song progresses, that is, as he moves toward expelling each *hebu*. The transition from sung to spoken discourse is a powerful metapragmatic sign—it indicates an overall shift in the roles that the curer and the boy's father play in the performance as the father moves from purely receptive involvement to sharing responsibility with the *wisidatu*, and the *hebu*, for producing the discourse.

All of the preceding elements—vocables, rattle rhythms, melodic contours, and the alternation of singing and speaking—lack denotative content. What is the role of verbally-coded speech? The referential content of the curers' terms is highly metapragmatic—the *wisidatu* and, to a lesser extent, the invading *hebu*, provide a virtually blow-by-blow characterization of the actions that are being effected at each step. The semantic content of these terms explicitly labels the identity and power of the singer as he declares that he is a curer, a person who knows as well as asserts his control over and ability to extract *hebu*. The denotative content of the songs also plays an explicitly metapragmatic role in connecting the curing performance with the preceding *nahanamu* ritual. This relationship is intertextual, in Kristeva's terms (1980; Todorov 1984); it links the two ritual performances in such a way as to provide a new reading of the *nahanamu*—from a *hebu*-centric perspective—as well as to explain what is taking place in the curing ritual.

If these explicitly metapragmatic terms are expressed in a curers' lexicon that is unintelligible to lay persons, however, what sense can the boy and his father derive from the text? The musical features indicate when the *hebu* is singing a particular stretch of text. Patients say that hearing the voice of the *hebu* is both terrifying and reassuring, since it is at this point that they come face to face—or perhaps voice to ear—with the force that has invaded their bodies. The *hebu*'s voice provides tangible proof that it is now under the control of the *wisidatu* and will soon be on its way. While this operation proceeds in a nuanced manner for the curer through the accumulation of the exoteric meanings of its terms, the power/knowledge of curers is indicated for noninitiates in a global fashion by its very unintelligibility. They are constantly reminded that the *wisidatu* possesses knowledge of and power over realms about which they are almost completely ignorant.

CONSTRUCTING SUBJECTS AND OBJECTS

Why is there such a pervasive contrast between explicit and implicit metapragmatic dimensions of Warao curing? Taking up this question entails addressing two of the issues invoked by the title of the paper—the nature of nonsense in a poetics of the body. While trying to figure out what was taking place in this performance, I spent several days with Mr. Medina and my two closest friends in the community, Mr. Torres and Mr. Alvarez, puzzling over its many facets. Mr. Medina participated late each afternoon, but he spent the earlier part of the day in the forest. I used a "boom-box" type tape recorder so that everyone in the house could hear. While transcribing, I recorded the curers' comments. I then went back through the text and elicited a translation into "everyday Warao." A third run through the material focused on the global patterning of the performance. Having gained a great deal of information on non-linguistic signals (musical patterns, rattle rhythms, body movement, and the like) during the previous steps, here I asked systematically about what Jakobson (1959) refers to as the intersemiotic relations between communicative channels. Both at this stage and in two subsequent passes through the tape, transcription, and exegesis, I asked for information regarding precisely what was taking place between the *wisidatu*, his helping spirits, the *hebu*, the quartz crystals, the patient, and, where relevant, the father. I also worked with Mr. Rivera—the father—and other individuals who are not *wisimo*.

This process revealed the tremendous difference between the information yielded by the implicit and explicit metapragmatic frameworks—even for individuals who had access to both. When assessments of what was taking place in the performance were based on denotative meaning, the *wisimo* gave me very precise and clear answers that they regarded as authoritative. These responses were based on inventories of what Austin (1962) refers to as "explicit primary performatives." In such constructions, the semantic content of the lexemes signals the illocutionary status of the action(s) performed—for example, "I promise to come on time." Here the dictionary-definition type meaning tells precisely what the curer is trying to do. When denotatively explicit forms were absent, the curers found it difficult to break phrases down into their component terms or to provide decontextualized interpretations of their function—that is, statements about what each element generally means or what effect it achieves. In reference to such elements, questions like "What's this?" or "What does this do?" seemed nonsensical and occasionally annoying.

What conclusions are we to draw from this difference? One could suggest that referential meaning is what really matters after all, and that the non-referential forms are simply aspects of the "staging" of the performance. Perhaps Saussure (1959[1916]) was right all along in suggesting that denotative sense constitutes linguistic meaning. Maybe Austin was on target in arguing that "primary explicit performatives" provide the model for "doing things with words." Clearly, these views reflect the privileging of sense—of denotative meaning—that has formed the core of dominant ideologies of language in the West at least since John Locke (1959[1690]) decreed that sense relations constitute the only dimension of language that is compatible with a scientific perspective. To point out the shortcomings of such a view of ritual discourse, I will draw on a distinction drawn by Kristeva (1984[1974]) in arguing that different ways of gaining awareness of what is happening in the performance—the two metapragmatic modes—are tied to contrastive ways of constituting the self. I will also argue that the tendency among students of ritual speech to collapse the distinction between denotatively- and non-denotatively-based modalities is tied to privileging the production of "meaning" over the constitution of social power.

Kristeva's two modes of textual production and reception

Kristeva distinguishes two contrastive ways in which texts function, which she refers to as *genotext* and *phenotext*. The genotext embodies what she terms *semiotic process*, a particular relationship between signifier, signified, and interpreting subject. In semiotic processes, the emphasis is not on what the signifier denotes, and the meaning does not emerge from one-to-one relationships between signifiers and signifieds. Many of the signs that comprise the genotext, which embodies the semiotic process, have no referential content; Goffman's response cries ("Ouch!") provide a case in point. The signified may also be related to the signifier through a contextual configuration, in which case the sign falls into the Peircean (1932) category of indexicality.

Crucially, the signifier also stands for the interpreting subject; subjects thus do not exist apart from signs, merely using them as tools to realize particular effects. It is rather the subject, the producer and receiver of signs, that is in focus. Response cries again provide an excellent example here: "Ouch!" and "Whoops!" do not denote an external element of reality, but rather draw our attention to the person who utters them. In the genotext, the subject does not enter into the semiotic process with a clearly defined identity that is shaped prior to and independent of the discourse. The subject is rather emergent in what Bauman and I refer to as *entextualization,* the process of shaping discourse into patterned and bounded text (see Bauman and Briggs 1990). Through the entextualization process, the self is constituted through its relationship with a complex array of signifiers. Crucially, the genotext draws heavily on those modes of signification, such as prosody and gesture, that are ordered into gradient distinctions along continua rather than clearly defined binary and discrete categories, such as phonemic or semantic units. The genotext thus focuses on just those signs that have so often defied linguistic analysis.

The phenotext, on the other hand, embodies what Kristeva calls *symbolic process.* The symbolic mode draws on the aspects of linguistic signaling that are more easily encompassed by linguistic theory. The phenotext is thus symbolic, in Peirce's as well as in Kristeva's sense of the term, involving shared and relatively context-free pairings of signifiers and signifieds. Here the emphasis is on the *signified,* and the signifier fulfills its traditional status as a formal means of conveying denotative content. Crucially, the signifier bears no direct relationship to the interpreting subject in the phenotext; the subject is rather shaped prior to the act of communication. The subject is either simply presupposed by the act of entextualization or is objectified as the signified (in self-reference). The language of scientific description aims at being quintessentially phenotextual, providing information about the real world through the use of terms with fixed, bounded meanings; this mode of signification attempts to render the identity of the speaker/writer and the context of utterance irrelevant.

The facets of *wisidatu* curing identified with implicit pragmatics—rattle rhythms, musical characteristics, movement, and vocables—are quintessential genotextual features. They lack denotative content, and they are not susceptible to glossing procedures that presuppose fixed, conventional, and context-free relations between signifiers and signifieds. They are the features by which the curer constitutes himself as a *wisidatu* and reestablishes his connection with the world of *hebu* each time he sings. This is not to say that the genotext moves from psychological and communicative indeterminacy to clarity and delineation. Through the operation of these genotextual features, the boundaries of the curer's self becomes far from coterminous with his skin. The "self" that signifies includes the helping spirits and the *hebu* as well; the auditory stream that emerges from the curer's body is a complex, constantly shifting construct, and its physical locus periodically shifts from the curer's chest, through his larynx, along the path formed by his breath, and into the rattle and the child—and then back again.

These signals are not segmentable since, unlike lexical and morphological units, we cannot cut up the stream of sound into distinct units and identify a particular set of meanings they convey. Rattle rhythms, musical patterning, and vocables are, rather, fused, and their functions become largely coterminous at a metapragmatic level. Moreover, these signifiers cannot be segmented from the "subject" who is producing them. They do not simply "represent" the *wisidatu*— they *are* him, at least with respect to his status as a spiritually engaged and powerful being. Nor is it easy to determine who is producing sound at any given point, since the sound is generated by the ever shifting corporeal interaction between the curer, his helping spirits, quartz crystals, and the *hebu*. The relative ambiguity regarding who is producing genotextual features reflects the lack of clear boundaries between these agents; in the genotext, these beings constitute themselves and each other in the course of a fluid interaction between overlapping subjectivities in the absence of distinct objects and addressees.

The richness of these features in providing an implicit metapragmatics is hardly coincidental: since these sounds and movements *are* the audible manifestation of invisible interactions, they provide the perfect index of this process. The *wisidatu* is thus not fully in control of the genotext. His own self is being produced in the process, and its shape is affected by the participation of the helping spirits, over which he exercises only partial control, and the *hebu,* beings that harbor malevolent intentions and with which the curer is engaged in an antagonistic and competitive relationship. The *wisidatu* is thus positioned *within* a genotext that is constituting his existence as a spiritually powerful being; he does not stand outside a process that is unfolding wholly in keeping with his directives.

The phenotext, on the other hand, is quintessentially embodied in the linguistic phrases that are expressed, primarily, in the curers' lexicon. This facet of the curing song is grammatically organized, and curers can provide morpheme-by-morpheme glosses of its denotative content. While the curer, his helping spirits, the quartz crystals, and the invading *hebu* participate in the process of forming subjectivities in the genotext, only the *wisidatu* and the *hebu* emerge at the phenotextual level. Here they enter the discourse as distinct and bounded identities that are fully constituted prior to the beginning of the performance. Highly marked line-final first-person pronouns (*iné*, 'I myself') draw attention to their assertions of identity. In the phenotext, subjecthood emerges in relationships between agents (the ones who effect actions) and patients (the recipients of those actions).[14] A number of grammatical features emphasize the agent-patient, asserting marked inequality in terms of agency and power.

While the genotext does not designate addressers or addressees, the phenotext regulates in explicit terms how parties enter the discourse. In the phenotextual dimension of the song, the grammatical structure defines the exchange of speaker and addressee roles between curer and *hebu*. The resulting exclusion of the patient and his father is inscribed into the song at an even more fundamental level by the unfolding of the phenotext in a lexicon that is unintelligible to noninitiates. Even a general idea of the semantic content of the song is of little use in deciphering the phenotext due to its reliance on subtle details of denotative meaning and grammatical patterning. Power and agency are thus encoded in the phenotext both at the level of particular syntactic and semantic features as well in the fact that the noninitiates are denied access to this domain.

BETWEEN GENOTEXT AND PHENOTEXT: GRAMMATICAL PARALLELISM

The preceding analysis provides a warning against conflating those elements of the performance that are denotatively coded and those that lack denotative content. Vocal and instrumental musical patterning, movement, the use of material objects, vocables, and such elements do not function here as means of disambiguating the semantic messages encoded in the text—they rather constitute a distinct mode of discourse production and reception. This distinction seems particularly important when the performance draws heavily on an esoteric lexicon, a common situation in ritual speech. Denotatively explicit and implicit metapragmatics produce different types of information, highly contrastive roles for participants, and distinct subject/object relations. One might ask how such sharply differentiated processes coexist from moment to moment in the same performance. Is there nothing shared between them? I believe that what we might call, with apologies to Jakobson (1981[1968]), the grammar of ritual performance and the ritual performance of grammar, provides just such a bridge.

Although curing songs invoke an esoteric lexicon, they use the same grammar as "everyday" Warao. Tacit knowledge of Warao grammar thus enables noninitiates to segment the linguistic stream and to discern syntagmatic and paradigmatic relations between units. With regard to the example of grammatical parallelism in lines 10–12, noninitiates are able to distinguish the five grammatically defined, paradigmatic "slots" into which particular morphemes (constituents of words) can be inserted. Non-specialists can also decipher the denotative content of the prefix (*hi-*, 'you'), the agentive suffix (*-tu*), and the final first person pronoun (*-iné*, 'I'). While some of the verb stems (such as *namina-*, 'know') are drawn from "everyday" Warao, use of the esoteric ritual prefix *aho-kʷa-* and a special sense of the term 'know' render the meaning of the stem more opaque. Thus, while the meaning of the line as a whole is unintelligible to the patient and his father, they are quite able to grasp the grammatical patterning—particularly since it is repeated in several lines. For noninitiates, the grammatical parallelism of curing songs comes close to what Saussure (1959[1916]) described as a system of "pure differences," a *langue* in which all that is relevant is that particular terms have contrastive meanings and not what those meanings might be. For curers, however, these relations are not purely differential but signify specific denotative features (see Benveniste 1971[1966]; Jakobson 1984). Denotative content plays a crucial role in the process of 'naming', 'softening', extracting the *hebu,* and getting it to say its piece, as it were. Thus, while parallelism provides curers with the framework used in building the semantics of curing and structuring how the therapeutic process will take place, it provides patients and their relatives with a means of knowing that progress is being made.

The role of parallelism in linking genotext and phenotext emerges as well from its close connection with the musical patterning of the song, as well as vocables and the curer's movements. As is apparent in Figure 2, melodic contours and rattle rhythms are contrastive in each section, thus paralleling the grammatical and semantic differences between sections; changes in the physical proximity of the curer and patient and the use of vocables also mark the transition between sections. All of these features join with grammatical parallelism in creating patterns of repetition that link each successive song in one performance and successive performances of curing songs.

For curers and spirits, all of these dimensions of the performance constitute what Peirce (1932) terms a diagram, a structural isomorphism between their respective patterns; the linear structure of the performance, including its succession of therapeutic actions, is thus mapped out not only by each of the individual semiotic modes but by their overall relationship as well. Since the curer can connect this diagram with the denotative content of words in curers' lexicon ('naming', 'grabbing', and so forth), explicit and implicit means of gaining awareness into and shaping the performance intersect for him. It is precisely this union of genotext and phenotext that is seen as generating the power needed to extract the *hebu* and effect a cure. In the case of the patient and his father, grammatical parallelism is not linked to the denotative content of the text, and a wide hiatus thus remains between genotext and phenotext.

Nonetheless, implicit and explicit metapragmatics do move much closer together for the father in Section 4. This dialogue moves from primary reliance on the curers' lexicon to limited use of "everyday" Warao. The father initially enters into the dialogue hesitantly, intermittently responding by simply repeating the *hebu*'s words. After the *hebu* has revealed the cause of his anger in "everyday" Warao—the premature consumption of palm starch during the *nahanamu* ritual cycle—the father moves to a truly dialogic engagement in the guise of commanding the *hebu* to depart from the community and leave his child in peace. While the father thus enters the dialogue through the implicit metapragmatic features that have provided him with access all along, the *hebu* provides just enough denotative content to enable the father to participate in the performance via explicit metapragmatics. This participation does not provide the sort of retrospective reflexivity that would enable the father to understand what has taken place in the earlier sections of the song; it rather enables him to grasp the *hebu*'s (and, we might guess, the curer's) view of the social conflict that is being cited as the cause of the illness.

CONCLUSION

Mr. Medina's performance clearly demonstrates the complexity of the issues of convergence between semiotic modalities and the role of semantics in curing. I would thus like to suggest that they can add significantly to our understanding of the general issues regarding the nature of ritual speech that I raised toward the beginning of this paper. Bloch (1974), McDowell (1983), Tambiah (1981), and others have argued that the "formal elaboration" of ritual discourse, as reflected in poetic elaboration, textual fixity, and intensive use of multiple semiotic modalities decreases the importance of semantic content.[15] The data on *hebu* curing, however, suggest that semantic content can continue to play a crucial role in ritual speech even when poetic, musical (instrumental and vocal), gestural elements are highly elaborated. 'Naming' the *hebu,* asserting the superior agency needed to extract it, and finding out what led it to attack the victim are all vital steps in effecting a cure. Denotative content plays a crucial role in each. Received statements regarding the marginalization of semantic content *do* seem to apply in the case of the patient and other non-specialists. As I have argued, their participation in the performance depends almost entirely on non-denotational elements.

Tambiah (1981) and other observers also stress the fusion of separate signaling media in ritual speech. The data I have examined suggest that dimensions which do not rely on denotative content are indeed integrated to a remarkable degree. They collectively form what I have termed, following Kristeva, a genotext, and they fit tightly together in providing an implicit means of shaping the therapeutic process, and understanding what is taking place. The individual components of the genotext would be ritually and metapragmatically ineffective if used in isolation from one another or from the performance as a whole. The explicit awareness that emerges from denotative content, on the other hand, is clearly set apart from this process of fusion. Not only is it patterned quite differently from the genotextual features, both in terms of its formal structure and functional role, but it affords a vastly different means of shaping the performance and grasping its progression. The nature and power of *wisidatu* curing is based on maintaining the distinctiveness of these two ways of constructing the performance rather than on their fusion. It is this gap—and the exclusion of non-specialists from production and reception of the phenotext—that enables *wisimo* to generate social power through curing.

Warao healing performances also point out the need to rethink a common association between denotative content and conscious accessibility on the one hand, and non-denotative elements and unconscious or subconscious processes on the other. In a fertile paper, Silverstein (1981) suggests that linguistic features which possess denotative content can be broken down into discrete grammatical categories, and presuppose parameters of the social and linguistic context (rather than creating aspects of the context themselves) are most likely to fall within the "limits of awareness" of speakers. I have shown that forms which meet these three criteria are accessible in special ways to curers, particularly as revealed in their ability to gloss forms and to explicate their role in the curing performance. Since such features as melodic patterns, rattle rhythms, vocables, and movements do not engender this type of awareness, it would be easy to place them outside of the limits of awareness. We could draw in this connection on Jakobson's (1981[1970]) assertion that the complex types of formal patterning evident in poetic texts operate beyond the conscious awareness of author and audience, constituting a type of "subliminal verbal patterning." We could similarly follow Sapir's (1949[1935]) association of "referential symbolism" with conscious elaboration and "condensation symbolism" with "the unconscious spread of emotional quality."

I have chosen to avoid these interpretive routes for a number of reasons. First, by denying that "native speakers" or "members of society in the course of their daily lives" possess an interpretive hold on what they say and do, scholars create interpretive and textual hierarchies that place scholarly discourse on a higher plane in the economy of interpretation and truth-telling than can be achieved by the discourse they analyze. These rhetorical strategies thus provide ready techniques for reserving textual authority for scholars.

Second, formulations that locate these types of textual features in residual categories ("the unconscious," "subliminal patterning," etc.) seem to deny that features which are not coded denotatively provide participants with insight into what is being said and done. I have shown that semantically nonsensical aspects of ritual speech operate metapragmatically as well, constituting both ways of saying and doing *and* ways of knowing what is being said and done, and of attempting to shape its social and discursive effects.

Third, the models of consciousness, subjectivity, agency and the like that are presupposed by these approaches generally remain fuzzy, implicit, and highly undertheorized. Moreover, they are often based on reductionistic assumptions which suggest that only discursive processes (and probably types of social action in general) that can be expressed explicitly—that is, broken down analytically and paraphrased In denotatively-explicit terms—build awareness of discursive properties and processes. The result is not only to privilege denotation, but also to assume that genuine reflexivity is predicated on the central role of individual subjects who enter the scene fully formed and clearly defined and who shape but are not shaped by the discourse; a notion that has come under increasing attack in post-structuralist literary scholarship and other fields.

A fourth problem relates to the way these models place meaning and reflexivity squarely in individual, self-contained isolated minds and/or in simple dyadic relations. I have argued that the genotext emerges in an interaction between an array of different selves which are being shaped in the performance. Characterizing such discourse features as components of a communicative act that originates in one mind and is "expressed" for the benefit of someone else, as assumed by Saussure's (1959[1916]:11–12) model of the "speech circuit" or Jakobson's (1960) outline of the components and functions of the communicative event, is thus highly problematic. I would argue that this view of discourse grossly distorts the nature of the features that make up the genotext, even if we argue that the "addressees" are spirits. Such models similarly fail in the case of discourse reception—as they listen to the performance, the child and his father participate actively in the construction of subjectivity and performativity, and the boundaries between the interpreting self and interpreted others are open and fluid. Note that the distinction between discourse "production" and "reception" is problematic in the case of the genotext in curing performances; when spirits speak through the larynx of the curer, these two facets are difficult to distinguish and even harder to assign to particular participants.

Fifth, an equally problematic assumption suggests that speakers must be capable of decontextualizing their understanding of a particular body of discourse from that discourse itself as well as the social and historical conditions in which it was produced; they must additionally be able to recontextualize it in a vastly different discursive setting. For linguists, anthropologists, sociologists, psychologists, and many other practitioners, this generally means that "informants" or "subjects" must be capable of recontextualizing such reflexive awareness in the form of answers to the investigator's questions in order to be accepted as genuine (see Briggs 1986). While curers are quite capable of performing this operation for explicit metapragmatics, this procedure works very poorly for implicit metapragmatics.

A final assumption, which has been criticized by Foucault (1972[1969]), seems to suggest that the production of "meaning" and its accurate decoding form the focus of both the discourse itself as well as the process of studying it. I have suggested, rather, that the production of supernatural and social power is constitutive of curing performances and that such power is generated, in part, by *withholding* denotative meaning from some of the participants. As Foucault (1973[1963]) has argued for Western medicine and Taussig (1987) for South American "shamanism," curing is not just "about" making people well—it also forms a crucial means of (re)producing relations of power. Taussig has explicitly addressed this question in his analysis of the Kuna birth chant. Drawing on a different analytic perspective, he nonetheless seems to reach the same conclusion that I have suggested in my analysis of Mr. Medina's performance: "This is where we must differ with the great classical tradition yearning for harmony, narrative closure, and structural integrity, that recurring Western tradition which would 'explain' the magic of healing rite as bound to the restoration of balance and the resolution of contradiction" (1993:25–26). Native American curing performances seem to be as productive of "meaningless" elements, communicative indeterminacy, and incomprehension as they are of meaning, communicative order, comprehensibility, and cognitive coherence. The need to know who is doing exactly what to whom where and why at each and every point and what it "means" thus seems to be more closely tied to the way that Western metadiscursive practices derive their authority by positing hidden dimensions of order and meaning and proceeding to find (read "construct") them than the nature of the metadiscursive practices they attempt to "explain."

My invocation of Foucault in this context may seem a bit strange. He called, after all, for analyses that focus on "relations of power, not relations of meaning" (1980[1972]:114). I have indeed been deeply interest in questions of language, as well as of music and of movement. Those *bêtes noires* decried by Foucault as well as by Derrida (1974[1967], 1977)—"meaning" and "communication"— have indeed played a role in my analysis as I have attempted to discern what Mr. Medina's song might "mean" to the various participants and what it might "communicate." As I have spelled out in the preceding paragraphs, however, my analysis does not rest on a semiotic or linguistic eufunctionalism. I do not simply assume that producing "meaning" or creating "communication," whether it might link individual to individual, mind to body, or human to spirits, is what the performance is all about, nor do I then go about the functionalist enterprise of seeing how what is said, sung, and done serves these ends. I would follow Foucault in arguing that strategies for the creation of relations of power play a crucial role in *wisidatu* curing. I am, however, no less skeptical of the sort of eufunctionalism which would suggest that each element of the performance is constituted by its status as a strategic means of realizing the end of generating power. I have rather attempted to show how contrastive facets of the performance are associated with quite different modes of creating subjectivity and agency. "Power" similarly assumes different forms and different degrees of importance when viewed from different perspectives on what took place. We would not want to follow Foucault in seeing hegemonic or dominant discourses as necessarily more normative, ordered, and non-contradictory than the discourses they seek to control or displace (see Taussig 1992:48).

With respect to the genotext, Mr. Medina is clearly in control in the sense that he is singing the song that sets the curative process in motion; the complex inter-action of invisible participants similarly takes place in his body. Nevertheless, power in this sphere is not constituted as a zero-sum game in which the agentive control of one party (the curer) rules out or diminishes the control of others (the spirits, the boy, or his father). Clearly, Mr. Medina attempts to determine the trajectory (getting rid of the spirits). While he provides an auditory and physical space for the participation of spirits, the sounds that emerge reflect the 'will' of these spirits. While he attempts to determine the character of their participation, *wisidatu* often fail in such attempts. In a narrative collected by Roth (1915: 336–38) regarding the first *wisidatu,* the *hebu* assert that *wisimo* will be able to cure some—but not all—of their patients. Since the production of sound and the movement of spirits is a complex process that is not fully under the control of the practitioner, indeterminacy remains; even the most experienced and success-ful practitioners face a sense of angst each time they begin to treat a patient, knowing that they may well fail. In the genotext, questions of power and agency are not foregrounded. Even after the performance had ended, the outcome had been determined, and we had listened several times to the recording, genotextual features never permitted Mr. Medina or other *wisimo* to calculate how much control accrues to each participant at any one point in time. When it comes to the phenotext, however, questions of power and agency are precisely what is in question. The relative claims of *wisimo* and *hebu* to determining the fate of human bodies is explicitly constituted as a zero-sum game in which the curer must render the *hebu* powerless by asserting his own power. As I noted above, the exclusion of non-specialists from the phenotext creates a crucial power differential in performances.

One of the most problematic aspects of the use of communicative, semiotic, discourse-based, and similar approaches in the study of ritual speech is a tendency towards adopting a synchronic bias and viewing the contextualization of discourse in rather narrow terms. Investigations of curing often construe performances as if they were analytic bubbles, focusing almost exclusively on what takes place between the beginning and end of the event; everything that occurs before and after the performance is either overlooked or assigned a secondary status as "background information." I would argue that this approach renders it much more difficult to simultaneously pursue an interest in the creation of relations of power and a close analysis of curing performances. Questions of power cannot be adequately addressed if they are seen as determined in isolated synchronic instances, no matter how many of these units might be examined or the breadth of the time span along which they are distributed. The (re)production of power in Warao curing performances hinges both on how discourse features shapes interactions that take place *in situ* and on how they relate the performance to words and actions that take place before and after the curative event itself.

Through the course of the seven songs, a variety of connections are made to the inauspicious *nahanamu* ritual cycle and the events that led up to it. The semantic content of the phenotext represents these discursive precursors, such that interpretations of the causes and effects of these events which serve the political interests of the three *wisimo* in the community emerge in the voices of *hebu*. Briefly put, Mr. Torres, the boy's grandfather, and an ally were making a bid for gaining a leadership role in the Mariusa community that would equal or surpass that of the *kobenahoro* ('governor') of the region and his backers. At this particular point, the two men were pursuing two strategies for gaining power. First, they had approached government officials of the Delta Amacuro State in nearby Tucupita, requesting that they be appointed as *komisario*. Unlike *kobenahoro*, who are invested with power by Warao communities, the Venezuelan government designates the *komisario*, charging them with representing the national government in their local communities. This bid not only threatened to shift the balance of power in the Mariusa region away from the *kobenahoro*, but to increase the penetration of the state into the lives of Mariusans. Second, the ritual dances that conclude each *nahanamu* constitute the hierarchical ranking of male leaders for the coming year. By holding a *nahanamu* that would rival the one sponsored by the *kobenahoro*'s supporters, Mr. Torres and his ally attempted to augment their externally imposed power with local legitimacy. By stealing some of the palm starch when the two men were in Tucupita and using it in their own *nahanamu,* the *kobenahoro*'s followers counter-attacked. The guests who insisted on eating the palm starch at Mr. Torres' *nahanamu* were, as you might imagine, low-ranking supporters of the *kobenahoro.*

Clearly, the failure of the *nahanamu* seriously undermined the two men's attempt to gain legitimacy for their new roles. When Mr. Torres' grandson was struck by *hebu* sickness, injury was added to insult, as it seemed as if the *hebu* had also become angry at the two men. Much of the broader political significance of the curing performance thus lies in the way it attempts to reinterpret what happened in the course of the *nahanamu.* The *hebu* declare that their anger was caused by the theft of the palm starch and the 'borrowing' of a sacred rattle by the *kobenahoro*'s followers; it was then compounded by the usurpation of the remaining palm starch by guests affiliated with the *kobenahoro.* Mr. Torres and his community are thus presented as the blameless victims of the *hebu*'s wrath rather than as its causes. The intertextual links that imbue the curing performance with tremendous political significance also extend forward in time, attempting to shape future discourse and social action. As the father dialogues with the *hebu,* he becomes aware of the source of the *hebu*'s anger. Moreover, the *hebu* assert that the father must lead the community in collecting the palm starch needed to bring the ritual cycle to successful completion. The voices of the *hebu* thus serve not only to reinterpret the political significance of the failed *nahanamu,* but to prompt the community to work towards hosting a more ritually and politically effective *nahanamu.*

Bauman and I have used the term *recontextualization* to point to the social and political as well as formal dimensions of such intertextual connections. Establishing such links asserts rights to extract discourse from one setting, to insert it with a particular type of authority in another situation, and to transform its formal and functional properties in such a way as to shape its impact on the new setting(s) (Bauman and Briggs 1990; Briggs and Bauman 1992). The social and political importance of this recontextualization process points once again to the importance of the distinction between the genotext and phenotext. It is the phenotext, with its explicitly metapragmatic content, that has the ability to create these intertextual links. The genotext crucially shapes what is taking place and how the participants become aware of this process, and the semiotic fusion that constitutes it enables participants to connect different aspects of the performance. Genotextual elements do not, however, provide resources that can be used in representing discourse that takes place in other settings, and it is very difficult to recontextualize the genotext. The genotext is difficult to grasp analytically in that even the most highly skilled practitioners lack an explicit metalanguage for describing and interpreting it. Herein lies much of the value of the contrast between phenotext and genotext for the creation of relations of power. While non-specialists enjoy access to the genotext, it is this dimension of the performance that is least useful outside the curing context.

The phenotext, on the other hand, holds the key to bringing other discourses into the performance and for using it in shaping what will be said and done in the future. The phenotext is precisely the dimension that is most stratified socially, in that *wisimo* hold explicit metapragmatic keys to its workings, while non-specialists have virtually none. Yet non-specialists are not completely in the dark with regard to the intertextual thrust of the performance. In the course of the spoken dialogue, Mr. Rivera is told in "everyday" Warao what happened during the *nahanamu*, why the *hebu* 'grabbed' his son, and what he should do. The point is rather that Mr. Medina—and presumably the *hebu* as well—determine point by point which connections they will allow Mr. Rivera to make by virtue of which phrases they choose to restate in "everyday" Warao. While they accordingly draw him into the recontextualization process, which features of the performance he can recontextualize and how he may do so remains largely within their control. *Wisimo* thus carefully determine the process of recontextualization, both with respect to the way that the performance provides a means of representing other discourses and the manner in which the ritual discourse itself will be (re)presented in subsequent discursive events.

I began this paper by addressing some key issues that have arisen in the study of ritual discourse. While I turned initially to the formal patterning of curing performances in addressing questions of semiotic fusion and semantic interpretability, I used these data in pointing to the ways that different types of subjectivity and agency are created. I went on to suggest some of the limitations of a narrow semiotic or communicative interpretation of this process. The social effects of ritual discourse do not emerge automatically from formal and functional properties of the discourse. Practitioners use complex arrays of formal features in shaping the ways in which patients and other community members will be able to gain access to the discourse. I argued that the social effects of this control become much more evident when the power of ritual discourse for representing other discursive events is comprehended. Eschewing nonetheless the sort of functionalism that would explain all discursive features as strategies for maximizing power, I argued that the genotext of Mr. Medina's performance constitutes an arena in which issues of power and control are much more complex and indeterminate.

I draw two more general observations from these findings. First, adequately grasping the nature of curing performances draws us into posing basic questions regarding the production and reception of discourse in general as it shapes and is shaped by bodies, minds, and social relations. Research in this area can accordingly offer rich insights into the sorts of questions that interest anthropologists, literary critics, and linguistics. Second, practitioners generally find it necessary at present to choose between close formal and functional analysis of particular, situated discursive events on the one hand and focusing on broader questions of the creation and reproduction of relations of power on the other. I have attempted to show that the study of curing performances can only address these broader questions—and deal adequately with particular cases—when investigators are able to join close analyses of formal and functional patterning with explorations of the means by which relations of power are created and maintained. Rather than simply juxtaposing heretofore opposing modes of analysis, however, the real value of this undertaking will emerge in the way such work can contribute to both of these scholarly frameworks.

ACKNOWLEDGMENTS

My primary debt in this paper is to the residents of the Mariusa region, especially to Manuel Torres, Santiago Rivera, José Félix Alvarez, María Rivera, José Medina, and Manuel Rivera. Mr. Torres and Mr. Alvarez were particularly generous in taking the time to explore this curing performance in detail. H. Dieter Heinen and Julio Lavandero greatly assisted me in planning my work in the Delta Amacuro. The Instituto de Investigaciones Científicas in Caracas and the Universidad de Oriente in Cumaná provided intellectual stimulation and institutional support. Thanks are due Vassar College for a sabbatical leave, a Mellon Grant for Faculty Development, and grants from the Salmon and Travel Funds. The support of the Linguistics Program of the National Science Foundation and the Wenner-Gren Foundation for Anthropological Research, Inc. are also deeply appreciated.

I feel particularly fortunate in having received a wealth of fascinating responses to earlier drafts of this paper. In addition to providing me with an extraordinarily thoughtful and detailed editorial reading, Carol Laderman and Marina Roseman organized the session at the Annual Meeting of the American Anthropological Association in New Orleans (in 1990) in which this paper was originally presented, and I would like to thank the discussant, Barbara Tedlock, for her commentary. Audiences at the Five-College Faculty Seminar on Folklore (Northampton, Mass.), the Department of Anthropology at Brandeis University, and the South American Indian Conference, Bennington College provided stimulating reactions. Past drafts benefited greatly from the generosity of a number of individuals who took the time to comment on the paper: Asif Agha, Mac Chapin, James Howe, Webb Keane, Joel Kuipers, Carlo Severi, Edward L. Schieffelin, Joel Sherzer, and Michael Taussig.

NOTES

1. In view of the complex restrictions regarding the use of Warao names, particularly those of shamans, I use pseudonyms in this paper.

2. Mr. Torres was initiated as a *wisidatu* shaman, and he thus does have some training in dealing with *hebu*. His main speciality, however, is *hoa,* and he does not attempt to remove *hebu* from individual patients.

3. Sherzer (1983:134) takes a more nuanced and charitable stance on Lévi-Strauss' article. While he faults Lévi-Strauss for assuming that the patient can understand the language of the chant, he argues that "ordinary Kuna" hear *ikar* in many contexts, grasp their "purpose and general structure," and can understand the parts of the texts. He thus concludes that Lévi-Strauss is "no doubt correct in the more abstract sense that the patient's general knowledge of the nature of the text and how it works is psychologically effective."

4. In order to sustain my analysis of the subtle ways that shamanistic practices are used in creating subjectivity and agency, I must include a number of Warao terms in the text. I attempt to define each term at the point it first appears in the chapter.

5. A number of conventions are used in the text. Lines are marked by musical and poetic features. Expressions that lack referential content have not been translated. A colon following a vowel indicates vowel elongation. Words enclosed in parentheses are not clear, and the transcription is accordingly uncertain.

6. Here the *hebu* is speaking not of his friend but that of the shaman's; the person is question is the boy's grandfather, Manuel Torres. The allusion in the next line is to Mr. Torres' status as a 'master' not only as a *hoarotu* and *wisidatu* as well as a practitioner in *domu,* which one can gloss very roughly as 'bird magic'.

7. Clearly, the musical transcription in Figure 2 suffers from the problems commonly associated with transcribing non-Western music in conventional staff notation. All pitches are approximate; many are microtonal pitches that lie between Western intervals. An x replaces a standard notehead when the note lies closer to the speech end of the speech-song continuum (see List 1963) and the pitch is thus indistinct. With respect to the transcription of the rattle rhythms, shorter and steeper lines indicate more rapid revolutions; the thicker lines indicate increased volume. My gratitude to Marina Roseman for her assistance in musical transcription and analysis, and to Peter Kienle for computerized notation using Finale 3.0.1.

8. *Waiya* is often used metonymically with reference to curing songs for *hebu* sickness as a whole.

9. The three shamans did sing for the spirits during the *nahanamu.* Rather than calling them and offering them tobacco smoke and palm starch, however, they simply announced that palm starch was being collected and that they would soon be inviting them to come. This attempt to prevent disaster was, obviously, not successful.

10. As Osborn (1966b) notes, this suffix both nominalizes a verb stem (transforming a verb into a noun), and marks it as agentive (i.e., as capable of performing a particular action) and singular.

11. Word stress generally falls on the penultimate syllable in Warao (see Osborn 1966a:114). A stress shift to the last syllable in the final word in each phrase is common in Warao song.

12. This statement pertains only to the textual and musical dimensions of the songs. The accompanying actions and their effect on the patient's experience clearly differs greatly with the change in orientation from the abdomen of the child to his head—extracting *hebu* from the child's head involves no physical contact, while the rattle makes forceful contact with the abdomen when *hebu* are lodged in this area.

13. For some *hebu,* the lack of a spoken dialogue following the third section of the song does not signal the failure of the shaman's efforts to extract it. In such cases, the *hebu* simply leaves after voicing its identity in Section 3.

14. Beyond the use of active, transitive verbs, the agent-patient relationship is emphasized through the use of three affixes. A second-person prefix (*hi-*) at the beginning of lines 6–12 and 16–18 states that the shaman is performing these actions on his interlocutor—the *hebu.* Lines 9–12 and 15 make use of an agentive suffix (*-tu*), thus nominalizing the verb stem and stressing his role as the performer of the action. Finally, when *iné* appears following the verb at the end of lines (as in 9–12 and 15–16), a sort of syntactic surprise value renders the speaker focal.

15. Clearly, Tambiah's position on this issue is complex. In his article on "A Performative Theory of Ritual" (1981), he argues that the fusion of semiotic modalities and poetic elaboration produces an "atrophy of meaning." In his *Buddhism and the Spirit-Cults in Northeast Thailand* (1970), however, he shows how denotative content plays a central role in one ritual and thus enters into the "total" village ritual.

REFERENCES

Austin, J. L. 1962. *How To Do Things With Words.* Cambridge: Harvard University Press.

Bahr, Donald M., and J. Richard Haefer. 1978. Song in Piman curing. *Ethnomusicology* 22:89–122.

Barral, Rev. P. Fr. Basilio de. 1964. *Los indios guaraunos y su cancionero: historia, religión, y alma lírica. Biblioteca "Missionalia Hispanica,"* vol. 15. Madrid: Consejo Superior de Intestigaciones Científicas, Departamento de Misionología Española.

Basso, Ellen. 1985. *A musical view of the universe: Kalapalo myth and ritual performances.* Philadelphia: University of Pennsylvania Press.

———. 1988. The trickster's scattered self. *Anthropological Linguistics* 30:292–318.

Bateson, Gregory. 1972[1955]. A theory of play and fantasy. In his *Steps to an ecology of mind,* 177–93. New York: Ballantine Books.

Bauman, Richard. 1977. *Verbal art as performance.* Prospect Heights, Ill.: Waveland Press.

Bauman, Richard, and Charles L. Briggs. 1990. Poetics and performance as critical perspectives on language and social life. *Annual Review of Anthropology* 19:59–88.

Benveniste, Emile. 1971[1966]. *Problems in general linguistics*. Translated by Mary Elizabeth Meek. Coral Gables, Fla.: University of Miami Press.

Blacking, John. 1985. The context of Venda possession music: Reflection on the effectiveness of symbols. *Yearbook for Traditional Music* 17:64–87.

Bloch, Maurice. 1974. Symbols, song, dance and features of articulation: Is religion an extreme form of traditional authority? *Archives Européennes de Sociologie* 15:55–81.

Bourdieu, Pierre. 1977. *Outline of a theory of practice*, translated by Richard Nice. Cambridge: Cambridge University Press.

Briggs, Charles L. 1986. *Learning how to ask: A sociolinguistic appraisal of the role of the interview in social science research*. Cambridge: Cambridge University Press.

———. 1988a. *Competence in performance: The creativity of tradition in Mexicano verbal art*. Philadelphia: University of Pennsylvania Press.

———. 1988b. Disorderly dialogues in ritual impositions of order: The role of metapragmatics in Warao dispute mediation. *Anthropological Linguistics* 30:448–91.

———. 1992. Generic *versus* metapragmatic dimensions of Warao narratives: Who regiments performance? In *Reflexive language: Reported speech and metapragmatics,* ed. John A. Lucy, 179–212. Cambridge: Cambridge University Press (forthcoming).

———. 1993. Metadiscursive practices and scholarly authority in folkloristics. *Journal of American Folklore* 106:387–434.

———. 1994. The sting of the ray: Bodies, agency, and grammar in Warao curing. *Journal of American Folklore* 107(423):139–166.

———. n.d. The "Effectiveness" of dialogue: Meaning, interaction, and power in Kuna and Warao curing. Manuscript.

Briggs, Charles L., and Richard Bauman. 1992. Genre, intertextuality, and social power. *Journal of Linguistic Anthropology* 2:131–72.

Buckley, Thomas. 1984. Yurok speech registers and ontology. *Language in Society* 13:467–88.

Chapin, Macpherson. 1976. *Muu ikala:* Cuna birth ceremony. In *Ritual and symbol in Native Central America*, ed. Philip Young and James Howe, 57–65. University of Oregon Anthropological Papers.

———. 1983. Curing among the San Blas Kuna of Panama. Ph.D. diss., University of Arizona.

Derrida, Jacques. 1974[1967]. *Of grammatology*. Translated by Gayatri Chakravorty Spivak. Baltimore: John Hopkins University Press.

———. 1977. *Limited, Inc.: abc...*. Baltimore: Johns Hopkins University Press.

Foucault, Michel. 1972[1969]. *The Archaeology of knowledge*. Translated by A.M. Sheridan Smith. New York: Harper & Row.

———. 1973[1963]. *Birth of the clinic*. Translated by Alan Sheridan Smith. New York: Vintage.

————. 1982[1972]. *Power/knowledge: Selected interview and other writings, 1972–1977,* ed. Colin Gordon. New York: Pantheon.

Friedrich, Paul. 1972. Social context and semantic feature: The Russian pronominal usage. In *Directions in sociolinguistics: The ethnography of communication,* ed. John J. Gumperz and Dell Hymes, 270–300. New York: Holt, Rinehart and Winston.

Frisbie, Charlotte J. 1980. Vocables in Navajo ceremonial music. *Ethnomusicology* 24:347–92.

Goffman, Erving. 1974. *Frame analysis.* New York: Harper and Row.

————. 1981[1978]. Response cries. Reprinted in *Forms of talk,* 78–123. Philadelphia: University of Pennsylvania Press.

Grice, H. P. 1975. Logic and conversation. In *Syntax and semantics,* vol. 3, Speech acts, ed. Peter Cole and Jerry L. Morgan, 41–58. New York: Academic Press.

Gumperz, John J. 1982. *Discourse strategies.* Cambridge: Cambridge University Press.

Hinton, Leanne. 1980. Vocables in Havasupai song. In *Southwest Indian ritual drama,* ed. Charlotte J. Frisbie, 275–305. Albuquerque: University of New Mexico Press.

Hymes, Dell. 1965. Some North Pacific Coast Poems: A problem in anthropological philology. *American Anthropologist* 67:316–41.

————. 1979. How to talk like a bear in Takelma. *International Journal of American Linguistics* 45:101–6.

Jakobson, Roman. 1959. On linguistic aspects of translation. In *On translation,* ed. Brower, Reuben A., 232–39. Cambridge, Mass.: Harvard University Press.

————. 1960. Concluding statement: Linguistics and poetics. In *Style in language,* ed. Thomas A. Sebeok, 350–77. Cambridge, Mass.: MIT Press.

————. 1978[1935]. The dominant. In *Readings in Russian poetics: formalist and structuralism views,* ed. Ladislav Matejka and Krystyna Pomorska, 82–87. Ann Arbor: Michigan Slavic Publications.

————. 1981[1968]. Poetry of grammar and grammar of poetry. In *Roman Jakobson: Selected Writings. Poetry of grammar and grammar of poetry,* vol. 3, ed. Stephen Rudy, 87–97. The Hague: Mouton.

————. 1981[1970]. Subliminal verbal patterning in Poetry. In *Roman Jakobson: Selected Writings. Poetry of grammar and grammar of poetry,* vol. 3, ed. Stephen Rudy, 136–47. The Hague: Mouton.

————. 1984. La théorie saussurienne en rétrospection. *Linguistics* 22:161–96.

Kristeva, Julia. 1984[1974]. *Revolution in poetic language.* Translated by Margaret Waller. New York: Columbia University Press.

Kuipers, Joel C. 1990. *Power in performance: The creation of textual authority in Weyewa Ritual Speech.* Philadelphia: University of Pennsylvania Press.

Laderman, Carol. 1987. The ambiguity of symbols in the structure of healing. *Social Science Medicine* 24:293–301.

————. 1991. *Taming the wind of desire: Psychology, medicine, and aesthetics in Malay shamanistic performance.* Berkeley: University of California Press.

Langdon, Margaret. 1978. Animal Talk in Cocopa. *International Journal of American Linguistics* 44:10–16.

Langer, Susanne K. 1953. *Feeling and form*. New York: Charles Scribner's Sons.

Leach, Edmund. 1976. *Culture and communication*. Cambridge: Cambridge University Press.

Levinson, Stephen C. 1983. *Pragmatics*. Cambridge: Cambridge University Press.

Lévi-Strauss, Claude. 1963[1949]. *L'efficacité symbolique*. *Revue de l'Histoire des Religions* 135:5–27. Reprinted in English as "The Effectiveness of Symbols." In his *Structural Anthropology*, 186–205. New York: Basic Books.

———. 1966. *The Savage Mind*. Chicago: University of Chicago Press.

List, George. 1963. The boundaries of speech and song. *Ethnomusicology* 7:1–16.

Locke, John. 1959[1690]. *An essay concerning human understanding*. New York: Dover.

Malinowski, Bronislaw. 1935. *Coral gardens and their magic*. New York: American Book Company.

McDowell, John. 1983. The semiotic constitution of Kamsá ritual language. *Language in Society* 12:23–46.

Neher, Andrew. 1962. A physiological explanation of unusual behavior in ceremonies involving drums. *Human Biology* 34:151–60.

Olsen, Dale A. 1973. Music and shamanism of the Winikina/Warao Indians of Venezuela: Songs for curing and other theurgy. Ph. D. diss., University of California, Los Angeles.

———. 1975. Music-induced altered states of consciousness among Warao shamans. *Journal of Latin American Lore* 1:19–33.

Osborn, Henry A., Jr. 1966a. Warao I: Phonology and morphophonemics. *International Journal of American Linguistics* 32:108–23.

———. 1966b. Warao II: Nouns, relationals, and demonstratives. *International Journal of American Linguistics* 32:253–61.

Peirce, Charles S. 1932. *Collected papers of Charles S. Peirce*. Elements of logic, vol. II. Cambridge: Harvard University Press.

Romero-Figueroa, Andrés. 1985. OSV as the basic order in Warao. *Linguistics* 23:105–21.

Roseman, Marina. 1988. The pragmatics of aesthetics: The performance of healing among the Senoi Temiar. *Social Science Medicine* 27:811–18.

———. 1991. *Healing sounds from the Malaysian rainforest: Temiar music and medicine*. Berkeley: University of California Press.

Roth, Walter E. 1915. An inquiry into the animism and folklore of the Guiana Indians. Bureau of American Ethnology, 30th Annual Report for 1908–9, 103–386. Washington: Government Printing Office.

Rouget, Gilbert. 1977. Music and possession trance. In *The anthropology of the body*, ed. John Blacking, 233–39. London: Academic Press.

———. 1980. *Music and trance.* Translated by Brunhilde Biebuyck. Chicago: University of Chicago Press.

Sapir, Edward. 1949[1935]. Symbolism. In *Selected writings of Edward Sapir in language, culture and personality,* ed. David G. Mandelbaum, 564–68. Berkeley: University of California.

Saussure, Ferdinand. 1959[1916]. *Course in general linguistics,* ed. Charles Bally & Albert Sechehaye. Translated by Wade Baskin. New York: McGraw-Hill Book Company.

Seeger, Anthony. 1987. *Why Suyá sing: A musical anthropology of an Amazonian people.* Cambridge: Cambridge University Press.

Sherzer, Joel. 1983. *Kuna ways of speaking: An ethnographic perspective.* Austin: University of Texas Press.

Silverstein, Michael. 1976. Shifters, linguistic categories, and cultural description. In *Meaning in anthropology,* ed. Keith Basso and Henry A. Selby, 11–55. Albuquerque: University of New Mexico Press.

———. 1981. The limits of awareness. Sociolinguistic Working Paper 84. Austin: Southwest Educational Development Laboratory.

———. 1993. Metapragmatic discourse and metapragmatic function. In *Reflexive language: Reported speech and metapragmatics,* ed. John A. Lucy, 33–58. Cambridge: Cambridge University Press.

Strawson, P.F. 1952. *Introduction to logical theory.* London: Methuen.

Tambiah, S. J. 1970. *Buddhism and the spirit cults in Northeast Thailand.* Cambridge: Cambridge University Press.

———. 1973. Form and meaning in magical acts: a point of view. In *Modes of thought: Essays on thinking in Western and non-Western societies,* ed. Robin Horton and Ruth Finnegan, 199–229. London: Faber and Faber.

——— .1977. The Cosmological and performative significance of a Thai cult of healing through meditation. *Culture, Medicine and Psychiatry* 1:97–132.

———. 1981. A Performative theory of ritual. *Proceedings of the British Academy* 65: 113–69.

Taussig, Michael. 1987. *Shamanism, colonialism, and the wild man: A study in terror and healing.* Chicago: University of Chicago Press.

———. 1992. *The nervous system.* New York: Routledge.

———. 1993. *Mimesis and alterity: A particular history of the senses.* New York: Routledge.

Todorov, Tzvetan. 1984. *Mikhail Bakhtin: the dialogic principle.* Translated by Wlad Godzich. Minneapolis: University of Minnesota Press.

Turner, Victor. 1967. *The forest of symbols: Aspects of Ndembu ritual.* Ithaca, N.Y.: Cornell University Press.

Wilbert, Johannes. 1972. Tobacco and shamanistic ecstasy among the Warao of Venezuela. In *Flesh of the gods: the ritual use of hallucinogens,* ed. Peter Furst, 55–83. New York: Praeger.

————. 1973–1974. The calabash of the ruffled feathers. *Artscanada* 30:90–93.

————. 1987. *Tobacco and shamanism in South America.* New Haven, Conn.: Yale University Press.

Wilbert, Werner. 1986. Warao herbal medicine: a pneumatic theory of illness and healing. Ph.D. diss., University of California, Los Angeles.

8

"PURE PRODUCTS GO CRAZY"

Rainforest Healing in a Nation-State

Marina Roseman

S ongs stretch parameters of everyday speech—intonation, duration, accent, stress, timbre, interlock and separation of voices, silences—to extraordinary dimensions, enabling sentiments and values otherwise suppressed or ineffable to take momentary shape. Dance stylizes gestures of daily life, manipulating effort, shape, weight, duration, and direction to trace forms and meanings otherwise inappropriate or inexpressible. In this movement from the ordinary to the extraordinary, performance becomes performativity; act, enactment; and the transformative power of ritual is literally and figuratively set in motion. In such symbolically and emotionally charged performance contexts, members of a society are often able to face their demons and desires; here they can reveal their misfortunes and their wishes, in whatever symbolic currency these may be locally defined.

Song and dance, combined in the culturally demarcated zone of ceremonial performance, intertwine sensory modalities (motion, color, sound, odor, tactility) to move participants from one experiential status, such as illness, toward another: health. Drawing upon a decade of research among Temiar rainforest dwellers of peninsular Malaysia, in this essay I will show how the affective power of such healing rituals are embedded in complex historical and social relations.

233

Temiar healing performances, though often oriented toward a particular individual's suffering at a particular moment in time, are also social healings addressing the scars of history.

Temiar cultural history and social relations are crystallized in their healing songs and dances, received during dreams from the animated "spirits" of their physical and social environment. Dreamers, given the leeway of individual revelation in this relatively egalitarian society, dream their songs in response to personal and historical experiences. Temiar musico-choreographic genres thus vary according to geographical location, historical time period, and even individual dream song composer-receivers. They range from those associated with Tiger Spirits (mamug) to those associated with mountains and rivers (tanga:y), from those emerging from the annually blossoming fruit trees (pɛnha:y, tangɔ:y, nɔŋtahon) to those which flow from commodities (like airplanes or canned sardines) and concepts (like statehood or nationhood) brought into the forest by more recently arriving foreigners, or "out-foresters."

I focus on musico-medical practices surrounding a healing song given by the spirit of one of these newer, postcolonial entities: the spirit of the State of Kelantan. Aspects of Temiar cultural history, political stances, and medical perspectives are embodied in the ritual songs, actions, and paraphernalia given to Abilem Lum, a Temiar medium and healer, by his spiritguide, Sri Kelantan, "the Princess of the State of Kelantan" in 1991.

I begin by introducing the Temiar geographical environment and demographic history as it is encapsulated in the altar Abilem Lum built for the Spirit of the State of Kelantan. In the following section, the process whereby Temiars encounter and engage with spirits, receiving songs to use in healing, is examined through the transcript and exegesis of the dream narrative in which Abilem recounts his meetings with the Female Spirit of the State of Kelantan. I investigate the multiplicity of her ritual directives, as they interweave the disjointed components of contemporary Temiar life in the nation-state of Malaysia, where "Pure Products Go Crazy."

The next section transcribes, describes and interprets the ritual texture of segments of a healing ceremony recorded in 1992, during which Abilem sings the song of the Spirit of the State of Kelantan to heal an infant suffering from constipation. This healing performance directed toward a particular infant displays Temiar concepts of illness etiology and treatment, and enacts preventive and therapeutic social healings for a social group traumatized by their encounters with deforestation, Islamic religious evangelism, and the transformation of their economy from generalized reciprocity to mercantile and capitalist systems of exchange.

FROM UPSTREAM TO DOWNSTREAM (AND BACK AGAIN).

3:00 P.M. in a lowland rainforest Temiar settlement, August 1992. Abilem Lum, back from the temporary dwellings upstream where his village members have their rice fields this year, goes out to a small structure located about twenty feet in the direction upstream from his house.

This small structure is close to the logging road that separates the homes of the approximately sixty village residents from their rubber holdings across the way; but it is obscured from casual sight by clumps of lowland brush and scrub trees. Unlike Abilem's wood plank and zinc-roofed government-issue home, this tiny house is built from traditional Temiar building materials: walls made from flattened and interwoven bamboo; thatched roof; lashed bamboo slats for the floor; all set on a foundation of wooden pillars raising it about four feet above the ground. Carrying his cigarette lighter, Abilem climbs up into the doorway. Fitting his five-foot, four-inch frame inside the tiny three-by-two-foot entrance, squeezing by the ritual ornaments hanging in the center of the interior space, Abilem spreads the folds of the cotton Malay sarong he wears as he seats himself cross-legged.

From the structure's eaves hangs an ornament akin to those that grace a Temiar dwelling when a singing and trance-dancing ceremony is held. Traditionally made from fragrant, moist, freshly gathered leaves and flowers, the suspended tənamuʔ (from the Malay term tamu, 'guest') provides an inviting, forest-like spot where visiting spirits from forest and settlement are thought to first alight during nighttime ceremonies. Summoned by the songs they have given to people in their dreams, these spirit guests are coaxed to join the people's musical gathering. The flowers and leaves strung from the tənamuʔ in this small altar built near Abilem's house are made from colorful but odorless plastic, the material Barthes has termed "the magical substance of the twentieth century."

Abilem has begun to perform a ceremony which will join the strands of his life as a rainforest dweller in contemporary Malaysia into an uneasy confluence. Abilem's life, never straightforward or "simple," has increasingly become a jumble of contradictions. In his dreams, the spirit of the state of Kelantan has sung to him. Kelantan is one of the eleven Federated States of Peninsular Malaysia. The state of Perak first recognized British colonial control in 1874; the nine original sultanates joined with the Straits Settlements of Penang and Malacca in the Malayan Union in 1948. Kelantan became a state within the independent Federation of Malaya in 1957.[1]

The female princess-spirit of the state of Kelantan has asked Abilem to gather the diverse ritual paraphernalia joined here under the roof of the small house she

Figure 1. Abilem offering incense, inside the altar for Sri Kelantan.

requested he build for her. She has asked this son of a semi-nomadic people not to stray too far, not to be gone too long, for he must return to her altar.

Her request helps legitimate Abilem's difficult, uneven transition to a more sedentary life in the Government Regroupment Project for Aboriginal Peoples. As often as possible, at 3:00 p.m. (marked by his wristwatch) he must light both store-bought Chinese incense and indigenous incense made from beeswax or from resinous *kamiyan* roots. If he keeps her altar well, and sings her song during nighttime singing and trance-dancing ceremonies, then she will keep her Temiar grandchildren safe and healthy as they move into a strangely reconfigured future.

Temiar dreams come from their engagement with the spirits of the sound-, motion-, and odor-filled landscape of the 2500 acres of lowland and highland rainforest in peninsular Malaysia through which their small communities of 25 to 150 people have traditionally been scattered. The approximately 12,000 Temiar are Orang Asli or "Original Peoples," indigenous Mon-Khmer speaking populations dwelling along the rivers in the forest still remaining in the center of the Malay peninsula.[2] Temiars move through this landscape—interacting with its landforms, flora, fauna, and other inhabitants—while hunting, gathering, fishing, preparing fields of tapioca tubers or hill rice, or harvesting.

Dreams ($p\varepsilon\,?p\,\jmath\,?$) that follow these daily activities, and dream songs received therein, later form the basis for community-wide singing ceremonies ($p\varepsilon h n\jmath\,:h$).[3] The Temiar animistic cosmological orientation homologies humans, who have head, heart, odor, and shadow souls, with other entities such as trees (with their leaf and root souls), or mountains (with their crest and cave souls). The head, heart, odor and shadow souls of the forest landscape, its flora and its fauna, are bound during daily life, but can become unbound "spirits" in the realms of dream, ritual, trance, and illness. This theory of personhood onto-logically grounds the act of communication and flow of information between the Temiar and other forest entities, realized in the form of gifts of song and other types of knowledge which are received from these entities during dreams.

Within the context of the contemporary Malaysian nation, the over 84,000 Orang Asli comprise less than one percent of Malaysia's current population of nearly 17 million (1989 estimate).[4] The balance of Malaysia's population includes 55% Malays, 33% Chinese, and 10% Tamil Indians (Department of Statistics, Malaysia 1983). Orang Asli status within the nation of Malaysia, like that of many indigenous minorities in amalgamated nations, lies suspended amidst Malaysia's often conflicting goals. These involve, on the one hand, Malaysia's competition in the international economy, with its demands upon rainforest land, timber, and hydraulic power, along with the increasingly intense religious activities of the Islamic Malay majority in states like Kelantan.

On the other hand lies Malaysia's celebratory approach toward cultural differ-ence in its expressive, performative dimensions, except when this cultural difference implicates rights to resources. These approaches are subsumed in a Governmental rhetoric of Orang Asli "integration," "sedentarization," and "development," often overlaying an agenda of land and resource appropriation (Nicholas 1990; Gomes 1990).

Mirroring the population of Malaysia, the state of Kelantan overarches cultur-ally diverse and economically competitive populations of Chinese Buddhists, Hindu Tamils, Malay Muslims, Christians of various ethnic identities and reli-gious sects, and predominantly animistic Orang Asli.[5] Abilem draws upon the multidimensional "Spirit of the State of Kelantan" to counteract the effects of living in a multicultural, indeed transnational, world in which the "pure prod-ucts have gone crazy."[6]

Temiars have long engaged with peoples and things from beyond the forest. They call themselves the "people of the forest," ($s\varepsilon n\,?\jmath\,:y$ $s\jmath r\jmath k$) in contradis-tinction to more recently arriving foreign "out-foresters" or $g\jmath b$. These latter include Austronesian-speaking maritime peoples, first arriving about 2000 years ago and mixing in varying degrees with Temiar and other aboriginal Austroasiatic speakers of the Malay peninsula to become the people now known as Malays. Temiar dream songs record their interactions with this cultural category of the "Other." For the Temiar the Other includes British colonials, Chinese and Tamil workers brought to work British mines and plantations; the Japanese occupying Malaya during World War II; anthropologists of varied descent, and Malays in their post-independence roles as mainstream Islamic population as government and as administrators. Songs sung during Temiar healing rituals now include those received from the spirits of the tunnels built by the Japanese, as well as those from market goods arriving from downriver Malay settlements, such as the salt-dried fish and canned sardines that replace fresh fish which is increasingly absent from rivers contaminated by the combined effects of deforestation.

Born in Perak, Abilem now lives in his wives' village, itself part of a larger Orang Asli Regroupment Scheme. Orang Asli traditionally ranged across territorial areas suited to their varied subsistence practices. Today, Temiars and other Orang Asli are posed as "tenants-at-will" on "aboriginal areas" and "aboriginal reserves" or "regroupment projects" whose size and location, indeed continuity of existence, remain at the discretion of state and federal governments.

Temiars rose to national consciousness during the post-World War II "Emergency" (1948–1965), when the British and then the Malaysian government sought to counter Communist insurgents taking refuse in the jungle.[7] The British colonial administration sponsored strategies to regroup and resettle Orang Asli *outside* the deeper jungle areas, resulting in wide-spread disease and death (Carey 1976). This strategy was replaced by jungle forts: colonial outposts which courted Orang Asli with food, medicine, supplies, wireless communications, and radio programs in order to influence them to remain pro-Government.

Subsequent Malaysian national policy regarding Orang Asli, even after the Emergency, has officially been guided by national-security concerns. Yet, "National Security" policies of aboriginal regroupment, sedentarization, and integration into the national economy (and mainstream Malay population's Muslim religion) became convenient screens for other agendas when the value of Orang Asli land and resources increased as Malaysia industrialized. Jungle forts became hubs for regroupment schemes located *within* the rainforest. Orang Asli gained increased access to limited forms of cosmopolitan health care, education, and communications through the regroupment schemes, but gradually lost the expanded territory and diversified ecological zones that supported their lifestyle of hunting, gathering, fishing, and shifting cultivation. The settlement where Abilem now lives, associated with one such Orang Asli Regroupment Scheme, is a consequence of this expanding government influence upon Orang Asli movements and residence.

For Temiar hunter-horticulturalists dwelling along the rivers that drain from the forested mountain center of the Malay peninsula down to the coastal plains, "upstream" (teh) is traditionally associated with things of the jungle, in both their benevolent manifestations as spiritguides (gonig;hala:ʔ) and their malevolent manifestations as illness agents (mɛrgaːh). Upstream also implies its opposite, "downstream" (rɛh), the direction of the marketplace, big towns, and "out-forester," or non-aboriginal Others. Jungle and marketplace each constitute a realm of things, people, and experiences both positively and negatively charged.

Temiars have long traded with "out-foresters," exchanging jungle products such as sandalwood, resin, rattan, medicinal herbs, and fruit for items such as salt, iron, and cotton cloth in earlier times, batteries, Adidas shorts, or cash more recently.[8] These items rarely lose their status as things of "foreign" or "recent" (gɔb) origin, as opposed to "original" or "ancient" (manah) items. Within the Temiar cultural system of illness and health, foreign items from "downriver" carried "market" illnesses associated with the Malays. Curry powder, salt, canned milk, sugar, and other items that have since become staples in Temiar diets are also the first to be removed from a person or family's diet in times of illness or ritual danger.

Increasingly, Temiars face their cosmology gone wild: "market" illnesses now come from Chinese and Malay logging camps *upstream,* from whence only forest illnesses once emerged. Indeed, Abilem's village is situated downriver from logging camps staffed by Chinese workers. Nearby, large rubber plantations run under the Government's rural development scheme, FELCRA, are worked by Tamils, Malays, and Indonesians. Across the logging road that runs by the Temiar villagers' homes are small Temiar rubber landholdings encouraged by Government resettlement schemes. Women and children, in particular, tap and press the rubber, regularly handling a "foreign" product associated with illness in Temiar etiological categories.

In this world gone topsy-turvy, a traditional medium and singer/healer like Abilem Lum seeks to minister to his people. Illnesses considered to have "forest" etiologies are treated with songs, dances, and ritual paraphernalia associated with "forest" spirits; illnesses with "foreign" etiologies are usually treated with musico-choreographic and ritual techniques learned from spirits associated with downstream and the marketplace. Often, both are called into play.

In several ceremonies I documented in the 1980s, Abilem counterbalanced the leaf ornaments of taŋɔːy, the rainforest spirit of the Rambutan Fruit Tree, suspended from a circular frame hanging on one side of the room, with leaf ornaments and ceremonial paraphernalia from pɛhnɔːh gɔb—the Temiars' version of what they call "Malay-type" ceremonies—which hung on the other side of the room. In these healing performances, he alternated between song genres and movement styles associated with the Fruit Season jungle spirits, and Malay-type spirit ceremonies. Thus, he said, would he honor both sets of spiritguides, that they not become envious of one another. And thus would he treat his people—suspended between two worlds. In this way, Temiar *bricoleurs* grapple with the radically shifting circumstances of their increasingly diminished forest refuge.

The altar that Abilem's spiritguide, the Princess of the State of Kelantan, requested he build, combines objects associated with Chinese dragons, Malay metalwork, archeological objects associated with the ninth and tenth-century Srivijayan Hindu-Buddhist presence in Southeast Asia, and items associated with the forest. These heteroglossic items, speaking with the many voices of the increasingly multicultural Temiar world, are joined within the altar, their conflictual referents tenuously bounded yet barely stabilized by both the relatively enclosed shapes of the conical/circular tənəmuʔ, hung with its plastic leaves and flowers, and the rectangular prayer shelter. The conical shape of the tənəmuʔ, resembling that of a mountain, Temiars say, funnels the spirits' energy into the human realm. Through ritual practice, Abilem attempts to hold this cultural heteroglossia in a dynamically balanced tension, so that he may act as the "medium" for what he considers to be its "integrative" healing potentials, and thus to heal patients suffering from its potentially disintegrating forces.

PURE PRODUCTS GO CRAZY

Whenever I recorded Temiar singing, I would later elicit a narrative recounting the dreaming which the song was initially received. The Temiar term nɔŋ, or "path," encompasses more than the song melody and vocabulary that arise during the encounter between Temiar dreamer and the familiar spirit. Rather, this "path" or "way" given by a particular spiritguide might include dance movements, particular leaves and flowers for use in ornaments, or other performance parameters, such as the amount of light or darkness the spirit is comfortable with during its arrival in the ceremonial arena. With these markers, the spiritguide marks a "path" through the dense forest environment, enabling the dreamer-singer and, in performance, the chorus, to wɛdwəːd nɔŋ, 'follow the panther.'

In the following interview, Abilem discusses the ritual directives Sri Kelantan gave him. Embellished over the course of several dreams, her directives combine a multiplicity of seemingly disjunctive items and activities:[9]

Marina: I'd like to ask, how did it come about, that you made the prayer house over there?
Abilem Lum: Because, in the very beginning, my brother-in-law Sandang, along with the schoolteacher Adaay, asked us if we would have a ceremony for the annual

fruits, at the time of the durian *fruit, the ripening time—sort of like the rice-planting time of festivities—for the spirits of our origins, we forest people of Kelantan. So we held a singing and trance-dancing ceremony at the annual flowering of the fruit trees. We ask for their help; it's something special to us from our origins, the original religion of we forest people who have our origins in Kelantan.*

So she told me the story, Princess Kelantan of the Holy Place of the Water-dragon-snake, she ordered me to make a prayer house. We've never made prayer houses, we forest people. So she came out of her Holy Place to help us however she could. She requested I make it, so I could light incense sticks inside the prayer house, and offer the burnt resin incense, kəmiyən. *Sri Kelantan wanted all kinds of things: she wanted two chickens as offerings; I've never made chicken offerings. We had never offered incense sticks in Kelantan, either.*

Princess Kelantan of the Holy Place of the Water-dragon-snake[10] incorporates the imagery of the *naga,* the mythological water-dragon-snake fundamental to Indic mythology (Bosch 1960) The *naga,* linguistically temiarized through glottalization and/or nasalization (naga:ʔ or daŋa:ʔ), has previously emerged within Temiar spirit cults, particularly in the genre Salɛmbaŋ.

Temiars often spoke of having observed Malay spirit seances, which draw upon the Hindu-Buddhist and animist substratum interwoven with the later-arriving Islam in traditional Malay religious orientations (Cuisinier 1936; Laderman 1991). Temiars of Betis, Perias, and Berok Rivers, for example, still remember receiving instruction from a powerful Malay medium, Raning, who lived at Kuala Betis until World War II. Offerings of chickens, chicken's blood, and the use of eggs in spirit rituals are associated with Malay-type ritual orientations by Temiars.

Salɛmbaŋ, a genre that Temiars associate with Malay-type ceremonials, originated around 1926, during a period of heavy flooding. The *naga,* flowing downriver in the floods, is said to have given the genre to a Temiar man named Seliloh. Accoutrements that Temiar associate with Malay-type spirit seances are used in Salɛmbaŋ, including the rotation of the head to go into trance, certain kinds of leaves in the ornaments,[11] popped rice divinations, and a musical partnership between the medium and his interrogator, a drum-playing accomplice named the *mindok* (Winstedt 1927:306; Roseman 1991:99–105).

Salɛmbaŋ also conjoins referents implicating the mystical dragons of Chinese mythology. Benjamin (personal communication) suggests that the term Salɛmbaŋ derives from the Hakka *selum-von,* "underwater dragon-snake."[12] the threads drawn together in Sri Kelantan's altar thus conjoin Malay, Chinese, and autochthonous Temiar "forest" orientations, as evidenced, for instance, in the two types of incense—Chinese stick incense and indigenous roots and resins—

that Sri Kelantan requests. Abilem has cut out the cardboard dragons on the wrapper enclosing the Chinese incense sticks, and includes them in the ritual paraphernalia gathered in Sri Kelantan's altar. The interview continues:

Abilem: I dreamt Sri Kelantan gave this to me so I could work to guard the safety of our land: the head souls of the fruits, the head souls of the bananas, of our food, of the rice, the spirits of all kinds of things. Their spirit-substance.

So I dreamt she pointed out: "You, help me by making offerings of kəmiyən *resin; I will be expecting this . . . And I, too, will help all of you, whatever illnesses you face. When you help me, when you ceremonialize, when you treat people, I will safeguard all of you—the well-being of you forest people, we who have our origins in Kelantan. So for building me the Altar of Kelantan here, I give you my hair ornament."*

She gave the Altar of Kelantan. So I received the things she gave. I depend on her to help us with all the illness of the land here, all the stones of the land, the winds, whatever difficulties, whether from the water or whatever types of illness agents they may be. That is what we hope for from Sri Kelantan. That she would hold this land, the place of our community here, and guard it.

. . .

Marina: When did you dream that dream?
Abilem: I dreamt it last year, this year, not yet a full year, I think it was twelve months. Nearly a year ago.
Marina: Is that hair ornament there, inside the prayer house?
Abilem: It is.
Marina: I saw something like a keris, *a Malay ceremonial knife, the long piece of metal; is that the hair ornament?*
Abilem: No, that's Hang Tuah's ceremonial knife.
Marina: Hang Tuah's keris!
Abilem: Yes. . . .
Marina: . . . How did you find them, on the ground, or . . . ?
Abilem: I met them over here, across the logging road, in the forest, over in the direction of the rubber trees.
Marina: Over there?
Abilem: Yes.
Marina: Had you already had the dream before you found them?
Abilem: First I dreamt, then I met the hair ornament and the knife.
Marina: The two of them?
Abilem: Yes.
Marina: The one, you mentioned earlier, Sri Kelantan's hair ornament. The other you mentioned . . . ?

Abilem: Ti? Sadu:n.
Marina: Sadu:n.
Abilem: Over there, I met it there. That's the origin of Ti? Sadu:n.
Marina: Ti? Sadu:n.
Abilem: Yes.
Marina: Is that a person?
Abilem: A person, like a Malay.
Marina: Like a Malay, that one?
Abilem: Yes. A holy person.
Marina: Female?
Abilem: Male.
Marina: Male?
Abilem: Yes.
Marina: A Minister, by his title?
Abilem: Minister[13] Sadu:n.
Marina: Minister of the Water . . . ?
Abilem: Minister of the Water. Minister of the source of this river here, the Berok River.

. . .

Marina: When you met the hair ornament, you met the two of them, Princess Kelantan and Minister Sadu:n?
Abilem: Two.
Marina: The one, Sri Kelantan, is she a forest woman?
Abilem: A female . . . naga:?, an underwater dragon-snake, like a forest woman too, a Snake King with holy origins.
Marina: But she's not Malay.
Abilem: Not Malay.
Marina: Not Chinese?
Abilem: Not Chinese.
Marina: No.
Abilem: But her ancestry is shared by the Chinese. The Chinese, too, pray to her, at the Altar of the Mother in Pulai.
Marina: So, you got those two pieces of metal, then you made the house.
Abilem: Then I made the house.
Marina: She herself, she ordered you to make the house?
Abilem: She ordered, she ordered that I should make a prayer house, that I guard it, I should offer kamiyan resin incense regularly.

Both Sri Kelantan's haircomb, and the ritual knife Abilem attributes to the legendary Malay hero, Hang Tuah, are made from metal. These items recall the trade relationships that have conjoined forest peoples and out-foresters for centuries; one of the important early trade items Temiars received through Malays were metals, particularly for knife blades. The forest woman, Princess Sri Kelantan, is joined in the altar by a Malay minister, Sadu:n, associated with the river—the route linking downstream's marketplace with the jungle.

Sri Kelantan is a "forest woman," but her ancestry, Abilem comments, is "shared by the Chinese," who "pray to her at the altar of the Mother in Pulai." In the Chinese town of Pulai, about 10 miles from the rapidly growing frontier town of Kuala Betis, Abilem reports having seen an altar which contains a bottle holding the photograph of a Temiar woman. He calls this the "Altar of the Mother." He may have seen a Chinese ancestral altar incorporating a Temiar woman that intermarried into a Chinese family.[14]

Though she appears like a woman of the forest, she is also associated with the underwater dragon-snake. In the altar he has constructed, in addition to Sri Kelantan's metal hairpin, Abilem places an archeological find from nearby limestone caves. This Buddhist votive tablet dates from the ninth or tenth century A.D., a period of the Srivijayan Hindu-Buddhist kingdom's influence in peninsular Malaysia. The Temiars discovered the cave before it was subsequently disturbed by plantation workers in the area. Three types of tablets were in the cave, but the one that Abilem chose to make the centerpiece of his altar is an ovoid-shaped tablet with a standing figure, curving and graceful, that he identifies with Sri Kelantan. The tablet represents Avalokitesavara as Protector of the Faithful.[15] For Abilem, this tablet, from a cave, the mountain's correlate of the "heart soul", was indeed from "ancient times", but represented Sri Kelantan, who appears in his dreams with the body of a curvaceous, beautiful young woman.

The antiquity of the tablet, and its prior home in the "heart" of the mountain, legitimate Abilem's sense of Sri Kelantan as an indigenous forest entity who encompasses the more recent "out-foresters" in her jurisdiction. The tablet is placed on a tray suspended from the tanamuʔ. The Temiar altar incorporating this tablet inverts the sacred geography as it appeared from the perspective of the outforester Malay kingdoms. When Malay royalty met with the peoples in their sphere of influence, each people had their place under an umbrella—the Chinese under one, aborigines under another. The politics of space is reconfigured by Abilem, who symbolically brings the Malays and the Chinese, the Hindu and the Buddhist, under *his* umbrella, in the form of the circular leaf ornament known as the tanamuʔ. Within Sri Kelantan's altar, through her countenance, Abilem positions himself and his people—the ancient, autochthonous aboriginal peoples of Malaya—in the center of the mandala: this representation of the spirit world that he has constructed.

Abilem brought the *tɘnɘmuʔ* in Sri Kelantan's altar back from a ceremony held to mark the end of a mourning period at another nearby Temiar settlement. In Sri Kelantan's altar, the plastic flowers of the *tɘnɘmuʔ* are imbued with the Temiar ritual sensibility valuing brightly colored flowers, shimmering leaves, and cooling plant sap.

As the interview continues, Abilem speaks about the ritual "division of labor" between his Annual Fruit Tree spiritguides, and Sri Kelantan, associated with the underwater-dragon snake. *Tɘŋɔːy*, the spirit of the Rambutan Fruit Tree, has jurisdiction over illnesses from the fruits, and those affecting head souls. Sri Kelantan has jurisdiction over illnesses associated with things lower and inner: tree trunks, earth, river, internal "winds," and heart souls. These illness sources are associated with the Malays.

Marina: Did she also direct you to make the central hanging flower ornament, like the one that hangs during singing ceremonies? I noticed there's a plastic one in the prayer house.

Abilem: She gave it to me so I could make the central hanging ornament, so that they could trance-dance, so that I could help sick people. If I ceremonialize, I try to help treat illnesses, Sri Kelantan can also help. That's all that she promised.

Marina: What illnesses is Sri Kelantan able to help with?

Abilem: The type of sicknesses . . . If it's an illness from the flowers, here, I ceremonialize with the Way of the Annual Fruit Trees.

Marina: Oh.

Abilem: If it's illness . . . mmm . . . from the tree trunks, like from the ground here, sort of like ghosts . . . , for that, I ceremonialize Malay.

Marina: But those two . . . Does Sri Kelantan watch over the Annual Fruit Way of the Jungle and the Malay Way?

Abilem: Tɘŋɔːy has a forest feel to it. Sri Kelantan is from the Holy Place of the Naga:ʔ.

Marina: Hmm.

Abilem: Haven't you ever met that naga, the underwater dragon snake?

Marina: Is it like Sɘlumbaŋ, that naga?

Abilem: Yes, Sɘlumbaŋ. The Dragon-watersnake King Naga:ʔ. That is Sri Kelantan, the Water-snake King, Sɘlumbaŋ, like Sɘlumbaŋ, that's what we ceremonialize.

Marina: But when you sing the Way of Sri Kelantan, you don't do any of the head-whirling, as is done in trancing of Temiar's "Malay-style" ceremonies, or things like that . . .

Abilem: You'll notice, when I "return home" from trancing, alter on during this evening's coming ceremonies, I'll sing the Fruit Way first to cause it to return home;

then, after that, follows Sri Kelantan. One after the other. . . . The Fruit Tree spirit is also important, but that one's specialty is our head souls.
Marina: Oh.
Abilem: The other one, Sri Kelantan here, helps in cases of illness such as when we are hit by ghosts, satans, all sorts of jins. *From the earth, from the trees. Or from the water, from wherever . . .*
Marina: Oh. If one is hit by illness from ghosts, from jin, *from the ground, does it hit one in the head soul, or does it hit one in the heart soul, or . . . ?*
Abilem: It hits us in the heart.
Marina: Oh.
Abilem: It hits differently, that one, it's type . . .
Marina: It hits in the heart . . .
Abilem: Yes . . .
Marina: . . . in the breath[16] *. . .*
Abilem: . . . in our bones.
Marina: In the case of the baby the other night, that couldn't defecate . . .
Abilem: Yes?
Marina: What was that sickness?
Abilem: That was a ghost, as well.
Marina: A ghost as well.
Abilem: Yes.
Marina: Not an illness of the head soul, that one?
Abilem: Not of the head soul; rather, a ghost. So when the baby tried to evacuate its bowels, they were tied up, it was held back.
Marina: Oh.
Abilem: Something like that, it's a case of illness connected with the river . . .
Marina: Oh.
Abilem: . . . a case connected with wind, this type of illness, under the orders, the jurisdiction of the ghost group here. The jurisdiction of Sri Kelantan. Its origins are in the wind.[17]

Through the discourse of illness, the medium Abilem confronts the problems faced by Temiars in a polyethnic nation-state. Together, Sri Kelantan and Taŋɔːy handle the multiplicity of contemporary dangers: those from fruits and flowers, affecting the head soul, and those from tree trunks, earth, wind, and river, affecting the heart soul and the bones. Sri Kelantan's altar brings items associated with Malays, Chinese, and Temiars together. During healing performances, her songs are sung along with those of the Fruit Tree Spirits. In Sri Kelantan, this group of Temiars have crystallized their sense of endangerment in contemporary times, and developed a rubric for encountering the complexity of the times. At the conclusion of a ceremony, both *Taŋɔːy* of the forest fruits, and Sri Kelantan of postcolonial Malaysia are sent home or "returned," by singing the songs that each has given.

A HEALING PERFORMANCE

In 1992, Abilem held singing and trance-dancing ceremonies on several consecutive nights in a large structure built by village residents from traditional bamboo and leaf thatch, and situated between Abilem's wood and zinc house and the long road. The songs included those from the Annual Fruits genre (*taŋɔːy*), a genre associated with the spirits of dead humans (*cincɛm*), and Sri Kelantan. Toward the end of each evening's ceremony, the mother of the constipated infant brought the child forward, cuddled in her lap. Abilem sang over the child, while a chorus of women beating bamboo tubes responded interactively. In his song, he invokes Sri Kelantan, asking her to shine out clearly and open the obstruction in the child's bowels.

His healing ministrations occur two or three hours after each ceremony's commencement, after he has brought a collection of spiritguides, through song, into the ritual realm. By then, the evening's ceremony has already reached several climactic moments, as male and female dancers progress from strolling, swaying dance movements to the shudders and double-paced jumping-in-place that mark the deeper transformations of trance. Some of the dancers, transported to the point where their head souls momentarily detach to dance with the spirits, leave their bodies strewn across the dance floor. Other dancers guard the bodies of those thus entranced. As each trancer indicates through slight motions the return to his or her earthly body, they raise the trancers and, supporting them by the waist and shoulders, dance them back to consciousness. Towards the later part of the evening, after trancers have returned to the sidelines, the mother brings her ailing child forward for healing ministrations.

Abilem employs a variety of ritual vocalizations as his spiritguides move through him. For Temiars, the heart soul is the locus of stored memory, thought, and emotion. The head soul is associated with vocalizations; the spiritguide's head soul moves through Abilem as he vocalizes. The most predominant form of ceremonial vocalization is 'singing' (*gənabəg*).

Sri Kelantan's song has three cyclically recurring melodic phrases which form repetitive strophes (Figure 2).[18] Temiar use the same term, contextually delimited, to refer to a song phrase, a strophe, or an entire song: *ɲag*, 'mouthful.' Extemporaneous song texts, employing genre-specific vocabulary, are fit within the melodo-rhythmic contours of these three phrases. A verse need not include all three song phrases.

Figure 2. Sri Kelantan (see pp. 248–251).

Intermittently, another type of song phrase, *jɛnhoːk*, occurs. *Jɛnhoːk* song phrases start on a repeated high pitch and then descend; these song phrases are used to work in lengthier portions of song text that otherwise would not fit within the three melodic phrases of the strophe.[19]

Just as songs are termed "paths" that knowledgeable spiritguides chart through the dense jungle, so too, melodic contour is discussed in terms of landscape and river contour. Melodies rise, fall, cut straight across, or wind sinuously; a good song, like a good hike, alternates types of terrain. What Temiars describe as the disorientation of illness is counterbalanced by the sense of being "located" on paths inscribed in song.

Abilem also engages in 'conversational speech' (*tɛhnuh*) with other participants, and in formally 'spoken' invocations (*bacaːʔ*). In song text, as well as spoken invocations, he variously describes or directs the actions of the spirit-guide, or requests its assistance. Sometimes, directing his speech toward the illness agent, he speaks harshly (*ʔɛ-ʔaːl*) to frighten it away.

Some of Abilem's vocalizations are directed internally: one vocalization, a sharp, sudden "*ʔ a h   !,*" reopens his ears, for in his entranced relationship with the spirit singing through him, he sometimes feels as if his ears are "stuffed," and he can no longer hear the bamboo tube percussion. When he wipes the sweat off his face, clearing and renewing his energy, he often exclaims, "*s w a m !*" A soft, momentary whistling on the out-breath helps him "catch his breath" on the inhale.

Other vocalizations embody sonic action: 'blowing' cools the patient; 'sucking' helps extract the illness agent, bringing it to the patient's body surface, so it can be drawn out into the medium's hand, or swept away with a leaf whisk. Towards the end of the session, his hand successively strikes the bamboo floor while increasing in distance from the patient as he draws the illness out and away. The sounds of the leaf whisk swept across the infant to clear it of illness, waving in the air to spread the cool rejuvenating liquid that flows, like sap, from the spiritguides, or slapped in a direction away from the patient as the illness agent is released back into the cosmos, add to the dramatic musical "score" of the interaction between medium and spiritguide, illness agent and patient.

Each song phrase vocalized by Abilem is interactively responded to by the female chorus, who also bat pairs of bamboo tubes in a duple, high-low rhythm (Figure 2). The pulsating sounds of the bamboo-tube percussion iconically replicate the oscillating sounds of rainforest birds and insects, on the one hand, and the interior sounds of the beating heart, on the other. Temiars say the sounds of these instruments, bringing them into dual awareness of the pulsing jungle and their pulsing hearts, transport them across the boundaries of inner and outer, facilitating the detachability and permeability of trance. The rhythms, continuous, familiarized in their repetition, give trancers a sense of constancy throughout their travels. Positioning "foreign" illness agents and new concepts, like statehood, within these repetitive rhythms conjoining forest and body, past and present, renders new concepts and commodities less strange, more manageable.

In the song text that follows, Sri Kelantan speaks and sings, through Abilem, over the constipated child.[20] Sri Kelantan's first song phrase (see line 2-1, below) is marked by the beginning vocables "*tuy ʔəh tuy*," 'over there, on the other side.' Mediums, entered by their spiritguides, speak of a double-consciousness, as if their own heart souls were moved slightly to the side while the spiritguide sings through them. Repeated throughout the song, the phrase "*tuy ʔəh tuy*" becomes less significant semantically, and more important for its grammatic parallelism as a metapragmatic indicator of the beginning of song phrase one, and thus a new verse. To preserve this sensibility in the transliteration that follows, I have not translated it.

This song phrase is also characterized by the beginning vocable *yəh* (no semantic translation), and the closing vocable *yeʔ* (first person singular pronoun). In Temiar, verbs are unmarked for tense, number, or gender; and subjects (especially pronouns) can typically be omitted. The result is that there may potentially be substantial ambiguity as to the subject of any utterance, an ambiguity that Abilem Lum exploits fully in the present text. The song text embodies in its language the dialogical conjunction of the medium Abilem Lum with his spiritguide Sri Kelantan. A single utterance is susceptible of various interpretations and can be translated in different ways.

"*Sandiŋ Sari Kalantan!*" could thus be parsed as a first person, auto-referential nominative statement: "I, Sri Kelantan, arrive!" or as a third person,[21] other- or exo-referential nominative statement: "Sri Kelantan arrives!" or as a second person, exo-referential term of address: "Sri Kelantan, arrive!" Abilem juggles the two sets of distinctions, declarative or imperative on the one hand, and auto- or exo-referential on the other. This polysomy embodies the double identity of the medium-as-*hala:ʔ* (entered by the spiritguide) and the spiritguide-as-*hala:ʔ* (entering the medium). In the text here I alternate among translations to preserve the double-consciousness. This textual conflation of self-referential and other-referential replicates the entanglement of self and other, forest and non-forest, in the moments of mimesis and alterity that constitute spirit-mediumship.

Abilem begins the first verse of Sri Kelantan's song on the third song phrase (1–3, first verse, third melodic contour) by welcoming all participants, human and spirit, and establishing the presence of Sri Kelantan as she spreads her light across the land of Kelantan. Ritual energy is musically intensified as Abilem raises the pitch of the ceremony, literally, by swinging his melody up an octave above the tonic, in the fourth verse at line 4-1. He redefines this previous tonic as the fifth above what becomes the new tonic, now approximately a perfect fourth higher in pitch than the initial tonic:

1-3   Welcome! I, Sri Kelantan, dance, spreading my light.

> *Abilem stops singing and converses with some*
> *young Temiar men, who tie up my toppling microphone.*
> *Whistles*
>
> *Conversational Speech:* Where's the leaf whisk I just had?
> *Whistles*
>
> *Conversational Speech:* Oh, the palas leaf came undone!
>
> *Blows; sucks*
> *Whistles*

2-1   *Yəh, tuy ʔəh tuy,* far across Kelantan *ye?*

> *Chorus member:* (voice breaks)
> *[Abilem] Conversational Speech:* It's still not right!
> Start beating those tubes, you!
> *Whistles*

2-2   I see truly: the flowers bend and shiver here, and later, on the other side.

> *Whistles*

3-1   *Yəh, tuy ʔəh tuy,* let it open and soften like the morning dawn, *ye?!*

> *Spoken: Swam!*
> *Whistles*
> *Claps leaf whisk*
>
> *[Raises pitch, using the octave above the tonic to modulate up,*
> *making the previous tonic now seem like a dominant to the new tonic]*

4-1   *Yəh, tuy ʔəh tuy,* enter and soften *ʔəh !*

> *Spoken:* See truly!

4-2   Feel the moisture I spread from the shaken leaves, my grandchild.[22]

In the song text, Abilem often sings in the imperative, as he simultaneously proclaims and requests that the child's intestines will soften (line 4-1). The illocutionary power of words manufactures agency in the world to counteract the patient's intestinal obstruction. Metaphors of opening, spreading, softening abound: Sri Kelantan spreads "like a flash of light she slants through from behind the clouds" (line 5-3); elsewhere, she orders, "Let it open and soften like the morning dawn" (line 3-1). The waving of leaf ornaments adorning the dancers (line 6-1), and the swaying movement of picking flowers, one by one, from side to side (line 6-3), adds to the imagery of soft pliability as the song continues:

5-1   Yəh, tuy ʔəh tuy, shivering, softening yeʔ

Spoken: Spread like a flash, you!

5-2   Enter truly into the spirit of my grandchild.

5-3   Sri Kelantan spreads; like a flash of light she slants through from behind the clouds.

6-1   Yəh, tuy ʔəh tuy, the leaf ornaments in my waistline wave as I dance.

Blows

Spoken: Swam!

6-2   Only you may enter truly here![23]

6-3   I myself, picking flowers from side to side, one by one.

7-1   Yəh, tuy ʔəh tuy, shaking, softening yeʔ

Blows; sucking

7-2   Sri Kelantan, see clearly!

Whistles

Often a descriptive phrase replete with expressives[24] sets the evocative stage for an imperative, as the descriptive image below, "picking flowers from side to side" (line 8-1), sets the stage for the imperative, "Enter, flow into my grandchild" (line 8-2). Here, the flower imagery prepares the way for an order associated with the moistening, refreshing liquid kəhyɛk that flows, like plant sap, from the spirit world into the human realm during song ceremonies. The detachable head soul of the spirit is mobilized through the medium's vocalizations; the moisture thus flows into the patient through the medium's singing and blowing. The liquid also flows through the leaf ornaments and the medium's leaf whisk (4-2, 11-1). Plant imagery extends the metaphors of softening and opening the patient's constricted intestines, as Sri Kelantan describes the opening, blooming, and blossoming of flower buds (lines 10-1, 11-3, 13-2):

8-1   Yəh, tuy ʔəh tuy, picking flowers from side to side

Spoken: Swam!

8-2   Enter, flow into my grandchild

Whistles; blows

8-3   I dance gracefully.

9-1   Yəh, tuy ʔəh tuy, from afar: soften yeʔ!

Spoken: See clearly, you!

Whistles; blows

9-2   Return, truly, head soul of my grandchild;

Whistles; sucks

9-3   I dance from afar

Blows

10-1 Yəh, tuy ʔəh tuy, from afar: bloom, my buds!

Spoken: Light it up, you, Sri Kelantan!

10-2 Spreading truly through the head soul of my grandchild;

Sucks

10-3 I dance from afar.

11-1 Yəh, tuy ʔəh tuy, liquid shaken from the leaves softens

Vocalization: ʔ ə h !
Sucking; blows

11-2 I open at dawn, glimmering; then at sunset, glowing from the west, I illuminate the east

Whistles

11-3 As I dance, the buds of my grandchild blossom one by one.

12-1 Yəh, tuy ʔəh tuy, I, Kelantan, see multitudes dancing.

Blows

Spoken: Arrive truly, you!

12-2 Arrive truly, my Sri Kelantan!

Whistles

13-1 Yəh, tuy ʔəh tuy, my grandchild is so weak;[25]

Sucking; blows

13-2 Feel your spirit blossom as my water sprays, my grandchild;

Blows

13-3 As I, Sri Kelantan, do dance truly!

In the following lines of song text, Abilem polysemously entangles the twisted intestines of the patient, the turning of the dancers, and the swirling (lɛŋwiŋ) sensibility of trance. The swaying, side-to-side motion of flower picking (12-3, 15-1), like the soft sway of the motion of leaf whisks worn in dancers' waist bands (lines 6-1, 20-J) intensifies in the twirling, whirling motions associated with the experience of deeper trance (14-1, 19-2, 20-J). This twisting and turning, when kept within the proper ritual bounds, is the dangerous pleasure described as the experience of the trance state. In this dizzying, whirling space, which Temiars describe as the transformation (lɛslaːs) of trance, differences and distinctions cease to be problematic; in treatment, invoking this space of swaying, shuddering, shivering, and swirling is said to counteract and soften the hard knot of the illness of constipation. If carried to excess, however, it becomes a crazed swirl, tying up the intestines, or leading a trancer into the illness of soul loss:

Whistles

14-1 ɣəh, tuy ʔəh tuy, waving and softening yeʔ

Vocalization: ʔ a h !
Sucking

14-2 It enters, swirling, from my leaf whisk[26]

Blows

14-3 Spreading, arriving, in the moisture of my shaking leaves.

15-1 ɣəh, tuy ʔəh tuy, the buds are soft and weak yeʔ;

Spoken: Welcome, you all!
Blows; sucks

15-2 My flowers open, spreading afar;

Blows

15-3 I dance gracefully.

16-1 ɣəh, tuy ʔəh tuy, the moisture of the leaves softens

Sucking; grunting
Draws hands away across the floor

Whistles; blows
Vocalization: ʔ a h !
Whistles
Blows

Immediately following the first song phrase of the sixteenth verse evoking the images of softening leaf moisture, Abilem intensifies his sucking to draw the illness out, grunts to intimidate the illness agent, and pulls his hands away from the patient. The sound of his hands thumping across the bamboo floor slats marks the moment of illness extraction, followed by a clapping of his hands as he releases the illness agent back out beyond the confines of the community. In his closing imagery, he develops the contrast between soft sway and healthful waving motions, and the excessive twisting and turning of illness:

19-1 ɣəh, tuy ʔəh tuy, softening my flowers;

Sucking
Spoken: Twisting!

19-2 So twisted, turning; hey you, stop tying it up!

Blows

19-3 Enter, my Sri Kelantan.

20-1 ɣəh, tuy ʔəh tuy, from afar: soften yeʔ.

Sucking
Blows

20-J [*Singing, Jɛnhoːk*]
You illness agents, return this patient's head soul from its crazed swirl to a soft sway!

[*Jɛnho:k transforming to "spoken"*]
Don't make sickness, don't act maliciously!
Arrive truly, Sri Kelantan; remember [us]!

Blows
Blows through fist;
Blows.

This final phrase (20-J) begins as a *jɛnho:k*—a song phrase that starts with a repeated high pitch, then gradually descends melismatically. As the intonation curve flattens, the phrase shifts into the category of vocality "formal speech," in the subcategory of a "request." Abilem asks Sri Kelantan to remember her wards, and guard them from illness. The bamboo tube percussion then slows, and Abilem begins to sing a song from the Annual Fruits way, the Way of the *Bəko:d* Fruit. The illness of constipation, an illness of wind and earth, must be treated by Sri Kelantan, who conjoins forest ways with those of out-forester Malays and Chinese. But her presence must be counterbalanced by a song of the Annual Fruits, a way of the jungle.

MUSIC, DANCE, AND SOCIAL HEALINGS

. . . But when we started singing
Those good foolish songs of ours,
Then everything was again
As it always had been.
. . .
Once more we were just young men:
Not martyrs, not infamous, not saints.
This and other things came into our minds
While we kept singing.
But they were cloudlike things,
Hard to explain.

—Primo Levi, "Singing"
3 January 1946

In the swaying, swirling space of trance and dream songs, Temiars situate their encounters with the spirits of the forest, and, increasingly, with concepts, commodities, and persons from outside the forest. As Temiars grapple with their marginalized and politically disempowered role in the polyethnic state of Kelantan, the medium Abilem gathers the multiple voices of the contenders— forest people, Malays, Chinese—within Sri Kelantan's altar. A turbulent bidirectionality is compressed in the process of nationalization: cultures and languages are simultaneously centralized and standardized in what Bakhtin refers to as a centripetal motion (1981), and diversified in a centrifugal motion as the peoples of alternative class, ethnic, gender, or other marginalized groups pull language innovation and expressive culture in other directions. It is this dynamic of multiple directionality, simultaneously centrifugal and centripetal, that Abilem seeks to direct. In Temiar terms, it is described as *lɛŋwi:ŋ*, the dizzying, swirling motions—internal and external—of the trance that accompanies contact with the spirit world.

Temiars struggle with decreasing access to land and natural resources and attempt to adjust to the alternate social configurations that accompany mercantilism and capitalism. Yet their song ceremonies continue to express and reinforce, in the dimension of sound and movement, the cultural logic of generalized reciprocity found in traditional forms of Temiar exchange, which promote the diffusion of resources throughout the social group. A spirit's song enters the group through the voice of a single medium, but is diffused in its repetition, line by line, by the interactive choral response (Figure 2). In this performance format, the Spirit of the State of Kelantan is diffused throughout the social group, even while the commodities and political processes associated with nationalization may promote increasingly restricted networks of distribution.

Voices of initial singer and chorus intertwine, Temiars say, when the initial singer's song phrase ends, descending "from the sky," while the chorus's phrase ascends "from the earth," as in Figure 2, from Marker 13-3, end of measure 1. Their positions are reversed when the chorus's phrase ends, descending "from the sky," while the initial singer's next phrase ascends. This occurs, for example, in Figure 2, from Marker 13-3, end of the second measure, into the beginning of 14-1. In such interactive musical moments, traditional Temiar reciprocal relations of self and society, male and female, human and cosmos, are restated, despite the changing lifestyles and value systems that increasingly impinge upon Temiar life in modernizing Kelantan.

These ceremonies—like the moments described in Primo Levi's poem about singing with his fellow inmates during the Holocaust—are arenas in which Temiars remind themselves, in the codes of sound, movement, color, and odor, who they are and how the world works. Here, space and time are restructured in the motions and durations of vocalized sound and body movements; boundaries are crossed, differences are both stated and undermined.[27] This is the arena in which "foreign" spirits are brought into Temiar habitats, where these strange new things, peoples, and concepts can be repositioned within the rhythms paced by the bamboo tubes and paths traced by melodic contours.

The Spirit of the State of Kelantan is musically defined in contradistinction to the Spirits of the Annual Fruits through the structure of the tone row or "steps" (laŋkah, "the space from one footstep to the next") from which her melody is constructed. The Spirit of Kelantan sings in an anhemitonic pentatonic[28] mode. Her melodies emphasize intervals of a whole step (or major second), and, in particular, use step-wise motion within the range of a major third (Figure 3, Example 7).[29] In contrast, songs of the Annual Fruits employ chromaticism, using a preponderance of half-steps and minor thirds in their melodies (Figure 3, Examples 1 through 6). Sri Kelantan's song does not contain the smaller half-step interval found in tone rows of the more than twenty songs of the Annual Fruits genre that Abilem has composed (or "interposed") since receiving his first from the Rambutan Fruit Tree in a dream during the mid-1970s. The tone row used to construct the melody of Sri Kelantan's song thus musically indexes her difference from that which has gone before, just as her altar materially indexes Abilem's response to the new experience of citizenship in the political framework of the nation-state.

Sri Kelantan's "steps," or scalular formation, do not exist in a referential vacuum. Viewed in intertextual relationship with other songs and genres within Abilem's personal repertoire of dream songs, and with those of other geographically and historically situated Temiar song genres, the tone row contains meaningful information at a level of specificity of the sign that, when carefully linked with ethnographic and ethnohistorical data, provides "keys"—in more than a musical sense—to Temiar cultural and historical experience.

When intertextually compared with other Temiar spirit song genres, Sri Kelantan's anhemitonic pentatonic tone row and melodic configuration exhibit a musical similarity with the genres Salɛmbaŋ and Pɛnhaːy.[30] Reviewing ethnographic interview data quoted above, we recall that Sri Kelantan's full name, given in her dream communication with Abilem, is Sri Kelantan of the Holy Place of the Naga King. While "Taŋɔːy has a forest feel to it," Abilem tells us, "Sri Kelantan is from the Holy place of the Nagaːʔ... The Dragon-water-snake King Nagaːʔ. That is Sri Kelantan, the Water-snake King, Salumbaŋ, like Salumbaŋ, that's what we ceremonialize." While Abilem recognizes that "her ancestry is shared by the Chinese," the Water-snake King, in Abilem's pantheon, maintains her character as a "forest woman.... Not Malay.... Not Chinese."

Sri Kelantan has emerged at a time of social upheaval and transformation for Malaysian rainforest peoples. Ethnohistorically, Salumbaŋ also references a time of social upheaval and dangerous transformation: the Great Floods of 1926. Formal musical parameters, here the distinctive tone rows of two genres Salumbaŋ and Sri Kelantan, are supported by ethnographic and ethnohistorical evidence. The anhemitonic pentatonic tone rows of Salumbaŋ and Sri Kelantan, within Abilem's and possibly the Temiar's musical repertoire, would

Figure 3. Tone rows of the Annual Fruits genre (Examples 1 through 6) compared with Sri Kelantan (Example 7).

seem then to encode spirit-mediated cultural responses to periods of social upheaval and change.

Interestingly, whenever Abilem sings Sri Kelantan, including during the healing performances of August 1992 held for the constipated infant, Abilem usually sings a song of the *Cincɛːm* genre. He learned this song from his paternal grandfather, born in Perak at Jalong, site of origin of *Cincɛːm*. *Cincɛːm* also ethnohistorically references a time of social upheaval in the 1930's, when Temiars were experiencing diasporic incursion through the increase in Islamic Malay settlement in upland areas.

Cincɛːm's tone row varies from that of Sri Kelantan; the historical experience of adjustment is expressed, rather, in ritual practices associated with the genre: those with whom *Cincɛːm* becomes familiar must abstain from eating wild boar. *Cincɛːm*'s admonishment legitimates the contemporaneous struggle Temiars were having with alterity as manifest in negative "out-forester" judgements regarding their non-participation with such Islamic prohibitions as eating pork.

Sri Kelantan's 1990's admonishment to attend to a stably situated altar similarly legitimates Abilem's and his fellow villagers' struggle to adjust to government-supported sedentary housing and lifestyle.

From information gleaned in interview and from observing healing performances, we find Abilem calling upon Sri Kelantan "in cases of illness traced to "ghosts, satans, and *jins*" from the earth, trees, water, and wind, affecting, as in this case, things lower and inner; the Fruit Tree spirits handle cases concerning head souls. The correlations among parameters of varied cultural dimensions—formal musical parameters such as tone rows and intervalic emphases, ritual admonishments such as food restrictions, historical contingency of emergence during periods of social upheaval, and illness etiology and treatment, constitute convergent data articulating Temiar cultural codes broadcasting distress.

The Temiar data demonstrates an independently variable relationship among parameters such as musical form, performance practice, ritual restrictions, and historicity in the cultural construction of meaning. Boas recognized the historical particularity and independent variation of parameters he termed *Race, Language, and Culture* (1966 [1940]); his subsequent call for ethnographic and ethno-historical detail would well be heeded by scholars too quick to seek an essential meaning for "the half-step" or "a tone row" divorced from the complexities of its musical, social, and historical contexts.

While tone row construction and melodic activity indexes similarities between some spirit song genres and differences among others, fundamental elements of performance practice remain the same within all Temiar musico-ceremonial genres. In particular, these include the vocal interaction between initial singer and interactive chorus, as well as the duple-based rhythms of the bamboo-tube and baranɔʔ or batak drum percussion (Figure 4). Sri Kelantan's multiplicities, expressed in different channels—from tone row to performance practice—subsume the turbulent heteroglossia of Temiar contemporary everyday life in ritual confluence. She contains the paradoxes of the river, the route that links these forest people with the deeper jungle and the outforest gɔb, both of which bring knowledge as well as illness, fortune as well as misfortune.

In this rainforest congress of the spirit world, Abilem petitions: "Don't make sickness, don't act maliciously! Arrive truly, Sri Kelantan; remember us!" Sri Kelantan's song, directed toward the healing of a particular individual, effects a social healing for a group traumatized by the dislocations of "regroupment." Community members join to choreograph and orchestrate their animated spirit world, bringing the presence of invasive outforesters temporarily under their control in this ritual space. Temiars resist passivity in the face of diminishing resources when they manipulate the song phrases and stylized gestures of the healing arts.

Figure 4. While singing a song from the Annual Fruit Tree genre, Abilem plays the *barənɔʔ* drum. His repetitive duple rhythm elaborates that of the bamboo-tube percussion.

This places Temiar dream song and ritual performance within the framework of musical genres that maintain dignity in the face of nearly overwhelming odds. African American spirituals, for example, and later, the blues, transformed the sadness lingering from experiences of slavery and loss into masterful play within expressive mediums. And the South African sung-poetry of *difela* (Coplan 1988) transforms the demeaning circumstances of migrant miners into heroic epics. Similarly, Puerto Rican *salsa* (Roseman 1983) symbolically intertwines the multiple and seemingly contradictory identities of Caribbean islanders now living in the hothouse of New York City, in its polyrhythmic, polytimbral musical combinations of Afro-Cuban percussion, Puerto Rican musical genres, and urban jazz horns. Temiar musical mixes help make sense of otherwise incomprehensible juxtapositions, as well, by deftly crossweaving the multiple cultural codes available in such musical parameters as tone row, melodic contour, interaction and delegation of voices, instrumentation, and rhythmic pulsation.

Temiars invent a poetics from the clash of competing societies. Through such creations, cultures carve their musics of survival, and gain the strength to carry on. Refreshed by the cool liquid of the spirits, "lightened" (hayɔ̌ʔ) as if a load were removed—"empowered," to use a cosmopolitan metaphor—Temiars return to the realm of daily life.

ACKNOWLEDGMENTS

Field research with the Temiars of Kelantan and Perak was conducted in 1981–82, 1991, and 1992, under the auspices of the Social Science Research Foundation, the Wenner Gren Foundation for Anthropological Research, the National Science Foundation, and the Research Foundation of the University of Pennsylvania. Additional travel funds were provided by Universiti Sains Malaysia and Malaysian Air Lines (1991). My thanks to these sponsors and to the Universiti Kebangsaan Malaysia, Muzium Negara, Jabatan Hal Ehwal Orang Asli, Socio-Economic Research Unit, and Persatuan Orang Asli Semenanjung Malaysia (POASM, Orang Asli Association of Peninsular Malaysia), whose officers and staff shared their extensive knowledge and services with me.

Temiars and other Orang Asli throughout Malaysia have been wise and patient teachers and friends, opening their homes and their experiences to me; my gratitude to them, and to host families of Wan Afidah and Satria Ahmad; Ahmad Sahlan; Dr. Mat Hussin bin Hassan Gul; Pamela Sodhy; and Sharifah Zaleha bin Syed Hassan.

NOTES

1. The Malaysian nation was formed in 1963. It included peninsular Malaysia (which attained independence in 1957), plus the formerly British Singapore, Sabah (North Borneo), and Sarawak (Northwest Borneo). Singapore was separated in 1965 to alleviate tensions between that city's Chinese majority and the Malays, who maintained administrative control of the Malaysian government (Andaya and Andaya 1982; Nagata 1979).

2. Temiars, speakers of an Austroasiatic language related to Cambodian, are poised at the southern end of the Austro-asiatic continuum of contemporary Indochina, where they have been enveloped by the Austronesian (Malayo-Polynesian) speakers of Mainland and Insular Southeast Asia. Temiar constitutes one dialect among 16 linguistic groups or dialects spoken by the two-thirds of the Orang Asli who are Austroasiatic speakers. The remaining third are Austronesian speakers of roughly 4 Malay dialects collectively termed Aboriginal Malay (Diffloth 1975, 1979; Benjamin 1976; Wurm and Hattori 1983; Roseman 1991:17–19).

3. Temiar orthography follows Benjamin (176) with slight changes. Vowel length is indicated with a colon: /a:/, vowel nasalization is indicated with a tilde: /ã/. Vowels (in their short, non-nasalized forms): /a/ as in English f*a*ther, /ɛ/ as in English b*e*t, /ə/ as in English th*e*, /e/ as in English b*ai*t, /ɔ/ as in English *o*r, /ɨ/ high central half-rounded voicoid, approximately English "t*u*ne", /u/ as in English b*oo*t. Consonant nasalization: /ɲ/ = /ny/; /ŋ/ = /ng/ as in English si*ng*; /ʔ/ = glottal stop, as in Brooklynese "li'l" for "little."

4. See Bellwood 1985, Benjamin 1976 on Temiar linguistics and archaeology; Solheim 1980 on the historical "origins" of the Orang Asli, or aboriginal peoples of Malaysia; Roseman 1991:17–19 on the historical relationships between Austronesian and Austroasiatic speakers; Benjamin 1985 for theories on the early eco-cultural and linguistic interactions among Malays and the diverse groups of Orang Asli.

5. Judith Nagata (1979) discusses the complex relationship among ethnic, religious, class, occupation, and educational status that define the shifting categories of ethnic identity cursorily listed here.

6. From the William Carlos Williams poem *For Elsie* (1923), highlighted in Clifford 1988:1–17. Clifford links the poem to a discussion of colonialism, transnationalism, and the inventive poetics of the twentieth century.

7. On this complex historical moment, see Jones 1968, Roseman 1980, Leary 1989, Nicholas 1990.

8. Gianno (1990) charts, for example, the history of the resin trade among the Semelai, another Orang Asli group.

9. Interview conducted in Bawik, August 31, 1992 (Tape 92-0C3 tr 2).

10. Temiar, *Sari Kelantan Karama:d Raja Naga:ʔ;* In Malay, Sri Kelantan Raja Naga.

11. Temiar, *calɨn.*

12. An associated Temiar term, *limbaŋ,* designates the primordial flood reported in a version of the creation myth collected by Benjamin (1967:38). Yuan Ke (1993) discusses dragons in Chinese mythology.

13. Abilem has shortened and Temiarized (with a glottal stop) the Malay title for minister, Menteri, to *Tiʔ.*

14. See Carstens 1980 on the Chinese Malaysians of Pulai.

15. Dr. Pattaratorn Chirapravati (1994:191, ft. 1; 558, fig.100) identifies this as a Type II Buddhist votive tablet of the Srivijaya period, 9–10 centuries A.D. She belies the cave was a forest refuge or pilgrimage site for Buddhist monks. The cave at Gua Berhala (Temiar also refer to this as Batu Chawas), Ulu Kelantan, has recently been studied by a team of archaeologists led by En. Adi Haji Taha from the National Museum in Kuala Lumpur (Adi Haji Taha 1993:77, 78 fig. 10). I am grateful to Oliver Wolters for further reflections on the significance of this site.

16. For Temiars, heart (*hup*) and breath (*hinɨm*) are associated due to their physical interiority and duple rhythms.

17. On the winds in Malay illness etiology and treatment, see Laderman 1991.

18. In the musical transcription in Figure 2, and in the song translation, below, these three melodic phrases are identified by a dash followed by the numbers -1, -2, and -3. Strophes (or verses to which these three phrases belong) are numbered prior to the dash, as they occur consecutively within the overall song. "4-2" would thus refer to the second melodic phrase of the fourth verse.

19. The *jɛnhoːk* phrase is identified in transcription and translation by a "-J."

20. Recorded in August 1992 (Temiar tape collection 92-OC5 track 1).

21. In many mainland Southeast Asian languages, Mon Khmer as well as Tai, the third person is regularly used as a first person in formal or polite utterances, like the "royal we" but not limited to pronouns. The range of person-referring forms includes pronouns, proper nouns and titles, kinship terms, and common nouns. To index formality, politeness, hierarchy, etc., singular first-person can thus be replaced by: first-person plural exclusive (we two), first-person plural inclusive (we all), or third person: name, title, kinship term, definite description of the speaker. Similarly, third person substitutes for second person, or the second-person plural exclusive/inclusive substitutes for the singular to indicate respect, politeness, etc. While Temiar social organization and language use are more egalitarian than that of many mainland Southeast Asian court and plains cultures, the Temiar language does differentiate among kinship terms of reference and address, and also employs the second-person plural inclusive/exclusive in substitution for the singular, to index formality and respect. Abilem sometimes employs these devices, as in the phrase "*Sandiŋ ɲɔb Sɛri Kɛlantan!*": "Arrive, you [plural exclusive] honored Sri Kelantan!" He may employ the oscillation between first and third person, as well, not only to embody the dual identity of the medium/spiritguide, but also to index the formality of the situation and the status relations between medium and spiritguide (i.e., non-familiar, if you will). My thanks to Frank Proschan for pointing out these comparative dimensions.

22. Abilem's spiritguide addresses the patient, a 6-month-old infant, as his grandchild, though he addresses Abilem as his father.

23. Only the spiritguide, not the illness agents, should be inside the child.

24. Expressives, words built through reduplicative play, are discussed in Diffloth 1976 and Roseman 1991:157.

25. Verses 13 and 14 are transcribed in Figure 2.

26. The spiritguide both describes ("it enters"; "it swirls") and declares ("Enter!" "Swirl!") simultaneously.

27. For further discussion of the transformative properties of music and movement, see Roseman 1990; Porter 1992; Nattiez 1990:118; Ness 1992.

28. A pentatonic tone row has five tones; the modifier anhemitonic describes the spacing between those tones, in this case, no "hemi-" or half-steps. The standard measure used in this description is the half-step of Euramerican tempered tonality. While limited in its crosscultural investigative capabilities, it maximizes broad scholarly communication. The half-step varies in hertz according to its placement in frequency range within the tempered scale, but is considered to be equivalent to 100 cents.

29. Intervals are a measure of the distance between tones, whether heard sequentially or simultaneously. They are commonly described by the number of half-steps they contain. A half-step, often referred to as a minor second, is generally equivalent to the distance between middle C and the D-flat (or C-sharp) just above it. Such intervals are found in tone rows and melodies of the Annual Fruits genre. Two half-steps, often referred to as a major second, describe the distance, for example, between middle C and the D above it. Sri Kelantan's melodies emphasize the whole steps, in descending order, from A to G, E to D, and D to C. A minor third contains three half-steps: for example, from middle C to the E-flat above it. This interval is emphasized in Annual Fruit genre melodies. Sri Kelantan's tone row contains a minor third between G and E; other melodies also emphasize whole-step activity within the range of a major third, from E to middle C.

30. For a chart comparing tone rows of Temiar musical genres, see Roseman 1995a:5, Figure 3.

REFERENCES

Adi Haji Taha. 1993. Recent Archeological Discoveries in Peninsular Malaysia (1991–1993). *Journal of the Malaysian Branch of the Royal Asiatic Society* 66(1):67–98.

Andaya, Barbara and Leonard Andaya. 1982. *A History of Malaysia.* London: Macmillan.

Anderson, Benedict. 1991 [1983]. *Imagined Communities: Reflections on the Origin and Spread of Nationalism.* Rev. ed. London, New York: Verso.

Bakhtin, Mikhail M. 1981. *The Dialogic Imagination: Four Essays by M. M. Bakhtin,* ed. M. Holquist. Austin: University of Texas.

Bellwood, Peter. 1985. *Prehistory of the Indo-Malaysian Archipelago.* New York: Bellwood.

Benjamin, Geoffrey. 1976. An Outline of Temiar Grammar. In *Austroasiatic Studies,* pt. 1, ed. P. Jenner et al. Honolulu: University Press of Hawaii.

———. 1985. In the Long Term: Three Themes in Malayan Cultural Ecology. In *Cultural Values and Human Ecology in Southeast Asia,* ed. Karl Hutterer. Ann Arbor, Michigan: University of Michigan, Center for South and Southeast Asia Studies.

Boas, Franz. 1966 [1940]. *Race, Language, and Culture.* New York: Free Press.

Bosch, Frederik David Van. *The Golden Germ: An Introduction to Indian Symbolism.* Gravenhage: Mouton.

Carstens, Sharon. 1980. Images of Community in a Chinese Malaysian Settlement. Ph.D. diss. Cornell University.

Carey, Iskandar. 1976. *Orang Asli.* Kuala Lumpur: Oxford University Press.

Chirapravati, Pattaratorn. 1994. The Cult of Votive Tablets in Thailand (6th to 13th centuries). Ph. D. diss. Cornell University.

Clifford, James. 1988. *The Predicament of Culture: Twentieth-Century Ethnography, Literature, and Art.* Cambridge: Harvard University Press.

Coplan, David. 1988. Musical Understanding: The Ethnoaesthetics of Migrant Workers' Poetic Song in Lesotho. *Ethnomusicology* 32(3):337–367.

Cuisinier, Jeanne. 1936. *Danses magiques de Kelantan.* Paris: Institute d'Ethnologie.

Dentan, Robert K. 1992. The Rise, Maintenance, and Destruction of a Peacable Polity: A Preliminary Essay in Political Ecology. In *Aggression and Peacefulness in Humans and Other Primates,* ed. J. Silverberg and J. P. Gray. New York: Oxford University Press.

Diffloth, Gerard. 1975. Les langues Mon-Khmer de Malaisie, classification historique et innovations. *Asie du Sud-Est et Monde Insulindien* 6(4):1–20.

———. 1976. Expressives in Semai. In *Austroasiatic Studies,* pt. 1, ed. Phillip N. Jenner et al., 249–264. Honolulu: University Press of Hawaii.

———. 1979 Asian Languages and Southeast Asian Prehistory. *Federation Museums Journal* 24, n.s.:3–16.

Endicott, Kirk. 1983. The Effects of Slave Raiding on the Aborigines of the Malay Peninsula. In *Slavery, Bondage, and Dependency in Southeast Asia,* ed. A. Reid and J. Brewster. Brisbane: University of Queensland Press.

Gianno, Rosemary. 1990. *Semelai Culture and Resin Technology.* New Haven, Ct.: The Connecticut Academy of Arts and Sciences.

Jones, Alun. 1968. The Orang Asli: An Outline of Their Progress in Modern Malaya. *Journal of Southeast Asian History* 9(2):268–292.

Laderman, Carol. 1987. Destructive Heat and Cooling Prayer: Malay Humoralism in Pregnancy, Childbirth and the Postpartum Period. *Social Science and Medicine* 25(4):357–366.

———. 1991. *Taming the Wind of Desire: Medicine, Psychology, and Aesthetics in Malay Shamanistic Performance.* Berkeley, Los Angeles: University of California Press.

Leary, John. 1989. The Importance of the Orang Asli in the Malayan Emergency 1948–1960. Working Paper Number 56. Clayton, Victoria: The Centre of Southeast Asian Studies, Monash University, Australia.

Levi, Primo. 1988. *Collected Poems.* Translated by R. Feldman and B. Swann. London: Faber and Faber.

Nagata, Judith. 1979. *Malaysian Mosaic: Perspectives from a Poly-Ethnic Society.* Vancouver: University of British Columbia.

Nattiez, Jean-Jacques. 1990. *Music and Discourse: Toward a Semiology of Music.* Translated by Carolyn Abbate. Princeton: Princeton University.

Ness, Sally Ann. 1992. *Body, Movement, and Culture: Kinesthetic and Visual Symbolism in a Philippine Community.* Berkeley, Los Angeles, University of California Press.

Nicholas, Colin. 1990. In the Name of The Semai? The State and Semai Society in Peninsular Malaysia. In *Tribal Peoples and Development in Southeast Asia,* ed. Lim Teck Ghee & Albert G. Gomes (Special issue of the journal *Manusia & Masyarakat*). Kuala Lumpur: University of Malaya, Department of Anthropology and Sociology.

Porter, James. 1992. (Ballad-) Singing and Transformativity. *Scandinavian Yearbook of Folklore 1992* 48:165–180.

Roseman, Marina. 1980. Malay and Orang Asli Interactions: Views from Legendary History. Unpublished paper, Department of Anthropology, Cornell University.

———. 1983. The New Rican Village: Artists in Control of the Image-making Machinery. *Latin American Music Review* 4(1):132–167.

———. 1984. The Social Structuring of Sound: The Temiar of Peninsular Malaysia. *Ethnomusicology* 28(3):411–445.

———. 1989. Inversion and Conjuncture: Male and Female in Temiar Performance. In *Women and Music in Cross-cultural Perspective,* ed. Ellen Koskoff. Urbana: University of Illinois Press.

———. 1990. Head, Heart, Odor and Shadow: The Structure of the Self, Ritual Performance and the Emotional World. *Ethos* 18(3):227–250.

———. 1991. *Healing Sounds from the Malaysian Rainforest: Temiar Music and Medicine.* Los Angeles, Berkeley, Oxford: University of California Press.

———. 1995a. *Dream Songs and Healing Sounds: In the Rainforests of Malaysia.* Washington, D.C.: Smithsonian/Folkways Recordings SF CD 40417.

———. 1995b. Singers of the Landscape: Song, History, and Property Rights in the Malaysian Rainforest. *American Anthropologist* 97(4): - . [Reprinted in *Culture and the Question of Rights in Southeast Asia: Forests, Coasts, and Seas,* ed. Charles Zerner. Washington, D.C.: Woodrow Wilson Press, i.p.]

Scheper-Hughes, Nancy and Margaret M. Lock. 1987. The Mindful Body: a Prolegomenon to Future Work in Medical Anthropology. *Medical Anthropology Quarterly* 1, n.s.(1):6–41.

Solheim, Wilhelm G., II. 1980. Searching for the Origins of the Orang Asli. *Federation Museums Journal,* n.s. 25:61–75.

Williams, William Carlos. 1986. *The Collected Poems of William Carlos Williams, Vol. I: 1909–1939,* ed. A. W. Litz and C. MacGowan. New York: New Directions.

Winstedt, R.O. 1927. The Great Flood, 1926. *Journal of the Malay Branch of the Royal Asiatic Society* 5:295–309.

Wurm, S.A., and S. Hattori, eds. 1983. *Language Atlas of the Pacific Area,* pt. 2. Map 37: Peninsular Malaysia. G. Benjamin, compiler. Pacific Linguistics, Series C., no. 66. Canberra: Australian Academy of the Humanities and the Japan Academy.

Yuan Ke. 1993. *Dragons and Dynasties: An Introduction to Chinese Mythology.* Translated by K. Echlin and Nie Zhixiong. London: Penguin.

9

FROM DIAGNOSIS
TO PERFORMANCE

Medical Practice and the Politics
of Exchange in Kodi, West Sumba

Janet Hoskins

The healing of illness is a spectacle in a great many societies, an occasion for beating drums and gongs, inviting large groups of people, and staging spirit seances, dramatic dances, and night-long oratorical competitions. The patient, who often lies in the middle, only semi-conscious, is surrounded by a host of invisible enemies and hidden friends, and an elaborate narrative is sung or spoken to portray the shadowy conflicts between warring figures within his or her suffering. The sick bed is transformed into a stage, and the patient, his or her family, and ritual specialists called in to assist them are transformed into players, opening their secrets up to public scrutiny and acting out their efforts to resolve them before an audience of human and spirit on-lookers.

I begin not with the performance—the dramatic staging of healing as a culturally orchestrated theater of suffering, whose moral has yet to be discovered—but with the more humdrum moments that precede it. The dramatic performances of healing take place against a background of other, less spectacular forms of medical treatment. My focus is the diagnostic decision which can lead either toward performance or away from it, and especially the moral consequences of this decision.

There are three questions that I ask about the diagnostic decision to move to performance in Kodi:

1. Is the movement to performance undertaken only in the case of failure of other traditional remedies?
2. Is the primary goal of the performance to cure the patient?
3. What else is going on at an elaborate performance, which may concern participants other than the patient him or herself?

It might seem reasonable to suppose that "performative resolutions" occur only after the failure of other means, if we accept the idea that ritual therapy serves primarily as a form of "hope in the face of despair," and offers psychological consolation rather than effective technical devices.[1] The data outlined here show, however, that while traditional remedies are highly effective in some cases, they are ineffective and even dangerous in others. This case study of the Kodi people of Eastern Indonesia demonstrates that the movement to performance is not simply related to the severity of the illness or injury, or to the capacity of private healers to treat it.

Since success rates vary for all forms of therapy, conducted both by private healers and public performers, a more important determining factor would seem to be how widely the net of collective responsibility is cast in each particular case. Public performances may be undertaken for patients who are already well on the road to recovery, or who are in fact mortally ill, and die soon after the proceedings. Since the performance is not invalidated by either of these outcomes, it is not realistic to insist that a ritual frame is the same thing as a medical practice. While each of these performances is filled with rhetorical calls for recovery, this is—at one level—simply rhetoric. Something else is being accomplished at the performance. We might wonder whether the effectiveness of the performance is really focused on the patient at all. Is the presence of illness a pretext for the resolution of long standing problems, within which the patient's suffering is just a starting point for a much wider investigation?

I will return to these questions later, once they have been grounded in case material that details the experience of illness and cure in a particular society.

THE SETTING: KODI SOCIETY AND EXCHANGE

I investigate this problem among the Kodi people of Sumba, Eastern Indonesia. At the time of my fieldwork in the 1980s, the majority of the 50,000 Kodi people were followers of the indigenous religion, the worship of *marapu* (ancestors, spirits and deities) who live in the tombs, gardens and houses along the west coast of the island. Social life in Kodi is organized by exchange obligations which obtain between ancestors and their descendants, wife-givers and wife-takers, and members of different houses who have formed reciprocal agreements for mutual assistance. A house is made up of the agnatic descendants of a single founder and the women they have married. It is located in a clan village which is the cult center for several hundred people, although they may live widely dispersed in inland garden hamlets. The extensive character of exchange obligations, and their tendency to be stretched out over long periods of time, means that almost all forms of social tension gravitate in some way around issues of exchange—promises to give gifts which were not fulfilled, duties to make offerings which were not carried out, debts which were acknowledged by one party but not by another.

Healing and the process of diagnosis is implicated in the politics of exchange, but in a complicated way: Some forms of illness and injury are diagnosed as "social diseases," a term which has here a very different sense from the one our society gives to this label, where it designates a narrow category of sexually transmitted diseases. In Kodi, "social diseases" (literally, *hadu pata tana* or "diseases related to custom") require elaborate performances, and call upon a network of kin and affines to bring contributions to a sacrificial slaughter. Other kinds of diseases (including, as we will see, the most common sexually transmitted diseases) are considered treatable by more mundane means—herbal potions, massage, the burning of scented barks or the rubbing of coconut oil on parts of the body. The seriousness of an injury and its ability to threaten life is not given as much importance as is the *location of its occurrence*—whether a fall on a steep mountain path or inside the ancestral house—since the location can determine the number of other people involved in its causation. Causation has serious consequences for treatment, determining whether procedures are used to open the patient up to everyone, making even the most intimate acts public knowledge, or close him off from the collective gaze. The problem of location brings us back to the very definition of the "social," since the "social disease" is the one which implicates not only a few individuals but a much larger corporate group.

Thus classification of illnesses and injuries in Kodi is based on causes, not on symptoms. A traditional healer examines his or her patient, listens to an account of the symptoms of distress, but also asks a number of other questions: Who has been made unhappy within the group? What ceremonial obligations have been neglected? Are there promised exchanges which have been delayed? What special requests from ancestors or wild spirits might not have been fulfilled? The physical signs of illness may provide clues to causes, but often they are described only rather vaguely as "fevers" (kalawaro) which show the "heat" of invisible disapproval. Ultimately the healer's diagnostic decision refers to afflicting spirits or other agents of destruction (notions of pollution and contamination, witchcraft, poison or bad magic), and not to the ailment itself.

I discuss three specific cases which show different relationships between the process of diagnosis and the movement to performance. Illness is enmeshed in the politics of exchange in all three cases, but only two were subject to ritual mediation. One, although serious, required more direct action on the part of the patient. The other two, because of their relation to wider contexts of social life, cast the patient in a passive role and lead us to question the usual assumption that the patient is really the beneficiary of the ritual process. In the terms of modern medical practice, my three cases concern venereal disease, mouth cancer, and a slight injury to the head from a fall, but in terms of Kodi ritual practice they concern pollution through a private act, arrested exchange, and unfulfilled obligations to the ancestors. The differences between these conceptualizations— the tension between the vocabulary not only of medicine but also of most "medical anthropology," on the one hand, and the indigenous set of categories, on the other—are real subjects of this discussion.

KODI PRACTITIONERS PUBLIC AND PRIVATE

What we call "medical practice"—the treatment of illnesses and injuries—is accomplished in Kodi by both private practitioners (*tou tangu moro,* "people who apply medicines") and public performers (*rato marapu,* "priests," *tou parupu kaloro* "diviners," and *tou ta liyo,* "orators").

Private healers divide into practitioners of specific therapies—bone-setters, makers of poultices of charcoal powder and leaves for tropical ulcers, herbalists who prepare "binding medicines" to stop bleeding after childbirth, and people who perform massage and ask patients to imbibe teas or apply healing oils. Many private healers deal with only one form of ailment, and most claim that they received the secret of these medicines from a dream or vision given them by an ancestral spirit. They are called in for specific problems, and are usually paid afterwards only if the affliction has responded to treatment.

The term for medicines, *moro,* designates colors which range from blue to green. It also has the meaning of "raw," "uncooked" or "unprocessed." Traditional herbal preparations, especially healing leaf pastes, are often greenish in color, and through this term they are linked both to folk technologies of indigo dying, and to a complex of "blue arts" associated with midwifery and witchcraft (Hoskins 1989). Much of this knowledge is inherited through the maternal descent line (*walla*), although membership in houses and ancestral villages is patrilineal. Both men and women practice as bone-setters, herbalists, and

Figure 1. A diviner performs a public interrogation of the spirits by lunging with a spear toward the right front pillar of the house as he proposes a series of reasons for the spirit's anger. When the spear touches the pillar, he has struck the truth, and can follow up with more questions (1980, photograph by the author).

masseurs, but only women serve as midwives and indigo dyers, while men predominate in the treatment of flesh wounds. No private healer would tell me the precise combination of ingredients culled from roots, barks and leaves that he or she used, but many told me some of the ingredients. The thick, curved vine of the *kahi kyara* creeper was used to treat impotence, the inside kernel of cottonwood was placed in coconut oil to fight fevers and infections, and a milky tree resin was sometimes given for dysentery. Private healers practiced most often on their own close kin, and some claimed greater efficacy for members of their own house and clan.

Public performers, on the other hand, cannot practice in their own homes. They must be summoned to another house or village, and serve as mediators between the human community and the *marapu*. They do not deal in any topical treatments, and in fact their approach to illness is basically that of a psychotherapist: They propose a "talking cure" whereby all the possible causes are exposed in a divination, as spirits are interrogated in turn and the reasons for their anger are determined. Divination occurs in a group setting, usually with all family members sitting near the right front pillar of the house, as the diviner constructs his interpretation of the spirits' anger from responses received from a spear which he holds with one arm stretched along its shaft as he lunges toward the pillar. He names a series of ancestors, local spirits and guardians of ritual protocol. When the spear strikes, he has pronounced the name of the offended spirit, and he must establish how it fits with evidence of neglected obligations supplied by his audience. In many ways, his role seems more that of the catalyst for a group-therapy session than that of an independent diagnostician, since after each revelation he goes back to the family members, who discuss and evaluate it and provide him with more information to continue the search. The public performer does not claim to receive visions or any direct supernatural experience. He is only the spokesman of the spirits, the "lips told to speak, mouth told to pronounce." The shamanistic voyage to the upperworld to atone for infractions discovered is delegated not to the performer, but to a sacred object, the drum played during the night-long singing ceremony (Hoskins 1988). The performer is thus always an outsider, whose participation in determining collective guilt and assessing its costs is only vicarious.

THE EFFECTIVENESS OF TRADITIONAL REMEDIES

Medical science has long recognized that many traditional remedies are highly effective. Kodi private healers make infusions and pastes from roots and barks which relieve headaches, dull pain in the joints, and lessen toothache. They prepare a poultice of charcoal from burned coconut shells which is highly absorbent, and reduces the inflammation of tropical skin ulcers. The use of herbal preparations to ease pain, protect injuries from flies, and allow clean healing within a splint or leaf paste is part of a tradition of local treatments which demonstrate "significant scientific knowledge discovered and preserved within the folk tradition" (Mitchell 1982a:6).

The dangers of some traditional remedies must be considered in relation to the benefits of others. Massage, for instance, is highly effective in setting bones, and can also be used to treat muscular strain and aches. Its use in village abortions is effective, but involves considerable danger to the life of the mother, since it is usually so vigorous that internal bleeding is provoked. Kodi midwives say that they can prevent pregnancy by "turning the womb around," and then reverse this process with another vigorous massage if conception is desired (See Laderman 1984:78–79 for a similar practice in Malaysia). Although sometimes this type of therapy is successful, I also encountered many women who said it had failed—and blamed their own barrenness on inexperienced masseuses. It is evident that topical remedies have variable success rates, but these are not the only (or even the most important) criteria in deciding when to use them. Through the study of diagnostic decisions made in three specific cases, we can explore Kodi notions of when a topical remedy is appropriate, and when the more complex ritual resolution to a "social disease" is required.

THE THREE CASES

Case 1: Secret Exchanges

My first case concerns a young man, Rende Kaha, who experienced extreme pain in urinating and had a bloody discharge from his penis. He did not, however, consult a diviner, or even come to the local clinic until after he had tried to carry out the traditional treatment.[2]

The Kodinese recognize that gonorrhea is a sexually transmitted disease which men acquire from women, and call it *hadu waricoyo* ("woman disease") or, somewhat more delicately, the "betel-nut disease" (*hadu hamama*), because betel nut is a common adjunct to courtship. The bloody discharge is explained as a result of menstrual contamination. According to native theory, placing the penis in contact with blood causes it to fester and produce a "blood clot" which must be returned to another woman by the same means that it was acquired.

David Mitchell, an Australian doctor who spent several years on Sumba, writes:

> This "treatment" is actually quite painful to carry out, and seems unlikely to be successful, but successful or not, it is certain to pass on the infection. With "treatments" like this it is not surprising that there is a great deal of gonorrhea in certain parts of Sumba (1982a:4).

The social meaning of the disease obviously plays on submerged hostilities between men and women. In searching for another woman to "receive the blood," the victim is also exacting a kind of indirect revenge on the one who contaminated him. Rende Kaha did this by trying to seduce a widow who was the clan sister of the girl he believed infected him. This particular choice of a victim to "carry away" the disease was motivated by his desire to "send the disease back into the house where it came from" (*bali la uma pa wali*). As the doctor's notes indicate:

> Women are supposed to avoid intercourse during their menses, but the men believe that unscrupulous women will deceive men and have intercourse during the phases of the menses when the flow is slight, either from

an excess of sexual desire, or out of malicious or vengeful intention to contaminate the man concerned. (Mitchell 1982b:10)

The Sumbanese do not formally recognize the fact that women can get gonorrhea from men, since they rarely display the same symptoms. But the impact of the disease on female fertility is acknowledged indirectly, though a metaphoric relationship between female bleeding and male bleeding.[3]

Venereal disease is said to have originated with the bleeding of super-incision. Superincision was performed up to about 50 years ago on all young men as they approached the age of marriage. A group of adolescent boys were taken down to the riverside and the top of the foreskin of their penises was cut open (*topolo*). Youths who bled extensively and became infected during these rites were told to "remove the water of the knife" (*halingyo wei kioto*) by having sex with an older woman or a slave. If this was not immediately effective, the would could be reopened with a knife and another effort could be made four days later to transmit the infected blood to a different woman (Needham 1990: personal communication). This "water from the knife" was believed to burn or sear the womb, and make a woman unsuited to bear children. For this reason, a boy's sexual initiation was usually entrusted to someone who was considered dispensable in the reproduction of the clan.

After these early experiences, however, a young man is expected to court a number of attractive young women of appropriate rank, one of whom he will eventually marry. The danger that he might spread the disease to them is not considered. The spread of the disease from one or two older women to a number of young men, and from them on to younger women who were trying to conceive lineage descendants was almost inevitable given these ideas. The effect in areas where gonorrhea is most prevalent is a considerably lower population growth rate (Mitchell 1982b:7).

Kodi believe that the unmediated exchange of infected blood between men and women blurs the distinction between the sexes, whose complementarily otherwise depends on difference. What is natural in a woman's body is alien and dangerous in a man's. The term for the blood clot produced as part of venereal disease, *manuho,* is also the term used for a fetus, or miscarried child, so that the experience of male bleeding seems to be associated with the idea of an inappropriate male pregnancy.

Rende Kaha refused to see a doctor before he had tried to pass on the disease, because he reasoned that antibiotics could not help until the blood clot had been transferred back to a woman's body. He interpreted the ailment as an act of aggression against him on the part of the girl he courted, because he had hesitated to commit himself to paying a large brideprice. If they had been official sweethearts, sanctioned by an initial gift of betel and a horse, their dispute would have required a formal negotiation. But since this was still just a liaison, he preferred to seek retribution on his own, and there was no movement to public performance. Only two persons were involved, so reciprocity could be direct and unmediated, without summoning up the great machinery of a ritual resolution. However, he chose to exact his revenge by choosing a woman closely related to the one he believed had acted as an aggressor against him, so a private act of revenge nevertheless retained a social dimension.

Case 2 (Pati Mbebe): Falling Into Memory

In this case it is shown how even a minor injury can serve as a signal from the invisible powers that something is wrong. Pati Mbebe, a young girl visiting her ancestral village of Bondo Maliti for a ceremony, slipped off the veranda of an important cult house. Immediately, a diviner and orators were called to investigate the case. The girl had only a small bruise on her forehead, but falling within the house dislodges the *hamaghu* or vital spirit,[4] and creates an imbalance among all the members of the house. It was interpreted as a sign of a lapse in the protection extended by the ancestral spirits to all of their descendants. The causes of the fall had to be determined before special sacrifices could be performed to "lift up her spirit" and restore it to its proper place in the house.

Diviners questioned the spirits in the rhythmic cadences of ritual speech, using parallel lines which together express a common metaphoric image (Hoskins 1988a):

Pena ba takoki lala bilu nikaya	How could she slip from the cloth bound at the waist?
Pena ba tanoma talu wairo nikya	How could she shatter like an egg fallen to the ground?
Enga nengyo pa kawico kadoru	There must have been a reason to pull on the nerves.
Enga nengyo pa tukiyo kambihya	There must have been something to make the skin twitch.
Ngandi a ndewa touna ura dadinya	So we need to bring back her personal spirit and birth fate,
Tahi la kemba waru ndara mu	Placing it at the withers of the horse,
Ngandi la kahele tete da	Bringing it bound to the bridle rope.

Her slight injury was interpreted as a "guilty twitch" for the collective conscience. It testified to the presence of a deeper offense that was struggling to come to the surface. The spirit who caused the girl's temporary soul loss was angry about something else, and even after the girl recovered this spirit could continue to plague her kin group with problems until the human community responded to its pleas. Members of the cult house were assembled at the *mata marapu* (source of the spirits) a large pillar in the front of the house. Then, the diviner began to lunge against the pillar with a spear held outstretched in his arms. He asked a series of questions of the spirits, using the intermediary of the spear to "cut through" to the cause, and then asked the drum played during the ceremony to embark on its own shamanistic voyage to the upperworld to seek absolution (Hoskins 1988b, 1993). The diviner began by inviting a large number of spirits to join the family sitting on the mats, promising that all that was hidden in the past would now be revealed:

Henene maka pa bunggero ha rou kalama	Now is when we open the tightly woven bundles of coconut leaves.
Henene maka pa manihi ha tugha touna	Now is when we sift through the poisonous root tubers.
Pa kawakaho kalambo wenggu	Even the loincloth must be unfolded.
Pa bunggero kapepe wenggu	Even the basket must have its lid raised.
Maka ambu tomango paneghe	So do not bury your words!
Maka mabu mbuningo patera	So do not conceal your speech!

After several hours of questioning, it was determined that the girl "wakened from her sleep, remembered as she walked" (*pada la manduru, ape la halako*). Her stumbling recalled the guilty awareness of a death which had not been ritually processed. Several years before, another young girl who had married into the house died while pregnant. Since Kodinese classify this as the "death of two bodies," it was inauspicious for her to have gone to her grave without a separate ceremony for the soul of the lost child. She was said to have "died bringing along a funeral shroud in her womb" (*mate ngandi ghabuho ela kambu dalo*), because the child was still wrapped in the placenta and had never been fully presented to the world. Without this ceremony, the souls of both mother and child could not come to rest in their graves, but remained the wandering prisoners of the sun and moon, looking down at their own kin in resentful reproaches.

Pati Mbebe's fall thus revealed the presence of ghosts, who had caused several other misfortunes over the years. Speaking now with the voice of the dead mother, the diviner elaborated other events in which the unhappy ghost had tried to contact her descendants, with no success. A tool shack had burned down three years before, destroying the offering platform and rice basket used in harvest rituals. The ghost confessed that it was her hand which "grew hot with anger, burned red with rage" and caused the fire to bring those objects, as companions, into her heavenly prison:

Maka na londo ba dikyaka	Now they sit with me
Kalete limya lodo	On the hand of the sun.
Pa ole nggu ba dikyaka	Now they join me here
Kahonga witti wyulla	Astride the feet of the moon.
Todi jomondanika lombo loko	So I blocked the edge of the river.
Hapa domodaka ela hupu mara	So I stopped the path beside the bay.

The loss of these objects made it impossible to perform the proper rites for the harvest, and crops of corn and rice had been meager for the past few years. Until the diviner had found the ghost and confronted her, no one knew which ceremonies needed to be performed to restore their lost fertility.

The diviner promised that he had now traveled the full pathway of recent misfortunes. "There is nothing that has not received our mark, there is nowhere our hoofprints haven't tread" (*njaingo njapa hala touka kanda, njaingo nja ka koka oro ndara ma*) in the journey to seek the truth. Members of the house promised to hold a pig feast and singing ceremony (*yaigho*) for the dead mother and child after the harvest the following year, but prayed for a temporary return to prosperity so that these plans could be realized. The reply to their request, read in the divination of chicken entrails, confirmed that now the ghost was satisfied, and she would return the soul of the girl who fell if others made an effort to return the other lost soul—that of the dead fetus. The rite finished with a celebration of anticipated well-being.

Case 3 (Guru Manu): Closing of the Mouth

Guru Manu, a local schoolteacher, suffered from swellings and bleeding of the lips, tongue and teeth. As a Christian convert identified with education and modernity, he first sought treatment with antibiotics at the government clinic. After many weeks, his condition failed to improve and the doctor concluded that he had cancer of the mouth. Since government health workers could offer no more assistance, he sought help from private healers with local medicines (*moro kodi*), solutions of leaves and barks which were poured into the sores.

Like the Javanese doctor at the clinic, local practitioners associated the disease with his consumption of betel and tobacco.[5] They suggested that "his betel pouch was not shared enough"—he had neglected certain exchange obligations.

Figure 2. At a yaigho, the singer takes findings of the diviner, sets them to the rhythms of the drums and gongs, and lets the spirits of the musical instruments carry this message to the upperworld. His singing alternates with spoken commentary by the diviner, who expands and elaborates the account (1980, photograph by the author).

The inflammations and lesions were linked to a betel quid which had "gone bad," because it had not been exchanged with those who deserved a share of his own prosperity.

A few days after he had tried a particular potion given to him by a herbalist from Balaghar, some of the sores broke open and he was able to open his mouth for the first time in a month. Thinking a cure was at hand, the family sent a pig and a cloth to the herbalist as payment, and invited him to come to a meal of celebration. The herbalist came, bringing along a friend who was a diviner. A chicken was killed and when its entrails were examined the augury was not positive. "The poison is deeper inside you, and my medicine cannot reach it all," the herbalist said. "I can heal the surface but not the inside of the wounds, so the infection will return." The diviner indicated that the deeper problem dated back to the death of Guru Manu's oldest daughter three years before, and would require a more complex investigation. Within a week, Guru Manu's condition was much worse.

The family decided to sponsor a ritual healing, including a full *yaigho*. The words of the diviner were then repeated, set to the rhythm of the drums and gongs, and sung for a while night so they could be heard by the invisible spirit audience of *marapu*. Christian prayer meetings had failed to alleviate his condition, and the many unconverted members of his lineage insisted that a traditional ceremony was the only way to identify the enemies whose attacks could spread to his wife, children and other relatives as well. Although a full recovery was not anticipated, the rite would bring to light hidden conflicts, and offered an occasion for summoning help and assistance from kin networks in a time of hardship.

Diviners determined that Guru Manu suffered from ancestral disapproval and resentment on the part of his maternal relatives. Guru Manu was seen as stingy. He had not contributed to efforts to rebuild his own lineage house, or that of his mother's brother. His father had died young, so Guru Manu had been raised since the age of twelve by members of his mother's village in Balaghar. His education in Christian schools and teacher's college had come through the sponsorship of his maternal uncle in Balaghar, but after that uncle died he did not go back to visit the family. None of his cousins—sons of this adoptive father—had continued their studies or gone into government service, so he was the only wage-earner in the whole village. They felt that Guru Manu had used his conversion to Christianity as an excuse not to contribute to their own feasts, neglecting the "debt of honor" which he had contracted to his earlier benefactor. No specific person was named in the Balaghar household, but it was suggested by the diviner that the path of exchange leading back to that house had been disturbed:

Pena inde ape la halako	Didn't you remember as you walked away
A punge ghaiyo pa dadi	The tree trunk of your birth?
Inde pada la manduru	Didn't you wake from sleep and see
A mata wei pa hialo	The source of your own blooming?
Na wongo wei pa inu	Who gave you water to drink?
Na wongo ngagha ha muyo	Who served you rice to eat?
Mono ndara ndali magho	Even the horse shies at his own shadow
Mono bangga nggoko ngingyo	Even the dog barks at his own reflection

Pene ba inde lembera paduki	So why didn't you go back to visit?
Pene ba inde palako hamama?	So why didn't you stop to chew betel?
Bali ela lete oro mburu	Returning to the steps you came down
binye oro loho	and the door you came out.

Guru Manu had not paid a social visit to the family in Balaghar in all the years since finishing his teacher's training. He had not brought them gifts from the city or sent their children to school, thereby failing to reciprocate the food and care he had received in his youth. The text evokes the theme of guilty self-knowledge ("The horse shies at his own shadow, the dog barks at his own reflection") which should have prompted an earlier realization of this debt, before his mouth became closed with disease.

In Kodi, betel, as the "stuff of sociality," is given a positive value as long as that sociality is properly channeled, but when social obligations are neglected, then the betel quid itself is said to fester and turn bad. The alkaline juice of the morsels which normally neutralize stomach acidity and act as an astringent begins to "burn" with the ire of imbalanced debts. Guru Manu's obligation to reciprocate his mother's brother's family for helping with his schooling turned the betel he received along with other gifts into a poison within his mouth.

The diviner did not accuse the mother's brother's group of literally poisoning him by applying substances to the sirih fruit or areca nut itself. Instead, the spirits had "taken him in their own way" (*deke mangu wubingikya*) by transforming a positive potency into a negative one. While reciprocated gifts are cooling and soothing, unreciprocated ones cause a "heating" of the body and (in this case) sores and lesions which appeared in the mouth, seen as the location of the crime. As Guru Manu's wife explained, "The people from his mother's brother's village kept talking about all the rice and betel that he was given during those years. They fed him and he simply swallowed the food, without thinking about replacing it in the mouths of future generations." The "poison" which appeared in his betel quid was therefore not a physical substance, a mixture of roots and barks bought from a herbalist, but a social substance, a backlog of resentments which went unnoticed. The "forgotten betel quid" grew bad because its social intent—the flow of mutual assistance between houses and villages—was not respected.

His illness made it possible to appeal to everyone gathered in the house to contribute toward ritual efforts and rectify what he had overlooked. Members of his patrilineage pledged to begin building their cult house in the next dry season, counting on a contribution from his descendants. The Balaghar contingent was also willing to be conciliatory, denying and specific responsibility for his illness

Figure 3. The drums and gongs played during a *yaigho* receive a ritual payment of betel fruit and areca nut on the morning after the ceremony, to thank them for serving as intermediaries and to restore harmonious relations between people and spirits (1980, photograph by the author).

but accepting the argument that exchange relations had broken down. They brought a large pig to the *yaigho,* and received the countergift of a horse. It was unusual to reciprocate directly, particularly in a time of hardship when the family could always delay counterpayments. This show of generosity on both sides served as a public (if implicit) acknowledgement of the bad feeling which had existed, and a first step toward dealing with it.

The *yaigho* was held when Guru Manu was already seriously ill, and no longer capable of speaking. The diviner finished with a powerful statement to the effect that all of those present would be joined together by the experience of witnessing his suffering and hearing the drums and gongs. "We all row to the same rhythm now; we all strike to the same beat" (*mera a bohe, hama a tuku*), the singer repeated, as refrain echoing through the night. The music itself was said to dissolve certain tensions, through its non-discursive power to unite the senses in a common project of social and bodily movement. (Hoskins 1988b).

After the rite was finished, Guru Manu wrote a note to his oldest daughter saying, "Now at least my debts will not drag you into the same early grave." She cried when she read the note, because it also acknowledged the fact that he realized his own death was near. One month after these final exchanges were completed, Guru Manu died. His funeral showed that the bonds of exchange had been renewed. The sons of his maternal uncle brought large buffaloes to the funeral sacrifice, showing that their ill feeling had passed, and their respect for the deceased remained.

CONCLUSIONS

These three cases demonstrate three very different relations between healing, social process and their mediation. They demonstrate that forgetting not only helps to create a "psychology of guilt" within the mind of the person who remembers, but can also be socially constructed as a "biology of guilt" which takes the form of particular physical disorders which require ritual redress.

The case of Rende Kaha contrasts with two other cases where the decision was made to move to performance. The distinction was made not on the basis of the severity of the affliction, or the prognosis for cure. Instead, it was made on the basis of how the affliction was interpreted within the idioms of the politics of exchange which posit a moral theory of illness.

The social evaluation of where guilt lies and how to atone for it involves a judgment of which ailments are "private" or "individual," and which ones are "public" and part of collective responsibility. Gonorrhea, which we euphemistically call a "social disease," is not a social disease in the same sense on Sumba, but is the result of a pollution experience. It is dealt with through an effort to pass it on, which underscores mistrust between men and women but does not require a group intervention. The pattern taken by Rende Kaha's personal revenge still betrays a perception of collective responsibility, in that he tried to return the disease to the house of the woman who infected him. These sexual exchanges were not made part of the public domain, however, and without the exchange of marriage gifts they are not subject to ritual mediation.

In the second case, a relatively minor injury was interpreted as a sign of greater troubles hidden below the surface, and these were extensively probed in a divination which focused on neglected obligations to ancestors. In the third, a fatal illness was perceived as an opportunity to repair relations across affinal lines, between a nephew, adopted by his uncle, and the sons of that uncle. The form that the disease assumed—the mouth swollen shut in pain—presented an image of arrested reciprocity. The patient's neglected cousins did not have to act directly to exact their revenge with poison. They could allow their wounded pride to fester on its own in the betel quid, bringing Guru Manu to a belated recognition of his own carelessness.

The theme of the exchange or subversion of substances is played out in different ways in each case. Native theories of venereal disease begin with the polluting contact between male sexual organs and female blood, and prescribe a return of the blood to another woman which is supposed to cure the infection. On the battleground of sexual conquests—like the battleground of traditional headhunting—a counterstrike is preferred to a negotiation.

In dealing with ancestors and affines, longer term effects are believed to follow from continuing discord, so the move to performance is needed. All the members of the ancestral house of Bondo Maliti were threatened when Pati Mbebe fell down. One living soul was being dislodged by a dead one, and an outside diviner was needed to re-open communication with a silenced voice—the ancestral ghost who had been forgotten. Retrospectively, this single minor misfortune was used to explain a number of other disasters and bring the community together to face them with renewed hope.

Guru Manu's fatal illness could not be reversed. But the ritual performance given for him acknowledged the sins of the past and re-opened blocked pathways for exchange, restoring the possibility of a new cooperation between affines. Betel provided a language for expressing the denial of sociality, since it is required for social interaction and the exchange of all valuables between affines.

The proper flow of exchange had been disrupted in each of these cases. In the first, the proper timing of sexual encounters was violated by a woman who accepted advances from a lover at the wrong time of the month. In the second, a young girl lost her balance in the house because of an imbalance in mortuary rites which kept the floorboards of the veranda slightly askew. In the third, a man who failed to repay the help he received from his maternal village was "poisoned" by the contents of his own betel pouch, since he had denied its proper social function. Returning blood, losing balance, refusing betel—all are united in their concern with the contours of social relationships, and not so much with the symptoms and suffering of the patient at hand.

Cosmopolitan medical practice is primarily centered on the patient as a psycho-biological entity, and thus often is oblivious to the social context. In order to understand healing in non-Western contexts, we must first "de-center" the emphasis on patients and symptoms, and focus instead on social factors—such as the kinds of reciprocity that they embody. In Kodi folk medicine, venereal disease is mediated through the negative reciprocity of counter-infection; a bruised head is treated with returning a forgotten spirit to the generalized reciprocity which operates within a house; and a fatal mouth infection requires a meeting of kin and affines in the friendly, balanced reciprocity of the exchange of betel pouches.

Healing rites performed on these occasions were not ultimately concerned with curing, if we define "cure" in the narrow sense of restoring the victim to health.

Instead, it seems to me that the ultimate goal of the rite is to repair social relations and "heal the group" even when the suffering individual cannot be saved.

Public performance offers a very different sort of frame for what in our society is called "medical practice," and may cause us to question the validity of this category for cross-cultural study. Private healers in Kodi acknowledge that they heal only a certain kind of illness, while public performers heal a wide range of ailments with a common arsenal of oratory and participatory theater. The trappings of elaborate performance—music and dance, sacrifice and divination—are used for an intensified dramatic effect, but this parade of signs may serve to confuse certain issues of substance. Singers, dancers and orators are summoned to repeat and reiterate points in a complicated visual and auditory experience intended to dissolve difference into consensus. Moral unity becomes the unity of audience, the shared sensory stimulus, and the evocative dramatic presentation. It is through this aesthetic impact of performance that the group is recreated and reconstituted, often over the body of the patient and often without much hope of alleviating his suffering.

NOTES

1. This was the often implicit assumption of an earlier tradition of medical or psychological anthropology, which spoke of the "'faith' of the patient in the power of the healer, and made the success of the "cure" depend on that faith. Kiev's (1964) edited volume titled *Magic, Faith and Healing* reflects this orientation. Even Victor Turner's classic "A Ndembu Doctor in Practice" argues that although the real focus of the Ndembu doctor is "remedying the ills of the corporate group," the basis of his efficacy for individual patients is psychological. A more sophisticated approach to the complex concept of "medicine's symbolic reality" is found in Kleinman, Eisenberg and Good (1978), which stresses how the ideas of "health" and "cure" are socially and culturally constructed.

2. Because of the sensitive nature of this ailment, my data here come not from the patient himself, but from the doctor who treated him at the clinic. The names of all patients in this paper are pseudonyms.

3. In 1968–69, the Health Service in West Sumba conducted a mass survey and treatment campaign against yaws, accompanied by examinations of urethral smears of 211 men in the Wanokaka district. A total of 90.5% tested positive for gonorrhea (Mitchell 1982b:4). Although it was not possible to examine women as well, fertility questionnaires revealed that 42% of the women had become infertile after the age of twenty-five (Mitchell 1982b:6). The doctor in charge concluded that although gonorrhea did not contribute seriously as a cause of death or chronic invalidism, its demographic effect was dramatic.

4. The theme of soul loss is a common one in Southeast Asian societies. The Kodi *hamaghu* or vital spirit is a cognate of the Malay-Indonesian idea of *semangat,* and is believed to be located at the fontanelle, where small infants will often have a slight dent in their skulls at birth. This is the site of vulnerability, since the *hamaghu* can be lost due to serious illness, injury or a supernature attachment by witches. The soul has another, more durable part, called the *ura ndewa,* which is located in the swirls of hair at the crown. This is the ancestral soul which can be reincarnated in future generations, and is associated with patrilineal transmission. The Kodi sometimes speak of the *hamaghu* as the "female soul" since it was created by the Great Mother Who Binds the Forelock (*Inya Wolo Hungga*) while the *ndewa* is the "male soul," crafted by the Great Father Who Smelted the Crown (*Bapa Rawi Lindu*). Both men and women have double souls of this kind, as a sort of residual pattern which admits to both vulnerability and an enduring social identity. The gender implications of this theory of souls and spirits are explored in Hoskins (1990).

5. Chewing the betel fruit along with areca nut is widely believed by the Kodinese to have beneficial effects: It is said to strengthen the teeth, reduce cavities, stimulate attention, reduce drowsiness, aid in digestion and prevent stomachache. The juice of betel leaves is used in treating eye infections, and its leaves are placed on wounds and sores to prevent infection. Betel chewing has a wide distribution in Southeast Asia, and medical research has authenticated its effects (Reid 1985:535). But if it is true that betel quid provides some bacteriological protection against intestinal parasites and water-borne diseases, it is also correlated with higher incidence of mouth cancer, particularly among those who put tobacco into the quid or store it under the lip (Reid 1985:536).

REFERENCES

Hoskins, Janet. 1988a. In The Lips Told to Speak, the Mouths Told to Pronounce. *To Speak in Pairs: Essays on Ritual Language in Eastern Indonesia,* ed. J. J. Fox. Cambridge: Cambridge University Press.

———. 1988b. The Drum Is the Shaman, the Spear Guides His Voice. In Issue on Healing in Southeast Asia, ed. Carol Laderman and Penny van Esterik. *Social Science and Medicine* 27(8):819–828.

———. 1990. Doubling Deities, Descent and Personhood: An Exploration of Kodi Gender Categories. In *Power and Difference: Gender in Island Southeast Asia,* ed. Jane Atkinson and Shelly Errington. Stanford: Stanford University Press.

———. 1993. *The Play of Time: Kodi Perspectives on Calendars, History and Exchange.* Berkeley: University of California Press.

Kleinman, Arthur, and Leon Eisenberg and Byron Good. 1978. Culture, Illness and Care: Clinical Lessons from Anthropological and Cross-Cultural Research. *Annals of Internal Medicine* 88(2):251–258.

Kiev, Ari. 1965. *Magic, Faith and Healing.* New York: The Free Press.

Laderman, Carol. 1984. *Wives and Midwives: Childbirth and Nutrition in Rural Malaysia.* Berkeley: University of California Press.

Mitchell, David. 1982a. Fold Medicine in Sumba: A Critical Evaluation. In *Indonesian Medical Traditions: Bringing Together the Old and New,* ed. D. Mitchell. Melbourne: Monash University Press.

———. 1982b. Endemic Gonorrhea in Sumba. Paper presented at the Asian Studies Association of Australia, Fourth National Conference, Monash University.

Reid, Anthony. 1985. From Betel Chewing to Tobacco Smoking in Indonesia. *Journal of Asian Studies* 44 (3):529–547.

Turner, Victor. 1964. A Ndembu Doctor in Practice. In *Magic, Faith and Healing,* ed. A. Kiev. New York: The Free Press.

10

DYING AS MEDICAL PERFORMANCE
The Oncologist as Charon

Megan Biesele and Robbie Davis-Floyd

I think *everything* in the universe is interconnected. And there are some interconnections we haven't been conscious of, and they'll come out sooner or later. Probably later, because knowing the AMA's grip on things, it's going to take a long time, and it's going to take a lot of people who aren't afraid to speak out for what they really believe in. . . . a lot of people who are *simpatico* with this new way of living, with this wholeness of living.

—Margaret Bell

INTRODUCTION

In November 1990 a 70-year old woman, whom we will call Mrs. Margaret Bell, entered the hospital suffering from severe dehydration following chemotherapy. She had been diagnosed with colon cancer with metastases to the liver in July of 1990. Having been admitted, she was convinced of her ability to recover. Shortly after she left the hospital after a ten-day stay, she became determined to die. By her own report, the oncologist's words played a significant role in this transformation. As she explained her experience, his dramatically ritualized and repeated pronouncement of her terminal status, reinforced by other aspects of her hospital experience, eventually integrated itself in her mind as a primary "failure" that added heavy symbolic weight to the other "system failures" (of blood sugar and electrolyte balance) she was experiencing. The terminal diagnosis quickly came to form one primary piece of a new reality matrix—a matrix that held her death to be imminent and her task not to be attempting further healing but preparing herself for death.

In an interview, the oncologist primarily involved in her treatment shed light on this transformative moment: he called the task of announcing terminal status one of the central responsibilities of the cancer physician. In fact, he identified the doctor-patient interaction surrounding this announcement and its reception as a main determinant of "a good death." It was clear to us as observers that the physician, whom we will call Dr. Henderson, had his most profound and anxiety-laden communication with the patient during the three days it took him to get her to accept the message that she was going to die. This freighted communication stood in marked contrast to the kind but brief and distant contacts the doctor had previously had with Mrs. Bell during her examination and chemotherapy sessions. The announcement of terminality seemed to be a key performative element in the oncologist's ritual role.

This inquiry into the performed roles of oncologists has an increasing number of parallel and complementary studies in the anthropology of biomedicine. These studies, both articles and books, deal centrally with issues of communication and empowerment in the relationships among patient, physician, and supporting others (Baer 1987; DiGiacomo 1987, 1992; Fisher and Todd 1983; Good 1991, 1993; Good et al. 1990; Kleinman 1988; Romanucci-Ross et al. 1983). In this article, we address both the humane purpose behind proper communication of the terminal diagnosis—helping the patient to prepare herself spiritually and to make the best use of remaining time—and the role this communication plays in reinforcing the claim laid by the medical establishment to ritual and symbolic hegemony over the bodily processes of life and death.

This study is based on interviews conducted with Mrs. Bell during her last month of life and with Dr. Henderson, her oncologist. Additional data come from intensive observation of the patient and her interactions with others during the five months between her diagnosis and her death,[1] and from conversations with several people, including another physician involved in the case. A specific context for the interpretation of interview data is provided through an account of a central episode—one of two hospitalizations—during Margaret Bell's illness.

THE CANCER PHYSICIAN'S ROLE
IN TECHNOCRATIC SOCIAL DRAMA

The cancer physician plays a key role in the social drama scripted through the interplay between the medically defined disease he diagnoses, on the one hand,

and the family affected by that diagnosis and its sequelae, on the other. In cases considered terminal, he is often called upon to perform not as healer, but as conductor to the other world. In the popular view, oncologists as a class are alternately celebrated for their willingness to play the part of the necessary "bad guy," the bearer of the tidings of death, and condemned for their reputed unwillingness to include the patient as part of the healing team (Buckman 1986; Henriques et al. 1980; GIVIO 1986). Some are further characterized as heartless technical automatons unable to relate humanly to patients and families or as intent on speeding the patient to an early death through self-fulfilling prophecies (Siegel 1986). Still others, however, have come, in the course of helping dying patients, to seem like compassionate and competent conductors to the world of death, performing the important role of lessening pain and fear (Good et al. 1990). Because death is so often not only the literal but also the symbolic—i.e., expected—outcome of cancer, oncologists inevitably take on roles that carry ritual as well as medical freight. Dr. Henderson's performance, in fact, seemed to encompass aspects of the role of Charon in Greek myth, who ferried the souls of the dead across the River Styx.

This last comparison illustrates a critical point. Despite biomedicine's departure from shamanism, religious and medical practices align themselves again when an unknown such as cancer, and the fear of its outcome, is involved. Indeed, until AIDS came on the scene, cancer reigned as the most feared disease in twentieth-century America (Sontag 1990:16). We contend that this unity of medical and religious roles is operative for cancer doctors even where individual patients have histories of personal religious practice to help them through the period of dying. The symbolic and ritual dimensions of the cancer doctor's role thus are subjects of interest to anthropology. Mrs. Bell's experience illustrates the ways in which these symbolic and ritual dimensions of the physician's role can both enable the transformative process of dying and reinforce powerful tenets of the American technocratic model.

As one of us has written elsewhere, the technocratic model of life processes is an important part of the American core value system which conceptualizes the human body as a machine, giving primary responsibility for its repair and maintenance to medical technicians (Davis-Floyd 1987, 1990, 1992). The technocratic model expresses two key dualistic organizing principles of American culture: the Cartesian separation of mind from body, and the belief (growing ever stronger in the West from the Renaissance on) in the possibility and the benefits of human separation from and control over nature, including the body. The medical management of birth and death are key phases in the development and reinforcement of this model. For example, the rituals that enact this technocratic core value system include the medical procedures through which birth is conducted (Davis-Floyd 1992). Through powerful and expressive symbols (e.g., the IV, the electronic fetal monitor, the epidural) these rituals dramatically show the birthing woman that she is not only separate both from her baby and from her dysfunctional body-machine, but also dependent on the institution's more perfect machines to control the birth of her baby, society's product.

Likewise, a dramatic hospitalization experience focuses enormous socialization pressures on an ill, and thus liminally receptive, individual. It is instructive, then, to observe the elements of performance used by the hospital team, as led by the oncologist, in inculcating the patient with the core values of technocracy and in aligning her own perceptions and models of her illness and its meaning with those of the hospital staff. These performance elements include "strange-making",[2] time disruption (Zerubavel 1981), and the symbolic distancing of practitioner from patient usual in hospital practice (Konner 1987; Stein 1990). In the particular case of Mrs. Bell, they also included other multivalent aspects of her experience, such as being awakened in the middle of the night three nights in a row to be weighed, being left helpless in the bathroom until she almost fainted, being kept hungry the night of her admission because a salmonella epidemic had brought in a record number of patients all at once, and feeling obscurely persecuted by the staff for falling sick on a holiday (Thanksgiving).

Melvin Konner (1987) has written eloquently of the pressures on hospital personnel that lead to such omissions and discomforts for patients. But he also identifies such care-less practices, which often are the rule rather than the exception in American hospitals, as part of an intentional pattern of socialization for medical students. He notes that during their journeys of initiation (residencies), students learn their roles as medical doctors from watching and imitating hospital practice—its manners perhaps as closely as its techniques. Both stem from the American core-value principle of separation, as the separation of mind from body is mirrored on a larger scale by the separation of physician from patient. The messages of the relative powerlessness and dispensability of the patient are impossible to ignore.

The fact that most female patients are treated by male physicians also has symbolic repercussions. The relatively higher status of men in American society reinforces the drama of the doctor's role for a woman patient in ways that are further disempowering. In Margaret Bell's case the symbolism was particularly poignant, as she had herself aspired to be a doctor. But on the advice of a male medical school professor, in her early twenties she settled on a career in medical technology. She came rather quickly to the conclusion that medical technology was second best to the primary medical role she wanted, but then she contracted serious viral hepatitis through her technology laboratory and felt set back too much (both physically and through loss of time) to contemplate a full medical-school education.

These and other aspects of Margaret Bell's history worked to ensure her profound socialization into the technocratic biomedical model, bringing her to the 1990 hospitalization with a predisposition towards a mechanistic approach to diagnosis and treatment. Nevertheless, as a result of years of working for a well-known holistically oriented nutritionist, she had also developed strong respect for the holistic approach to healing. Where the technocratic model is based on principles of separation and mechanicity, the holistic paradigm is based on principles of interconnectedness and organicity (Davis-Floyd 1992:Chapter 4). This dichotomy set up a structural tension in Bell's own life—a tension that also structured the drama of her death. Yet in turn, this structural tension was ultimately resolved through the manner of her dying, for she partly chose, and was partly persuaded by her family, to live out her remaining weeks at home in ever deepening connection with her family, and to die there. This resistance to the full application of the technocratic model to her illness and death (which might have resulted in the applying of "heroic measures" in the hospital, and a lingering death hooked up to machines) led the patient and her family to feel that she had died "a good death" in spite of the disappointments encountered in treatment—a judgment with which the physician eventually concurred.

Although her death in the end was a holistic one, along the way she very nearly chose the much more technocratic approach of retaining full control over the dying process through consciously choosing euthanasia. This consideration sheds further light on the symbolism of the oncologist's role. At one point, when euthanasia was most seriously seen as a viable option, his role as Charon seemed on the point of actualization. Although in the end he did not actually "ferry her across," it seemed clear to us that his perception of his role was informed by ancient models transmitted to him through centuries of Western literature and art and subtly codified in medical school pedagogy regarding the treatment of dying patients. There was an old, sure inevitability about the dramatic performance by this young doctor that went far beyond his physical treatment of the illness. Exploring how these ancient models were used in the service of modern American values is a primary thematic concern of our article.

We will also ask how symbolic analysis can point the way to dynamic *new* uses of the power of symbol and drama. We suggest that medical paradigms may actually be challenged by restructuring performative models. This is in fact the sort of challenge to the medical establishment presented by contemporary holistic healing philosophy and practice. Holistically oriented medical practicioners and writers like Norman Cousins (1979, 1989), Bernie Siegel (1986), and Simonton et al. (1980), emphasize empowerment of the patient; the social support of friends and family; and good communication among doctor, patient, nursing staff, and religious practitioners. Most significantly, these writers promote dramatic visualization and relaxation techniques to enhance mind-body integration and redefine negative expectations positively. Though few such practitioners are anthropologically sophisticated, what they advocate amounts to a return to concepts of traditional healing and shamanism in which religious and medical healing work is united by practitioner and ceremony and the healing energy is readily available to all participants (Katz 1982).[3]

CASE STUDY: A CENTRAL EPISODE IN THE DRAMA OF ONE DEATH

Margaret Bell was born in 1919 and grew up in a family that encouraged and enabled her to pursue a college and post-graduate level of education. But the value placed on her education, although high, was not as high as that placed on the education and careers of her brothers. This discrepant valuation was consistent with American historical forces during her formative decades, and is unremarkable except that her family did transcend the general ethos by allowing her to attend a university and work away from home. Her medical career was similarly unremarkable for a woman at that time: having been channelled into medical technology by a professor's remark, the commitment of time she had made to that career would most probably have kept her from full-scale medical education even had she not contracted hepatitis.

Notwithstanding her professional marginalization, Bell was active in the early work on the Rh factor in blood ("A technician walking the rhesus monkeys," she used to fume). For many decades in the biochemistry of nutrition, she worked hand in hand with physicians and nationally known researchers on the discovery and testing of new vitamins and nutritional therapies. Her academic and career experience on the sidelines of male achievements led her into active promotion of "continuing education for women," before the advent of Betty Friedan and the women's movement. Her three daughters report that, due to their mother's example, they were privileged to experience not a moment's worry over whether their own academic and career aspirations were as worthwhile as any man's. Until her cancer diagnosis at age 70, Margaret Bell still worked every day in a groundbreaking nutritional therapy clinic associated with a biochemical research unit in a major university.

As anthropologist Susan DiGiacomo, herself a cancer patient, has noted:

> Biomedicine as commonly practiced in the U.S. simultaneously individualizes its treatment of disease symptoms and routinizes dealings with the patient, so that the afflicted person is transformed from an integrated and fully functioning adult to a collection of diseased body parts. Further, biomedical opinion holds that sick people are less than fully competent adults

simply by virtue of being physically unwell. The first difficulty of the patient, then, is not getting a fair hearing for his or her point of view concerning the illness and its treatment; it is getting the doctor to recognize that the patient, has, in fact, a point of view at all . . . Thus, from the outset, the afflicted person is required to accept a reduced and defective patient self constructed for him or her by the doctor. (1988:4)

Accordingly, when Margaret Bell became a patient, her lifetime involvement in medical science and therapy was suddenly of no consequence to the decision-making associated with her treatment. She was immediately demoted to passive status by the hierarchically structured routines and rituals of her first oncologist's practice (he was later dismissed by Bell and her family in favor of Dr. Henderson). Moreover, in spite of Bell's desire to try it, this first cancer doctor refused to consider the relatively new interferon therapy as an adjunct to chemotherapy (surgery and radiation had previously been ruled out).

Mrs. Bell's husband, Dr. James Bell, taught cell biology and had done pioneering research in cancer chemotherapy and electron microscopy early in his career, yet he was similarly sidelined by the ritual unapproachability and unquestionable aura of authority with which the first doctor surrounded himself. Sidelined and passive they remained during the first frightening weeks after Mrs. Bell's diagnosis until their eldest daughter arrived home. Strongly oriented towards a holistic philosophy and a feminist stance, this daughter immediately began to push for better communication with the physician, and soon Mr. and Mrs. Bell began to feel as if they had a right to be included on the healing team. At that time, through the help of a close friend, the family contacted Dr. Henderson, who agreed after evaluation to provide a new combination therapy of chemotherapy and experimental interferon on a twice-weekly basis—a treatment that was being successfully used in another city by a colleague of Henderson's on cases like Bell's. This colleague, whom we call Dr. Abdul, had also evaluated Margaret Bell and was glad she was able to find a physician in her own town to administer the treatment.

Bell and her family settled into a routine of chemotherapy ups and downs with the familiar good and bad appetite days of the week. The mood for some time was very positive, as Bell was absolutely determined to combine excellent nutrition, exercise, and positive visualization techniques to help her body and mind work together to fight her cancer. She was surrounded by an extremely supportive group of friends and family. Her primary caregivers soon welded themselves into an efficient team, working hard to leave no stone unturned in investigating the latest research about colon and liver cancer, preparing nutritious meals, ensuring the patient's rest and comfort, and providing both diversion and loving concern. And for several months the medical news was positive, as Margaret responded well to the combined therapy and did not experience undue discomfort. This scenario seemed to all concerned to be a healthy blend of the biomedical and holistic approaches, with each complementing and working to enhance the positive effects of the other.

Sometime in October, however, the side effects of chemotherapy began to take their toll. Also, the indicators of tumor activity reversed their hopeful downward trend and began to rise again. Although Margaret pursued her program of daily swimming and walking, and although each meal was carefully planned and prepared by her family, her health began to go downhill. By the end of November she became dehydrated from uncontrollable diarrhea, and, at the family's suggestion, with which Dr. Henderson concurred, she entered the hospital to have her fluid balance corrected. She was admitted on her 71st birthday, November 20, 1990, just before Dr. Henderson left town on his Thanksgiving holiday.

When admitted, Margaret assumed she would be in the hospital for a few days and then resume her program of combined interferon and chemotherapy. As it turned out, she had an exhausting ten-day struggle in the hospital to regain physical equilibrium. This struggle was not made easier by the fact that for the first crucial days she was seen exclusively by medical students and doctors unfamiliar with her history. Also, it became clear through routine tests that an incipient diabetic condition was beginning to give her trouble, and insulin was started. It took some time for the dosage to be regularized, and during this period Margaret's weakness and instability dictated that she remain in the hospital.

After her first night, which taught her and her family that she needed more constant care than could be provided by the nursing staff, her daughters took turns sleeping on the floor, so that they could help her to the bathroom, make sure she was comfortable, and run interference when there were unreasonable staff interruptions of her sleep, such as the 3 A.M. weighing sessions.[4] There were also difficulties with her IV-line which made her family feel that she needed more than ordinary supervision.

Many of the interruptions took the form of what seemed to the family to be a kind of "hazing" of Mrs. Bell as a patient. For example, a male nurse exhibited total disregard for the pain of a chemotherapy rash on her hands, grasping them roughly after she had begged him not to, saying, "Of course it doesn't hurt!" The rapid turnover of staff, which meant that each new nurse who came on the ward had to be familiarized with her weaknesses and special needs, gave her and her family a profoundly uneasy feeling that it was "us against the world" of the hospital. Some nurses seemed friendly and compassionate, but more were bored, indifferent, condescending, and even hostile. Especially upsetting was the sense the patient felt of being punished for having "difficult veins." Every time one of the nurses had a hard time replacing the IV-line, an expert was called in who brooked no failures and whose very stance bristled with disapproval and censure. A huge woman known to the family as "the IV-nurse from hell," she struck terror into the hearts of all, looming as a truly frightening possibility every time a change in IV had to be made.

Socially, Mrs. Bell's hospital stay was all that could be desired. She was never left alone for more than a few minutes, and when she was napping there was a vigilant family member on guard outside her door to request visitors to come back another time. When awake and feeling well enough, she gladly received many visitors, as well as a wallful of cards and a roomful of flowers and gifts. Though she realized she had had a serious setback, she assumed that she was on track with her original plan of treatment, and was determined to keep right on listening to her visualization tapes, reading Bernie Siegel, taping her memories for her daughters, making lists of gifts to give at Christmas, and anticipating how good it would be to get back to home cooking after the boring hospital food. She greatly enjoyed visiting with her daughters, who clearly had all inherited their mother's ability to see humor in adversity. By the time Thanksgiving was over, her room was quite the party place on the oncology wing.

Thus it came as a shock to hear from Dr. Henderson on Monday when he returned from his holiday that there would be no more treatment. After examining her and reading her charts, he told Margaret without preamble that "resistance had developed," that she couldn't handle the treatment, and that there was nothing else known that could help her.

This was Act I in a dramatic three-day attempt to get Mrs. Bell to accept the "fact," as Dr. Henderson saw it, that she was going to die. On this first day, the stage as one of us (Biesele) observed it was set as follows: the eldest daughter sat on the window ledge at her mother's bedside. The doctor sat slumped in a chair in the furthest corner of the room, his posture suggesting both earnestness and a lack of ease. Mrs. Bell and her daughter became suddenly anxious, both because they had waited six tension-filled days for this particular doctor to answer some questions about acute problems that had developed in the hospital, and because this was the first time in their three-month association with him that they could remember him actually sitting down with them. (His earlier talks had been careful and calm, not lacking in communicative mutuality, but he had conducted them on his feet, while examining Mrs. Bell on a raised table, for instance, or passing by in the hall while his nurse administered chemotherapy.)

After briefly discussing her blood sugar and dehydration problems, Dr. Henderson said that Margaret Bell was "in a terminal phase." He said that she would be getting no more chemotherapy because of the resistance, as seen in the elevated CEA level (a blood indicator of tumor activity) and on the CT scan, which revealed no appreciable shrinkage of tumors. Mrs. Bell drew herself up with what dignity she could muster, and said that she accepted the diagnosis but did not consider herself "terminal." She said that she was still fighting. The daughter by her own admission was "glaring" at the doctor and silently applauding her mother's spirited answer. Mrs. Bell then asked the doctor, with a sourness quite uncharacteristic of her, whether he thought nutrition could play a role in healing. The unwillingness of the medical profession to consider nutritional approaches had been a long-time sore topic with her both professionally and personally, so when Dr. Henderson answered with the single word, "No," the atmosphere became very quiet—and very charged. Mrs. Bell said, "Then that's all I have to say to you for now," and Dr. Henderson stood and went out the door.

Early the following morning he returned for Act II. He seemed more rested than the previous day and quite energetic, like a person who knows he has a job to do and feels equal to the task. He said clearly that she was "terminal, and that isn't necessarily bad. One can prepare oneself for death." Mrs. Bell's response surprised even her daughter, who (though she had long ago thrown in her lot with the self-healing philosophies and had been listening to the personal empowerment tapes right along with her mother) thought that by now the diagnosis of terminality was quite clear. Mrs. Bell said, "What I want to know is how are you and Dr. Abdul going to build me up so I can continue chemotherapy?" Dr. Henderson appeared to realize at that point that Mrs. Bell and at least some of her family were still reacting at that point with denial, and he just left it. Indeed, her daughter said, "It was as if she had not heard what he said." Before he left the room, Mrs. Bell requested a look at the CT scan taken a few days earlier and the addition of a vitamin-C infusion to her IV bottle. Dr. Henderson quietly agreed to both requests and departed.

Later that day, when Dr. James Bell was sitting with his wife, Dr. Henderson returned with the CT scan of her abdomen. In technocratic diagnosis, the CT scan, as external, "objective" evidence obtained by tests and machines, constitutes a defining source of "authoritative knowledge" (Jordan and Irwin 1990)—that is, knowledge that forms the basis for decisions made and actions taken. It was apparent that the liver was largely taken over by tumors. The nursing staff did add an ascorbic-acid solution to the IV, though at a much lower percentage than that recommended by Mrs. Bell's nutritional-therapy colleagues. Mrs. Bell spent a quiet afternoon listening to her husband read to her: her eyes were bothering her and reading was difficult, though it never had been before. She seemed untroubled by this annoyance.

Meanwhile, the family "cheering squad" (as they called themselves) went into action and rallied around the telephone, checking out every possible lead. Much of the activity centered around the question of whether Dr. Abdul in the neighboring city concurred with Dr. Henderson's assessment of "resistance." When at last it was ascertained that he did, and had in fact already told Dr. Henderson that further treatment seemed counterindicated, Mrs. Bell's daughters began to confront for the first time the probable reality that their mother was going to die. This is how the stage was set as Dr. Henderson and Mrs. Bell went into the last act in their joint drama: acceptance of terminal status by the patient.

Early on Wednesday morning, when Mrs. Bell's middle daughter was with her, Dr. Henderson came back a third time. Mrs. Bell asked him what treatments she would be getting when she got out of the hospital. The question was in the context of possibly continuing Vitamin-C infusions via a periodic IV-drip. He said, "I'm not recommending any. It's important for you to not just keep trying quackery but to think about your death." Margaret then said, "Oh, so you're saying I'm really terminal?" Dr. Henderson replied, "You've been terminal since you got your diagnosis in July."

Later the middle daughter encountered Dr. Henderson in the hall, and said "She's finally accepted it." He said, "I was beginning to get worried."

On the afternoon of the same day, when the eldest daughter was with her mother, Dr. Henderson again came in and repeated for a fourth time that she was terminal. It was as if he needed to reassure himself that she had indeed accepted her status. And perhaps he also wanted to make sure that the eldest daughter, who had been the primary caregiver, had, like her sister, accepted it too. To this eldest daughter, it seemed as though her mother was behaving as if she were receiving the news for the first time. When the doctor left, Mrs. Bell said, "I wish he'd told me before, so I could have gotten my study in order." The daughter, who later said that leaving a chaotic study behind after her own death had always been an uneasy thought, began to feel guilty for her own part in promoting—perhaps overpromoting—the stance of positive resistance to a grim prognosis. Had she robbed her mother of enough time to put her affairs in order? If the doctor had "known" her mother was terminal ever since her diagnosis, had her own positive outlook kept him from informing the family until now?

Yet the family remained open, even after that third day, to any desire Mrs. Bell expressed to try alternative therapies in keeping with her nutritional convictions. Dr. Bell and the eldest daughter made an appointment with Dr. Henderson on Thursday morning, largely for the purpose of obtaining his blessing on such alternative therapies. He agreed readily, but repeated that she was terminal and all that was realistically left as an option was "symptom management." The daughter asked whether great pain was to be expected or rather a quiet death from liver failure. Dr. Henderson said the latter, and that it would be relatively "comfortable."

Finally Mrs. Bell's condition stabilized and she asked to end her ten-day hospital stay and go home. In the days that followed her discharge from the hospital her family continued to strive to balance her diet and regime of care with her ever-more-complex physiological needs. She went by car and wheelchair to the one doctor in town who would agree to provide the high concentration of Vitamin-C infusions she wanted to try. These infusions, along with the soothing atmosphere of this "New Age" doctor's clinic, had a restful and apparently cleansing effect on Mrs. Bell's state of mind and body. But by about mid-December even this doctor was unable to find a vein capable of holding a needle, and he suggested that it would be best to "take a rest and come back after Christmas." This news was received gravely by the whole family. Mrs. Bell began another alternative therapy she learned of through the nutrition clinic, one she could take at home orally, but this time she seemed to act without conviction. In the oral history her daughters had been recording for some months there suddenly appeared the motif of acceptance of death.

At this time, one of us (Davis-Floyd) asked to move beyond the observer's role, to formally interview Mrs. Bell about her current experience. This interview turned out to be decisive. With her main caregiver, her eldest daughter, absent, Mrs. Bell was able to speak without hesitation about her readiness to die. She spoke of having no fear of death, only of the messiness of dying and the burden she was putting on her family. Reaching over and emphatically tapping the recorder taping the discussion, she said repeatedly, "If I could, I would just push this button and turn myself off." She confessed that she was only continuing with the latest alternative nutritional treatment to please her family and her community of holistically-oriented friends. After saying this in the interview, she found the courage to say it to her friends and family as well. (As the anthropologist left, teary-eyed, the eldest daughter asked her at the door, "Are you telling me it's time to stop cheerleading?" and the anthropologist answered, "Yes.")

Sometime between her discharge on December 2 and the interview on December 21, Margaret Bell had completed the process of cognitive restructuring that accompanies all lasting major perceptual shifts (d'Aquili et al. 1979; Laughlin et al. 1990); in other words, her cognitive system had reconstellated around the diagnosis of terminality. When asked in the interview what were the deciding factors in this process, she answered that it was the combination of seeing the CT scan and the many repetitions by the doctor that she was terminal. In the days following the interview, her behavior consistently expressed the thoroughness of this process of cognitive restructuring. Her clear-eyed acceptance of death's inevitability enabled her family too to relax into the next phase. Said one family member, "It was as if the whole house stopped fighting and gave a sigh of relief."

The routines of care did not cease, but they were carried out under a different aegis, that of easing a loved one the best way possible into another life. Norman

Cousins died at this time, and though they found that "very sad," it did not cause the family the consternation it might have a month before. No longer was Bernie Siegel read in the house; his new videotape arrived and remained unopened. Instead, family members took turns reading from books about near-death experiences and what they can teach us about "the other side." Mrs. Bell found it soothing to hear this sort of thing read to her before she napped.

The oral history was completed with all that she found important, and was transcribed by a family friend. The rituals of Christmastime, particularly caroling and church music, were brought to the house by the choir in which Mrs. Bell had sung for twenty years. Mrs. Bell talked more and more often of the plans for her memorial service, and Christmas music figured prominently in them.

At this time too, Mrs. Bell told her eldest daughter, and some of her friends, of her interest in euthanasia. She had a conviction of its rightness in "hopeless cases" (her words) like her own, and even a vision of its aesthetic potential. She spoke about this with conviction with the clergyman she had chosen to conduct her memorial service. In general, people were awed but respectful of her views. Shortly before Christmas a good friend close to medical networks made the family aware that Dr. Henderson himself was not unwilling to discuss the matter. Mrs. Bell made an appointment to see him, saying that she had just enough strength to leave her house one more time.

In the end, after this consultation, family debates, and a pivotal conversation with a compassionate woman doctor/friend, Mrs. Bell's decision was made in favor of her family's peace of mind and legal safety. But she had made her convictions fearlessly known. And through the discourse surrounding this decision she finally came to terms with allowing herself to be taken care of to the end, at home, by her family (who firmly desired that). Throughout, she insisted that heroic measures never be taken on her behalf and had filed a "Durable Power of Attorney for Medical Care" with her lawyer and her physician. Her desires were honored, and after last visits from virtually everyone she wanted to see, she died peacefully at home on January 1 with her eldest daughter by her side.

But the debate about euthanasia nevertheless illuminated the symbolism of choice and empowerment involved in the dying process. Margaret Bell had resisted her dismal and eventually terminal prognosis stoutly. Only twice during the difficult five months she lived after her diagnosis did she give in to brief expressions of dismay when anyone else was around. She took just as positive an orientation toward her death once she had accepted its inevitability:

> It's that I'm a realist, and I know enough about what the body does under different circumstances to be able to see myself going down day by day, in the strength department and in every department—my eyes are really bad. . . . I'm a realist, and I call things as I see them.

This attitude was partly connected with Mrs. Bell's unstoppable research orientation. She was interested in monitoring her condition up to the last in order to understand it, even to the final phases of systemic breakdown. She said that she found the ways in which her vision was distorted at the end, for instance, "captivating to watch. It doesn't bother me that I can't read any more." The existence of the euthanasia option, she said, means that one doesn't have to be afraid of carrying this learning process so far that one's quality of life becomes intolerable.

DR. HENDERSON AND MRS. BELL: A CONTRAPUNTAL DIALECTIC BETWEEN PHILOSOPHY AND PERFORMANCE

In a telephone conversation with Mrs. Bell's eldest daughter after the last office visit, Dr. Henderson opened the topic of his own understanding of Mrs. Bell's views on euthanasia by saying, "I know what she wants—she wants to exit stage right." The performative reference of this statement, combined with the discovery that Dr. Henderson was working toward a doctorate in philosophy in order to pursue a strong academic interest in the ethics of euthanasia, led us to request a formal interview with Dr. Henderson.

The interview was conducted a week after Mrs. Bell's death. Early on, Dr. Henderson had remarked, "Dying is not something that happens to you. It is still something you can participate in." It quickly became clear that Dr. Henderson was committed to the social support of the dying in a profound way, and that he found his own niche as a cancer doctor to be just there, defining the limits of science clearly so that patients could prepare themselves for their deaths by completing their connections with life. What galvanized him was practicing "medicine" on patients, which for him included taking full responsiblity for "taking care of them until they die," as opposed to surgery, which he said was "just slice-of-time oriented . . . where you do not have to take care of the whole patient, where you are either successful or not in that limited slice of time. It does not seem to be as rewarding."

He said that medicine, as opposed to surgery,[5] "should be good at knowing when the battle is lost and you need to change directions and provide some comfort. . . . It is trying to do everything you can and still be the court of last resort for a lot of people." A period of practice in a small Mennonite community had helped form his outlook in this regard: he characterized it as a community with "no loss of connection. . . . The diagnosis of cancer was a signal that someone needed to be taken care of and hardly anyone went out of this little community to be taken care of." He went on to say that had he been in a big city he would have continued in academic medicine—doing hematologic cancer protocols, etc. "But I don't think I would have been as satisfied as I could be now because academic communities are so disjointed from the community of the patient that you can't provide total care. All you can do is provide heroic care." He preferred, he said, that there be "some look over the long term even if it's only a couple of weeks. I'm not here to say, 'Well, I have nothing to offer you and you need to go someplace else.'" It was clear that the "long-term look" and "total care" meant for this doctor something different from what such terms might mean coming from a family pediatrician, for example. They had a great deal to do with mediation of the dying process once curative medicine had reached acknowledged limits. In Mrs. Bell's case it was clear from the way Dr. Henderson went into action at the time of his announcement of the diagnosis of terminality that his sense of his role was centered just there—an observation confirmed by his own words in the later interview:

> What the patient's whole life is has a lot to do with how they are going to live the rest of their life. Some will be satisfied with facing the end of treatment and some won't. They will want to do other things. . . . The greater likelihood a patient has of being cured the more adamant I am about trying to get them to take chemotherapy. But if there is no cure rate we are really just talking about quality.
>
> Dying is an event we all have to go through and it seems to me you are shortchanged if you don't [have the chance to] do the things you would regret not doing if you didn't know about it . . . You look at what you have to leave people. And that is all you can do. You leave something. You leave whatever you do through your connections. . . .
>
> So, I do believe a lot can be made of the death. It can be a good death. [But in our culture] it has been hidden. It has been suppressed by medicine. Medicine has held out a hope that has been unrealistic. . . . People still die . . . too often in the hospital, too often not aware of what has happened to them. And they are older, and separated from their families. It's partly medicine and it's partly society.

Asked how he thought modern physicians—particularly oncologists—might help alleviate this problem in the social dimension of dying, Dr. Henderson said, "You have to develop some kind of philosophy that allows you to . . . get into somebody's life, to participate in someone's life. . . ." But he went quickly into the difficulties this approach involves for physicians:

> There are certain penalties you have to pay for being connected. One of them is that you will have feelings for a person, whatever happens to them. On balance that is okay . . . but it's just not easy sometimes. I can't see not doing this but I can see doing less of it. It is where I keep contact with what happens. I'm not sure it's a strength. It's just something I do. . . . The

greatest amount of suffering in someone's life may occur toward the end of that life so there is a need. And filling that need is what I feel fairly comfortable with. It's a good sense, you know. You get reinforced every now and then. We have had people who have had good deaths and we have participated in that to some degree. I think people's lives are better for that—it's just not as dramatic or visible as getting your appendix out. So there is reinforcement. There is a commitment to helping people at that time in their lives.

When asked about the limits he had to set in order to keep on doing this difficult thing, he responded that the main limit was an adherence to scientific facts. He named these same scientific limits as a source of occasional escape from the personal emotional pressures of oncology. He called clinical medicine

a detective game requiring . . . understanding of the whole patient. . . . I took a hematology/oncology rotation when I was a senior medical student. I don't know why I was particularly struck by it except that it was exciting medicine. You could make diagnoses right away just by looking at blood films. . . . Hemologic malignancies: it's intellectually challenging. There are obscure diseases like certain kinds of anemias—interesting. Sickle-cell disease is the best-defined genetic disease there is . . . So that is scientifically pure to some degree. Some of the hereditary anemias and some of the clotting disorders are almost pure science. You can see a defect and you know what the molecular effect is and you can follow it all the way up to what happens on the physiological level. So that's fun and is a good foil for some of this other stuff. A relief. I enjoy it and it's fairly simple. There are some sophisticated tests you can do but still you don't always need an NMI scan. You can just look at the blood and take a person's history and physical exam, so it fits together well for me. However, a lot of the hemologic diseases are fatal.

At almost every point in the interview, as here, the narrative arrows, returning, pointed toward death. As this was clearly a focal point in Dr. Henderson's perception of his role, we asked how his medical-school training had prepared him to handle it. He answered that in medical school "it's not as intense since you are not the one who is primarily responsible. . . . Now I find since I am primarily responsible for patients that it has become difficult, an emotional effort, to help people die." The age limit he placed on his practice was born of hard experience with himself: "I couldn't stand to see kids die. I couldn't stand to deal with their parents. It was just overwhelming—it was just too much for me. I just couldn't stand to see children who were terribly disfigured and disabled, probably because I didn't know enough."

He also admitted limitations in the area of interacting with patients, speaking admiringly of "Sandie," the nurse who administered chemotherapy in his clinic. "She's wonderful. She is a buffer for me: she has much more physical contact with the patients." He surprised us by saying he had found her by placing a personal ad for a cancer-clinic nurse. Sandie seemed a highly approachable pillar of human strength, performing routine chores and tests with the outpatients which clearly would have taxed Dr. Henderson beyond his specialist's role. She "ran interference" with a vengeance, making it virtually unnecessary for Dr. Henderson to have contact with patients or families as often as was usually necessary during the course of chemotherapy. We talked with her and found that she connected her own ability to do what she did with her experience in taking care of a father who died of cancer.

In a recent study of American oncologists, Good et al. (1990) find that these oncologists perceive themselves as mandated "to instill and maintain hope." In contrast, in Margaret Bell's case, both Sandie and Dr. Henderson seemed to have developed into professional hope-withholders. They worked in structural symmetry: Dr. Henderson ran interference for her (as she for him) by acting out his role as the scientific arbiter for treatment decisions. However, he was somewhat "unavailable" (at least on Mrs. Bell's twice-weekly session basis) to discuss the case as it progressed. Sandie herself could be asked questions at each session, but the answers took time to come back, as most of them had to go through Dr. Henderson. By the time the answers did come back, the original impetus for the question had often faded and the emotional charge lessened, making Sandie's "patient contact" less trying for her than it might otherwise have been.

Meanwhile, Sandie performed the maintenance and treatment tasks routinely, and this in itself was patient therapy, as it at least acknowledged the ongoing physical needs of the patient. The performance aspects of Sandie's job made it highly didactic: her kind but businesslike demeanor conveyed, more clearly than words could, what kind of job she saw herself engaged in. It was, like Dr. Henderson's job, one of facilitating dying more often than fostering life. She silently taught the patient and family what their job was too.

Sandie's lesson at first was not easily absorbed by the Bells. Mrs. Bell was distressed that she was not able to discuss with Sandie or Dr. Henderson the holistic-healing philosophy that was animating a whole other side of her self in her struggle against her disease. She and her family were shaken by the realization that in the entire oncology profession of their large city they had been able to discover only this single young doctor willing to administer an experimental treatment combination, but that even he stopped short of enthusiasm for "mind-made health." They were uneasy with the split between home, where one could take a hand in one's own healing, and clinic, where one could not. It wasn't that their holistic views were overtly denigrated in the clinic, but rather that the atmosphere at the clinic allowed them no conversational room to even bring up the philosophies of Bernie Siegel and Norman Cousins.

Characteristic features of biomedicine as described by a number of social scientists include a hierchical physician-patient relationship in which the physician protectively contains his authoritative knowledge within the community of biomedical practitioners, doling out small pieces of information to the patient while maintaining a general unwillingness to share this knowledge and information (Fisher and Todd 1983; Jordan and Irwin 1990; Klein 1979; Lyng 1990). Susan DiGiacomo (1987) poignantly describes her five-year struggle not only with Hodgkin's disease but also with the resistance her physicians demonstrated toward keeping her fully informed. An anthropologist and Ph. D. candidate at the time of her initial diagnosis, *she* desired a collegial relationship with her physicians in which knowledge and information would be shared and treatment decisions mutually decided upon, while *they* sought to enforce a strict hierarchy in which she would follow the treatments they prescribed without asking too many questions. So pervasive is this approach in biomedicine that Stephen Lyng, in envisioning an ideal "countersystem," suggests that in such a system "the practitioner's primary role would be educational, while the patient would assume primary responsibility for selecting a diagnosis and treatment regimen from among the various alternatives presented" (1990:61).

Like DiGiacomo, throughout the course of her illness Mrs. Bell keenly felt the disjuncture between the technocratic approach to healing and her own. This sense of disjuncture was intensified by her personal lifetime commitment to the idea of nutritional support for the immune system. She had doubts throughout the course of chemotherapy about whether she could fruitfully discuss nutrition with either her doctor or her nurse, doubts that were finally confirmed in the hospital during the dramatic announcement of terminality. The question she blurted out, "Do you believe that nutrition can play a role in healing?" was one she had been longing to ask for months, as the answer would precisely define the limits of their system of shared beliefs. Dr. Henderson's flat "no" cemented the disjuncture, making impossible any kind of conceptual reconciliation between Margaret Bell's own beliefs and those of the medical personnel treating her, ultimately augmenting her sense of hopelessness.

In other words, although Mrs. Bell and her family continued to pay every good attention to her diet, the sense of dissonance created by the total devaluation of this practice by the medical profession intensified her alienation from a part of herself. In Kleinman's (1988) terms, this situation constitutes a failure of conversation, a failure of the healer to empathetically enter into the patient's own discourse concerning her lived experience:

Of all the tradecraft of the physician, nothing more effectively empowers patients. The very act of negotiation, if it is genuine, . . . necessitates that at the very least the physician show respect for the patient's point of view. The real challenge is for the physician to engage in negotiation with the patient as colleagues involved in care as collaboration. The practitioner begins this phase of care by elaborating an explicit comparison between the lay model and the professional biomedical model. The physician can determine points of disagreement. . . . [H]e must be prepared to hear out their criticisms. . . . [H]e must expose his uncertainty and the limits of his understanding, as well as his critical reaction to relevant popular and commercial images. . . . The negotiation may end up in a compromise closer to the patient's position, a compromise closer to the doctor's position, or a joint lesson in demystifying professional and public discourse. (Kleinman 1988:243)

Such a joint lesson in demystification was precisely what Bell was longing for. The psychological trauma of her illness experience stemmed from the total lack of this kind of mutual negotiation, which she experienced as an extreme philosophical tension and an ultimate putdown—a powerful argument in support of Kleinman's conversation-centered approach to healing.

It was not until after Mrs. Bell's death that anyone involved in the process was to hear Dr. Henderson speak the word "holistic." During our interview with him, Dr. Henderson spoke favorably of humanizing trends in medicine's approach to death stemming from the hospice movement and a "network of holistic medicine." Yet two of his main judgments about holistic medicine were decidedly negative:

> If you ask, "Do these [alternative treatments] have a function for the patient?" the answer is that they do. They provide a level of proof that no matter what they do this disease is not going to go away. . . . One study in the *New England Journal of Medicine* showed that non-traditional and traditional treatments had the same success rates. The proof is . . . the lack of effectiveness, the fact that they are going to die . . . It is a proof of mortality, basically, and there is nothing we have that will rescue them from it.[6]

At one point in the interview, Henderson added,

> I think people do get the idea that what [Siegel] is saying is that if you can think about it you will get better, if you will it enough, when in fact this is not the case. In fact, that gives even the wrong meaning in that you end up with patients who blame themselves for their disease, which is just entirely wrong.[7]

This potential for creating guilt in patients, he said, together with holistic healing's mindless positive attitude (which he characterized as "ice-cream sundaes") obscures the real message:

> What Siegel is saying is that whether you have a diagnosis of a cancer or not, that should not keep you from living your life. There are still things to do, and [you] may be able to tune into the connections you do have. Relationships are still important, maybe more important. . . . [And Siegel] is emphasizing the emotional content by shaving his head to be sympathetic with those patients having chemotherapy, hugging his patients, and being in contact, sharing their feelings.

There was a certain wistfulness detectable in Dr. Henderson's acknowlegment of his own very different orientation to patient treatment, as he noted, "I haven't come to that point . . . I just recommend hairpieces instead."

This acknowledgment points up the structural tension in Dr. Henderson's own working philosophy—fascinatingly, the same tension that structured Margaret Bell's experience of illness and death. In his own words, he values connectedness and seeks for patients to be connected with both their families and himself. Yet his orientation to diagnosis, treatment, and interaction with patients is highly technocratic; his words express, and his behavior enacts, a more-deeply held valuation of distance and separation. The pure science of complex tests is "fun," "a relief" from the strain of human commitment. And although Dr. Henderson verbally expresses human commitment both to patients and their families and in professional writings and talks, he does not physically enact this commitment through companionship, or conversation, or head-shaving, or loving touch. In other words, he does not engage patients in two-way explorations of the experience or meanings of their illnesses.

In this, he is not alone. As Arthur Kleinman notes in *The Illness Narratives,* at the heart of healing lies the potential for a powerful dialectic that can draw the practitioner into the patient's experience and so can make of illness and treatment a rare opportunity for moral education. But instead, the modern medical-care system

> does just about everything to drive the practitioner's attention away from the experience of illness. The system thereby contributes importantly to the alienation of the chronically ill from their professional care givers and, paradoxically, to the relinquishment by the practitioner of that aspect of the healer's art that is most ancient, most powerful, and most existentially rewarding. (1986:xiv)

CHARON'S DISCOURSE: A CONVERSATION-CENTERED
APPROACH TO THE ISSUE OF EUTHANASIA

Participation in dying through consciously living the last months or days of life seemed a cornerstone of Dr. Henderson's philosophy, whether he was referring to his own or to more holistic approaches. It was of a piece with his attitude toward euthanasia, though this attitude was far from simple or completed in his mind. "Euthanasia is interesting," he began. "Euthanasia is a good death, bringing about a good death. That's what we do." He went on to explain the legal constraints and ultimately to illuminate through his own ambivalent musings the moral confusions that keep most doctors from active involvement with what they may humanely believe in:

> I think the difference between passive and active is artificial. I don't know if you know what they generally consider the distinctions. . . . Actively agreeing about somebody's death is allowed if you meet certain criteria. Actually it's done much more *sub rosa* than you might consider. If you meet certain criteria of intractable suffering and a terminal disease, then a physician under certain circumstances is allowed to end that patient's life. We are [legally] allowed to do that [in the U.S.]. We also have something called passive euthanasia which is if death is inevitable and you are taking steps to relieve suffering and that speeds up the time of death, then that is okay . . . [But] if you look at intent, then there is no difference between passive and active euthanasia.
>
> I have a lot of difficulty with killing patients, ending suffering by putting the patient to death, mostly because I don't think the patient is likely to be suffering if his other aspects of medical care are handled properly. Another issue in a good death is whether timing is important. To my way of thinking, timing isn't that important, that a physician should participate in hastening a patient's death. . . . It's important to the patient not to be a burden any more. You have fulfilled all your obligations, you've taken care of all your connections, life is not going to be worth a damn any more . . . and it's time to check out. That's not metaphysical. That is very much tied into what that person is, and that is assisted suicide, [an act that] is for convenience and I'm not willing to do that . . . Whether society should say at some point that a patient has a right to do that is probably something I would not object to, but that has to be a societal decision . . . not a medical decision. . . . I think there is something about the separation between medicine and society that has to continue.

These and other considerations were in the background of Dr. Henderson's interaction with Margaret Bell in the final days before Christmas, 1990, when she made the appointment to discuss euthanasia with him. At that time he did not make these issues clear either to the patient or to her family, partly because another physician came on stage at this moment. A compassionate woman doctor, whom we will call Ann Walker, was a colleague of Dr. Henderson's and thought very highly of him. She offered to discuss the issue of euthanasia and the practical problems involved with the family at home after Mrs. Bell had expressed her views to Dr. Henderson at the clinic. Dr. Henderson appeared happy to have Dr. Walker take on this chore. In the absence of full information at that time regarding his views on euthanasia, the family assumed that Dr. Henderson was taking the easy way out to protect himself legally. This assumption was reinforced by Ann Walker's surprisingly ready acknowledgment that she knew she was being "used" in this way; however, she pointed out, she didn't care, as she had her own strong convictions about patients' rights.

When Ann arrived on December 22 to talk to Dr. Bell and his eldest daughter, her words hit them "like a bolt of lightning." She was compassionate and caring, but this was "the most intense family learning experience we had ever had." The eldest daughter woke up very quickly to the fact that the practical details of her mother's intention were far from easy and that they would not, as she had assumed, be carried out by a physician or a nurse, as Mrs. Bell was no longer hospitalized and was choosing to die at home. They would become the responsibility of the family, but as primary caregiver, she herself would have to carry them out. Even more astonishing was Dr. Bell's response, "Are we actually talking here about shortening her life?"

Swiftly it became apparent that Dr. Bell either had not been given or had not taken in the implications of Dr. Walker's visit. Just as swiftly he reacted with a perspective that had not been considered by the eldest daughter—the legal liability that could become a problem for family members. A recent case was in the news about a man who received a life sentence for helping his wife, who was suffering from AIDS, die. Dr. Walker explained her view that one way to resolve all this was to reassure Mrs. Bell that her natural course of death at home, no matter how long it took, would be no burden but rather a blessing in the eyes of her caregivers. Perhaps, she suggested, Mrs. Bell could perform this final act of trust in the love of her family. She also implied, but did not state, that Mrs. Bell's decision would be based as well on compassion for the difficulty a family member would find in actually physically assisting a beloved one to die. Enacting her stated high value on connection and patient empowerment, Dr. Walker hugged both husband and daughter as she left; she also left them with a prescription for morphine sufficient not only to ease pain but to cause death.

The turning point in this family drama came the next day when the eldest daughter was able to convey the substance of Dr. Walker's visit to her mother.

She did so in the context of a simultaneous illumination she was having about the necessity of her seeing the processes of caregiving through, for purposes of her own growth:

> I explained to my mother that I was experiencing the completion of our bonding by taking care of her as she died, and in so doing was eliminating a lifelong sense of incompleteness. I asked my mother to trust my desire to care for her to the end at home. I said that either of the other alternatives—giving her over to hospital care or helping to hasten her death—would be much harder for me personally than seeing it straight through.

She spoke of her own concern that since death is "the final stage of growth," there may be some reason for not hurrying that process. Mrs. Bell's final protest was that she was afraid her daughter's back would be hurt: "You will not be able to lift me tomorrow." Her daughter told us that "somehow the strength in my eyes convinced her otherwise, and then she gave herself over completely to trust in her family's ultimate care. The prescription was never filled."

Though the family's final decision was made in a context of poignant personal relationships, it mirrored in interesting ways the societal ambivalences outlined by Dr. Henderson in the interview after Mrs. Bell's death. At least some of the family members were clear on the humane intent of both active and passive euthanasia, and had supported Mrs. Bell's wishes throughout the course of her illness regarding avoiding intrusive or heroic measures. They were in tune with both Dr. Walker's and Dr. Henderson's views that the administration of progressively higher and eventually fatal doses of painkiller was acceptable and even expected in the hospital with terminal patients, comatose or not. But their ambivalence about personally "assisting suicide" coincided strangely with the legally disputed gray area in American society where some cases of "mercy killing" reached prosecution and others, perhaps many others, carried themselves to their conclusions in private.

By their own report, the family's courage in this regard never matched that of Margaret Bell, the uniqueness of whose attitude was attested to by her clergyman and many others. Her vision of euthanasia was an utterly positive and even joyful one, and if it had not been for her consideration of family members' feelings it might have been her final act of self-realization—an act she considered not only because she had not wanted to be a burden, but also because she "never liked messiness" and wanted to control the aesthetics of her death.

Yet the important point here is that the decision against euthanasia was reached in just the sort of egalitarian conversational context that Kleinman (1988) recommends. The consensual nature of that decision, the mutuality of its acceptance, and the family healing that the process of reaching it achieved stand as a powerful endorsement of the value of Kleinman's conversation-centered approach.

THE ONCOLOGIST AS CHARON:
ETHNOCONCEPTS AS CULTURAL CONTAINMENT

Anthropologists have identified the most destructive concomitant of illness as fear of the unknown. For example, drawing on the works of such earlier theorists as Lévi-Strauss (1967) and Turner (1967), Schieffelin (1985) describes Kaluli healing seances in Papua New Guinea as emergent social constructions that draw upon and actualize group knowledge about the unknown. He emphasizes that removal of chaotic fear through such dramatic social ordering processes lies at the heart of shamanistic cures.

Although in official American ideology, religion and medicine, like religion and state, split off from each other long ago, in praxis the physician, laden as he is not only with responsibility for the body but also with heavy ritual and symbolic weight, has enormous influence over the psyche as well—a shamanistic function of which American physicians themselves are often aware, and whose potential they sometimes consciously exploit (Spiro 1986).[8]

Correspondingly, one of the main services the American doctor provides is a cognitive system emergent in diagnosis and treatment (or lack thereof) that organizes and alleviates the chaos of fear. Perhaps he does this partly by taking into himself, as a ritual figure, all those unknowns of a mysterious disease process and of death, thereby relieving the patient of that wondering that is beyond her capabilities. As he is himself untrained in shamanistic myth and mystery, the full alleviation of such wondering is beyond the oncologist's capabilities, as well. Nevertheless, the ritual function of these doctors in Western society is consolidated by their exclusive control of authoritative knowledge—highly specialized scientific information—in spite of its conceptual emptiness/inability to explain. Yet the function itself is as simple and as old as the Christian idea of carrying another man's burdens for him, an idea shared by many ancient religions and healing traditions. It is as simple as piling symbolic unwanted baggage—disease, trouble, fear—on a symbolic camel and watching it walk off into the sunset.

"Man," wrote Suzanne Langer "can adapt himself somehow to anything his imagination can cope with, but he cannot deal with chaos" (1974:23). It was Malinowski (1925) who first made clear the roles of religion and magic in inducing socially agreed upon confidence in observances designed to keep chaos at bay. Expanding on Malinowski's insights, Turner (1967, 1974) and Geertz (1973) emphasized the processual nature of "reality," showing that ritual performances are not only models of what humans believe, but models for ensuring that they will believe it. "In these plastic models, men attain their faith as they portray it" (Geertz 1973:114). The metaphor of a camel loaded with symbolic baggage, for example, or any other metaphysical image used in a therapeutic context, can have the effect of lightening the load of mystery upon the ill person. The physician/healer whose ability to assume the load of chaos is consonant with general social belief in the effectiveness of such a maneuver will demonstrate a capacity to heal which may have little or nothing to do with specific knowledge of treatment or cures.

Seen this way, the oncologist's role must finally be understood as having profoundly mystical dimensions. This doctor is Charon in no mechanistic sense: morphine is ultimately no way out of the ethical dilemmas of his mandate. His task remains as hard as the task of the mythic thaumaturge has always been—harder, because he is also charged, today, with probing the furthest reaches of proliferating scientific fact to leave no healing possibility unexamined. Yet despite its medical connotations and emphases, the oncologist's role remains basically a social one. In effect, he does address the lived experience of illness as well as the mechanics of disease. As arbiter of both the potentials and the limitations of scientific medicine against a disease virtually synonymous with death, he holds the reins on what the unassisted patient and family both fear and dare to hope. The mystery they fear is clear; what they dare to hope for—new discoveries in the nick of time, the power of the mind to transcend statistics, the possibility that choosing the time and the manner of death may be an affirmation of life, the ultimate rightness of their hunch that death will be an opening-out rather than a closing-in—may be much more individual, a result of their histories as persons. But all individualism must be culturally contained, and this is where the cancer doctor's role has what is perhaps its central defining power.

The Greeks' model "of and for" dying was the Charon myth, the conceptual reality of which they expressed by burying their dead with *oboli* on each eyelid to pay the ferryman for passage to the Underworld. Just so does a modern cancer patient internalize her relationship to the cancer doctor's ritual power, once her own beliefs come into alignment with the technocratic model/myth. She gains, ultimately, the treasure of conceptual clarity, even if she must pay for it with the loss of individual hope.

We suggest that the power operating here is both social and religious. If a central act for many oncologists is the announcement of terminality and getting the patient to accept that diagnosis in the interests of "a good death," it is clear that defining "a good death"—known by anthropologists to be a social and religious preoccupation of societies in general (Fox 1973; Needham 1973)—has become at least partly the province of these specialists. If one realizes further that under certain conditions medical euthanasia may be permitted by our society, that these conditions are most often met in cancer cases, and that providing the means for euthanasia under these conditions is defined by at least some oncologists as "bringing about a good death," the implications of a role far beyond the medical one as contemporarily conceived are inescapable.

In the end, in Mrs. Bell's case, the question of who does Charon's actual ferrying, and to where, is left open. But some boatman figure standing ready to meet the dying passenger and carry her across seems just as necessary in our age as in ancient times.[9] If dying has become medicalized in America it has not done so without bringing elements of performance into the medical profession along with it. If "exiting stage right" is not yet actually condoned medically in America as a good death, it is at least a ready metaphor for evoking the performative aspects of dying and of attending those who die either as actor or audience.

Ideas about illness and healing are as precisely idiosyncratic to specific cultures as is verbal language. Ethnoconcepts form part of the cultural signature: though there may be variation within traditions, part of what holds the members of a culture together is the containment provided by such ideas. This containment holds true for people whether they live in traditional or in highly industrialized societies.

The heritage of the classical cultures of Greece and Rome held powerful sway in Euroamerican thinking for centuries. Economic fields such as medicine, politics, and law which have invested heavily in, and gained much from, this intellectual heritage, are slow to move toward "multicultural" (or even ethnohistorical within European tradition) awareness. They have the investor's unwillingness to learn of a possible threat to the return on their worldview. The science of anthropology goes largely unheeded by the science of medicine, for example, and *a fortiori* the ethnoscience of traditional peoples has little impact on medical practice, even as comparison or perspective.

But, as anthropologists often point out, a biomedicine that is trying to humanize itself could learn much from other conceptual systems and practices. The !Kung (Ju/'hoansi) of Botswana and Namibia, studied by Biesele (1979, 1990, 1992), for example, have a long and trusted heritage of altered-state healing by laying on of hands. In this tradition, religion and healing are inextricably linked—by the practitioners, the *n/omkxaosi* or "owners of medicine," who are seen as both doctors and religious technicians, and by the expectations of all who participate. Such high value is placed on *n/om* (an intangible potency or energy which is activated both from within the healers' bodies *and* from within the highly social context in which they work) that herbal medicine, though known, is relatively little elaborated. Faith is put instead in the transformative experience shared by patient and healer.

In Ju/'hoan healers' ideas of death and fate lies an even more striking contrast to Western medicine. For them, the power to kill a person lies in the hands of !Xu (God). A healer has no foreknowledge of what he can cure and what he cannot cure. He must just try to the limit of his strength and if he is defeated, the patient will die. No fault accrues to him if this happens: instead he is socially rewarded for having tried his best. For Ju/'hoansi or for Ju/'hoan healers, the strength of *n/om* is not a thing that one can augment by wishing or trying. It is a given. It is God-given. *N/om* is given to the healers through the whim of !Xu. It does not set its owners apart or above others in the society, and they do not receive material benefits for using it. They participate, as do all the people, in the dancing and singing which accompanies healing, for the pleasure of participation in a beautiful social event.

Further, *n/om* is conceived as a thing only multiplied, never divided, by being shared. Thus Ju/'hoan healers are not concerned that when someone dies they have not tried hard enough (as a physician who has not kept up with the latest medical journals might feel), since a certain equable fatalism releases them from personal responsibility. These factors, it seems, have important correlates in the realm of individual psychology and social structure.

First, *n/om* is not jealously protected, because sharing it redounds to the good of all. Nor are there material rewards to be had for exclusive control of *n/om* or its secrets. So a priesthood doesn't form, and egotism in the defensive sense does not characterize the social interactions of the *n/omkxaosi* with the ill. Second, the ultimate responsibility for life and death is far removed from these practitioners. They do not have to know everything. They can help ease the fear of sickness or of death, just as some biomedical doctors do, but they do not have to perform expert prognoses.

For these reasons, their role, even when dealing with grave illnesses like the recently introduced tuberculosis, does not define itself around an announcement of terminality or urgings to the patient to order her affairs. It is life- and hope-affirming throughout, holding to one source of hope—the patient's will to keep trying—as the indicator that effort should still be expended, that the patient should not be given up for lost.

It is here that Ju/'hoan traditional practices and newer holistic medical approaches in the U.S. most significantly converge. Neither treats the living patient as a "case." In both approaches the patient is an autonomous actor, her individuality valued, her inclusion on the healing team a given, her will and beliefs assumed to play strong roles in the healing process. But, contrary to the American holistic tradition's emphasis on acceptance as an important part of the dying process (Kübler-Ross 1975), in the Ju/'hoan tradition the sick are alive until proven dead, given the benefit of the doubt as long as they are still breathing (and sometimes even afterwards): they are culturally allowed the ability to make the miraculous recovery if it is in them—or if, as the Ju/'hoansi believe, it is in !Xu's will.

Returning to the Kalahari, and seeing the ease with which Ju/'hoan healers accept that death is ultimately out of their hands, Biesele was filled with compassion for doctors whose techno-scientific tradition forces them to incur so much personal responsibility. She remembered Dr. Henderson's words: "Since I have become primarily responsible for patients . . . it has become difficult, an emotional effort, to help people die."

Upon her return, Biesele told the story of Margaret Bell's death to a !Kung healer she had known and worked with, a man in his fifties we'll call Komtsa Kxao. Komtsa listened gravely to the story of how the last afternoon of Mrs. Bell's life was spent at home in a coma with her family present, and how she quietly slipped away in the evening. "Where was the doctor?" he wanted to know. "Well, they all knew she was dying so he wasn't there." Then Komtsa said, matter-of-factly and without a trace of criticism for the other medical tradition, "It's too bad she was so far away. If it had been me, I would have still been trying. If she could have been brought back, I could have done it."

Shortly after her mother's death, Mrs. Bell's eldest daughter had told us a strange story about hearing "garbled voices in the wall" above her mother as she lay dying, speaking incomprehensibly but so audibly that she actually went outside to see who was there, but found no one. It occurred to Biesele to ask Komtsa Kxao if he had any idea what these voices might have been. He responded, "Of course I know. It was the spirits coming to take Mrs. Bell. If I had been there, because I'm a *n/omkxao* I would have been able to speak their speech and ask them to bring her back."

We believe that Western "experts" have much to learn from such healers' ministrations to the ill, including their spiritual or humane approaches to the whole person. Other cultures, other traditions suggest more open paradigms of the healer than the technocratic biomedical model: in other models, it seems, the ferryboat to the other side can run both ways. Perhaps the role of Charon for Western physicians involved in terminal illness has a great deal to do with the privileged classical heritage in which they have invested. It's not just the myth, though myths are powerful; it is the whole complex of ideas about Cartesian rationalism and the human potential for control of both nature and fate which come down to us with the strength of unassailable Truth. Yet these ideas, like any ideas, are cultural constructs, and the physician who enacts the matrix they form by diagnosing in its terms only is imposing a very narrow and culture-specific view of reality on the life/death of his patient. Fascinatingly, the attempt to meaningfully move beyond this narrow matrix informs not only the philosophies of physicians and medical anthropologists who advocate conversation-centered approaches to healing (DiGiacomo 1987; Kleinman 1988), but also those of the advocates of holism so admired by Margaret Bell (Cousins 1982, 1989; Siegel 1986).

Dying is a physiological and often interactional event with profound religious, social, spiritual, and individual ramifications. Enactments of their cultural matrix by practitioners who wrestle with, talk to, or wait upon death, be they technocratic Western physicians, holistic Western practitioners, or traditional Ju/'hoan healers, work to ensure that, like giving birth, dying will also be a cultural performance.

NOTES

1. Our complete acceptance by Mrs. Bell and her family as anthropologists was certainly related to the fact that we were also close family friends.

2. Abrahams (1973) defines "strange-making" as making the commonplace strange by juxtaposing it with the unfamiliar.

3. We rely here on insights derived from our work with healing practitioners in more traditional contemporary societies whose roles combine the religious and medical; Biesele's with !Kung Bushmen of Southern Africa (1979, 1987, 1990a,b, 1992; Biesele and Katz 1986; Katz and Biesele 1980, 1987), and Davis-Floyd's with Mexican shamans (1982).

4. As Zerubavel (1981) has demonstrated, time in the hospital is organized to fit the needs of the staff, not the patient.

5. In biomedical parlance, "medicine" means generally and generically internal medicine, the central specialty of the field (Hahn 1985). Hahn reports that to "go medically" is to be conservative, to intervene more cautiously, to act non-invasively out of an ideal of "physiological wholeness." "Surgery" is perceived by biomedical practitioners as the extreme opposite, a mode of practice based on "invasive procedures, direct looking at and handling of the body's organs, and the virtues of aggressiveness, action, doing, mastery, conquest" (Stein 1990:40).

6. A recent study of oncologists and their discourse on hope found that, although they stressed the advantages of instilling hope and a positive attitude in their patients, they did not associate these with increased longevity but only with a better illness experience (Good et al. 1990).

7. This notion that we can make ourselves both sick and well—the "New Age" concept of patient responsibility for illness (Ferguson 1980)—has been interpreted by social scientists as "blaming the victim" (DiGiacomo 1992; Farrer 1988). DiGiacomo (1992) points out how neatly this concept articulates with the pre-existing tendency in biomedicine to "blame the victim" in a different way—"She failed her chemotherapy," "He ruptured his scar." Thus it can be easily coopted into the biomedical discourse, providing technocratic practitioners with yet another

means of retaining control by separating themselves from the patient and then defining the patient's experience.

8. Kleinman himself advocates such exploitation. He recommmends that physicians try to achieve "the highest possible placebo effect rates" (1988:245). His approach to psychotherapy involves establishing relationships that "patient and family come to believe in as of practical help and symbolic significance" (1988:245).

9. It is noteworthy that in this context some holistically-oriented practitioners have begun to specialize in facilitating death in much the same way as midwives facilitate birth. For example, harpist Theresa Schroeder-Sheker plays music and sings songs for the dying created by French monks in the 11th century to help the dying make a peaceful transition, as part of what Schroeder-Sheker terms "musical sacramental midwifery" (Harrington 1990).

REFERENCES

Baer, Hans A., ed. 1987. *Encounters with Biomedicine: Case Studies in Medical Anthropology.* New York: Gordon and Breach Science Publishers.

Biesele, Megan. 1979. Old K'xau. In *Shamanic Voices,* ed. J. Halifax, 54–62. New York: Dutton.

———. 1990a. *Shaken Roots: Bushmen of Namibia Today.* With photographs by Paul Weinberg. Environmental Development Agency, Johannesburg.

———. 1990b. Learning a 'New' Language of Democracy: Bushmen in an Independent Namibia. Nyae Nyae Development Foundation of Namibia, Windhoek, Namibia.

———. 1992. *"Women Like Meat": Ju/'hoan Bushman Folklore and Foraging Ideology.* Johannesburg: Witwatersrand University Press.

Biesele, Megan, ed. with R. Gordon and R. B. Lee. 1987. *The Past and Future of !Kung Ethnography: Critical Reflections and Symbolic Perspectives.* (Essays in Honor of Lorna Marshall.) Hamburg: Helmut Buske Verlag.

Biesele, Megan, and Richard Katz. 1986. !Kung Healing: The Symbolism of Sex Roles and Culture Change. In *The Past and Future of !Kung Ethnography,* ed. Biesele et al.

Buckman, Robert. 1984. Breaking Bad News: Why Is It Still So Difficult? *British Medical Journal* Vol. 288:1597–1599.

Cousins, Norman. 1979. *Anatomy of an Illness.* New York: Bantam.

———. 1989. *Head First: The Biology of Hope.* New York: E.P. Dutton.

Davis-Floyd, Robbie E. 1982. Myth, Ritual, and Shamanism: A Symbolic Analysis of Cultural Vitality in Mexico. Manuscript.

———. 1987. The Technological Model of Birth. *Journal of American Folklore* 100 (398):93–109.

———. 1988. Birth as an American Rite of Passage. In *Childbirth in America: Anthropological Perspectives.* Karen Michaelson and Contributors. Beacon Hill, Mass.: Bergin and Garvey.

———. 1990. The Role of American Obstetrics in the Resolution of Cultural Anomaly. *Social Science and Medicine* 31 (2):175–189.

———. 1992. *Birth as an American Rite of Passage.* Berkeley and London: University of California Press.

d'Aquili, Eugene G., Charles D. Laughlin, and John McManus, eds. 1979. *The Spectrum of Ritual: A Bio-Genetic Structural Analysis.* New York: Columbia University Press.

DiGiacomo, Susan. 1987. Biomedicine as a Cultural System: An Anthropologist in the Kingdom of the Sick. In *Encounters with Biomedicine: Case Studies in Medical Anthropology,* ed. Hans A. Baer, 315–346. New York: Gordon and Breach.

———. 1992. Metaphor as Illness: Postmodern Dilemmas in the Representation of Body, Mind, and Disorder. *Medical Anthropology* 14:109–137.

Ferguson, Marilyn. 1980. *The Aquarian Conspiracy.* Los Angeles: J. P. Tarcher.

Fisher, Sue and Alexandra Dumas Todd. 1983. *The Social Organization of Doctor-Patient Communication.* Washington, D.C.: The Center for Applied Linguistics.

Fox, James J. 1973. On Bad Death and the Left Hand: A Study of Rotinese Symbolic Inversions. In *Right and Left: Essays on Dual Symbolic Classification,* ed. Rodney Needham, 342–368. Chicago and London: University of Chicago Press.

GIVIO (Interdisciplinary Group for Cancer Care Evaluation, Italy). 1986. What Doctors Tell Patients with Breast Cancer about Diagnosis and Treatment: Findings from a Study in General Hospitals. *British Journal of Cancer* 54:319–326.

Good, Mary Jo Delvecchio. 1991. The Practice of Biomedicine and the Discourse on Hope: A Preliminary Investigation into the Culture of American Oncology. In *Anthropologies of Medicine: A Colloquium on West European and North American Perspectives,* ed. Beatrix Pfleiderer and Gilles Bibeau. Special Edition of *Curare,* 7:121–136.

Good, Mary Jo DelVecchio, Byron J. Good, Cynthia Schaffer, and Stuart E. Lind. 1990. American Oncology and the Discourse on Hope. *Culture, Medicine and Psychiatry* 14:59–79.

Good, Mary Jo Delvecchio, Linda Hunt, Tsunetsugu Munakata, Yasuki Kobayashi. 1993. A Comparative Analysis of the Culture of Biomedicine: Disclosure and the Consequences for Treatment in the Practice of Oncology. In *Health and Health Care in Developing Societies,* ed. P. Conrad and Eugene Gallagher. Philadelphia: Temple University Press.

Harrington, Maureen. 1990. The Medieval and the Modern, *Sunday Denver Post, Contemporary* Section, Sept. 23, 14–20.

Henriques B., F. Stadil, and H. Baden. 1980. Patient Information about Cancer: A Prospective Study of Patient's Opinion and Reaction to Information about Cancer Diagnosis. *Acta Chir. Scand.* 146:309.

Hertz, Robert. 1960[1909]. *Death and the Right Hand.* Translated by Rodney and Claudia Needham. London: Cohen and West. New York: The Free Press.

Katz, Richard. 1982. *Boiling Energy: Community Healing among the Kalahari !Kung.* Cambridge: Harvard University Press.

Katz, Richard, and Megan Biesele. 1980. Male and Female Approaches to Healing among the Kalahari !Kung. 2nd International Conference on Hunting and Gathering Societies, Dept. of Anthropology, Laval University, Quebec.

———. 1987. !Kung Healing: The Symbolism of Sex Roles and Culture Change. In *The Past and Future of !Kung Ethnography: Critical Reflections and Symbolic Perspectives,* ed. Biesele et al. Hamburg: Helmut Buske Verlag.

Konner, Melvin. 1987. *Becoming a Doctor: A Journey of Initiation in Medical School.* New York: Viking.

Kubler-Ross, Elizabeth. 1975. *On Death and Dying.* New York: Harper and Row.

Laughlin, Charles D., John McManus, and Eugene G. d'Aquili. 1992. *Brain, Symbol, and Experience: Toward a Neurophenomenonology of Human Consciousness.* New York: Columbia University Press.

Long, Susan O. and Bruce D. Long. 1982. Curable Cancers and Fatal Ulcers: Attitudes toward Cancer in Japan. *Social Science and Medicine* 16:2101–2108.

Lyng, Stephen. 1990. *Holistic Health and Biomedical Medicine.* State University of New York Press.

Moerman, Daniel E. 1987. Physiology and Symbols: The Anthropological Implications of the Placebo Effect. In *The Anthropology of Medicine,* ed. Lola Romanucci Ross, 156–168. South Hadley, Mass.: Bergin and Garvey.

Needham, Rodney, ed. 1973. *Right and Left: Essays on Dual Symbolic Classification.* Chicago and London: University of Chicago Press.

Romanucci-Ross, Lola, ed. 1983. *The Anthropology of Medicine: From Culture to Method.* South Hadley, Mass.: Bergin and Garvey.

Schiefflin, Edward L. Performance and the Cultural Construction of Reality. *American Ethnologist* Vol. 12 No. 4:707–723.

Siegel, Bernie S. 1986. *Love, Medicine, and Miracles.* New York: Harper and Row.

Simonton, O. Carl, Stephanie Matthews-Simonton, and James Creighton. 1980. *Getting Well Again.* New York: Bantam.

Stein, Howard F. 1990. *American Medicine as Culture.* Boulder: Westview Press.

Todd, Alexandra and Sue Fisher, eds. 1983. *The Social Organization of Doctor-Patient Communication.* Washington D.C.: Center for Applied Linguistics.

Zerubavel, Eviatar. 1981. *Patterns of Time in Hospital Life.* Chicago: University of Chicago Press.

INDEX